PENGUIN CLASSICS

THE COSMOGRAPHY AND GEOGRAPHY OF AFRICA

JOHANNES LEO AFRICANUS, born al-Hasan ibn Muhammad al-Wazzan in Granada in the 1480s, served as a diplomat to the sultan of Fez during the first two decades of the sixteenth century. In 1518 he was seized by Christian pirates in the Mediterranean, brought to Pope Leo X and baptised Johannes Leo two years later. Living in Rome in the 1520s, he wrote a number of works, including his masterpiece, *The Cosmography and Geography of Africa*, in 1526. He is said to have later reconverted to Islam and moved to Tunis, but the remainder of his life remains shrouded in mystery.

ANTHONY OSSA-RICHARDSON teaches English literature at University College London. He has previously held fellowships at Queen Mary University of London and the Wissenschaftskolleg zu Berlin. He has published widely on a variety of topics in literary and intellectual history, including two books: *The Devil's Tabernacle* (2013), about the Renaissance understanding of the ancient Greek oracles, and *A History of Ambiguity* (2019), about the ways in which readers from antiquity to the present have wrestled with multiple meanings in texts.

RICHARD J. OOSTERHOFF teaches history at the University of Edinburgh. He has held fellowships at the University of Cambridge and the University of Notre Dame, with briefer ones at the Houghton Library, the Huntington Library and the Warburg Institute. His first book, *Making Mathematical Culture: University and Print in the Circle of Lefèvre d'Étaples* (2018), studied the Renaissance learning that often accompanied cosmography. A second, co-authored book took on questions of invention and translation: *Logodaedalus: Word Histories of Ingenuity in Early Modern Europe* (2018).

JOHANNES LEO AFRICANUS
(AL-HASAN IBN MUHAMMAD
AL-WAZZAN)

The Cosmography and Geography of Africa

Translated and edited by
ANTHONY OSSA-RICHARDSON
and RICHARD J. OOSTERHOFF

PENGUIN BOOKS

PENGUIN CLASSICS

UK | USA | Canada | Ireland | Australia
India | New Zealand | South Africa

Penguin Books is part of the Penguin Random House group of companies
whose addresses can be found at global.penguinrandomhouse.com

This edition published in Penguin Classics 2023
003

Translation copyright © Anthony Ossa-Richardson, Richard J. Oosterhoff, 2023

The moral rights of the translators have been asserted

Set in 10.25/12.25pt Sabon LT Std
Typeset by Jouve (UK), Milton Keynes
Printed and bound in Great Britain by Clays Ltd, Elcograf S.p.A.

The authorized representative in the EEA is Penguin Random House Ireland,
Morrison Chambers, 32 Nassau Street, Dublin D02 YH68

A CIP catalogue record for this book is available from the British Library

ISBN: 978-0-241-54393-1

Contents

List of Maps and Illustrations

Maps

Illustrations

Introduction

The word 'unique' is overused. But the work you are holding, a geographical and historical guide to Africa from the Italian Renaissance, really is unique. It was the first full-length book about its subject, and the first book by a modern African, to reach print. It was also the starting point in Europe for knowledge about much of Africa until the nineteenth century. Due to the singularity of its author's life and the circumstances of its composition, the book crossed boundaries in an extraordinary fashion: not only from Africa to Europe, but from Islam to Christianity, and from Arabic and Berber to Italian and Latin – and beyond. It conjures urban bustle and rural desolation, culture and commerce, labour, slavery and war, magical herbs and strange animals, personal experience and the shocks of history. In doing so it participates in a rhetoric of exoticism that was already becoming implicated in colonial projects and the European appropriation of Africa, and yet at the same time it is not, like so many treatises of the Middle Ages and Renaissance, a mere catalogue of the exotic to titillate the educated: its earliest readers, like its readers today, were invited not only to imagine lands unknown, but to acknowledge the similarities, continuities with and relevance to the time and place they knew. The *Cosmography and Geography of Africa* is, in other words, significant to our understanding not just of Africa, but of the world.

WHO WAS LEO AFRICANUS?

The writer known to Europe as Johannes Leo Africanus was born al-Hasan ibn Muhammad al-Wazzan in Granada, probably around 1488.[1] His uncertain date of birth is only the first in a long series of biographical doubts. We know nothing of his family: his surname either means 'the weigher' – perhaps indicating that his parents worked for the *muhtasib* or market inspector in Granada – or it connects him to the Beni Wazzan tribe of Berbers, who had ties to the royal Marinid and Wattasid dynasties in Fez.[2] At some point in the early 1490s, either before or soon after the fall of Granada to the Christians (1492), his family emigrated to Fez; al-Wazzan's education took place there, and in his book he claims that 'he was not raised [in Granada] and does not even remember it' (1.32). The family would have been one among hundreds of thousands who left Spain for the Maghrib during the Reconquista, forming a powerful and prosperous Andalusi community in North Africa. As al-Wazzan himself tells us, his father was a landowner in the regions outside Fez (2.2.2.17, 2.2.5.29), while his uncle (2.1.5.7) served as an ambassador on behalf of the sultan, Muhammad al-Burtuqali – 'the Portuguese', a nickname derived from his seven years of captivity as a child in that country.

Our sole source of information on al-Wazzan's life in Africa is his own book. He learned the Qur'an by heart at school, and studied grammar, theology and *fiqh* (Islamic jurisprudence) at the Bou Inania madrasa, whose sumptuous buildings still stand today. We have records of the astounding library of manuscripts in Wattasid Fez but know little about the learned culture in which al-Wazzan was educated, for the sources remain obscure – many of them unpublished and untranslated.[3] Al-Wazzan was evidently precocious: by the age of sixteen, as he tells us proudly (2.1.5.7), his poetic skills impressed foreign rulers. Like his uncle, he worked as a diplomat for al-Burtuqali, but also for Muhammad al-Qa'im, an emir of Sous and founder of the Sa'diyan dynasty that later wrested control of Morocco from the Wattasids. The latter he refers to as 'ash-Sharif', indicating his status as *sharif* or noble descendant of the prophet Muhammad's family. On diplomatic missions Leo travelled all over the Maghrib, south to Timbuktu and other areas of sub-Saharan Africa – known in Arabic as 'Bilad as-Sudan', translated in the *Cosmography* as 'the Land of the Blacks' – and east to Egypt and Constantinople; at the end of his sixth book he lists the Arabian peninsula, Babylon, Persia, Armenia and Tartary as other destinations. He witnessed much of the warfare between the Wattasids, the Spanish and Portuguese Catholics, and the fearsome Turkish pirate brothers Oruç and Hızır Reis, both known to the West as Barbarossa. He also encountered the Ottoman emperor Selim I on his conquest of Mamluk Egypt in 1517.

In June 1518 a boat bound from Cairo to Morocco, with al-Wazzan on board, was seized by pirates, perhaps off the coast of Jerba – supposed by some to be the Island of the Lotus Eaters described by Homer – or else near Crete or Rhodes. The pirates were led by the Spaniard Pedro de Cabrera y Bobadilla, brother to the bishop of Salamanca, a confidant of Pope Leo X. Al-Wazzan was brought to the Pope within a few months. In November the Venetian politician Marin Sanudo noted Bobadilla's arrival at the papal court with a group of Moors, among them an 'ambassador from the king of Tlemcen', who had been captured on his return from congratulating Selim I for his victories in Syria and Egypt; Sanudo added that this man had some writings that the Pope wanted to have translated.[4] Al-Wazzan remained a prisoner in the Castel Sant'Angelo for a year and a half, until he agreed to convert to Christianity; the Pope baptised him at St Peter's Basilica on 6 January 1520, the Feast of the Epiphany. He gave al-Wazzan his own name, Leo, and christened him Joannes. A surname, 'de' Medicis', after Leo X's family, was never subsequently used. Instead he was Jo(h)annes Leo of Granada – or of Africa. This was the name that appeared on all his completed writings; Leo's birth name was not revealed until 1760, when the Maronite librarian Michael Ghaziri (or Casiri) discovered his Arabic signature on a manuscript, rendering it in Latin 'Alhassam Ben Mohamad Alvazan Fessanus'.[5]

Leo was evidently in demand at the papal court for his learning and languages, and, given the rise of the African kingdoms and the Pope's desire for a new crusade against the Ottomans, his knowledge of Islamic Africa would also have been of significant political interest. Over the next seven years he produced a rich body of work, above all his magnum opus, the *Cosmography and Geography of Africa*, written in Italian and completed in 1526. The word 'cosmography', meaning a description of the world (*kosmos*), had been adopted by fifteenth-century printers as the title of geographical treatises by the ancient writers Ptolemy and Pomponius Mela and the modern writer Aeneas Sylvius Piccolomini, better known as Pope Pius II. For al-Wazzan it seemed to correspond to a genre of Arabic geography practised by great medieval authors such as al-Bakri and al-Mas'udi, and which he hoped to emulate for a European audience. Beyond the *Cosmography*, Leo wrote at least two surviving treatises, one on Arabic prosody and the other on the lives of great Arabs and Jews.[6] There also seems to have existed a work, now lost, entitled *Epitome of the Muslim Chronicles*, referred to frequently in the *Cosmography*, and another on Muslim law. During most of this period he lived in Rome, where he could enjoy the modest collection of Arabic manuscripts in the Vatican Library, and mingle with notable scholars such as Egidio da Viterbo, Elia Levita, Alberto Pio and Agostino Giustiniani. But he also visited Florence, Venice and Naples, and spent time in Bologna, where in 1524 he collaborated on a trilingual Arabic-Hebrew-Latin dictionary with the Jewish physician Jacob Mantino ben Samuel.[7]

We know almost nothing about Leo's later life. Natalie Zemon Davis suggests he may be identified with the 'Io. Leo' listed in a Roman census of January 1527, living in a household of three. One ambiguous later reference places his departure, and reconversion to Islam, at the time of the sack of Rome in 1527. A more solid witness, the German scholar and subsequent papal secretary Johann Albrecht Widmanstetter, claimed in 1555 that 'Leo Eliberitanus' (Leo of Granada) had reconverted and moved to Tunis by 1532. Beyond this we are in the realm of fruitless speculation, at most a pastime for the scholarly imagination.

Admittedly, it is a pastime towards which Leo's work beckons us; historians seem to have the promise of a real person through the screen of the *Cosmography*, and so they debate the ambiguous evidence. Did he inwardly convert to Christianity, or was it a ruse? Did he really visit sub-Saharan Africa, or only repeat the reports of merchants?[8] Such questions feel especially pressing at a time when the identity and authenticity of writers have become paramount for us – when we argue over who has the right to tell a given story, and seek to elevate those whose voices have traditionally been erased. But the *Cosmography*, with its absences, equivocations and fictions, does much to withhold this real person. Many critics have focused on a story that closes its first book. Leo tells of a bird who, when the king of the birds came to collect his tribute, dived into the sea to live among the fish; when the king of the fish came for his tribute, the bird fled back up into the sky. He explains it as a parable for his own practice: 'whoever spies an advantage will always wait and go after it. For instance, if the Africans are being insulted, he'll come up with the obvious excuse that he was not born there but in Granada; or when the Granadans are being insulted he'll give another excuse, that he was not raised there and does not even remember it' (1.32). This story has always stood out from the book; in 1612 an Oxford preacher cited it as a good example of how *not* to behave.[9] Today we are better disposed to appreciate cunning, flexibility and ambiguity. Davis responds to the vignette by characterising al-Wazzan as a 'trickster', acknowledging slipperiness but keeping our attention on the man. Dietrich Rauchenberger, meanwhile, sees in it a portrait of Leo not as a trickster but as a Muslim who had found the means to retain his faith, the wings of his soul, even when living among the heathen fish.

Another approach might be to relocate the focus of our attention from the man to his book – to treat it as an object in its own right, with its own life and character, a bright painting rather than a besmeared window onto the world of the past. When one remembers the circumstances of its composition, in distant exile among infidels, with few textual resources to help, one is struck by the quality of the performance. First and foremost it is a performance of memory: of names, places, events, dates, numbers. Even though the latter are nearly almost prefixed with 'circa' (about), we might be inclined to distrust their accuracy. Could

Leo really remember, eight years after his capture, that the Oulad Dalim tribe in the Libyan desert numbered ten thousand men, including four hundred cavalry? Or that the governor of Tuggurt received an annual revenue of 130,000 ducats? Perhaps Leo had notes with him. Or perhaps the *Cosmography* was a different sort of performance, that is, a charismatic performance of authenticity, the claim to encyclopaedic knowledge combined with a flair for storytelling. If we want to entertain this suggestion, the important question is not so much what clues can be gleaned of the real Leo, but how the *Cosmography* conjures the author and his subject for its Italian readers.

AFRICA IN THE *COSMOGRAPHY*

The *Cosmography* is the first direct appearance in a European language of what Matthew Keegan calls the 'Islamic archive': 'a vast and multifaceted realm of cultural memory that includes the Qur'ān, *ḥadīt̲*, and a multitude of other Islamic texts and discourses'.[10] The Africa that it offered Christendom for the first time was not an objective reckoning – as if such a thing could exist – but a construction of late medieval Muslim thought: a physical landmass with countless towns and peoples, but also a storehouse of ideas, starting with the very idea of Africa itself. Despite al-Wazzan's extensive travels, his Africa is archaic, with the ocean running straight along from Jenne and Mali to 'Gaoga' in the east, probably present-day Sudan (1.2). In places he explicitly follows the ancient geography of Claudius Ptolemaeus (known in modern English as Ptolemy), and Leo's general division of the four parts of Africa corresponds to the *aqalim* or climatic zones delineated by Muhammad al-Idrisi in the twelfth century: the coastal plains and mountains of Barbary (Arabic: Maghrib, 'the west'), followed by the dry lands of Numidia (Arabic: Bilad al-Jarid, 'the land of dates'), the vast deserts of Libya (Arabic: Sahra, 'the desert'), and finally the many kingdoms of the sub-Saharan 'Land of the Blacks' (translating the Arabic Bilad as-Sudan) – including a famous description of Timbuktu, dripping with gold, jewels and books. Egypt was only disputedly part of Africa, but Leo includes it as a bonus. In the very first words of the *Cosmography*, he identifies Africa with the Arabic term 'Ifriqiya', although, as he admits, the latter name usually denoted a much smaller Islamic province centred around Tunis.[11] The result of these diverse sources is a rather ambiguous topographical and political entity not corresponding to any one single historical reality. Much less does it correspond to the structures we take for granted today, namely the nation states of Morocco, Tunisia and so on; these names do not appear in our translation, simply because Leo's categories are the four parts of Africa, and on a smaller scale the kingdoms of Marrakesh (2.1), Fez (2.2), Tlemcen (2.3) and Tunis (2.4). European place names pose less of a problem, with the exception of the frequent term 'Betteca' or 'Ebetteca', that is, Baetica, a Roman province in southern Spain; for Leo it means Muslim Spain, al-Andalus.

Beyond the geography itself, the most important topic in the *Cosmography*, from Leo's own perspective, is the many peoples of Africa. The two categories are impossible to disentangle: places in the Maghrib are frequently named after the tribes who occupied them, making the physical landscape a record of human communities. As with his geographical labels, Leo's demographic categories rarely map onto those with which we are now famil-iar: we look in vain for words like 'Tuareg' or 'Bedouin', and this difference is important to preserve.[12] His basic division in the book is between (1) the *Affricani bianchi*, the white Africans or Berbers, (2) the *Affricani nigri*, the black Africans south of the Sahara, and (3) the Arabs. All three groups, interestingly, are por-trayed as immigrants to Africa: beneath the differences between peoples is a similarity. Leo derives the Berbers indecisively from the Philistines, the Assyrians, the Sabaeans of the Arabian penin-sula, or an unnamed people of Asia; he traces the black Africans, following an ancient tradition, to Cush, Noah's grandson in Genesis 10:6, who in Leo's misremembering was also the grand-father of Philistim, progenitor of the Philistines. The Arabs, meanwhile, first invaded in the mid-seventh century under the command of the third caliph, 'Uthman ibn 'Affan, then migrated in huge numbers around the turn of the eleventh century, divided (according to Leo) into three main tribal groups, the Chachim, the Hilal and the Maqil. This was a picture derived from the earlier Arabic tradition over many centuries, above all the Andalusi-Tunisian polymath Ibn Khaldun (1332–1406). As Ramzi Rouighi has recently argued, it was Ibn Khaldun above all who had cemented the Arabic construction of the Berbers as a distinct ethnic category, a notion alien to the indigenous tribes themselves.[13] His *Kitab al-'Ibar* (*Book of Examples*) – with its long, encyclopaedic first book often copied and published separately as the *Muqaddimah* (*Introduction*) – remains the single most important source for Leo's thought.

Al-Wazzan's stated views of the Africans – and one may wonder to what extent such views form part of his performance for a Christian audience – are often pejorative and insulting, especially when it comes to the sub-Saharan peoples, whom he frequently describes as brutish, ignorant, lustful and uncultured. Indeed, he cannot be absolved on historical grounds from a charge of racism; no less than his European readers, he took for granted a hierarchy of peoples determined in no small part by their culture and physical traits such as skin colour. As recent scholars such as Chouki El Hamel and Michael A. Gomez have shown, such a hierarchy had been a commonplace in the Arabic world in which Leo was raised: for several centuries Muslim scholars in the Maghrib had sought to justify slavery with racialised constructions of African tribes as well as northern Europeans.[14] Leo himself does not explicitly make the same connection, but it is hard to suppose that his view was significantly different, for the Africa he describes is full of slaves, most of whom are either traded from the Land of the Blacks (e.g. at 5.7) or imported from the Slavic and Circassian peoples far to the north (e.g. 6.26). Moreover, al-Wazzan was attentive to the larger differences of power that enabled enslavement; for instance, in a bleak passage he describes the starving Berber villagers of Barca (Cyrenaica), forced to sell their sons to Sicilian merchants in exchange for grain (1.22).

That said, the pejorative comments on the black Africans cannot be read as the straightforward expression of racial superiority. The bulk of his criticisms occur in a chapter (1.32) devoted to the faults of *all* the Africans, one that appears immediately after a chapter on their virtues, each divided up according to the four regions. Thus the black Africans may be 'lacking all reason and worse than irrational ... living like animals without laws and rules', but they are also 'people of integrity and good faith ... without any malice', respectful of learning, and enjoying 'a better life' than any other people in the world. Meanwhile, Leo's own people, the 'white' city dwellers of the Maghrib, are painted in equally negative terms: 'poor, impetuous and cruel', 'credulous and simple-minded', 'illiterate and ignorant', and so on. As racist as Leo's assumptions likely were, this section is not a simple polemic: a better interpretation of the two chapters may be, again, as a rhetorical performance in an Arabic tradition of praise-and-blame, resembling somewhat the European scholarly exercise of arguing on both sides of a given question.[15]

The issues of race and slavery in the *Cosmography* cannot be isolated from the question of gender. Although al-Wazzan rarely focuses on the specific problems faced by African women, it is not hard to discern structures of power and systemic misogyny behind his descriptions, for instance in the grouping of women and slaves together as property of powerful men. He always has his eye out for the attractiveness and availability of local women, and his prose often adopts a knowing leer, as in Fuwwah, a town on the Nile, where 'the women enjoy such a freedom that their husbands do not know where they are all day; you can imagine the rest' (6.12). The humanity of female slaves is obscured still further than that of their male counterparts: in the mountains outside Marrakesh, they are sold for more than the men – though for half as much as camels – commodified as mere breeders and objects of pleasure (2.1.5.8). Leo innocently reports that in the Numidian province of Draa, the locals marry their black slave-women and produce children of mixed colour, but he fails to acknowledge any coercion or subjugation (3.5).[16]

Like so many of his peers and forebears, al-Wazzan's judgements on peoples, both positive and negative, turn primarily on questions of religion and *civiltà*, a difficult word that we have rendered as 'culture' rather than 'civility' or 'civilisation'. One of the first things that he tells his reader about a given city or mountain, after its size and location, is how *civile* or cultured it is. He explains what culture means (2.3.16): mosques, madrasas, hospitals, hammams, inns, as well as the shops of merchants and artisans. It represents the advanced life of a community, and is the result of wealth, either from natural resources (e.g. 2.1.5.1) or trade (e.g. 2.2.1.3); conversely, culture can be depressed, along with population, by excessive taxation (e.g. 2.4.1.15). Because it is linked to wealth, culture is also connected to class; in Fez, Leo writes, 'the inhabitants of the city, or at least the burghers, are very cultured' (2.2.2.12.8). These burghers or *ciptadini* (*cittadini* in modern Italian) are an important feature of his demography: they are not nobles or gentlemen, but prosperous city-dwellers who have come to play a part in the regulation of civic life. Some townsfolk aspire to being *ciptadini* but are too coarse and poor (e.g. 2.2.4.4, 2.4.1.20). It is clear that this class is where Leo's own sympathies lie, but he is also quick to praise skilled artisans, such as the coppersmiths of Ceuta (2.2.4.14) or the female weavers in the mountains near Fez who can make wool blankets as fine as silk (2.2.7.15). By contrast, he can be highly critical of the corrupt and despotic ruling classes in Fez and elsewhere; he is more interested in, and spends more time describing, the hierarchies of court officials (2.2.2.15, 2.3.10.2, and especially 6.25–42). No doubt the emphases of this performance appealed to al-Wazzan's early readers, themselves members of a powerful civic class but eager for knowledge of artisanal excellence and Muslim tyranny.

A great deal of Leo's geography is taken up with history, and valuably fills several gaps in the historical record. But the spatial organisation of the book means that the history is told only in fragments, and we seem to see in it the Islamic centuries of Africa as through a glimmering crystal, turning from one facet to the next to catch the light. Underlying his vision is a mood, not quite captured by the English scholarship on his book,[17] of melancholy and nostalgia, for, while the great kingdoms of West Africa were flourishing and expanding in the sixteenth century, the old powers of the Maghrib were in decline. Leo could look back to the golden age of Islamic empire – to the Almoravids (c. 1050–1147), the Almohads (1147–1244) and the Marinids in their heyday (1244–1358). We hear repeatedly in the *Cosmography* about the heroic warrior-leaders of these dynasties: Yusuf ibn Tashfin, 'Abd al-Mu'min, Abu Yusuf Yaqub al-Mansur, 'Abd al-Haqq I and Abu 'Inan Faris. The Almoravids and Almohads, both dynasties developed out of the uprisings of rural Berber tribes, had controlled much of the Maghrib and southern Spain, founding and expanding cities, commissioning splendid works of architecture, and cultivating theology, philosophy, jurisprudence and the arts.

After the fall of the Almohad empire, power in northern Africa fragmented into three main groups: the Marinids in the west, centred in Fez and Marrakesh, the Hafsids in the east, centred in Tunis, and the weaker Zayyanids in the middle, centred in Tlemcen. Of these the Hafsids proved the most resilient, lasting – with a couple of interruptions – until the Ottoman capture of Tunis in 1574; their survival may be attributable to their creation of local tribal coalitions, itself a necessary result of their separation from their own tribal (Masmuda) heartland in the Atlas mountains.[18] Closer to Leo's home, the Marinids swiftly imploded in the second half of the fourteenth century, and continued to contract and weaken in the fifteenth, giving way eventually to the fragile Wattasid sultanate in Fez, but also to smaller regional powers and to the incursions of the Portuguese and Spanish along the coast, which had begun with the conquest of Ceuta in 1415. Leo himself had a ringside view of these bouts, working in some capacity for both the Wattasids and the Sa'diyans. One figure who encapsulates the unsteady politics of the period is the shadowy Berber chief Abu Zakariya Yahya bin Muhammad-u-Ta'fuft (d. 1518). After helping his friend 'Ali ibn Washman overthrow the semi-autonomous regime in Safi, Yahya defected to the Portuguese as a vassal *alcaide* (governor) from 1511; his name features regularly in state correspondence of the period, although the Portuguese captains stationed in Safi regarded him with distrust.[19] Leo met Yahya on an official mission, apparently from both Muhammad al-Burtuqali and Muhammad al-Qa'im (2.1.4.2), in Tumeglast – perhaps present-day Gmassa – where Yahya had come to collect tribute on behalf of Manuel I of Portugal (2.1.3.7). Likewise, al-Wazzan witnessed warfare first hand, such as the 1515–16 battle with the Portuguese and Spanish at Ma'mura, after which, he wrote, 'the waves heaved with blood' (2.2.2.4). The rise of warlords like Yahya, and the losses to the Iberians (and later the Ottomans), were results of the slow collapse of centralised power. As the Moroccan historian and philosopher Abdallah Laroui put it fifty years ago:

> The two centuries between the death of the Marīnid sultan Abū 'Inān [in 1358] and the defeats of the Spaniards at Tunis (1574) and of the Portuguese at El Ksar (1578) are a period of deep-seated regression, which for this very reason may well be one of the most significant periods in the history of the Maghrib.[20]

The great early witness of this decline was, again, Ibn Khaldun, whose pessimistic reading of the decline of civilisations was thoroughly informed by his experience of Marinid decadence after the death of Abu 'Inan. One hundred and fifty years later, al-Hasan al-Wazzan, without any explicit theory of society and politics, lamented the past and ongoing destruction of the world he knew; for good reason Laroui writes that the *Cosmography* 'should be taken as a picture not of a static world but of a phase in a process'. Even as a young man Leo had fixated on the grave, attempting to compile all the epitaphs in the Maghrib for 'a work of many chapters on the grief, sadness and bitter fear of death' (2.2.2.13.2). Later in life, as he went about his diplomatic duties, he found himself constantly saddened by loss, especially in the province of Tamasna, ruined during the Lamtuna invasion of the eleventh century, and the areas surrounding Fez, ruined in the siege of 1411. Of Anfa (modern Casablanca) he writes that 'the sight made him weep despite himself' (2.2.1.3), while in Rabat he experienced 'a deep melancholy for the vast difference between the life of the world when was founded, and its life today' (2.2.1.9). Salé, near Rabat, lost 'two-thirds of its culture' during Christian occupation and the current inhabitants had no appreciation for its fine old columns and marble windows (2.2.2.2). Soussa 'is now almost entirely uninhabited' (2.4.1.29) and only a fifth of its houses and a few shops remained; Leo's party 'felt great compassion and pity' at seeing the town mistreated by the local rulers. Even in the Almoravid capital Marrakesh, 'one of the grandest and greatest cities in the world', the ruined kasbah, and its beautiful old library, were now haunted by 'pigeons, crows, owls' (2.1.3.9). In Roman exile, Leo was looking back to a time when he had already been looking further back, memory mingled with forgetting.

The history in the *Cosmography* is valuable but factually unreliable. Leo's narratives are often hard to contextualise against other sources, and are sometimes contradicted by them, especially in earlier centuries and more distant lands, for instance with his account of the twelfth-century Kurdish general and sultan Saladin (6.26). Geopolitical struggles are often rendered as personal dramas, impossible to corroborate, as when the fall of Ceuta to the Portuguese in 1415 is imputed to the fact that the Marinid sultan heard of the attack during a party and refused to stop dancing (2.2.4.14). National catastrophe thus becomes for al-Wazzan, as for so many premodern writers, the stage for a moral lesson.

The *Cosmography* is an image of Africa, but it is also an image of Leo himself – proud, learned and worldly. We need not, of course, take that portrait at face value: it was the last and finest touch of his performance. Personal reminiscence is interwoven with the geography and history throughout, giving us the charm of subjective colour on the features and events described. In Ramusio's edition of the text, al-Wazzan refers to himself in the first person, but in the manuscript he mostly uses the third. His word for himself, *compositore*, is particularly interesting, as it means 'compositor', 'composer', 'compiler', someone who puts materials together; as he remarks at 2.1.3.13, when he visited the mountain of Semede in Morocco, he had to write out legal documents for the locals because none of them could *comporre* (put together) two words. It is also clear that Leo distinguishes a *compositore* from an *auctore* (see for instance 1.25 and 2.1.6.8), which he always uses in the sense of a venerable authority such as Ibn Khaldun. But as noted by Oumelbanine Zhiri, one of the world's foremost Leo scholars, his frequent expression 'ipso compositore dice' renders the Arabic phrase, common in writings of the period, *qala al-mu'allif*, which just means 'the author says'. We have therefore translated *compositore* as 'author' and *auctore* usually as 'authority', though the reader should bear in mind the subtlety of the term.

These performances are rich and complex, but they do not add up to an 'authentic' African vision of Africa, if by authenticity we mean an unfiltered, pre-European image – a phantom of colonial desire. Rather, the *Cosmography*, no less hybrid and no less knowing than its author, anticipates the language and questions of its Christian readers. Such an entanglement, far from being a weakness, constitutes the book's primary power.

READERSHIPS

Oumelbanine Zhiri has rightly said that the *Cosmography* 'holds a place of the first rank in the European construction, from the Renaissance onwards, of an "African" realm of knowledge, and a study of the work is important for understanding the past as well as the present European notion of Africa and the Maghrib.'[21] This is partly due to the fact that it contained a huge amount of information unavailable elsewhere in Europe for a long time. Western scholars could read a little about the West Coast of Africa in Alvise Cadamosto's records of his 1455–56 voyages (first published in 1507), about Ethiopia in Francisco Álvares's *True Report on the Lands of Prester John of the Indies* (1527, first published 1540), and about Egypt, especially Cairo, in a number of pilgrimage reports of the period, as well as in Pierre Belon's fascinating *Observations of Many Singularities and Memorable Things* (1553). They could also read accounts of African battles in the chronicles of João de Barros, Damião de Góis and others. Other eyewitness accounts of Africa, such as those of Gomes Eannes de Zurara, Duarte Pacheco Pereira, Valentim Fernandes and André Álvares de Almada, would be published only centuries later.[22] In breadth and depth, al-Wazzan's only real rival was Luis del Mármol Carvajal, a Spanish adventurer and historian whose *Descripción general de África* (1573–99) borrows much from the *Cosmography* while adding important first-hand material.[23]

However, the attraction of Leo's work for European readers was not solely a result of its valuable data. Its style and mood, too, played a part. In particular, the book's authorial voice holds two contrasting approaches to the reader in creative counterpoint, the first insisting on the wondrous, marvellous, extraordinary sights and places of Africa, unlike anything its Italian readers could imagine, the second finding points of continuity and resonance with Italy and Europe more broadly. In other words, the *Cosmography* both pushes and pulls. 'In spring, anyone approaching will smell such sweet fragrances and odours from the blossoms of orange, lemon, citron and other fruit that it will truly seem a paradise on earth' (2.2.2.12.7). 'The author has seen . . . a canopy bed made entirely with needlework, covered on top with a fine net of pearls weighing forty-five pounds; even without the pearls, the bed went for 10,000 *sherifi*' (6.17). But the people of Fez 'wear simple caps on their heads, like those worn in Italy at night' (2.2.2.12.8), and 'the roofs of the mosques are all built like the churches in Europe' (2.2.2.11). We ought not to prioritise one approach at the expense of the other; the book's strength lies at least partly in its unresolved ambivalence.

The book proved to be of singular interest to audiences across Europe. In the Renaissance, plagiarism was the sincerest form of flattery, and we find whole chunks of the *Cosmography* repeated near-verbatim in the works of Mármol, Damião de Góis, Livio Sanuto, André Thevet and others. The French political theorist Jean Bodin praised the book, and the polymath Isaac Casaubon, having emigrated to England at the end of his career, filled his Latin copy with eager annotations, cross-referencing the Bible, classical literature and Arabic geography.[24] Many writers simply mined the work for information, from ancient African religion to contemporary wedding customs; Michel de Montaigne noted the nomadic practice of covering the mouth while eating, and much later the young Jean-François Champollion, who subsequently deciphered the Rosetta Stone, used Leo's account of Egypt in drawing up his own topography of the Nile. Since its translation by John Pory in 1600, English readers, too, have taken an interest, some of them very illustrious. It has often been suggested that Shakespeare's Othello, an exiled and converted Moor, was inspired by al-Wazzan. John Milton, certainly, in his sonorous list of future kingdoms spied by Adam from a hill in Eden, has three lines of names extracted from the *Cosmography*:

> Or thence from Niger Flood to Atlas Mount,
> The Kingdoms of Almansor, Fez and Sus,
> Marocco and Algiers, and Tremisen ...
> *(Paradise Lost*, XI.402–404)

Two centuries later, Herman Melville would, somewhat inevitably, fillet curious details about whales from one chapter. Perhaps the most surprising engagement with al-Wazzan by a literary writer was that of W. B. Yeats, who claimed at a séance in 1912 to commune with a spirit calling itself 'Leo Africanus'; upon consulting the 1896 edition of Pory's translation, Yeats was delighted to discover that Leo had been 'a distinguished poet among the Moors'. In 1986, readers of fiction were confronted with al-Wazzan in the novel *Léon l'Africain* by the Lebanese-French writer Amin Maalouf. The novelist borrows many vignettes and episodes from the *Cosmography*, but also adds details of his own, such as giving his hero a black, fourteen-year-old slave-girl as a lover. Of course, while casting our eyes over the long story of Leo's readership, we must not forget the present. In the early twenty-first century, readers across the world are clamouring for better access to, and greater understanding of, the words and worlds of peoples beyond the narrow canon of Western literature; our task, like Leo's, is to acknowledge both profound difference and a common humanity. It is in such a spirit that the present translation is offered.

THE TEXT

The text of the *Cosmography* has a complex and interesting history. The work was not published until 1550, when it appeared in an edition by the distinguished Venetian geographer Giovanni Battista Ramusio (1485–1557), as the first part of his three-volume collection of travel narratives, *Navigationi e Viaggi*

(*Navigations and Voyages*). This text, which Ramusio entitled *La descrittione dell'Africa* (*The Description of Africa*), was subsequently translated into French by Jean Temporal (1556) and into Latin by the Antwerp schoolmaster Jan Blommaerts or Joannes Florianus (1556). The Temporal translation is worth noting for its woodcut images, a few of which we have reproduced in this volume; the unknown artist was working purely from the text, rather than from any independent knowledge of Africa, but the woodcuts give us some idea of how contemporary European audiences might have visualised al-Wazzan's descriptions. Florianus's version was the one most widely read in the Renaissance, but unfortunately it was wildly inaccurate; a later German translator claimed to have spotted 'six hundred' errors in it, the usual Latin idiom for 'an awful lot'.[25] Indeed, in Florianus we find howlers like *Iudaeus* (Jew) for *giudice* (judge), and *ver* (spring) for *inverno* (winter), as well as many little deliberate additions, deletions and rewritings. It was this version that John Pory (1572–1636), a young associate of the geographer Richard Hakluyt, translated into English in 1600, preserving Florianus's errors and adding a few of his own.

Pory's text remains the only version in English until today. It was re-edited in the 1890s by the Scottish botanist and explorer Robert 'Campsterianus' Brown (1842–95) for the Hakluyt Society, in three volumes, with copious notes, many of which are still useful, and an introduction detailing the faults in the translation, although the text itself remains uncorrected. Commissioned in 1890, it was Brown's last work, and he died a year before it appeared in print.

In December 1931 a discovery was made that would transform historians' understanding of the *Cosmography*, when the first (and still the only) known manuscript of the work appeared at auction in Rome. The 957-page manuscript, now Biblioteca Nazionale Centrale di Roma, MS V.E. 953, is entitled *La cosmographia* [*sic*] *& geographia de Affrica*: this is the text we have translated, and consequently the title we have used. What it immediately revealed is that Ramusio had rewritten the text from beginning to end, mostly to improve its prose style, but also cutting salacious passages and emending in places.[26] The corollary for an English reader is that the Pory translation is at three, not two, removes from the original. The manuscript is not in Leo's hand, and shows signs of scribal error; it is also not the copy used by Ramusio, whose text has more accurate numbers in places and contains two substantial passages not in our manuscript (these have been included here, in square brackets). The manuscript is dated 10 March 1526, but so is the colophon at the end of Ramusio's edition, suggesting that the date is in fact that of the completion of the work, not the copy. In fact, there is a good reason to believe that the copy is somewhat later, for it incorporates at least one subsequent event, namely the accession of Abu Muhammad 'Abdallah II of Tlemcen in 1528 (see 2.3.1). Since there is no break in the manuscript here, perhaps the scribe incorporated marginal additions from Leo's autograph copy.

Soon after its discovery, the manuscript became attached to the Milanese Arabist and geographer Angela Codazzi (1890–1972), who had penned an unpublished study of Leo a decade earlier. An edition of the manuscript became her life's work, but although she became known across Europe as the foremost expert on the *Cosmography*, the edition was never completed. The closest it came was in England. In the late 1940s, the Hakluyt Society investigated the possibility of a new, dual-language edition of the *Cosmography*.[27] The Society's secretary, R. A. 'Peter' Skelton, asked E. W. Bovill, a historian with several works on Africa under his belt, to produce a translation and commentary in collaboration with Gerard Crone, with whom Bovill had previously worked on the Society's 1937 translation of the *Voyages of Cadamosto*. Codazzi, the Society's only Italian member, would supply the text; it was to be edited from the manuscript with variants from Ramusio's edition. Skelton's proposal for a five-volume edition was accepted, with some hesitation, by the Society Council in January 1962. Everyone waited for Codazzi to supply her text. But it did not come. Bovill died in 1966, Skelton in 1970, Codazzi in 1972.

Another publication associated with Codazzi was more successful, namely the 1956 French translation by Alexis Épaulard (1878–1949), which has been used by scholars for the past half-century as the standard edition of the work. Épaulard's correspondence with Codazzi until his death evokes a tense relationship: he hoping to work together and share expertise, she polite but aloof, unwilling to let her research be published under his name, or even to share her images of the manuscript.[28] The published translation uses Ramusio as its text, with only occasional reference to the manuscript, which Épaulard had studied for two weeks in June 1939; it was completed, and furnished with excellent notes, by a trio of specialists, Théodore Monod, Henri Lhote and Raymond Mauny. (These three were also to participate in the Hakluyt Society edition, although, as Skelton lamented, Lhote was by this stage 'persona non grata' among French scholars, perhaps for his 1958 book claiming extraterrestrial contact with the ancient peoples of the Sahara.) We have gratefully used the French notes (cited as 'Épaulard') in compiling our own, but the reader should turn directly to that edition for further information on certain historical details, and for fuller attention to the discrepancies between Leo's geography and the reality of modern Africa.

In 2014 the manuscript itself finally appeared in print, lightly edited by Gabriele Amadori. This is the text we have used for the translation, with additional reference to the high-resolution images of the manuscript online at the Biblioteca Nazionale's Biblioteca Digitale. We believe ours is the first ever translation directly from the manuscript, although we have allowed ourselves to emend where we have judged Ramusio's reading better. A new edition of the Italian, with the manuscript and Ramusio's text on facing pages, is currently being prepared by Andrea Donnini.

THE TRANSLATION

In this volume we have aimed to produce a clear and readable translation for a general audience, but a few words will be necessary on some of our strategies and word choices. Translating the *Cosmography* poses two unusual challenges. First, Italian was not Leo's native language, and the style is, at least by the standards of Renaissance humanism, inelegant and sometimes confusing. His sentences are not periodic or rhythmic, but instead consist usually of chains of simple statements joined by 'and', 'and so', 'but', 'therefore', 'because', and so on. We decided that rigidly preserving these structures, while philosophically defensible, would be grating for the general reader, and have therefore neatened up the sentences a little and cut some empty repetition; however, we have not rewritten to anything like the same extent as Ramusio, and in places we have permitted a little inelegance and stiltedness to remain. To give a flavour of the original, here is a passage, taken at random, from Leo's chapter on the town of Collo in present-day Algeria:

E il populo di la dicta terra vive in sua liberta simelmente loro vicini montanari e li ciptadini con li dicti montanarii sonno tutti in una lega contra el re di Tunis e il prencepe o logotenente del re che sta in Constantina li quali cercano continuo di potere subiicere la dicta terra ma non e stato mai possibile peroche ce sonno altissimi monti habitati da valenti homini. (2.4.1.7, MS 305r)

Literally translated this would turn out as something like:

And the people of the said town live in their freedom, likewise their neighbours the mountainfolk, and the citizens with the said mountainfolk are all in a league against the king of Tunis and the prince or viceroy of the king who lives in Constantine, who seek continually to be able to subjugate the said town, but it was never possible because these are very high mountains inhabited by brave men.

Whereas we have translated it:

They live in freedom, as do the neighbouring mountainfolk, with whom the citizens are allied against the king of Tunis and his prince or viceroy in Constantine. These two are always trying to subjugate the town, but have never succeeded, because the mountains are very high and their inhabitants are brave.

Likewise, we have permitted elegant variation in passages with a repetitive vocabulary; for instance, 'dopoi El Mansor la renovo

li muri e fece ivi uno hospitale *bellissimo* e uno *bellissimo* pala-
tio per logiamento delli soi soldati e anchi uno *bellissimo* templo
dove fece una *bellissima* sala ornata di marmori intagliati a
musaicho' (2.2.1.10, italics added), which we have translated
as 'Al-Mansur later renovated the walls and built a *very fine*
hospital, a *magnificent* block as barracks for his soldiers, and
a *splendid* mosque with a hall adorned with inlaid marble
mosaics'. On similar grounds, we have tended to omit Leo's
near-universal use of the word 'circa' (about) before numbers.

The second challenge is that, to communicate key terms of
Muslim culture, Leo often chose corresponding words from
classical or Christian culture. For instance, his usual word for a
mosque is *tempio*, 'temple', and for a caliph *pontifice*, 'pontiff'.
This was a brilliant stroke of familiarisation for an audience that
might otherwise have been daunted by words and concepts for
which they had no equivalent. (The practice is inconsistent: occasionally we find *moschea*, *califa* and so on in Leo's text.) However,
we live today in a global society, and a gesture intended to draw
Leo's readers in would now have the opposite effect. We have
therefore rendered these words with the more usual term in English, feeling that it would be too jarring to a general reader for a
caliph to be called a pontiff, and so on. Most of the Arabic words
have become sufficiently naturalised to need no explanation, but
others may need a gloss. Here is a full list:

caliph, for Leo's 'pontefice' (pontiff). The supreme religious
    and political authority of an Islamic region.
Eid al-Fitr, for Leo's 'Pascha' (Easter). The feast of breaking
    the fast at the end of Ramadan, also called Eid es-Seghir in
    Morocco.
hammam, for Leo's 'stufa' (stove or bathhouse). The public
    baths, modelled on the Roman baths, that represent an
    important feature of any large Muslim city.
imam, for Leo's 'sacerdote' (priest). In Sunni Islam, the imam
    is not a priest in a church hierarchy, but the prayer leader in
    a mosque.
ksar, for Leo's 'castello' (castle). A fortified village of a
    recognisable type in North Africa.

madrasa, for Leo's 'collegio' (college). An institution of higher
   learning, focused on jurisprudence.
minaret, for Leo's 'turre' (tower), where appropriate. The
   tower adjacent to a mosque and used for the call to prayer.
mosque, for Leo's 'tempio' (temple).

By contrast, where the Arabic term would be too obscure for
an English reader, or when the English term does not misrepre-
sent the meaning, we have translated more directly, sometimes
with a footnote. For instance, when referring to the *mahr* or
bride price used in Muslim marriage ceremonies, Leo's word is
dote, which we have rendered literally as 'dower'; likewise, we
have translated *consulo*, his term for the *amin* or head of a trade
guild, as 'consul'.

   Arabic personal names and tribe names have been rendered
using modern conventions, using a ' for the *ayin* and a ' for the
hamza; for instance, 'Abd al-Mu'min is our spelling of Leo's
Habdulmumen.[29] With our readership in mind, we have priori-
tised accessibility over regularity in transcribing place names.
Where there is a standard English form (e.g. Algiers, Marrakesh, Timbuktu) we have used that, and where there are
competing alternatives we have preferred forms with less
French influence (e.g. Tuggurt for Touggourt, Jerba for Djerba).
Otherwise we have given modern Arabic forms, using *al-* for
the article except where *el* has become the norm; for instance
we use the French-tinged 'Oued el Abid' instead of 'Wad al-
Abid'. In a few instances we give both the Arabic and the
European forms in the title of a chapter, e.g. 'Sabta (Ceuta)'.
The forms used by al-Wazzan himself have also been provided
in a separate index. We have followed Leo's inconsistent gemin-
ation of the Arabic definite article: for instance 'at-Tawil'
(ettauil) and 'ash-Sharif' (Esserif), but 'al-Sheikh' (El Saic).

   Finally, a few other notes on our choice of words, spelling
and punctuation. When Leo uses words in Arabic, Persian,
Latin, Berber and Hausa, we have retained them, supplying a
gloss in brackets whenever Leo himself does not. We have done
the same for Italian or Arabic words that have no English equivalent, notably the terms for units of measurement, the *cantar*, the

ratl, the *scorzo* and the *canna* – usually defined in the text – and for coinage, as follows:

baiocco. An Italian silver coin, roughly 100 to the ducat; Leo means the silver dirham, which was likewise around 100 to the gold dinar (see 2.3.10.2).

ducat (*ducato*). The gold dinar or *mithqal* (strictly a measure of mass, equal to 4.25 grams) widely used in the Islamic world.

duppuli. This word seems to denote a Hafsid gold dinar, since it is only used in Book 2.4 (the kingdom of Tunis). Apparently a form of *doppio* or *doppia*, 'double', the name of a number of European gold coins from the period; compare *dobla*, *doubloon*, etc.

quattrino. A copper coin worth (in Leo's time) a quarter of a *baiocco*; Leo may mean either a copper coin like the *fals* or a fractional dirham.

sherifi (Leo's *srafini* or *seraphini*). An Ottoman ducat used in Egypt, sometimes rendered *seraph*. Equivalent to the *zecchino* (*chequin*, *sequin*).

Terms for settlement types we have consistently rendered with the following words: *cipta*, city; *terra*, town; *terrecciola*, little town; *castello*, ksar; *casale*, village; *habitatione*, settlement. That said, Leo himself does not always use these terms consistently; for instance, he refers to Larache (2.2.3.3) as both a *cipta* and a *terra*.

Leo usually gives dates according to the Arabic calendar, dated from the *hijra* of AD 622 (AH 1, or *Anno Hegirae* 1). We have supplied the equivalent date in the Christian calendar in brackets; except where we had more specific evidence, we give the latter as a range of two years, since the two calendars are not synchronised. It is worth noting, from the one or two instances where Leo gives both forms, that he did not know the correct means of converting dates between calendars, and where appropriate and possible we have supplied correct dates in a footnote.

All brackets in the text are added by us. Square brackets indicate textual lacunae, but also subheadings in the three chapters on Fez (2.2.2.11–13) and one on Tlemcen (2.3.10.1), introduced by Ramusio to break up the text. The other divisions are Leo's own, although we have added the numeration. Round brackets supply brief glosses, including fuller personal names, alternative renderings of place names, dates in the Christian calendar and translations of non-Italian words.

NOTES

1   For the reasons for this dating, see 2.1.4.2, note 60 (pp. 472–3).

2   Natalie Zemon Davis, *Trickster Travels*, 18, prefers the first explanation (originally advanced by the founder of modern Leo studies, Louis Massignon), while Dietrich Rauchenberger, *Johannes Leo*, 28–9, proposes the second. The latter points out the concentration of Berbers in Granada, and notes that the adjective 'Affricano', which Leo applies to himself in the *Cosmography*, usually denotes the Berbers, not the Arabs, in Africa.

3   See, e.g., Mohamed B. A. Benchekroun, *La vie intellectuelle marocaine sous les Mérinides et les Waṭṭāsides, XIIIe, XIVe, XVe, XVIe siècles* (Rabat, 1974), 8–9; see also 57 on the Fez library.

4   Marino Sanudo, *Diarii*, ed. F. Stefani, 58 vols (Venice, 1879–1902), XXVI, col. 195.

5   Michael Casiri, *Bibliotheca arabico-hispana Escurialensis* (Madrid, 1760), I, 172.

6   These treatises are preserved in a single, neatly written manuscript in the Laurentian Library in Florence, Plut.36.35; page images are available on the library website. The treatise on prosody was edited by Angela Codazzi as 'Il trattato dell'Arte Metrica di Giovanni Leone Africano', in *Studi Orientalistici in Onore di Giorgio Levi Della Vida*, vol. 1 (Rome, 1956), 180–98. The other work has recently been translated into French by Jean-Louis Déclais and Houari Touati as *De quelques hommes illustres chez les Arabes et les Hébreux* (Paris, 2000).

7   This dictionary is now Real Biblioteca del Escorial, Spain, Manuscritos árabes MS 598.

8   For the sceptical view, see Pekka Masonen, *The Negroland Revisited*, 189–94.

9   Thomas Anyan, *A Sermon Preached at S. Maries Church in Oxford, the 12. of July. 1612* (London, 1612), 22.

10   Matthew L. Keegan, 'Digressions in the Islamic Archive: Al-Ḥarīrī's *Maqāmāt* and the Forgotten Commentary of al-Panǧdīhī (d. 584/1188)', *Intellectual History of the Islamicate World* 10 (2022), 82–118, at 85.

11   On 'Ifriqiya', see Davis, *Trickster Travels*, 125–6. The name is used only once in the rest of the *Cosmography* (in 1.13).

12   Dominique Casajus, 'Les noms de peuples ont une histoire', in *Léon l'Africain*, ed. François Pouillon, 103–17.

13   Rouighi, *Inventing the Berbers*.

14   El Hamel, *Black Morocco*, 60–90, and Gomez, *African Dominion*, 43–57.

15   The fourteenth-century Moroccan traveller Ibn Battuta includes a similar section on the Land of the Blacks (*Travels*, IV.965–6). Leo himself mentions an example of this Arabic genre at 2.4.1.13.

16   On women and Islamic slavery, see especially El Hamel, *Black Morocco*, 11–12 and 17–58.

17   See, however, Guy Turbet-Delof, *L'Afrique barbaresque dans la littérature française aux XVIe et XVIIe siècles* (Geneva, 1973), 57–8, and the conclusion of Federico Cresti, 'Il Maghreb centrale agli inizi del XVI secolo: Strutture politiche, economie urbane e territorio nella *Descrittione dell'Africa* di Giovanni Leone Africano', *Africa* 53.2 (1998), 218–38, at 236–7.

18   Loimeier, *Muslim Societies in Africa*, 48–9.

19   Matthew T. Racine, 'Service and Honor in Sixteenth-Century Portuguese North Africa: Yahya-u-Ta'fuft and Portuguese Noble Culture', *Sixteenth Century Journal* 32.1 (2001), 67–90.

20   Abdallah Laroui, *The History of the Maghrib: An Interpretive Essay*, trans. Ralph Manheim (Princeton, 1977), 227, 299.

21   Zhiri, '"Il compositore"', 65.

22   For more information, see John Thornton, 'European Documents and African History', in *Writing African History*, ed. John Edward Philips (Rochester, NY, 2005), 254–65.

23   A little later, one can add Duarte Lopes' *Relatione del reame di Congo et delle circonvicine contrade* (Rome, 1591) and two more derivative works, Diego de Torres' *Relacion del Origen y Sucesso de los Xarifes y del Estado de los Reinos de Marruecos, Fez, etc.* (Seville, 1586), and Jean-Baptiste Gramaye's *Africa illustrata* (Tournai, 1622).

24   Now British Library, shelfmark 793.d.2.

25   Georg Wilhelm Lorsbach, *Solemnia academica* (Herborn, 1801), 7.

26   See Zhiri, 'Leo Africanus, Translated and Betrayed'.

27 British Library, Hakluyt Society Archives, Mss Eur F594/6/1/15.
28 Biblioteca Comunale Centrale di Milano, Carte Codazzi, fasc. 70/14.
29 The exception is unidentified names, which we have left as given; but these are rare.

Timeline

Further Reading

The editions we have consulted are the following, in date order:

La descrittione d'Africa, in *Navigationi e Viaggi*, ed. Giovanni Battista Ramusio, vol. 1 (Venice, 1550).

Description de l'Afrique, tierce partie du monde, trans. Jean Temporal (Lyon, 1556). The source of our images.

The History and Description of Africa and of the Notable Things Therein Contained, trans. John Pory, ed. Robert Brown, 3 vols (London, 1896, reissued by Cambridge UP, 2010).

Description de l'Afrique, trans. Alexis Épaulard, ed. Alexis Épaulard, Th. Monod, H. Lhote and R. Mauny (Paris, 1956).

Dietrich Rauchenberger, *Johannes Leo der Afrikaner: Seine Beschreibung des Raumes zwischen Nil und Niger nach dem Urtext* (Wiesbaden, 1999). Books Four and Five.

Cosmographia de l'Affrica (Ms. V.E. 953 – Biblioteca Nazionale Centrale di Roma – 1526), ed. Gabriele Amadori (Rome, 2014). Our source text.

In addition to the Pory *History and Description*, there have been excerpts in English translation found in:

A. R. Allen, *Leo's Travels in the Sudan* (London, 1962): parts of Book 5, adapted from Pory's translation.

John O. Hunwick, *Timbuktu and the Songhay Empire* (Leiden, 2003), 272–91: parts of Book 5, from Ramusio.

Pierre Joris, 'From *Travel Diaries*', in *Poems for the Millennium: The University of California Book of North African Literature, Volume Four*, ed. Pierre Joris and Habib Tengour (Berkeley, 2012), 179–82: parts of Book 1 and Book 2 (Fez), from Épaulard.

Oumelbanine Zhiri, 'Leo Africanus's *Description of Africa*', in *Travel Knowledge: European 'Discoveries' in the Early Modern Period*, ed. Ivo Kamps and Jyotsna G. Singh (London, 2001), 249–57: parts of Book 1, from the manuscript.

There are only a few items in English worth reading on Leo Africanus: above all Natalie Zemon Davis's first-rate biography, *Trickster Travels: A Sixteenth-Century Muslim Between Worlds* (New York, 2006), but also Pekka Masonen, *The Negroland Revisited: Discovery and Invention of the Sudanese Middle Ages* (Helsinki, 2000), 167–214, especially on Leo's knowledge of sub-Saharan Africa. On Leo's early translators, two items should be consulted: Oumelbanine Zhiri, 'Leo Africanus, Translated and Betrayed', in *The Politics of Translation in the Middle Ages and the Renaissance*, ed. Renate Blumenfeld-Kosinski et al. (Ottawa, 2001), 161–74, and Crofton Black, 'Leo Africanus's *Descrittione dell'Africa* and its Sixteenth-Century Translations', *Journal of the Warburg and Courtauld Institutes* 65.1 (2002), 262–72. Unfortunately much other English work on Leo is reliant on the faulty 1600 translation by John Pory. For a non-scholarly work of travel that follows in Leo's footsteps, see Nicholas Jubber, *The Timbuktu School for Nomads: Across the Sahara in the Shadow of Jihad* (London, 2017).

The major work on al-Wazzan is mostly in other European languages; above all one should mention Oumelbanine Zhiri, *L'Afrique au miroir de l'Europe: fortunes de Jean Léon l'Africain à la Renaissance* (Geneva, 1991), much of it about the *Cosmography*'s readers; Dietrich Rauchenberger, *Johannes Leo der Afrikaner* (see list of editions above), an impressive study with a focus on Books Four and Five; and the conference volume *Léon l'Africain*, ed. François Pouillon et al. (Paris, 2009), especially the early chapters. Valuable shorter items include Federico Cresti, 'Il Maghreb centrale agli inizi del XVI secolo: Strutture politiche, economie urbane e territorio nella *Descrittione dell'Africa* di Giovanni Leone Africano', *Africa* 53.2 (1998), 218–38, and Oumelbanine Zhiri, '"Il compositore" ou l'autobiographie éclatée de Jean Léon l'Africain', in *Le voyage des théories*, ed. Ali Benmakhlouf (Casablanca, 2000), 63–80.

For work on subjects related to this book, the following may be of interest (we have limited our list to accessible English titles). On Maghribi history, Jamil M. Abun-Nasr, *A History of the Maghrib in the Islamic Period* (Cambridge, 1987), remains a classic and reliable account; see also Matthew T. Racine, *A Most Opulent Iliad: Expansion, Confrontation and Cooperation on the Southern Moroccan Frontier (1505–1542)* (San Diego, CA, 2012), Maya Shatzmiller, *The Berbers and the Islamic State: The Marinid Experience in Pre-Protectorate Morocco* (Princeton, 2000), especially the chapters on the origins of the Berbers, and on the Moroccan institutions of the madrasa, *waqf* and taxation, and Chouki El Hamel, *Black Morocco: A History of Slavery, Race, and Islam* (Cambridge, 2012). An older but very readable account of Fez in the period leading up to Leo is Roger Le Tourneau, *Fez in the Age of the Marinides*, trans. Besse Alberta Clement (Norman, OK, 1961). On Islam in Africa, see Roman Loimeier, *Muslim Societies in Africa: A Historical Anthropology* (Indianapolis, 2013). For architecture, see Jonathan M. Bloom's splendid *Architecture of the Islamic West: North Africa and the Iberian Peninsula, 700–1800* (New Haven, 2020). For West Africa, see, in addition to the works by Hunwick and Masonen mentioned above, two recent books, Michael A. Gomez, *African Dominion: A New History of Empire in Early and Medieval West Africa* (Princeton, 2018), and Toby Green, *A Fistful of Shells: West Africa from the Rise of the Slave Trade to the Age of Revolution* (Chicago, 2019). For those interested in the primary sources, the indispensable English volume is *Corpus of Early Arabic Sources for West African History*, ed. N. Levtzion and J. F. P. Hopkins, trans. J. F. P. Hopkins (Cambridge, 1981), still in print. On the Berbers, see Michael Brett and Elizabeth Fentress, *The Berbers* The Peoples of Africa (Oxford, 1996) and Ramzi Rouighi's revisionist *Inventing the Berbers: History and Ideology in the Maghrib* (Philadelphia, 2019). Kathleen Bickford

Berzock, ed., *Caravans of Gold, Fragments in Time: Art, Culture, and Exchange Across Medieval Saharan Africa* (Princeton and Oxford, 2019), is a lavishly illustrated guide to the culture of the Sahara as Leo would have known it. On Mamluk Egypt see Carl F. Petry, *The Civilian Elite of Cairo in the Later Middle Ages* (Princeton, 1981) and *Protectors or Praetorians? The Last Mamlūk Sultans and Egypt's Waning as a Great Power* (Albany, NY, 1994).

Finally, in our endnotes, we occasionally adduce other early accounts of Africa and its history, in translation where possible. These are: (1) Abu Salim al-Ayyashi, *Voyage de l'Imam el-'Aïachi depuis le Pays des Aït-'Aïach, dans le Maroc, jusqu'à Tripoli, et retour*, trans. Adrien Berbrugger, in *Exploration scientifique de l'Algérie*, 40 vols (Paris, 1844–81), IX, 1–164; (2) Ibn Battuta, *The Travels of Ibn Battuta*, AD 1325–1354, 5 vols (London: Hakluyt Society, 1958–2000); (3) Pierre Belon, *Travels in the Levant*, ed. Alexandra Merle, trans. James Hogarth (Kilkerran, 2012); (4) Alvise Cadamosto, 'Voyage from Venice to Cape St Vincent' (1455), in Robert Kerr, ed., *A General History and Collection of Voyages and Travels Arranged in Systematic Order*, 18 vols (Edinburgh, 1811–24), II, 203–45; (5) Felix Fabri, *Evagatorium in Terrae Sanctae, Arabiae et Egypti peregrinationem*, ed. Konrad Dieterich Hassler, 3 vols (Stuttgart, 1843); (6) Jean-Baptiste Gramaye, *Africa illustrata* (Tournai, 1622); (7) Muhammad al-Idrisi, *Géographie*, trans. Pierre-Amédée Jaubert, 2 vols (Paris, 1836–40); (8) Taqi al-Din al-Maqrizi, *Durar al-'Uqud al-Faridah* (Beirut, 2002); (9) Abu al-Hasan 'Ali al-Mas'udi, *Les prairies d'or*, trans. C. Barbier de Meynard and Abel Pavet de Courteille, 9 vols (Paris, 1861); (10) Duarte Pacheco Pereira, *Esmeraldo de situ orbis*, ed. and trans. George H. T. Kimble (London, 1937); and (11) Arnold Von Harff, *The Pilgrimage*, trans. Malcolm Letts (London, 1946).

Acknowledgements

In a pandemic period of global isolation and confinement, it has been the greatest pleasure to correspond with the world's experts about a treatise that embodies travel and exploration. For their insights into linguistic, historical, cultural, architectural and other aspects of the *Cosmography*, and for their support and encouragement of the project more generally, we'd like to thank Mohammad Al Attar, Mohamad Ballan, Lars Behrisch, Francisco Bethencourt, Jonathan Bloom, Lucinda Byatt, Jeremy Dell, Rachel Holmes, Shamil Jeppie, Matthew Keegan, Dilwyn Knox, David Nirenberg, Valentina Pugliano, Ramzi Rouighi, Ulinka Rublack, Lameen Souag, Nicholas Warner, Natalie Zemon Davis, Oumelbanine Zhiri, and most of all Andrea Donnini, who fielded dozens of textual and critical queries. We'd also like to thank library staff at the Biblioteca Comunale Centrale di Milano and the British Library for their assistance. The translation and research were supported in part by Anthony's year-long fellowship at the Wissenschaftskolleg zu Berlin, for which we are both profoundly grateful.

THE COSMOGRAPHY AND
GEOGRAPHY OF AFRICA

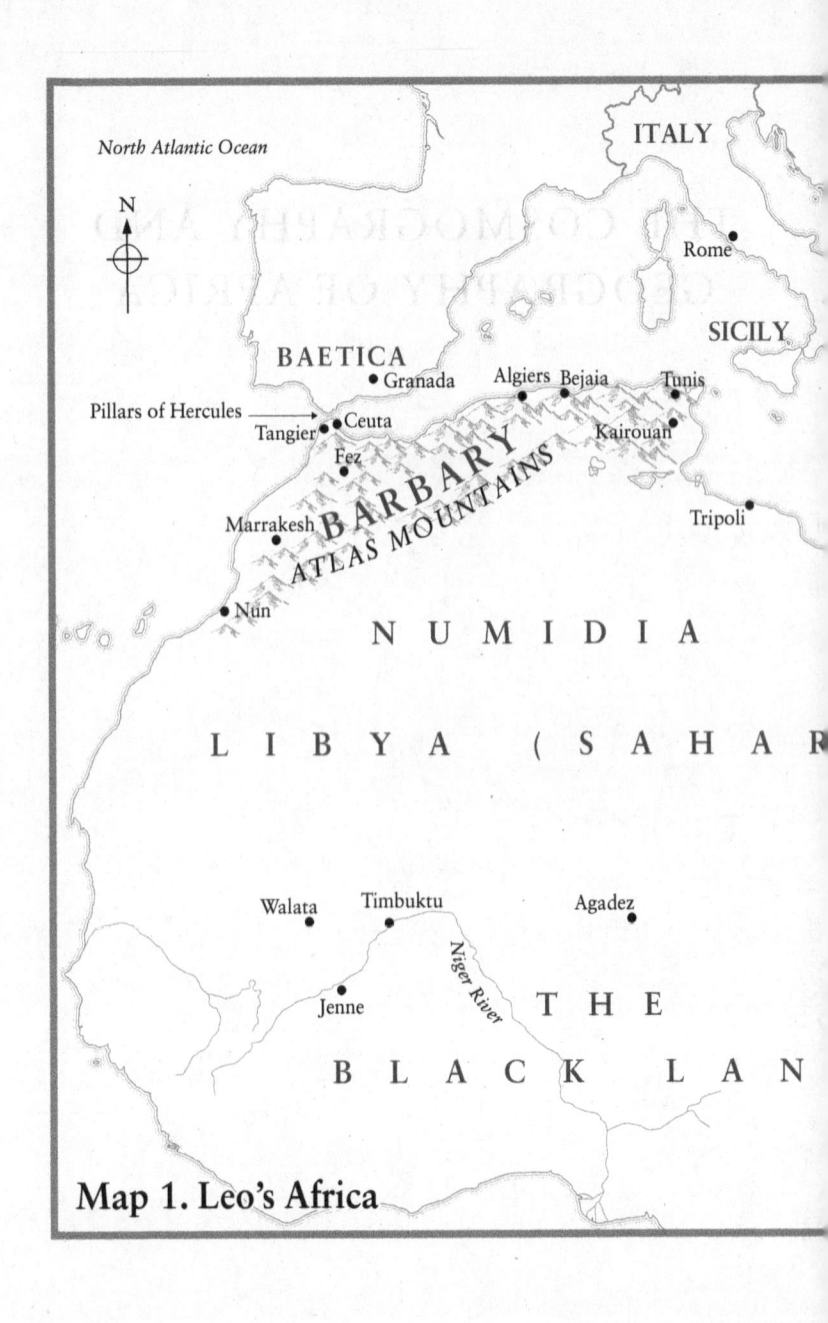

Map 1. Leo's Africa

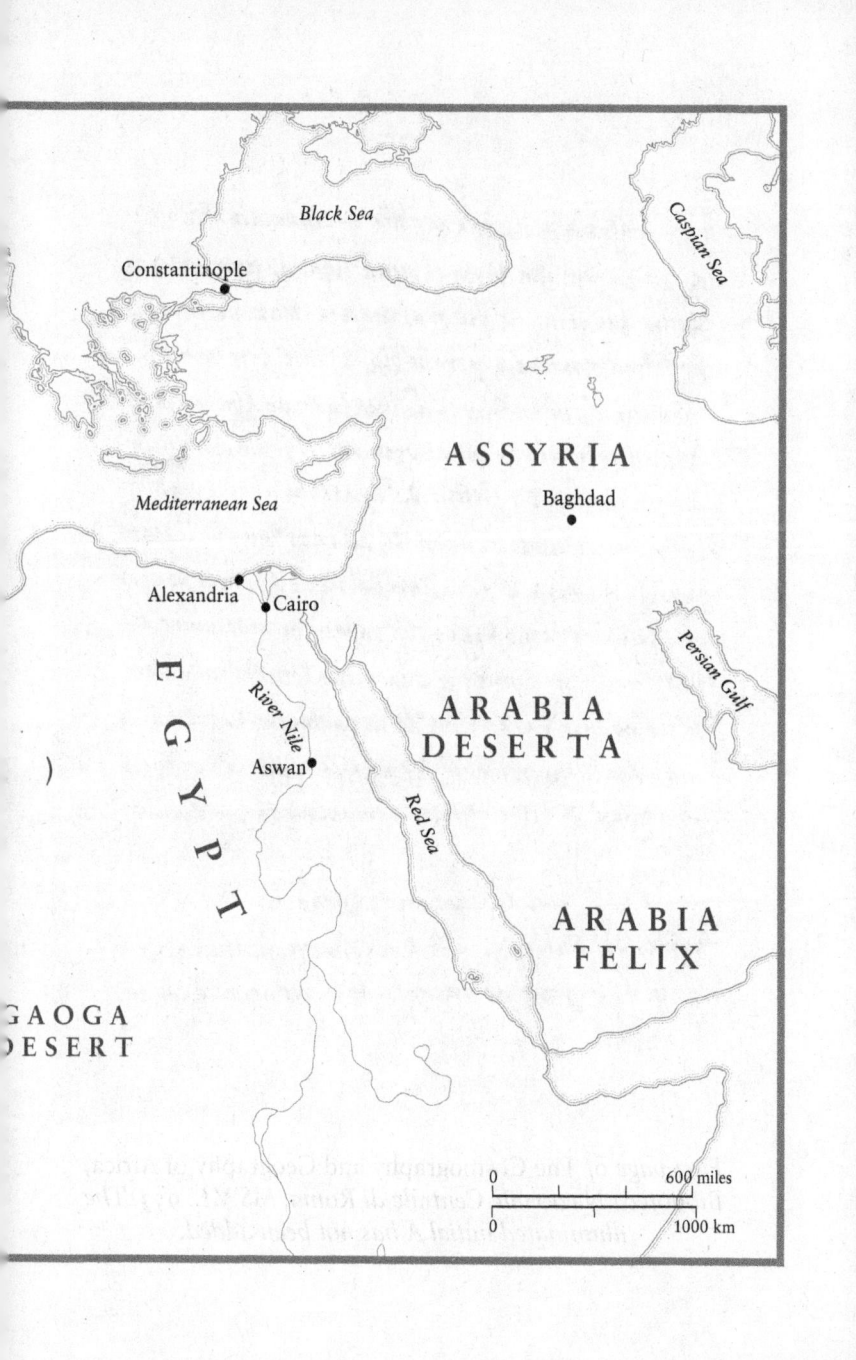

ffrica in lingua arabica e chiamata ifrichia
dicta da Faracha Verbo el quale significa separauit e
sonno due opinione per qual causa fu chiamata ifrichia
la prima opinione e perche questa parte de la terra e
separata da la europa e da una parte de Asia con lo ma
re mediterraneo e la ltra opinione e per la quale fu chi
amata ifrichia Da Ifricus Re di Arabia felice e lo quale fu
lo primo che ando ad habitare in la dca Parte de lo xtiano
pero che fu rupto e descacciato dal Re de Asiria et non pos
sette induieto al suo Regno cosi passo in Suria lo fiume del
nilo cum li suy exerciti e ando uerso ponente in tanto ch
se fermo in le parte uicine de la cartagine e per tale ca
usa li Araby non uengono per Affrica se non la Regione di
cartagene e nella Affrica la chiamono la parte occiden
tale.

De li Termini di Affrica

Appresso li Doctory Affricany e cosmografi Affrica e Ter
mine de la parte de oriente in lo fiume del nilo comen

BOOK I.

INTRODUCTION

1.1. Introduction

Africa is called in Arabic *Ifriqiya*, from the word *faraqa*, meaning 'he separated'. There are two opinions on the origin of this name. The first is that this part of the world is separated from Europe and Asia by the Mediterranean; the second is that it was named after Ifricus,[1] king of Arabia Felix, who was the first to settle in that part of the world, since he had been defeated and driven out by the king of Assyria and could not return to his kingdom. Ifricus raced across the Nile with his army and travelled west to the part near Carthage, which is why the Arabs call only the region of Carthage 'Africa', whereas they call the whole of Africa 'the Western Part'.[2]

1.2. The boundaries of Africa

According to African scholars and cosmographers, Africa is bounded to the east by the Nile, stretching north from the tributaries of the lake in the Gaoga desert, to the lowlands of Egypt where the Nile flows into the Mediterranean. It is bounded by the Nile Delta to the north, extending west to the straits of the Pillars of Hercules.[3] The western border stretches from these straits near the ocean down to Nun, the furthest town of Libya on the ocean. The southern border extends from Nun, along the ocean that surrounds the whole of Africa, as far as the Gaoga deserts.

1.3. The divisions of Africa

According to our scholars and cosmographers, Africa is divided into four parts – Barbary, Numidia, Libya and the Black Land. Barbary begins to the east at Mount Meiies,[4] the furthest point of the Atlas range 300 miles from Alexandria; bounded to the north by the Mediterranean, it extends from Mount Meiies as far as the Pillars of Hercules. The western part runs from those Pillars along the ocean to the other end of the Atlas mountains, that is, where the Maghrib begins on the ocean near the town of Massa. The southern part is bounded by the Atlas mountains, on the side facing the Mediterranean. This is the noblest part of Africa, where the cities are, and where the people are white and capable of reason.

The second part is called Numidia in Latin, but the Arabs call it Bilad al-Jarid, that is, 'the Land of Dates'. It begins in the east at al-Wahat, a region 100 miles from Egypt, and extends west as far as Nun on the ocean; to the north it is bounded by the south-facing Atlas mountains, while the southern regions are bordered by the sands of the Libyan desert. The Arabs naturally call all the lands in which dates are grown by the same name since they are all of one terrain.

The third part is called Libya, though Arabic has no word for it but *Sahra*, 'desert'. It begins from the Nile to the east, on the borders of al-Wahat, and extends west to the ocean; to the north it borders Numidia, where the dates are grown, and to the south it borders the Black Land.

The fourth part, the Black Land, begins to the east at the kingdom of Gaoga and extends west to Walata on the ocean. To the north it borders the Libyan desert and is bound by the ocean to the south. These are places unknown to us, but, even so, we have acquired much knowledge of them from the merchants who venture from these regions to the kingdom of Timbuktu. Through the middle of the Black Land flows the river Niger, which issues from a huge lake in a desert called Seu to the east, and extends west until it enters the ocean. According to our cosmographers the Niger is a branch of the Nile that vanishes underground and re-emerges at the lake. Others say that it issues from the western region of the mountains and flows east into a lake; but this opinion is false, because we have sailed from the kingdom of Timbuktu in the east, following the water down to the kingdoms of Jenne or Mali west of Timbuktu.

The principal kingdoms of the Blacks are those on the river Niger. It should be noted that the part of the Black Land lying across the Nile – that is, from its eastern bank to the Indian Sea, bordering the Red Sea to the north, in other words the area adjoining the straits of Arabia Felix[5] – is not held by our cosmographers to be part of Africa, for many reasons given in their long treatises. Latin speakers call this region Ethiopia. From it come certain friars whose faces are branded with fire, whom one sees throughout Europe, especially in Rome. This country is governed by a ruler like a patriarch whom the Italians call *Pretegianni* (Prester John).[6] Most people in this region are Christians, but there is a Muslim ruler who controls a large part.

1.4. The divisions of the kingdoms of the four parts of Africa

Barbary is divided into four kingdoms. The first is Marrakesh, which is divided into seven regions: Haha, Sous, Guzula, Marrakesh, Doukkala, Haskoura and Tadla. The second is Fez, which also has seven regions: Tamasna, Fez, Azgar, al-Habat, er-Rif, Garet, Al Haouz. The third is Tlemcen, which has three regions: the mountains, Tenes and Algiers. The fourth is Tunis, which has four regions: Bejaia, Constantine, Tripoli and Zeb, which is partly in Numidia. The region of Bejaia was always in contention between the kings of Tunis and Tlemcen; in modern times it was made a kingdom by itself, until the capital city was captured by Count Pedro Navarro in the name of Ferdinand of Spain.

1.5. The divisions of Numidia, the Land of Dates

This part of Africa is less well developed, and so cosmographers and historians have not assigned any kingdoms to it, since its regions and settlements are very far from one another. For instance, Tesset, a Numidian town of 400 homes, is 300 miles across the Libyan desert from the nearest settlement; such a thing hardly merits the title of a kingdom. There are, however, some places like the other regions of Africa in regard to the quality of their settlements, such as the state of Sijilmasa in the part of Numidia near Mauretania, the state of Zeb near the kingdom of Bejaia, and Bilad al-Jarid near Tunis; therefore the author will briefly note these places, one by one, in the third book of this work. The rest, beginning in the Maghrib, are: Tesset, Waddan, Ifran, Akka, Draa, Tabelbala, Todgha, Ferkla, Sijilmasa, Beni Gumi, Figuig, Tuat, Tesebit, Tigurarin, M'zab, Tuggurt, Ouargla.

The province of Zeb has five cities: Biskra, al-Borgi, Nefta, Tolga and Doucen. Bilad al-Jarid also has five cities: Tozeur, Gafsa, Nefzawa, al-Hammah and Gabes. East of these provinces are the isle of Jerba, Gharyan, Msallata, Misrata, Tawergha, Ghadames, Fezzan, Awjila, Bardoa and al-Wahat. These are the names of the famous places of Numidia, from the ocean in the west to the borders of the Nile.

1.6. The divisions of the deserts between Numidia and the Black Land

Our people do not give these deserts any names, but divide them into five parts. Each part is named after the people who go there to graze their flocks, in other words the Numidians,[7] who are of five tribes: Zanaga,[8] Wanziga, Terga, Lamta, Bardoa. There are also areas with particular names from some good or bad quality, such as Azawad, a desert named for its wretched dryness, and Aïr, named for its temperate fertility.

1.7. The divisions of the Black Land, kingdom by kingdom

The Black Land is divided into many kingdoms; some of them are unknown and unvisited, but the author will explain which we have visited and which the merchants visited but not us. He himself has been to fifteen kingdoms of the Black Land, but there are three times as many, some known and neighbouring those he has visited, others unknown and far away. Here are the names of the kingdoms he has been to, beginning in the west and extending east and south: Walata, Jenne, Mali, Timbuktu, Gao, Gobir, Agadez, Kano, Katsina, Zazzau, Zamfara, Wangara, Bornu, Gaoga, Nubia. These are the fifteen kingdoms, most of which are on the river Niger. Merchants who journey from Walata to Cairo travel through these kingdoms, which is a safe route, though longer. These kingdoms are far from one another, separated either by desert or by the Niger. Formerly each kingdom had its own ruler, but in the author's time they were all controlled by three powers – the greater part ruled by the king of Timbuktu, a smaller part by the king of Bornu, and another part by the king of Gaoga. The ruler of Dongola also had a little state of his own bordering these kingdoms, and to the south are many other kingdoms: Bito, Jemiam, Dauma, Medra, Gorhan.[9] Those that have good governors and rulers are rich and often visited, but the others are worse than animals.

1.8. The settlements of Africa and the races of their inhabitants

According to the cosmographers and historians, Africa was formerly uninhabited, except the Black Land; Barbary and Numidia remained uninhabited for many centuries. All the inhabitants, that is, the whites, were named al-Barbar, derived, according to many scholars, from *barbara*, a word that means 'mumbled' in Latin, since the African language is meaningless to the Arabs and sounds like animal noises.[10] Some say that *barbar* is a repetition, for *bar* in Arabic means the desert. They say that long ago, King Ifricus, when he was defeated by the Assyrians or Ethiopians, fled into Egypt with his enemies in pursuit; unable to defend himself, he took counsel with his people on how to provide for their safety, and everyone cried out *Al-bar bar!*, that is, 'The desert, the desert!', meaning that their only recourse was to cross the Nile into the African desert. This explanation agrees with those who say that the Africans are descended from the people of Arabia Felix.

1.9. The origins of the Africans

Historians disagree about the origins of the Africans. Some say they come from the Philistines and were driven out long ago by the Assyrians, fleeing into Africa, which they found pleasant and fertile, so they stopped there. Others say they come from the Sabaeans, a people of Arabia Felix, who, as we said above, were driven out either by the Assyrians or by the Ethiopians. Others say that the Africans were native to some part of Asia, and that their enemies declared war on them; fleeing towards Greece, which was then uninhabited, they were pursued by their foes, so they crossed the sea of Morea[11] and arrived in Africa, where they stopped, while their enemies stopped in Greece. This discussion concerns only the origins of the white Africans, that is, those who inhabit Barbary and Numidia, but the Africans of the Black Land are all descended from Cush, son of Ham, son of Noah; the white and black Africans are therefore entirely of the same origin, since they all come from the Philistines. The Philistines are also descended from Mizraim, son of Cush, and also from Sheba, son of Raamah, son of Cush.[12] There are so many other opinions that I cannot remember them all, for it has been ten years since I've seen or opened any work of history at all.

1.10. The divisions of the white
Africans into many peoples

The inhabitants of Africa are divided into five peoples: the Sanhaja,[13] the Masmuda, the Zanata, the Hawwara and the Ghomara. The Masmuda live in the western part of the Atlas mountains, from Haha to the River of the Slaves;[14] others live on the south side of the Atlas, others in the plains. They have four provinces: Haha, Sous, Guzula and the region of Marrakesh. The Ghomara live in the mountains of Mauretania on the Mediterranean, and they rule the entire coast of er-Rif from the Pillars of Hercules east to the borders of the kingdom of Tlemcen, which in Latin is called Caesarea. The Masmuda and the Ghomara live by themselves, separate from other peoples.

The other peoples are mingled in the settlements all across Africa, but they can tell each other apart and are always at war among themselves, especially those in Numidia. Many authorities say that these five peoples once lived in tents in the countryside, but that long ago they fought a war, and all those who lost retreated into walled towns and became the vassals of those who remained in the countryside. This is proven by the fact that many of those in the country speak the same way as those in the towns; for instance, the Zanata in the country speak like the Zanata in the towns, and likewise with the others.[15]

These three races or peoples – the Zanata, the Hawwara and the Sanhaja – are all found in the countryside of Tamasna, alternating between peace and war following their past rivalries. Their princes reigned throughout Africa; the Zanata, for instance, drove out the house of Idris, the true rulers and founders of Fez. They were of a tribe called the Miknasa, but then the Maghrawa, another tribe of Zanata who lived in Numidia, arrived and drove the Miknasa from the kingdom of Fez. Some time later there came from the Numidian desert a Sanhaja tribe called the Lamtuna; they drove the Zanata from Fez, despoiled the entire region of Tamasna, and exterminated every tribe in Tamasna except those of their own stock, whom they made to live in Doukkala.[16] It was the princes of the Lamtuna who built the city of Marrakesh. Then al-Mahdi, a preacher of the Harga, a Masmuda tribe, rebelled and kicked the Lamtuna out of the kingdom. When the preacher died, one of his disciples was elected, 'Abd al-Mu'min of the Beni Ouriaghel, a Sanhaja tribe;[17] the kingdom remained in his house for around twenty years and he ruled almost all of Africa. Then he was deposed by the Beni Marin, a Zanata tribe, and the kingdom belonged to them for seventy years before they were expelled by the Beni Wattas, a Lamtuna tribe, who had existed for the entire time that the Beni Marin ruled. The Beni Marin constantly waged war against the Beni Zayyan, the house that ruled Tlemcen, from the Maghrawa tribe of the Zanata. And so the Beni Marin often fought with the Hafsid kings of Tunis, who belonged to the Hintata tribe of the Masmuda.

From all this, anyone can see how each of these peoples of Africa have played their part in these regions. It is true that the Ghomara and Hawwara peoples did not vie for dominance, although they did rule in particular regions, as can be seen from the chronicles of the Africans. This period when all these tribes ruled came after they had joined the Muslim sect. Before this they all lived apart in the countryside, each group in the desert or towns favouring their own faction; the countryfolk raised animals while the townsfolk plied their trades and farmed the land.

The five peoples are divided into 600 tribes, as is seen in the family tree of the Africans, a work by Ibn ar-Raqiq, the chronicler of Africa.[18] Many historians hold that the present king of Timbuktu, and the former kings of Mali and of Agadez, are descended from the Zanaga people, who live in the desert.

1.11. The diversity and characteristics of the African language

All the peoples mentioned above are divided into hundreds of tribes and thousands of settlements. They share a language they call *agual amazigh*, which means 'the noble tongue', whereas the Arabs of Africa call it 'the Berber tongue', that is, the native African language. It is distinct from and different to other languages, but it contains some words taken from Arabic, which some see as evidence that the Africans are descended from the Sabaeans, the people of Arabia Felix. Others hold that these Arabic words were found in the African language only after the Arabs invaded and dominated Africa; however, the people were so ignorant and illiterate that there is no authority to support either side. There are variations in the pronunciation and meanings of words. Those who are nearer the Arabs and deal with them have a great number of Arabic words. Almost all the Ghomara people speak a corrupt Arabic; many Hawwara tribes also speak corrupt Arabic, since they lived with the Arabs for a long time.

In the Black Land they speak various languages, one of which they call the Songhay tongue, spoken in many regions such as Walata, Timbuktu, Jenne, Mali and Gao. Another is called the Gobir tongue,[19] spoken in Gobir, Kano, Katsina, Zazzau and Wangara. A third[20] is spoken in the kingdom of Bornu, and it is similar to that of Gaoga. A fourth is spoken in the kingdom of Nubia, which is a sort of mixture of Arabic, Chaldean and Egyptian.[21]

However, in all the maritime cities of Africa from the Mediterranean to the Atlas mountains, the inhabitants speak corrupt Arabic, except in the kingdom of Marrakesh, where they speak the true Berber language, just as in the towns of Numidia near Mauretania and Caesarea. But those near the kingdoms of Tunis and Tripoli all speak corrupt Arabic.

1.12. The Arabs who live in the cities of Africa

A huge number of Arabs – 80,000 nobles and commoners – arrived in Africa in an army commanded by the third caliph 'Uthman (ibn 'Affan) in AH 24 (AD 645). When they had acquired many regions, almost all the princes and nobles returned to Arabia, except the general of the army, 'Uqba ibn Nafi', who stopped there and built the city of Kairouan.[22] For he was constantly wary of being defeated or betrayed in that coastal town of Tunis, suspecting that aid for the Africans would arrive from Sicily or Apulia; and so he retreated, with all the treasures he had won, to the desert 120 miles from Carthage, and there built the city of Kairouan. He ordered all his lieutenants to live in the citadels and fortresses of nearby towns, and to build them in those without. So it was done, and the Arabs remained safe and became citizens mingled with the Africans, who at that time spoke Italian because they had been ruled by the Italians for many years. For this reason Arabic was corrupted and spread in every city of Africa, as seen today when the Berbers mix with the Arabs. However, an Arab always notes his lineage on his father's side, as does a Berber; this is important as every notary and official will write a person's name alongside that of his lineage, or the name of his tribe, whether Arab or Berber.

1.13. The African Arabs who live in tents

The Muslim caliphs always forbade the Arabs to cross the Nile with their families and tents until AH 400 (AD 1009–10), when permission was granted by a schismatic caliph. For a schismatic had rebelled in Africa and ruled the city of Kairouan and almost all of Barbary, leaving the kingdom to his successors.[23]

The kingdoms and sects of the Arabs multiplied during the reign of the rebel al-Qa'im, the third caliph of that house,[24] so he ordered his slave and minister Jawhar[25] to march west with a huge army. With this army Jawhar conquered all of Barbary and Numidia as far as the province of Sous, collecting the tributes and profits from those kingdoms; then he returned to his master, the caliph al-Qa'im, and gave him all the treasure and goods. When the caliph saw his competence and faithfulness, it occurred to him to seek a still greater victory. So Jawhar offered his services, saying 'My lord, I promise that, just as I acquired the western region for your lordship, no less will I acquire for you the entire eastern region, that is, Egypt, Syria and all of Arabia, avenging the wrongs done to your ancestors by the Abbasids and exposing myself to every danger until you sit on the throne of your venerable fathers.'

The caliph immediately dispatched an army of 80,000 soldiers and gave them great riches. The slave went with them, crossing the desert between Barbary and Egypt, and, when he arrived at Alexandria, the viceroy of Egypt[26] at once retreated, fleeing to Baghdad to find his master the caliph.[27] Over just a few days, Jawhar conquered all the regions of Egypt and Syria. However, he remained wary, afraid that if the caliph of Baghdad arrived from Asia with his armies, his own army in Barbary would be under threat. With this in mind, he decided to build a fortress to which he could retreat from such violence and calamity; and so he founded a fully walled city, establishing there his entire guard and part of his armies. He gave it the name al-Qahira, that is 'compeller', commonly known in Europe as Cairo.[28]

Day by day villages and settlements grew up around the city to such an extent that one cannot find its like anywhere in the world. The slave Jawhar, when he realised that the caliph of Baghdad had made no provision against him, wrote to al-Qa'im, advising him that the region he had acquired was fully pacified and under guard, and that if his Highness should come in person to Egypt, his presence would be worth more than hundreds and thousands of soldiers[29] and would drive out his enemy the caliph of Baghdad from his caliphate and kingdom. On which advice the caliph prepared and set out for Egypt with a great army, leaving as the viceroy and general of all Barbary a prince of the Sanhaja people, who was his friend and household servant.[30] When the caliph arrived in Cairo he at once dispatched his army against the caliph of Baghdad. Then the viceroy of Barbary rebelled against his caliph and demanded obedience to the caliph of Baghdad, who gave him privileges and made him king of all Africa.[31]

The caliph of Cairo[32] knew this was very bitter news, since he was outside his kingdom against his will and had spent all the riches he'd brought with him from Barbary. He could not think of a solution. But one of his ministers,[33] a very learned man, counselled him with these words: 'My lord, if you would take my advice, I will find you an army of 400,000 people needing no payment; in fact, each person will instead pay you a ducat.' Hearing this news, the caliph cheered up immensely, and asked how it could be done. The minister replied: 'Lord, you well know that there are so many Arabs that Arabia cannot hold them; there is not enough for their animals and they are almost desperate, for the land is dry and insufficient. Give them permission to cross over to Africa and I'll put countless ducats in your hand.'

The caliph was very reluctant to do so, thinking that the Arabs would be the cause of Africa's ruin, and that neither he nor the rebels would be satisfied; but, seeing that he would in any event lose his kingdom, he considered that it would not be so bad to acquire a good deal of gold and have revenge on his enemy. So he made a decree throughout Arabia that any tribe wishing to cross over to Africa would be allowed to do so, so long as they paid one ducat per person and swore themselves the enemy of the rebel. The moment the Arabs heard this decree, they rushed to cross the border; they numbered around ten tribes, that is, almost half of Arabia Deserta, and also a few tribes from Arabia Felix.[34] There were around 50,000 fighting men and innumerable women, children and animals, although the chronicler of Africa Ibn ar-Raqiq has counted them all. Within a few months the Arabs had crossed the desert between Egypt and Barbary; first they besieged Tripoli, entered it by force and sacked it, killing as many as they could, and then they went and destroyed the city of Gabes. They also went to Kairouan, where the rebel forces had enough provisions to maintain themselves under siege for eight months; then the Arabs took the city by force, sacked it and killed the rebel forces.[35]

The Arabs shared the countryside among themselves and imposed huge tributes on all the towns, remaining rulers of all Ifriqiya until Yusuf ibn Tashfin, the first king of Marrakesh, came to power.[36] He very diligently gave favours to the rebel families,[37] until he had lifted the Arab dominion from the lands. The Arabs laid waste to the countryside, sacking and looting until the reign of (Abu Yusuf Yaqub) al-Mansur, the fourth king and caliph of Marrakesh, of the Almohad dynasty; the rebel families remained in these lands with the favour of the Arabs. Al-Mansur shrewdly headed for the region and defeated these rulers, bringing all the Arab princes to the western kingdom and giving them Doukkala and Azgar for settlements. He forced those of lesser status to live in Numidia; however, after a long time they were freed and began to dominate the region against the will of its elders, the Numidians themselves.

The Arabs in Azgar and other parts of Mauretania were all reduced to servitude, since Arabs outside deserts are like fish out of water; they were unable to cross the Atlas mountains into the desert because the passes belonged to Berbers and the country-side to other Arabs, so they gave up their pride and became shepherds and farmers, living in tents and paying tribute to the king of Mauretania. But those in Doukkala, because of their great number, never paid any tribute. Other Arabs refused to go with al-Mansur and remained in the kingdom of Tunis. After his house lost the kingdom, they became the rulers of the region until the reign of the house of Abu Hafs.[38] The Arabs reached an agreement with these rulers, taking their own share of the tribute and the profits of the kingdom alongside the king of Tunis. But he could not satisfy them, and even today they take a bite out of the kingdom along with the king, for he perceives their greater strength and gives them a share of his profits on condition of maintaining peace in the countryside. Those who are deprived of the king's provision go around waylaying and ambushing victims all the time, so there is never a safe route; when they have to travel from Tunis, merchants pay a company of gunmen to keep them safe from the Arabs, but they also have to pay a hefty duty to the Arabs funded by the king. Even so, Arabs who are not funded sometimes hold up and rob the merchants as they pass.

1.14. The divisions of the Arabs who went to live in Africa and were called Barbary Arabs

There are three Arabic peoples in Africa: the Chachim,[39] the Hilal and the Maqil. The Chachim are divided into the Athbej, Sumait and Sa'id tribes. The Athbej are divided further into the Dallaj, Muntafiq and Subai' subtribes, and these are divided in turn into countless generations.

The Hilal are divided into the Beni Amir, Riyah, Sufyan and Chisuin tribes. The Beni Amir are divided into the 'Urwa, Okba, Habra and Muslim subtribes. The Riyah are divided into the

Dawawid, Suwaid, Asja', al-Harith, an-Nadr and Kerfa sub-tribes, and these six into countless generations.

The Maqil are divided into the Mukhtar, ['Uthman and Hassan tribes. The Muhktar are divided into the Rawaha and Selim subtribes.][40] The 'Uthman are divided into the al-Hasim and Chinaua[41] subtribes. The Hassan are divided into the Dhawi Hassan, Dhawi Mansur and Dhawi 'Ubayd Allah subtribes. The Dhawi Hassan are further divided into the (Oulad) Dalim, Udaya, Berabish, Rahamna and 'Amr branches; the Dhawi Mansur into the 'Amarna, Menabha, Husein and Abu'l-Husein branches; and the Dhawi 'Ubayd Allah into the Kharaj, Hadaj, Thaaliba and Ja'wan branches. All these are divided into countless parts, which we cannot all record here.

1.15. The divisions and number
of the Arab settlements

The Athbej, who were al-Mansur's main captives, living in Doukkala and in the plains of Tadla, have in recent times been much troubled by the king of Portugal and sometimes by the king of Fez. They number 100,000 fighting men and more than half are mounted. The Sumait remain in the deserts of Libya near the kingdom of Tripoli, and rarely go to Barbary since they have neither place nor dominion there, but stay with their camels in the desert; they number 80,000 fighting men, mostly on foot. The Sa'id live in the Libyan desert and trade with the kingdom of Ouargla. They have innumerable animals and in the summer supply all the cities neighbouring their deserts with meat; in winter they stick to the desert and number 50,000 fighting men, although they have few horses. The Dallaj live in various places, but for the most part inhabit the borders of Caesarea and of Bejaia, receiving tributes and provisions from nearby rulers. Another, smaller part live in the plains of Adekhsan, on the border between Mauretania and the Atlas mountains, paying tribute to the king of Fez. The Muntafiq live in the plains of Azgar and are now called al-Khlot; they pay tribute to the king of Fez and number 8,000 well-equipped cavalry. The older and braver members of the Subai' live on the borders of the kingdom of Algiers, provided for by the king of Tlemcen, and many towns in Numidia are subject to them; they number 3,000 brave horsemen. They go to the desert in winter as they have many camels. The other part inhabits the plains between Salé and Meknes; they keep sheep and oxen and farm the land, paying tribute to the king of Fez. They number 4,000 brave and well-equipped cavalry.

1.16. The Hilal and their settlements

The largest Hilal tribe are the Beni Amir, who live on the borders of the kingdoms of Tlemcen and Oran and travel the desert of Tigurarin, receiving provision from the king of Tlemcen. They are a brave and wealthy people who number 6,000 fine and well-equipped cavalry. The 'Urwa, who live on the borders of Mostaganem, are wild men and thieves, travelling the desert badly clothed because they have neither provision nor territory in the kingdom of Barbary; they number 2,000 cavalry. The Okba live on the borders of Miliana and receive some provision from the ruler of Tenes, but even so they are great brigands, a wild race numbering 1,500 cavalry. The Habra, who live in the plains between Oran and Mostaganem, are farmers and pay tribute to the king of Tlemcen; they number 100 cavalry. The Muslim live in the M'Sila desert near the kingdom of Bejaia; they are thieves and brigands and receive tribute from M'Sila and other towns.

The Riyah are divided into, first of all, the Dawawid subtribe, who live in the Libyan deserts near Constantine and have a large territory in one part of Numidia. They are divided into ten branches, all strong, noble and well equipped, receiving a great provision from the king of Tunis; they number 5,000 cavalry. The Suwaid live in the desert near the kingdom of Tenes; they enjoy a great reputation and many territories, and the king of Tlemcen gives them a generous provision. They are strong, noble and well equipped. The Asja' are subject to many Arabs and a large number of them live in Garet with the 'Amarna tribe;

another part of them live with the Arabs of Doukkala in the neighbourhood of Safi. The al-Harith live in the plains of Haha together with the Chiadma and receive tribute from the Haha, a base and badly equipped people. The an-Nadr also live with them in the plains of Haha. The Arabs of Haha number 4,000 cavalry in total, but they are all badly equipped. The Kerfa live in various places, and have no capital, but live together with other tribes, especially the Manebha and 'Amarna; they are camel-drivers, bringing dates from Sijilmasa to the kingdom of Fez, from which they bring food back to Sijilmasa.

1.17. The settlements and number of the Maqil

The Rawaha subtribe of the Mukhtar, who live on the borders of the desert near Dades and Ferkla, are poor because they have few territories; but they are powerful foot soldiers who deem it a disgrace for one of them to be defeated by two on horseback. They are also great walkers, and can keep up with a horse even on a long trip. They number 500 cavalry and 8,000 on foot. The Selim live on the edge of the Draa River; they travel the desert and are rich. They always go once a year to Timbuktu with their merchandise and are favourites of the king; they have many farms in Draa and many camels, and number 3,000 well-equipped cavalry.

The al-Hasim live next to the ocean on the borders of Massa and number 500 poorly equipped cavalry; another part of them live in Azgar. Those in Massa are free men but those in Azgar are subjects of the king of Fez. The Chinaua live with the Khlot; they are also subjects of the king of Fez, but they are brave and well equipped, numbering 2,000 cavalry.

The Dhawi Hassan are divided into the Oulad Dalim, Berabish, Udaya, Dhawi Mansur and Dhawi 'Ubayd Allah tribes.[42] The Oulad Dalim live in the Libyan desert together with the Zanaga, an African people; they have neither territory nor any provision, but are poor thieves who often travel to the province of Draa to barter animals for dates. They are poorly equipped, numbering 10,000, with 400 on horseback and the rest on foot. The Berabish also live in the Libyan desert next to the province of Sous, and are numerous and poor; they have many camels and the territory of Tesset, but not enough money to shoe the few horses they have. The Udaya live in the deserts between Waddan and Walata, and control Waddan, as well as receiving tribute from the ruler of Walata in the Black Land. They are almost innumerable, estimated at more than 60,000, although they have few horses. The Rahamna live in the desert near Akka and have their own territory, travelling as far as Tesset in the winter; they number around 2,000 warriors but have few horses. The 'Amr inhabit the desert of Tagawst and receive some provisions from the community of the city there; they travel the desert as far as Nun and number 8,000 warriors.

1.18. The Dhawi Mansur

The 'Amarna tribe of the Dhawi Mansur live in the desert near Sijilmasa and travel through the Libyan desert as far as Igdi, receiving tribute from the people of Sijilmasa, Todgha, Tabelbala and Draa. They have many date farms in those places and live like kings; they have a great reputation and number 3,000 cavalry. Many base Arabs live alongside them, but, like the Kerfa and Asja', they have horses and many animals. Another part of the 'Amarna travel the Figuig desert and control certain towns and farms in Numidia, all of which pay them heavy tribute. In summer they go to live in the province of Garet on the eastern borders of Mauretania; they are noble and brave, and the kings of Fez, who marry their women, are like family to them.

The Menabha live in the same desert and control the Matgara and Reteb provinces in Numidia. They are also brave and noble, receiving some of their provision from the people of Sijilmasa; they number 2,000 cavalry.

The Husein tribe of the Dhawi Mansur live in the Atlas mountains and control many inhabited mountains, towns and ksars, granted to them long ago by the Marinid kings for supporting them when they began to rule. Their territory lies between the kingdoms of Fez and Sijilmasa, and their capital city is called Gerseluin; they also travel the Draa desert. They are a rich and brave people, numbering 6,000 cavalry, and there are many common Arabs as vassals in their company.

Some of the Abu'l-Husein live in the deserts of Draa and have a little territory there; however, the larger part of them are reduced to misery, and, with no capacity to support themselves in tents in the desert, they built wretched, starving towns in the Libyan desert, paying tribute to their kinsfolk.

1.19. The Dhawi 'Ubayd Allah

The Kharaj are a branch of the 'Ubayd Allah who live in the Beni Gumi and Figuig deserts, with many towns in Numidia under their dominion; the king of Tlemcen gives them provision and tries to keep them at peace, for they are thieves and brigands. They number 4,000 cavalry and in summer they usually go to live on the borders of Tlemcen.

The Hadaj live in the Angad desert near Tlemcen; they have neither territory nor provision, living solely from killing and robbing. They number 500 cavalry.

The Thaaliba live in the plains of Algiers and travel the desert as far as Tagdemt, having under their dominion the cities of Algiers and Dellys. In modern times, however, these cities were captured by the Turkish captain Barbarossa, who became king, and the Thaaliba were destroyed.[43] But they were noble and valiant on horseback, numbering 3,000 cavalry. Time has only treated them as it treated the others.

The Ja'wan live separately, one part with the Kharaj and another with the Hadaj, but they are treated as vassals even though they are kinsfolk.

It should be noted that the first two peoples, that is, the Chachim and the Hilal, are Arabs from Arabia Deserta descended from Ishmael, the son of Abraham, whereas the third people, the Maqil, are Arabs from Arabia Felix descended from Saba; among the Muslims the Ishmaelites are nobler than the Sabaeans.[44] Many poets have composed dialogues on the question of which people is nobler, each relating the virtues and benefits of his own people's customs. It should also be noted that the ancient Arabs, who lived before the Ishmaelites arrived, are called by historians Arabian Arabs, while the Ishmaelites are called Musta'rab, that is, Arabised Arabs, or to put it another way Arabs by accident, because they are not native. The Arabs who went to live in Africa are called Musta'jam or Berberised Arabs, since they went to live with a foreign people, until their own language was corrupted and their customs changed and became Berber.[45]

One would do better to consult the history of the Arabs by Ibn Khaldun, who produced a large volume on the family trees and origins of the Berberised Arabs; it can be seen just how weak the author's memory is on this subject. It seems to have been ten years since he saw any book on Arabic history, although, because he has met and conversed with almost all the Arab peoples mentioned above, some of the history remains imprinted in his memory.

1.20. The customs and ways of life of the Africans in the Libyan desert

The five peoples mentioned above – the Zanaga, Wanziga, Terga, Lamta and Bardoa – all of whom the Latins call Numidians, live in a similar manner, lacking all reason. They are very poorly clothed, wearing only a narrow patch of coarse wool that covers the smallest part of their body, and, in some cases, a piece of woven black cloth around their head. Their noblemen also wear long-sleeved shirts of blue cloth and silk, which merchants bring them from the Black Land. They only ride camels, putting the saddle between the hump and the neck and usually crossing their legs over the neck; sometimes they put their legs in straps without stirrups, carrying an iron attached to a cubit-long piece of wood that they use instead of spurs, albeit prodding the camel only on the shoulders. The riding camels are pierced through the nose like buffalos; through the piercing the riders put a plaited leather halter, used to guide the camels, like horses with bridles.

For beds they have only mats of slender reeds, and their tents

are poorly made of camel fur and a rough woolly material that grows among bunches of dates. As for their food, their tolerance for hunger must be seen to be believed, since they eat no bread or any kind of cereal but nourish themselves on camel milk. In the morning each of them drinks a bowlful of warm milk from a mug as it issues from the camel's teats; in the evening they prepare dry meat boiled in milk and butter, and when it is cooked everyone takes a piece in his hands and eats, drinking the broth with his hands instead of spoons, with a cup of milk each. They do not worry about water when they have milk; in the spring especially there are some who do not wash their hands or face for the entire season, during which they do not travel to the countryside where there is water, having milk instead. Moreover, the camels do not need water when they can eat grass. These peoples spend their whole lives either hunting camels or stealing them from their enemies; they do not stop in any one place for more than three or four days, letting their animals eat the grass there and then moving on.

Each of these peoples has a prince, whom they highly honour and obey like a king. They are all ignorant and illiterate, lacking any arts or graces; it is very hard to find a judge among them who can reason well. Some of them will ride five or six days in search of the judge's tent, since they do not study, nor do they even want to leave the desert for a town in which to study. Foreigners from the town who come to act as judges cannot abide such a life, and so there are very few learned men among them; but these few are well paid, and whoever knows a little can earn a thousand ducats, more or less, as a judge. Their noblemen all wear a black turban on their head, part of which covers their whole face except the eyes; when they eat they uncover their mouth for each bite, covering it again afterwards, for they say that just as it is shameful to vomit food up, so it is to put food in.[46]

The women are very coarse and fat, and not fair-skinned; they have fat buttocks and chests, but their waists are very slender. They are very homely in their speech and gestures, and sometimes let themselves be kissed, but one cannot fool around any further, because the men kill each other over such things. These peoples are very generous, but no traveller encounters their camps, for they do not use the main paths but their own secret ways in these places. They receive tributes from the caravans that cross their deserts and each camel load pays a piece of cloth worth one ducat.

Once, when the author was crossing the desert, his caravan stopped at the well of Arawan. The prince of the Zanaga appeared with 500 men riding camels and demanded his usual tax, but then invited the whole caravan to rest for a day or two in his camp. The merchants did not wish to lengthen the journey, as their camels were heavily loaded and the camp was about eighty miles off the route; nonetheless, they brought the camels with their burdens along the route and the merchants went with the prince to his lodgings. When they arrived at the main tent, the prince at once had many camels slaughtered, both young and old, and many lambs and ostriches which they'd caught along the way. The merchants informed the prince that he need not slaughter the camels, for they were only used to eating lamb; but he replied that, in his people's custom, it was shameful to kill only little animals for feasts, especially when they had new guests, and so he was obliged to kill the large animals. The entire meal consisted of roasted and boiled meats, and they cooked the ostrich meat in tajines, roasted with herbs and spices from the Black Land. They made a flatbread of millet or panicum and brought many dates and large jugs of milk. The prince himself sat with his kinsfolk and called all the literate and religious men to sit and eat with him; then he provided for the other merchants who sat beside them. As they dined, neither the prince nor his kinsfolk touched any bread, but ate only the meat and dates and drank the milk. Everyone around him marvelled at this, and the prince, noticing their reaction, said: 'Do not be amazed that we are not eating the bread, for we come from the desert where no grain grows, and we nourish ourselves on what does grow here. Every year we acquire a little grain for any stranger who may pass through our main tent; however, we do eat bread on festival days such as Eid al-Fitr and the Feast of the Sacrifice.'[47]

The author had no choice but to remain there with a few others for two days; on the third day the prince personally accompanied them to the caravan. He had killed so many animals for the merchants that their value far exceeded the tax he had received from them. In conversation the author recognised his nobility, but unfortunately he could not understand the prince's language, nor the prince his, and they had to communicate by an interpreter. What we have said of the life of the Zanaga is true precisely of the other peoples, that is, the four mentioned above who are scattered through the Numidian deserts.

1.21. The life and customs of
the Arabs in Africa

Just as the Arabs live in different places, so they have different characteristics and customs. Those who live between Numidia and Libya lead a most wretched and straitened existence, like the Africans living in Libya mentioned above, but the Arabs are more spirited. They habitually trade on their camels in the Black Land and have a great many horses, which in Europe are called Barbary horses; they constantly hunt deer, wild asses, ostriches, *lamt* (oryxes), *meha* (addaxes) and other animals. Most of the Arabs of Numidia are poets, always composing long poems narrating their wars and hunts; they also compose love poems of great elegance and sweetness, and their verses rhyme like the vernacular verses of Europe. They are generous people, but they cannot maintain a reputation because they are so far out of the way in the deserts. They are clothed like the Numidians, only their women differ a little in dress. The deserts where the Arabs now live used to be inhabited by the African peoples, but when the Arabs invaded Africa they drove out the Numidians with cruel wars; they settled in the deserts near the Land of Dates, while the Numidians went to live in the deserts near the Black Land.

The Arabs who live in Africa, between the Atlas mountains and the Mediterranean, have more resources and wealth, as can be seen especially in their clothes, the furnishing of their horses and the beauty and size of their tents; they also have fine horses but don't ride them like those of the desert. The Arabs till the soil and harvest a great deal of grain, as well as having innumerable sheep and oxen; for this reason they do not settle down in any one place, but travel to pasture their animals. These Arabs are naturally baser and more barbarous than those of the desert, but they are at least generous. Those who live in the kingdom of Fez are subjects of the king, to whom they pay tribute. Those in Doukkala and the kingdom of Marrakesh were at liberty until the Portuguese arrived at Safi and Azemmour, at which point the Arabs fell into strife and discord; the king of Fez destroyed one side and the king of Portugal destroyed the other, while the famine in Africa during those years nearly took care of the rest. So the wretched Arabs went to Portugal, agreeing to be the slaves of those who fed them. None of them remained in Doukkala.

However, the Arabs in the deserts near the kingdoms of Tlemcen and of Tunis lived like lords, since all their leaders received great provision from the king, which they shared among themselves to maintain unity. They are well clothed, their horses are well furnished, and their tents are large and beautiful. In the summer they travel to the borders of Tunis to receive their provisions from the king, and when October arrives they immediately buy necessities such as food, fabrics and weapons, carrying it all with them through the desert, where they stay all winter. In the spring they go hunting with dogs and falcons for all manner of wild beasts and birds; the author has many times lodged with them, and truly their tents are better furnished than many city dwellings with fabrics and copper, brass and iron goods. Despite being murderers and thieves, they are strong, generous and most elegant in their poetry and common speech, although their language has become corrupt – but then, what does elegance have to do with grammar? Some of their poets earn more than they ask from the rulers, because their verses in that rustic language have more grace and purity.

Their women dress well in black blouses with long sleeves, and, over these, black or blue lengths of cloth in which they wrap themselves up, fastened at the shoulders with silver clasps. They wear many silver rings in their large, fleshy ears, just as they wear rings and bracelets on their hands, as well as on their ankles, as is the custom throughout Africa. The Arab women wear black veils over their faces with holes for their eyes; when they see a man who is not their kin, they immediately veil their faces and speak among themselves. At home with their husband and family they keep the veils raised. When the Arabs travel from place to place, they carry their women in basketlike objects on their camels, furnished with fine carpets; these baskets are built like a platform and can hold only a single woman each.[48] Often, on the day of battle, they bring their wives to give them encouragement.

When they are to be married, the women have their faces painted, as well as their breasts and most of their arms from the shoulders to the fingers, believing this to be a mark of refinement; the Arabs took the practice from the Africans, for they never spoke of such a thing in Arabia, but when they came into Africa they adopted the customs of this region. By contrast, the wives of the city dwellers and nobles of Barbary remain as white as they were born. Admittedly, they sometimes take tints from burned gall and iron,[49] with which they colour the middle of their cheeks in a round spot like a coin; below the eyelashes they paint a triangle and above the chin an olive leaf, and some paint their lashes. They believe these daubs a mark of refinement, and the Arab poets and city-dwellers have praised the practice. But women do not wear this make-up for more than two or three days, as they are not permitted to be seen by the men of their tribe except their husband and sons, because the Arabs judge it a thing done deliberately out of lust.

1.22. The Arabs who live in the desert between Barbary and Egypt[50]

The wretched Arabs in the deserts between Barbary and Egypt lead a miserable life because it is a dry, harsh land. They keep sheep and camels but, lacking grass, the animals breed little. Through all the wide country there is nowhere to sow any grain, except a few towns or rather villages in the desert with date farms. The Arabs give the inhabitants of these villages considerable trouble, though they sometimes agree to barter their animals for dates and grain; this is not enough for the Arabs, however, for they are numerous and the villages are small with meagre fields. As a result, they constantly pawn their sons for grain to the Sicilians, who arrive in ships laden with grain to sell or barter for black slaves. Because the Arabs have nothing to pay them with, the Sicilians give them credit, holding as collateral the debtors' sons, whom they take with them back to Sicily; if they have not been given satisfaction by the appointed time, they take the sons for slaves and demand a new payment.

Because of their dire straits and poverty these Arabs are the worst brigands in the world. Nor is robbery enough when some foreign captain falls into their hands; first they rob him, then they sell him as a slave to the Sicilians. For this reason, no caravan has passed along the coast around that desert in over a century; instead they travel inland 500 miles from the sea, keeping well clear of these accursed Arabs. The author has passed along the coast by sea with three merchant ships, and the Arabs, when they saw them, ran towards the port to trade with the ships. But the merchants did not trust them, and would not even disembark until they had many of the Arabs' sons in their hands;

then they bought their lambs and butter and went on their way, fearing the pirates of Sicily and Rhodes.

This race is brutish, badly clothed and emaciated with hunger; God's wrath and curse seem always to hang over this accursed people.

1.23. The Shawiya or shepherds, an African people who travel like the Arabs

Many African tribes work hard raising sheep and oxen, most living in the foothills of the Atlas mountains, or in the mountains themselves. Wherever they live, they pay tribute to the local kings or to the Arabs, except those who live in the province of Tamasna, who are free and have considerable power. Some of these shepherds speak the African language, while others speak Arabic because they live near and do business with the Arabs. There is another tribe living in the countryside of Urbs, on the border between Tunis and Numidia, and whose prince dared to make war on the king of Tunis.[51] A few years later in AH 915 (AD 1509–10), the king's son left Constantine to collect his tribute from these people, but their prince arrived with 2,000 cavalry and defeated the army of the prince of Tunis, who was killed and his carriages sacked. When they had defeated him, this tribe acquired great renown. Many of those in the service of the king fled their homes and went to live in the countryside with the victorious people, until their prince became one of the greatest rulers in Africa.

1.24. The religion of the ancient Africans

The Africans of Barbary were idolaters like the Persians, who worshipped fire or the sun and kept temples dedicated to them. In these temples they always kept a flame burning day and night, tended and carefully watched lest it go out, as can be seen in the chronicles of the Persians and the Africans. The Africans of Numidia and Libya worshipped the planets and made sacrifices to them. Some of the Black Africans worshipped Guighimo, which in their language means 'the Lord of Heaven', and they had this fine idea on their own without being informed by any prophet or other person. Much later some of them became Jews and remained as such for a long time, while a few kingdoms among the Blacks became Christian until the sect of Muhammad arrived.

In the year AH 268 (AD 881–82) the Libyans became Muslim by means of certain preachers, causing them to fight great battles with the Blacks, until all the kingdoms of the Blacks bordering Libya became Muslim. So at present there are found some kingdoms where there are Christians, but those of the Jews were destroyed by the Christians and Muslims. All those who live by the ocean are heathen and worship idols; they have met and had dealings with the Portuguese. Indeed, the people of Barbary remained idolaters for a long time, until 250 years before the birth of Muhammad; at this point they all became Christian because the area around Tunis and Tripoli was dominated by certain Apulian and Sicilian lords, while the coasts of Caesarea and Mauretania were dominated by the Goths. In those times many Christian lords from Italy fled the Goths and went to Carthage, where they set up a new dominion. However, these Barbary Christians did not keep observance of the faith or the order of the Roman Christians, but rather the rule and faith of the Arians, one of whom was St Augustine.[52]

When the Arabs conquered Barbary they encountered Christian rulers, giving rise to many wars until the Arabs were victorious; the Arians returned to Italy and also went to Spain. A decade or so after Muhammad's death, almost all of Barbary became Muslim; but the people rebelled many times, rejecting the Muslim religion and killing their governors and imams. Whenever they received such news, the caliphs at once sent armies against the Berber renegades, until they captured the African schismatics who had fled from the caliphs of Baghdad.[53] Then the religion of Muhammad began to secure itself in Barbary, but with many heresies and differences among them, of which there will be further notice in my book on the religion and law of Muhammad, that is, on the most important things of his religion that are common among the Africans and Asians, if time does not prevent the present work from going ahead.

1.25. The African alphabet

Arab historians hold that the Africans have no alphabet besides the Roman one. When the Arabs conquered Africa, especially Barbary, where the culture of Africa was and still is, they found no other alphabet but the Roman; indeed, they conceded that the Africans had a different language but used the Roman alphabet, like the Germans in Europe. All the Arabic histories of the Africans have been translated from Latin; these are ancient works, some written in the time of the Arians and others earlier. They were written by authorities whose names the author has now frankly forgotten; they must have been long works, for their translators say 'such and such a thing appears in the seventieth book', which implies that the work has seventy books. However, the Arabs do not translate them in the original sequence, but rather draw up a list of the rulers' names and order the reign of each ruler or prince according to those of the Persian, Assyrian, Chaldean or Israelite kings. When the schismatics reigned in Africa they commanded all the Africans' books of history and learning to be burned, on the grounds that they had given the Africans their former pride, and so made them rebel and deny the faith of Muhammad innumerable times.

Other African historians say that the Africans had an alphabet of their own, but that, after Barbary was conquered by the Romans, the Italian Christians and the Goths, the Africans lost it because their rulers did not use it, and so the people willingly abandoned it, as happened with the Persians, who lost their alphabet and learning under the dominion of the Arabs. The Persians' books were burned on the orders of the Muslim caliphs, who doubted that they could become true Muslims if they still had their tomes of natural sciences and law and idolatrous religion; with this in mind they burned their books and treatises, and forbade learning.

Precisely the same occurred when the Romans and Goths ruled Barbary. It is proof enough that there is no alphabet but the Roman in any epitaph on tomb or wall in all of Barbary, in the ancient cities both on the sea and in the countryside. Despite all this, the Africans did have an alphabet of their own, but, when their enemies the Romans conquered them, they removed the signs and memorials from the Africans' buildings and put up their own, so no other memory would remain but their own. The Goths wanted to do the same with the buildings of the Romans, and similarly the Arabs with those of the Persians, and the Turks with the memorials of the Christians, destroying the painted figures in the temples. So also in modern times a ruler or caliph will construct a large building on which he spends tens of thousands of ducats; on his death he leaves the building unfurnished and incomplete, but his successor, another ruler or caliph, spends little on furnishing it, first removing the arms and signs of his predecessor who has constructed most of the building. There are some good men who leave up the arms of their predecessors and put their own underneath. It should be no surprise, then, that the African alphabet is lost, and that they have been using the Arabic script for the past 900 years. Ibn ar-Raqiq, the African chronicler, has discussed this question at length, that is, whether the Africans had an alphabet or not; he concluded that they did, and that 'whoever denies this can also deny that the Africans had their own language'. Ibn ar-Raqiq denies that a people can have their own language and books in a foreign alphabet.

1.26. The terrain of Africa

Just as Africa is divided into four parts, so it also has four different kinds of terrain. First, the Mediterranean coast, from the straits of Gibraltar to the borders of Egypt; throughout the coast there are mountains stretching 100 miles to the south, more or less, and between these and the Atlas mountains are plains and hills. Throughout the coastal mountains are found many springs of little rivers; after the plains and hills come the Atlas mountains starting at the western part of the ocean, and extending east as far as the borders of Egypt. After the Atlas mountains are the plains of Numidia where the dates grow, an almost entirely sandy country. After Numidia are the deserts of Libya which are all sand as far as the Black Land. There are also many mountains in the desert, but in their travels merchant groups avoid them, for there are many broad passes and plains between them. After the Libyan deserts is the Black Land, which is mostly plains and sand, except for the banks of the river Niger and all the places it waters.

1.27. On the fruitful places in Africa

All along the coast of Barbary are rather cold mountains where it sometimes snows; grain and fruit grow throughout, but little wheat, and the inhabitants eat barley bread most of the year. The spring water is cloudy and tastes of the land, especially on the borders of Mauretania. There are also many deep, thick woods in these mountains, full of good and bad animals. But the hills and plains between them and the Atlas mountains are very fertile lands where much grain and good fruit grow, for all the rivers flowing from the Atlas mountains to the Mediterranean pass through them; but there are few forests. The hills and forests between the Atlas mountains and the ocean are fertile, like the region of Marrakesh and the province of Doukkala and all of Tadla and Tamasna, together with Azgar, as far as the straits of Gibraltar.

The Atlas mountains are very cold and fruitless; little grain grows and there are dark woods in every part, but from them flow all the rivers of Africa. The springs in these mountains are so very cold in the summer that if any person should hold his hand under them for seven or eight minutes he will doubtless lose it, due to the freezing cold. The mountains are not equally cold in all their parts, since there are many almost temperate places where one can easily live, and these are well inhabited, as will be seen in the rest of this book, section by section. Other parts, such as those near Tamasna, are frozen and harsh, and therefore uninhabited and abandoned. The parts near Mauretania are also very cold, but the shepherds and other Arabs go there in summer to pasture their flocks; however, it is impossible to stay there in winter because it snows continually, and a north wind kills every animal there. Many people die in the mountain passes between Mauretania and Numidia.

Date merchants usually leave Numidia with their fruit and other goods at the end of October. Sometimes the weather catches them unawares in the mountains, leaving not a soul alive, for it starts snowing at night and in the morning all the caravans are found buried in the snow along with the trees in the wood. Not a single path or tree is left, nor any other sign as to where the dead bodies are.

The author has twice escaped, as if by a miracle, from the grave peril of the snow. It was sunset when the snow began to fall; some Arabs appeared on horseback, perhaps ten or twelve of them, inviting him to leave the caravan in haste and ride with them. The author wondered if by this invitation they meant to lure him into a wood and kill him for his possessions; but, luckily, before they took off he cunningly pretended to go and piss, hiding his money under a well-marked tree. He rode with them until around midnight, when they started questioning him to find out if he had any money on him. He replied that he'd left it in the caravan with one of his family; not satisfied with this answer they stripped him naked in the freezing cold, but, finding no cash, they returned his clothes and claimed they were just horsing around with him.

They rode for two or three hours more until, out of the darkness, they could hear the bleating of many sheep; they turned in that direction, where woods and high rocks posed another great danger, until they came upon high caves into which a group of shepherds had shrewdly led their flocks and made a large fire. The shepherds were afraid when they saw them, for they recognised the horsemen as Arabs; but then it occurred to them that, even though they were Arabs, in such fearful weather they could do no harm because the snow would prevent them from fleeing. After many humble entreaties by the Arabs, the shepherds explained to them how to escape the cold via the foothills of the caves, and showed them other caves, where they'd tied up their horses and furnished them with plenty of hay. So the author and the Arabs climbed up into the caves, which were very large. The shepherds gave them meat, bread and cheese to eat, and that night they slept by the fire half dead from cold and fear, especially the author, who had been stripped and searched just before they arrived.

When morning came they were bewildered to find the entrance to the caves stopped up with the drifts; but the shepherds comforted them, and they remained there for two days and nights while it continued to snow. The snow grew deeper over the caves where the horses were kept, but on the third day it levelled off, and the shepherds at once began with great diligence to remove the snow from the mouth of the cave, because they also had oxen there. When the caves were open they found the horses healthy, safe and hardy, with plenty of hay already there, for which they thanked God. That day there was a warm sun, and the next morning they recognised the route. The shepherds went with them, taking paths where they knew there would be less snow, even though it still came up to the horses' bellies, until they arrived at a town on the borders of Fez.[54] They were informed that the entire caravan had been overwhelmed by the snow, at which point the Arabs no longer had any hope of being paid, since, although they had gone to accompany and rescue the caravan, it was lost and their effort wasted. Therefore they took a Jew who had been in the company of their caravan with around fifty loads of dates, keeping him prisoner in their tents until he satisfied them for the whole caravan. As for the author, they took his horse and left him to walk, so he took a mule with a harness that the mountainfolk use, and on the third day he arrived at Fez bearing his bad news. It had, however, arrived before him, and he was thought dead like the others. No – fortune let him escape and tell his whole story in Italy. This was one of the greatest dangers he had ever experienced on a journey; it can well be seen from the story just how cold it is in the Atlas mountains.

Returning to our subject, there are warm and dry lands beyond the Atlas mountains, where the rivers from the mountains flow into the Libyan desert, dispersing in the sand and feeding into lakes. In this area are few patches of arable land, but there are countless date palms and a few other fruit trees.

On the borders of Numidia and Libya are other harsh and un-inhabited mountains, but in their foothills are forests of spiny trees that bear no fruit. There is neither spring nor river here, except a few almost unknown wells between these hills and the desert mountains.

Numidia is crawling with reptiles, scorpions and snakes, and every summer many die from their bites. Libya is also an arid desert, nothing but sand, with no spring or river or other water beyond a few deep salty wells, and even these are not found everywhere. In some places one can travel six or seven days without finding water except what is carried in skins on the camels; this is especially true on the route from Fez to Timbuktu or from Tlemcen to Agadez. Even worse is the current route between Fez and Cairo through the Libyan desert; likewise from Agadez to Cairo, but at least on that route one passes a huge lake where the Seu and Gorhan peoples live. But on the route from Fez to Timbuktu, which lasts five, six or seven days, there are a few wells either covered inside solely with camel hide or walled with camel bones as well. Merchants who make this journey face great peril except in winter, for either the sirocco or the south wind will blow, carrying so much sand that the wells are covered over and mountains pile up. Merchants journey in the hope of finding water en route, but find instead that every sign and trace of the wells is lost, so the entire caravan dies of thirst; one can still see their bones and those of their camels. Sometimes they manage to survive by killing the camels, taking their bowels and intestines and drinking the little water they can squeeze out; they occupy themselves with this until they find another well – or until they die. In the Azawad desert are the tombs of two men, one very rich and the other a mule-driver, beside an inscribed marble tablet; the mule-driver sold the merchant a cup of water for 10,000 ducats, but neither the buyer nor the seller escaped alive.

There are many dangerous animals in the desert, and also some that are harmless. This subject will come up again in the fourth part of this book, which discusses Libya and likewise the animals of Africa.[55] So that everyone can understand better and more clearly, the author will chiefly relate the dangers he encountered on his journeys through Libya, especially from

Walata to Cairo. Sometimes on these journeys they could not find the path to water, since the guides got lost; other times they found the wells full of sand or enemies blocking the way, and they had to preserve water because their supply for five days had to last ten. But to recount all the details of a single journey would require a work of a hundred pages.

There are also scorching areas in the Black Land, humid from the river Niger. All the regions bordering the river have very fertile soil where a huge amount of grain grows, and a great number of animals, but no fruit at all except a variety like chestnuts that grow on large trees. However, these are a little bitter and grow far inland from the river; they are called *goro* in their language.[56] Gourds, cucumbers and onions also grow in large numbers. There are no mountains or hills along the Niger, nor on the borders of Libya, but there are many lakes into which the river flows; around these are numerous woods containing elephants and other animals, as will be seen in more detail when the kingdoms of the Black Land are discussed.

1.28. The natural motions of the air in Africa and their effects

Almost everywhere in Barbary the rain and cold begin in mid-October, and it becomes much colder, like everywhere else, in December and January, although they warm themselves by the fire only in the morning. February is less cold, but often the weather will change five or six times a day; in March very strong winds blow in from the west and north, making the trees blossom with all kinds of fruit, while in April almost all the fruit start to ripen, so that in the plains of Mauretania they begin eating cherries at the end of April and start of May. After the third week of May they eat summer figs, and in the third week of June the grapes ripen and everyone eats apples, pears and apricots. Plums ripen between June and July. In August the autumn figs and jujubes start to ripen, but figs and peaches quickly arrive in September; after 5 August the grapes begin to dry in the sun, and if it rains in September all the remaining grapes are used to make wine and cooked must, especially in the province of er-Rif, as will be seen in more detail later on. In October, pomegranates and quinces are picked, and in November olives are harvested, but they do not pick them using ladders as in Europe, but by hand; for they cannot make ladders long enough to reach the branches, given that olive trees are very large and tall in this land, especially those of Mauretania and Caesarea, whereas those of the kingdom of Tunis are like European ones. When they want to gather the olives the men climb up on very long stilts and beat the branches so that the olives fall to the ground; but they are well aware that this beating is very harmful, for they strike the shoots of the branches until they break. By law the olives of Africa are gathered in abundance one year and not at all the next; there are other olives not good for making oil but only for eating, and all olives are either pickled or smashed and broken.

Whatever the duration and qualities of the other seasons, all three months of spring are temperate. According to the Africans, spring starts on the fifth night of February and lasts until 6 May. There is fine weather all season, but if it does not rain from 25 April to 5 May, the harvest will be very poor; that rain they call 'Nisan water',[57] holding it blessed by God, and many people devoutly keep vessels and phials of it in their homes. The summer lasts, they say, until 6 August, and it is extremely hot this entire time, especially during June and July. In all these months the weather is serene and fine, although in some years it rains in July and August, so the weather is bad; many fall sick with a steady fever and few escape. Autumn begins on 7 August and lasts until 5 November; the three months August, September and October are less hot, but the ancients called the month from 15 August to 15 September 'the days of the weather', because in August the figs, pomegranates and quinces ripen and the grapes dry. Winter lasts from 5 November until 4 February; at the start of this period they begin sowing the fields in the plains, but in the mountains they begin to sow in October. The Africans hold that the forty hottest days of the year begin on 2 June, and likewise that the forty coldest days begin on the second night of December. The Egyptians hold that the equinoxes fall on 6 March and

6 September and that the sun turns and goes back on 6 June and 6 December. Similarly, they adhere to this calendar in renting their lands and farms, and in sowing, harvesting, navigation and finding the planets.

They teach children more useful things in school. Many farmers and Arabs know the calendar and its principles but no letters, and the calendar was translated into Arabic from Latin, so now they call the months by their Latin names. So also, just the same, they have a huge book in three volumes called in their language *The Farmers' Treasure*, translated from Latin into Arabic in Córdoba at the time of al-Mansur, the ruler of Baetica;[58] this book discusses agriculture, sowing, planting, grafting and imitating every fruit, grain and vegetable. The author greatly marvels that many things in their language were taken from Latin that are no longer found in Latin itself. The histories and rules of the Africans, and all the works on Muslim law and religion, are regulated by the moon, and their year is 354 days long because six lunar months have twenty-nine days each.[59] However, their feast days and fasting periods occur at varying times, because the Arabic year loses eleven days from the Latin year and these eleven put the Latin year behind.

The last part of autumn and all of winter, as well as part of the spring, has stormy weather, hail, thunder and lightning, and there are still many places in Barbary where it snows and there are many storms. There are also three harmful, scorching winds: the levant, the sirocco and the southerly, especially when they blast in May or June, destroying all the grain and preventing the fruit from growing or ripening. Mist, too, greatly harms the grain, especially when it comes as the grain is in bloom, for sometimes it lasts all day. But in the Atlas mountains there are only two seasons – the six months of winter from October to April, and the six of summer from April to September – although the mountaintops are always covered in snow all year round.

In Numidia the seasons change more quickly, for the grain is harvested in May and the dates in October; from then until January is colder than the whole rest of the year. However, when it rains in September the dates are practically destroyed and the harvest is poor. The fields of Numidia must all be irrigated to be fit for sowing, and so when it doesn't rain in the Atlas mountains the rivers of Numidia remain dry and the fields cannot be irrigated. If the rain fails in October there can be no hope of a good harvest that year; if it fails in April, no grain can be gathered from the countryside, but the date harvest will be good even without rain. The Numidians give the date harvest greater importance than the grain harvest, because even an abundance of grain will be enough for only half the year, whereas with a good date harvest there will be grain as well, for the Arabs and camel-herders in the date trade bring an enormous amount of grain to barter for the dates.

In the Libyan deserts the seasons also begin in mid-August and the rains last until November, and then again throughout December, January and part of February; after this comes an abundance of grass and seasonal flowers, and throughout Libya many [. . .]60 and much milk and good vegetables to eat, so Barbary merchants journey to the Black Land at this time.

In the Black Land the seasons arrive earlier; there it begins to rain at the end of July, but it does not rain much and makes no difference, good or bad, for the fields are all fertilised by the Niger, just as in Egypt with the Nile. However, some mountains in the Black Land are fertilised by rainwater. The Niger floods in its season just like the Nile, starting on 5 June and lasting ten days, with another ten to recede. During the Niger's flooding one can go by boat to all the Lands of the Blacks and all the lowlands; the valleys and ditches become rivers, but the boats are very dangerous to sail, as we will see at more length in the fifth part of this work.

1.29. The age of men, its shortness and length

Throughout Barbary people live to the age of sixty-five or seventy. Few live longer, but there are some in the mountains who live for a century, or even longer, and are very healthy;61 the author has seen many men of eighty who plough the earth and hoe the vineyards, and likewise in the Atlas mountains he has seen men of seventy and eighty in battle, fighting and even beating younger men. In Numidia, the Land of Dates, they also live a long time, but they lose their teeth and grow weak from all the dates they eat, and their eyesight fails because the land is much vexed by the levantine wind, which stirs up sand and dust, making the inhabitants rub their eyes and damage them. The Libyans have shorter lives than those of other regions, but they are healthy and strapping until around sixty years old, although meagre and slender. In the Black Land their lives are shorter than the other races, but they remain strong with healthy teeth all their lives; however, they are very lascivious, like the Libyans and Numidians, although the people of Barbary are less strong.

1.30. The diseases that often afflict the Africans

Young boys and women often suffer from ringworm of the scalp, which is only cured with great effort. Over the course of the year, the men often have headaches without fever. Toothache affects many who eat hot broth and then immediately drink cold water. Also stomach ache, which in their ignorance they call heartache. A lot of people feel bodily pains many times a day due to drinking cold water. Sciatica and knee pain afflict many who often sit on the ground and walk without shoes. Few have gout, except for some rulers who drink wine and eat a lot of poultry. People are often burdened with scabies from eating too many olives and nuts and other melancholic foods. Sanguine people who sit on the ground suffer coughs and chills, especially in winter; it is great fun going to a mosque on a day when thousands are present, for if one person happens to cough just as the imam starts preaching, everyone else follows and nobody can hear anything.

The very cruel French pox with its pains and boils afflicts all of Barbary with sores, and few escape it. However, nobody has it in the countryside or the Atlas mountains, or among the Arabs or in Numidia; they do not even talk about it in Libya or the Black Land. But as soon as they have it they go to Numidia or the Black Land, where the air heals them at once. Nobody had ever witnessed this disease, or even heard it named, but when Ferdinand drove the Jews out of Spain, many of those who went to Barbary spread the disease, for they brought it from Spain; some melancholy Moors mixed with the Jewish women, and it grew little by little until in ten years no family was free of it. The first ones who had it were thought lepers and driven out and forced to live with the lepers; then, seeing that the number of infections grew daily, and discovering that the fault had come from Spain and that a great quantity of men now had it, those who had been driven out of their homes at once returned. The people of Barbary hold that this sickness originates in Spain, and they give it the same name as the Spaniards.[62] Others, especially in Mauretania and Tunis, as well as in Egypt and Syria, call it the French pox like the Italians; in these places, especially Tunis and Egypt, it has done great harm.

Some suffer pain in their ribs, but rarely. Genital warts afflict many, and they cannot cure the sickness of the testicles, that is, when they become swollen; this affects few in Barbary but many in Egypt, whose testicles grow quite large. It is said that such sickness afflicts the Egyptians because they eat so much gum and salted cheese.[63] Children often suffer epilepsy in Africa, but when they grow up they are cured; it also affects many women, especially in Barbary and the Black Land, but they foolishly believe that it is caused by spirits. The plague appears in Barbary every twenty or twenty-five years and strikes the people hard because they do not protect themselves from it, nor even have any remedy except to anoint themselves with Armenian earth. In Numidia this sickness occurs only every century, but in Libya and the Black Land it never comes.

1.31. The virtues and praiseworthy qualities of the Africans

The Africans living in the cities of Barbary, especially those on the coasts of the Mediterranean, take great care in their studies of the disciplines, especially in the humanities and in their theology and in matters of religion and law. Once they used to study the sciences of the ancients, that is, in mathematics, astrology and philosophy, but 400 years ago, many disciplines were prohibited by the teachers and rulers, such as philosophy and judicial astrology. The men of Africa living in the city are also devout in their faith and obedient to their teachers and imams. They take great pains to know the things necessary to their faith and continually come to make the usual prayers in their mosques, sometimes washing their whole body, as will be seen in the second book on the religion and law of Muhammad.

The city dwellers of Barbary and Africa are ingenious men when it comes to the well-ordered fine arts, and they make beautiful buildings and works that show their great ingenuity. They are people of integrity, without too much malice, virile men; what they say in your absence they'll repeat in your presence. They are valiant and spirited, especially those who live in the mountains and the countryside, and they are careful to keep their promises. They are jealous and scorn their own life when someone dishonours them, especially concerning their wives. They are people of great spirit in acquiring goods and honour, going all over the world to trade. Africans are found among the teachers and masters of learning in Egypt, Ethiopia, Arabia, Persia, India and Turkey; they are well received everywhere and honoured because they are up to the task, that is, each of them in their own profession or art. The city dwellers of Barbary are also honourable and modest people; they never speak dishonourable words in public and the youths greatly honour their elders in their conversation. The son in the presence of his father or uncle speaks neither of love nor of women, nor can he even sing any love songs around his elders. If they see a friend of the father or anyone else speaking of women or love, all the younger boys will leave at once. These are the good customs of the city dwellers of Barbary.

Those who live in tents, namely Arabs and shepherds, are generous and spirited people, compassionate, patient, sociable, homely, honest, obedient; they keep their promises, they are peaceful and cheerful, and they care little about amassing possessions. The mountain dwellers are generous, spirited, modest and honourable in communal life. The Numidians are more ingenious and cultivated, being given to virtue and to the study of law and religion; although unlearned in the natural sciences, they are well versed in arms, very spirited and sociable. The Libyans – both the Africans and the Arabs – are generous, peaceful and very obliging to their friends; we see their goodwill towards foreigners, and they are spirited, honest, sincere and trustworthy. The Blacks are people of integrity and good faith, kindly towards foreigners and eager to please; they are always cheerfully dancing and holding feasts. They are people without any malice and they greatly honour learned and religious men; that race enjoys a better life than all other Africans, and indeed all the other races that the author has ever encountered in the world.

1.32. The faults and nefarious behaviour of the Africans

The city dwellers of Barbary are like fleas in a midden: poor, impetuous and cruel. They are scornful people who, whenever a person has displeased them even a little, hold him for ever an enemy; they are so disagreeable that a foreigner can never gain their friendship. Beyond their studies they are credulous and simple-minded, believing all sorts of impossible things, and their common folk are illiterate and ignorant in their understanding of nature, holding every natural motion for a divine act. They are unruly in their way of life and their trade and conversation; they always speak with a loud, booming voice, and get into fights everywhere. They are base and held in contempt by their rulers, who have more esteem for their animals. They have no chiefs or sheriffs or magistrates or lawyers who can rule or advise them in anything to do with governance. They are very stupid and ignorant in trade, and have neither money changers nor agents for dispatching their goods from one town to another, since their merchants all want to stay with their goods, so, wherever the goods go, their owner goes. They are as greedy as can be; a large number of them have never welcomed a foreigner either out of kindness or for love of God; few repay the gifts they receive from others.

They are melancholy men, pleased by nothing, because they are constantly occupied with the effort of surviving amid the great poverty of those regions, where so little money can be made. Those who live in the mountains and countryside – that is, the shepherds and some of the Arabs – all live in exhaustion from labour, always wretched and in dire need. They are brutish thieves and lechers, and they cannot be trusted to pay their debts. They are ignorant of letters and, in all their dealings, and more cuckolded than roosters. Each man seeks out a lover for his daughter, and holds a feast for him, joining the boy's hand with the daughter's, or her sister's, and they become lovers. But as soon as she marries, her lover will no longer see her, fearing the hostility of her husband. Most are not true Muslims, nor even Jews or Christians; they know neither God nor saints, and do not say or know any prayers; they have no mosques or imams or learned men. Those few who are devout are lost among them, for they have neither law nor rule but seek pleasures without limits.

The Numidians lack any understanding of things, as they are very far from a natural way of life, being treacherous and murderous thieves without any conscience. A very base people, they travel to Barbary and take on every disgusting job; some clean and polish latrines, others are cooks or work in kitchens and stables, since for cash they will turn their hand to anything.

The Libyans are brutish people, illiterate and lacking any learning; they are thieves and brigands, living like wild beasts, without religion and rules. They live and have always lived in misery, and are the most treacherous people, especially with their possessions. They have long horns[64] and waste their lives in idleness, either hunting or warring among themselves; at other times, barefoot and naked, they pasture their animals in the desert.

The inhabitants of the Black Land are very brutish, lacking all reason and worse than irrational; moreover they are without wit and skill, knowing nothing and living like animals without laws and rules. Among them are many prostitutes and cuckolds, except some who live in the great cities, where there are a few with a little more rationality and human feeling.

The author feels deeply ashamed and conflicted to reveal the vices and faults of Africa, since he was nourished and raised there and is known as a blameless man. But every writer must tell things as they are, and as an author he finds himself in a situation similar to that described in *The Book of a Hundred Tales*. To relate it briefly, in one of these tales there was a man sentenced to be whipped, and he happened to be a great friend of the executioner. When he was led to where he was to be whipped, at the sight of his friend he was comforted and consoled, thinking that, because of their friendship, the executioner would take pity on him. But the executioner made the first stroke very hard and cruel. The man cried out: 'O friend, you mistreat your friend greatly!' But the reply came: 'My friend, have patience! I must do my duty as it should be done.'

It would be a greater scandal, however, if I were justly blamed and held to have most of their vices and faults, especially if I should find myself deprived of that small virtue and good that the Africans have. But I'll act like that bird also found in the *Hundred Tales* that could live underwater as well as on land. When the king of the birds arrived to demand tribute from them, the bird at once dived into the water and said to the fish: 'You know me, I'm always with you. That lazy king of the birds has demanded tribute from me – what do you make of that?' The fish replied: 'He demanded tribute from you? What an idler! Let him come to us: we'll show him what tribute he'll get from you!' So the bird remained there, most comforted and consoled. Then, after a year, the king of the fish arrived to demand his tribute. When the other fish gave him their tribute, the bird darted from the water and fled back to the birds, to whom he gave the same excuse.

From this tale the author infers that whoever spies an advantage will always wait and go after it. For instance, if the Africans are being insulted, he'll come up with the obvious excuse that he was not born there but in Granada; or when the Granadans are being insulted he'll give another excuse, that he was not raised there and does not even remember it. To tell the truth, he would have to deny the country that nursed and suckled him. At any rate, he has presented only the most public and general matters, which he could not have concealed even if he had wanted to.

Map 2. Marrakesh and Fez

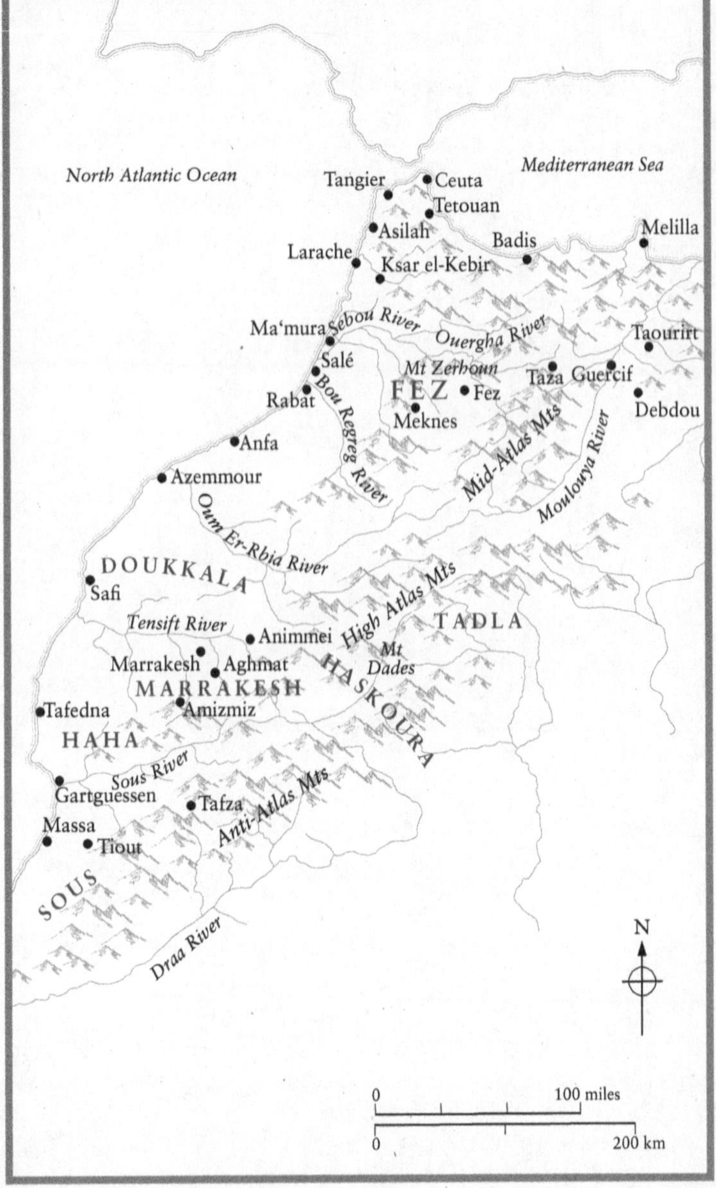

North Atlantic Ocean

Mediterranean Sea

Tangier
Ceuta
Tetouan
Asilah
Badis
Melilla
Larache
Ksar el-Kebir
Ma'mura
Sebou River
Ouergha River
Taourirt
Salé
Mt Zerhoun
FEZ
Fez
Taza
Guercif
Rabat
Bou Regreg River
Meknes
Mid-Atlas Mts
Debdou
Anfa
Moulouya River
Azemmour
Oum Er-Rbia River
DOUKKALA
Safi
Tensift River
Animmei
TADLA
Marrakesh
Aghmat
Mt Dades
High Atlas Mts
MARRAKESH
HASKOURA
Amizmiz
HAHA
Tafedna
Sous River
Gartguessen
Tafza
Anti-Atlas Mts
Massa
Tiout
SOUS
Draa River

N

0   100 miles
0   200 km

BOOK 2.1.

KINGDOM OF MARRAKESH

With the general overview of Africa out of the way, let us now discuss in detail the provinces, cities, mountains, terrains and plains, as well as their qualities, their climate and its effects, and the local habits and customs. Beginning to the west, Barbary will come first, and then a full account of Numidia, Libya and the Land of the Blacks. Then, likewise, the rivers and their names, courses and qualities, along with the unusual animals found in Africa; anyone with an open mind will be satisfied with all that the author, in the prime of his youth, and in the face of untold pains and grave dangers, visited and investigated in his travels.

2.1.1.1. Haha, the westernmost region of the world

The region of Haha ends at the ocean to the west and north; to the south it borders the Atlas mountains, and to the east the river Assif Inwal, which flows down into the Tensift, dividing Haha from the other regions.

2.1.1.2. The character of this land

Haha is a harsh land, with many high, craggy mountains, forests and valleys, and narrow streams. It is well populated and full of goats and donkeys, but fewer sheep, cattle and horses; little fruit grows there, not because the land is poor, but because the people are ignorant, for I have seen many places where grapes, figs and peaches flourish. They grow little wheat but large amounts of barley and millet, along with honey, which they eat without knowing to keep the wax too. There are many thorny trees that produce fruit somewhat like Spanish olives, which they call *argan* in their language, and from which they make a stinking, foul oil, used for food and fuel.

2.1.1.3. How the people of Haha live

These rustic people eat much barley bread, making it flat and unleavened and baking it in earthen pots like those used to cover cakes in Italy; only rarely do they use an oven. They also have a lazy dish called *asida*, often eaten at night, which is made as follows. First you boil water in a pot, then add barley flour and stir with a stick; when well cooked, place it in a dish and make a little hollow in the middle, adding a dash of argan oil. The whole family then comes to eat with their hands – no spoons. In spring and summer, they boil the flour in milk and use butter instead of oil. This is their evening meal, but during the day they eat bread and honey. In winter and spring they add milk and butter, and eat boiled meat with onions or beans, or, when they have guests, a food they call *couscous*.[1] They do not use tables, let alone table-cloths, but instead set a few round mats of [...] on the ground and eat on them.

2.1.1.4. The clothing and customs of this people

Most wear woollen garments that they call *al-kisa*[2] resembling the blankets used in Italy, which they fold around themselves, and they wrap woollen cloths around their buttocks and loins. On their heads they wear strips of wool about ten palms long and two wide, dyed with walnut root bark, twisted and wrapped around the head leaving the crown uncovered. Round double caps are worn only by old and learned men, not too tall, like the ones some doctors wear in Italy. Very few wear shirts, since they do not grow flax or even know how to weave it. They sit on the ground on hairy mats made of reeds; they sleep in hairy blankets ten to twenty cubits long, with the hairy side next to their bodies in winter, and outward in other seasons. Their cushions are made of rough woollen sacks, like those used to cover horses in Albania or Turkey. Most women go about with their faces uncovered. Their bowls are made of wood, not turned on a lathe, but carved out with a hammer and chisel, rather lazily and roughly, while their pitchers and jugs are of clay. It is the custom that unmarried men go beardless, shaving often, and growing a beard only after taking a wife.

The few horses they have run over the mountains like cats, unshod. They use both donkeys and horses to plough the earth. Many deer, goats and hares are found in the region, but they are not hunted. Wherever there is a stream, one finds a mill, though they also use small millstones in their houses, which the women turn by hand. They have no scholars or men proficient in any branch of learning except a few simple lawyers, and they lack any other ability: not a single doctor, surgeon, barber or even apothecary. Most of their remedies and medicines involve brutish enchantments, though they do have some barbers who circumcise their children. They have no soap, using ashes instead.

This wretched people are always and forever at war, so they cannot travel safely through the country, though a foreigner will come to no harm. If one of them wishes to travel he needs to be accompanied, either by a man of religion or by a woman from the opposite side. Justice in the region is unheard of, especially in the mountains where neither princes nor their deputies govern; their nobles, burghers and barons have, with great difficulty, been able to achieve some law within the walls of the towns. One finds few cities in the region, though there are many little towns, ksars and villages, large and small; I will describe the most famous of them one by one.

2.1.1.5. Tadnst

The ancient city of Tadnst was built by the Africans on a plain, with walls of rough clay bricks like all their homes and markets. It has 1,500 dwellings, and a stream winds around its walls.

There are a few markets for merchants and craftsmen who make necessary items such as the local clothes; one also finds fabrics and textiles from Portugal. Their only craftsmen are cobblers, blacksmiths, tailors and Jewish goldsmiths. The town has no inns, hammams, barbershops or anything of value.

When a foreign merchant comes to the city, either he lodges with an acquaintance or, if he doesn't know anyone, the local nobles draw lots to decide who will host him. The gentry take pleasure in generously hosting these foreigners, who usually leave a gift for the host when they wish to depart; a traveller who is not a merchant chooses whichever gentleman he pleases and lodges with him free of charge. A poor foreigner will stay at the hospital or another place in which they house the poor. In the middle of this city is a rather magnificent mosque of stone dressed with lime, an old building from when the land was governed by the king of Marrakesh. At the centre of the mosque is a large cistern; clerics and servants are appointed to maintain the mosque. Other mosques and houses of prayer are small and poorly built and looked after.

Around a hundred Jewish houses in the city do not pay a set tribute,[3] but instead present a regular gift to one of the town's gentlemen, each of whom looks after two or three Jewish houses. The majority of the city are Jews, and it is they who mint the coins, making sixty aspers from a single ounce of silver, a coin like the Hungarian fillér but square.[4] The city has no tax, customs or tax office, so when the community incurs some cost they share it between them, according to each person's means. In the year AH 918 (AD 1512–13) the city was laid waste and its inhabitants fled to the mountains and to Marrakesh. For the local Arabs had reached a pact with the Portuguese king's captain in Safi, wanting to give the city to the Christians; when the people discovered this they all fled together. The author saw the city in AH 920 (AD 1514–15) after it had been destroyed and its walls and houses razed, leaving it inhabited only by crows and owls.

2.1.1.6. Taqulit

The town of Taqulit comprises a thousand homes set on a mountainside. It is eighteen miles west of Tadnst, and a stream passes by it, on both sides of which are many gardens and orchards with all kinds of fruits; inside the town are many freshwater wells. There is a nice mosque, three hospitals for the poor, and another for the religious. The townsfolk are wealthier than those of Tadnst, for Taqulit has an ocean port called Aguz[5] where they sell large amounts of grain, since the town is by a splendid plain, and they also sell a lot of wax to Portuguese merchants. On account of this, the people are better dressed and their horses are finely outfitted.

When I was in this land, there was a certain gentleman in the city who led their council and was entrusted to manage the tribute paid to the Arabs, as well as their accords and treaties with the city; he was very rich, spending much on charity and alms, using his own wealth to help the people. For this he was well loved by the people, and elected head of the council. The author met this gentleman, who put him up in his home for eight days; he was a generous, charming man, living honourably, and he possessed many histories and chronicles of Africa. In the end, the poor man was killed in the war with the Portuguese, along with his adult son, in AH 923, which is the year of Christ 1514.[6] The town was destroyed and some people were captured, others fled and others were killed, as I have discussed further in my modern history of Africa.

2.1.1.7. Hadecchis[7]

The town of Hadecchis is eight miles south of Taqulit on the plain, with 700 homes; its walls are of rough stone, as are its mosque and other buildings. A slender stream flows through the town, with trellised vineyards on each side. It has many Jewish craftsmen, and the people, who are pederasts, are well dressed and ride good horses since they travel for trade. They strike silver coins and hold an annual fair that attracts all the mountainfolk, who are more like beasts than men. The fifteen-day fair brings together immense numbers of animals, wool, butter, honey, argan oil, ironwork and local fabric. The local women are the most beautiful creatures, very pale, plump, refined and friendly, while the men are cunning and loutish, ready to kill anyone who fools around with their women. For secular affairs, they have no judges or scholars to decide cases, but their leaders govern according to their whims; for spiritual matters, they have imams and lawyers to advise them. They pay no taxes or tariffs, just like the other towns.

The author lodged with an imam there; the man was a complete barbarian, but enjoyed Arabic oratory so much that the author stayed for a month, compelled by embarrassment – for he could not leave without the man following him out of a love of the Arabs, begging the author to stay longer and read out a little work of oratory – before returning to Marrakesh. The town was destroyed in the war with the Portuguese, and the inhabitants all fled to the mountains at the start of AH 922, the year the author left home, namely the year of Christ 1505.[8]

2.1.1.8. Ileusugaghen[9]

The town of Ileusugaghen, which comprises 400 homes, is set like a fortress on a lofty mountain ten miles south of Hadecchis. A stream passes below the town, which has no gardens, vineyards or other good crops either inside or outside, for most of its people are idlers. They all eat barley and argan oil, and go barefoot, except for the few who wear sandals of camel or cow leather. They are forever at war with the inhabitants of the countryside, and kill one another like dogs. They have no judges, imams or anyone else with legal authority, for they have no law or religion beyond what they share by word of mouth.

The whole mountain has no goods beyond huge amounts of honey, which they eat and sell to their neighbours, while they throw out the wax with their refuse. There is a small mosque, which can only hold 400 people, since they care little for prayer and show no devotion. When their men go about the square, or to the mosque or the shops, they bring their daggers and spears, for they are murderous cut-throats. The author was in this cursed city with ash-Sharif, who then became prince of Haha,[10] and who came to this town to make peace among its people, hearing their countless lawsuits and charges of murder and robbery. This prince had no judge or scholar with him, so he asked the author to see to these various cases. The author did so, as well as he could, as if he were their leader, in the prince's presence. The first man came before the author and began: 'This man killed eight of my kinsmen, and I killed ten of his; according to the custom of our ancestors, he owes me a certain amount of money to make peace.'

The other answered: 'You should give me that money, for you killed ten of my people, more than I killed of yours.'

'I can prove that I had a good reason for killing yours, since they took my land, which I inherited from my mother. But you killed mine without reason, simply to avenge your own dead, which you had no right to do since they had committed an unjust crime in taking the land.' They argued into the night, and by midnight neither party was even close to being done, shouting: 'Kill, kill!' The prince began to suspect foul play, and so in the middle of the night we mounted our horses and left for Iguil n Iguiguil. This town is still inhabited today, since the Portuguese could not reach them high on their mountain.

2.1.1.9. Tiout, Haha

Tiout is a small, brick-walled town, comprising 300 homes, on the plains among the mountains ten miles west of Ileusugaghen. Inside it are wells, little shops and a small house of prayer. Its inhabitants are all farmers; they have good fields for sowing barley and many orchards and gardens with grapes, figs and peaches, along with a huge number of goats, though there are many lions who ravage and eat them.

The author lodged one night outside town in a tumble-down farmhouse, tying the horses to a manger in one room, and foddered them with plenty of barley, since it was April. His men then stopped up the door with a mass of thornbushes, climbed onto the roof overlooking the courtyard, and went to sleep. When midnight came, two enormous lions arrived and tried to drag away the thornbushes covering the door; the horses heard and smelled the lions, and tugged with enough force to pull over the manger, one tearing its halter and making horrible noises. At first the author's party feared the horses would fall prey to the lions' jaws, and be ravaged and eaten; then they stopped worrying about the horses, for they feared that the building would fall because of all the noise, leaving them at the mercy of the lions. That night dragged on for a thousand years. When morning came they wondered in what state they would find the horses after all the kicking and biting, especially the author's mare; but without any delay they saddled up and rode back to the prince. The town has since been destroyed and the inhabitants could find no refuge, some being killed and others taken captive to Portugal in AH 920 (AD 1514–15).

2.1.1.10. Tesegdelt[11]

Tesegdelt is a rather large town of 800 homes, twelve miles south of Tiout on a high mountain. Being surrounded on all sides by towering cliffs, it needs no walls, much like Orte in Italy. A river passes below, with gardens and orchards of many kinds of fruit and especially walnuts. The inhabitants are wealthy and have so many horses that they pay no tribute to the Arabs, with whom they are continually at war, killing many. All the people of the surrounding countryside bring their grain into this city for fear of the Arabs.

The burghers have good practices and customs, and are especially generous, instructing their guards, whenever a foreigner enters, to ask if he knows anyone in town. If he says no, then the guards are to find him lodging as is their custom, and he will never spend a penny. The people are very devout and carefully observe their religion, having a handsome mosque in the middle of town, well run by the imams. They have a judge, a man learned in law, who passes judgement among them, except in criminal cases. They sow the fields on the mountain. The author stayed in that town for ten days with Prince Sharif in AH 919 (AD 1513–14).

2.1.1.11. Tagtessa[12]

The ancient town of Tagtessa is built on a high, round mountain twenty-four miles from Tesegdelt, and the road curves around it like a winding staircase. It has a stream below from which its inhabitants drink, and which appears from below about a mile and a half from the town, even though it is a good six miles away; the women fetch the water via a narrow path cut with iron in the fashion of a staircase. The inhabitants of this land are all brigands and cut-throats, and enemies with their neighbours; their fields and animals are on the mountains, and not a single horse is found in the town. The Arabs cannot cross the fields without a safe-conduct. All the woods are full of wild pigs. The author passed below this cursed town in a year of huge locust swarms; the grain was ripe, but there were ten times more locusts than ears of grain, so that one could only see the earth with the greatest of difficulty. That was in AH 919 (AD 1513–14).

2.1.1.12. Ait Daoud

The Africans built the ancient city of Ait Daoud on a high mountain fifteen miles south of Tagtessa, below a beautiful plateau. It has 700 homes and in the middle are many very cold, flowing fountains. All around it are steep slopes and frightening woods; many trees grow on the slopes. The town has many Jewish craftsmen, cobblers, dyers and goldsmiths. It is said that they are Jews of the tribe of David, but that after the Muslims took over the land they became Muslim. There are many men learned in the law here, most of whom know by heart the legal statutes and writings. The most marvellous was an old man who knew by heart a work called *al-Mudawwana*, which means 'compendium of laws'; it comprises three large volumes, constituting most of Malik's opinions on the legal tradition.[13] The town is widely known in the region for resolving disputes and drawing up contracts, and all the nearby people have recourse to it for these purposes. The jurists govern both spiritual and secular affairs, but the people disobey them when they advise in criminal matters, so their teaching doesn't help the people at all.

When the author arrived, he stayed with the town's lawyer, and at dinner there were many jurists present. After dinner, they began to consider certain questions about whether it was licit to sell endowments in order to meet the needs of the people.[14] Among them was an old man of great reputation, named Hegazzare in their Berber tongue. The author asked him what his name meant, and he answered, 'It means butcher.'[15] Asked why he had this name, he replied that he carved the law at its joints just as a butcher carves an animal at its joints.

The townsfolk have a hard life, subsisting on nothing but barley, argan oil and goat meat, without any wheat to speak of. The beautiful women are adorned in bright colours; the men are strong and passionate, nearly all with hairy chests, but very generous.

2.1.1.13. Qal'at al-Muridin, or the Fortress of Disciples

This little fortress sits atop a mountain between two other mountains just as high, with soaring crags between them and surrounded by forests. It is close to Tesegdelt and eight miles from Ait Daoud. One can only climb up to the fortress by a small, narrow path that goes a mile and a half up one side of the mountain. The town was built during the author's lifetime by the heretical leader and rebel, 'Umar as-Sayyaf,[16] who started out as a preacher in that province, but as more listened to him and his disciples grew in number he became a great tyrant. 'Umar as-Sayyaf ruled for two years and caused the land to be ruined. One of his wives killed him in his bed because she found him fornicating with her daughter, and realised that he was a faithless and lawless man. With him dead, his whole army was destroyed; the people rose up, killing his disciples and all his followers. One of his nephews was castellan of the town; since the people had risen up, he strengthened himself and those who escaped his uncle's army all went to the fortress. The people of Haha decided among themselves to raze it and remained there besieging the fortress for nearly a year without being able to do it any damage. To this day a deep hostility remains between the fortress and all Haha, and the man can only survive by robbery; he has some cavalry and he uses them to sally out, stealing animals, horses and people, for whom he charges a heavy ransom.

They cannot sow, till or rule even a patch of land beyond the mountain. They shoot arquebuses at the travellers who pass along the main road a mile from the fortress. The few animals they have are kept on the mountain. They keep the cursed body of 'Umar as-Sayyaf within the fortress and honour it as if he were a saint. When the author passed by with some of Prince Sharif's horsemen, they bombarded us from the fortress with their arquebuses, driving the group to the ground even though they missed. The author spoke with some former disciples who related everything about the heretic's life and his decrees contrary to public law; he wrote this down in the *Epitome of the Muslim Chronicles*.

2.1.1.14. Iguil n Iguiguil, a town in Haha

The small town of Iguil n Iguiguil comprises 400 homes; it was built by the ancient Africans on a mountain about a mile south of Ait Daoud. It is full of craftsmen of necessary things and surrounded by fields good for barley, producing considerable honey and argan oil. The only road leading up to the town is an extremely narrow, difficult path up the mountainside, which one can climb by horse only with great effort. The inhabitants are impressive with weapons, in constant conflict with the Arabs; they are always victorious since their land is well fortified on their mountain, and they are very generous. In this town they make many clay pots that are found in markets all over the region, of a kind the author thinks are made only there.

2.1.1.15. Tafedna

Tafedna is a fortress forty miles west of Iguil n Iguiguil on the ocean, built by the ancient Africans. It has 600 homes and a good port for smaller ships, where Portuguese merchants come to trade for wax and goatskins. The fields are all mountainous and yield barley. Beside the town runs a small river where the boats shelter when storms arise at sea, and it has very strong walls of brick and polished stone. The people levy customs and taxes, and their income is divided among those men who can defend the town. There are imams and judges, though they can do little about murders or stabbings, but normally, when someone is killed and his kinsmen find the culprit, they kill him – unless he flees the territory for seven years. After that, in order to return home, he must pay a fine to those owed restitution. The people of this town are very pale, natives and foreigners alike. Foreigners are honoured more than locals; they have a large hospital to accommodate them, though most lodge in the homes of burghers.

The author stayed in this town with Prince Sharif for three days, which felt like more than three years, because his rooms swarmed with fleas and reeked of goat dung and piss. The goats stayed outside during the day, but at night stood in the halls inside and slept in the bedroom doorways. The author did not sleep a wink during his three days there.

Now that the author has written of the famous towns of Haha in particular, he will describe the mountains, since most live in hamlets and villages in the mountains.

2.1.1.16. [Mount Ida ou Akal]

The mountain of the Ida ou Akal people is the first part of the Atlas, stretching east from the ocean to Iguil n Iguiguil and dividing the regions of Haha and Sous. It is a good three days across; the author has ridden the whole distance from Tafedna on the sea coast in the north to Massa in the south. The mountain is well populated with many hamlets and villages, whose inhabitants live off their goats, barley and honey. None of them wear shirts or sewn clothes, for they do not know how to tan leather or sew, instead draping cloth around their bodies. The women wear large, thick silver rings, four in each ear; some wear a thick clasp weighing an ounce and a half to fasten their cloth at the shoulder. Likewise, some rich and noble women wear big rings on their hands and even legs, though the poorer folk have iron or copper ones. They possess some small horses, unshod, which jump up and down like cats. The mountains are full of hares, goats and deer, but the people pay them no heed; they also have many springs and walnut trees.

Most of them ride like Arabs from one place to the next. They carry broad, curved daggers; their swords are broad and curved too, with a thick back like the sickles used to cut hay in Italy; each man carries three or four javelins. They have no judges or imams, men of learning, or mosques, being instead thieves, bandits and cut-throats. Prince Sharif mentioned in the author's presence that the people of this mountain have 20,000 fighting men.

2.1.1.17. Mount Demensera

This mountain also belongs to the Atlas. From the borders of the last mountain, it extends fifty miles east to Mount Nfifa in the region of Marrakesh, separating a large part of Haha from Sous, so that one must pass through it to get to the latter. It is well populated by a barbarous, beastly people, who keep horses and fight when their neighbours and the Arabs wish to come into their land. There is no town, ksar or house alone on the mountain, but there are several farms and villages, and some gentlemen keep a following to command. The mountain's fields are good for barley and millet, and many springs flow among the valleys on their way to the river Chichaoua. The people are well clothed and mine iron veins, travelling to trade on the profits. There are many Jews on the mountain too, who ride and bear arms, fighting on behalf of the mountainfolk who rule them. These Jews of Africa are called Karaim.[17] Tall mastic and boxwood trees, thick as walnut trees, as well as argan trees all grow on the mountain; all of which produce a bitter oil that they eat and burn. Many say that the mountain supports 25,000 warriors, on horse and foot. In AH 920 (AD 1514–15) the author passed by on his return from Sous, and thanks to Prince Sharif's letters of recommendation he was treated with great honour.

2.1.1.18. Mount Hadid, the mountain of iron

This mountain does not belong to the Atlas, as it begins at the seashore to the north and extends south along the river Tensift, dividing the region of Haha from Marrakesh and Doukkala. The Regraga people live here; it has huge forests and many springs, but despite an abundance of honey and argan oil they have only a little grain, supplied from Doukkala. Though poor, the people are good and devout; at the summit are many hermits who live on greens and water, all entirely honest, maintaining their faith in perpetual peace; when one of them steals from or attacks another, he is exiled for seven years. The people are very simple, and, when any chance event befalls one of the hermits, they treat it like a miracle. The Arabs nearby were a great nuisance to them, exacting a heavy tribute. The author says that when Muhammad, the current king of Fez, attacked the Arabs, they fled to this mountain. The king had aided the people by fortifying the mountain, so they killed the Arabs coming up the narrow passes; the wounded who turned tail were slaughtered by the king's army, and very few escaped. Then the mountainfolk brought the king of Fez the dead Arabs' horses, around 3,800 in total. Never again did they pay any tribute.

The author travelled there with the king's army in AH 921 (AD 1515–16). The mountain warriors numbered 12,000. There are many other mountains in Haha, but they are uninhabited, and we will pass over them to avoid getting too long and tedious.

This ends the first book, concerning the region of Haha, the province in Africa. Next is the second book, about Sous, across the Atlas mountains to the south and on the other side of Haha.

2.1.2. Sous

Sous is a region at the edge of Barbary, stretching from the ocean in the west to the sands of [. . .] in the south; it reaches the Atlas at the border of Haha to the north, and the great river Sous to the east, from which it gets its name. Let us go town by town, beginning in the west.

2.1.2.1. Massa

Massa comprises three small towns with walls of rough stone, built a mile apart from one another by the ancient Africans, next to the ocean at the point where the Atlas begins. Between them flows the great river Sous, which one can wade across in summer, though in winter their small boats are not up to crossing it. The three towns are in the middle of a palm forest, which is not wild but cultivated by the townsfolk. The dates are not very good, for they do not grow all year round. The inhabitants are all farmers who work the land during the two seasons of flooding, September and late April, and then harvest the grain in May. If the river does not flood during one of those seasons, then they cannot harvest grain from the fields. The towns have little livestock.

On the shore outside the towns is a mosque, which they hold in great devotion. Many historians say that from this mosque will come the righteous caliph foretold by Muhammad, as is found in the scriptures. Even more wonderfully, they say that, when the prophet Jonah was swallowed by a fish, it cast him up on the shore of Massa. The beams of the mosque are all made from the ribs of dead whales on the beach, and it is astonishing to see their size and hulking outlines. The common folk of the little towns say that every whale passing the mosque will die, on account of the power bestowed on the mosque by God. The author admits he had been among those who would not have believed it had they not actually seen the dead whales in great numbers. Later he spoke to an old Jew of the town, who told him that it was no wonder this happened, for about two miles out to sea there are large, sharp rocks; when a storm roils up the sea, it tosses the whales about and dashes them on the rocks, where they are torn up and die, and cast up nearby. This account now seems a little better than what the foolish people think.[18]

When Prince Sharif was in that town, a gentleman invited the author to dine with him in a garden outside the towns, and along the way he came across a rib set up like an arch, under which one could pass on a camel without brushing one's head. They say this rib has been there for 200 years. Along these shores one finds scattered the most excellent ambergris, which they sell to merchants from Portugal or Fez very cheaply at a ducat per ounce. The inhabitants claim to know that the whales produce it: some say it is their dung, others the sperm that the male releases when trying to mate with the female, congealed by the water. God knows what the truth is.

2.1.2.2. Tiout, Sous

Tiout is an ancient settlement built by the Africans on a splendid plain, divided into three parts each a mile from the other in a triangle, together comprising 4,000 homes. The river Sous passes nearby, and the soil is wonderfully fertile for wheat and barley as well as other grains and beans. They grow considerable amounts of sugar cane, but they do not know how to boil it properly or purify it, so all the sugar is black in colour; merchants come from Fez, Marrakesh and the Land of the Blacks to buy it. The town also has plenty of dates.

Their only money is raw gold, one ducat of which buys a certain amount of fine cloth; a little silver is found there, though the women all wear it to adorn themselves. They also use small iron pieces that weigh an ounce and are worth a *quattrino*. The only fruit found there are figs, grapes, peaches and dates; no olives, but they import oil from the mountains of Marrakesh, which sells in Sous at fifteen ducats for a *cantar* equal to 150 Italian pounds. Seven and a third of their ducats make up an ounce, which is equivalent to the Italian one, but their pound is eighteen ounces. They call the pound a *ratl*, with 100 *ratl* to a *cantar*. At the usual price, when not too expensive or cheap, three camel loads cost one ducat, where a load weighs 700 Italian pounds; this is in winter, but in summer they go for five or six loads per ducat. In this town they tan fine cordovan leather, known in Italy as Moroccan cordovan, selling a dozen hides for six ducats, or eight ducats in Fez.

Towards the Atlas mountains there are many villages and hamlets, while the south is uninhabited, since those plains and fields belong to the neighbouring Arabs. In the middle of the principal town stands a rather large mosque, inside which flows part of the river they direct nearby. The townsfolk are fierce, always at war among themselves, rarely at peace. They elect three upstanding men to rule them, from each of the three towns, holding office for three months each.

Most are dressed in the fashion of the people of Haha, and others wear cloaks, shirts and turbans of white cloth. A *canna*[19] of thick cloth like the Frisian is worth a ducat and a half, while for four ducats one can buy twenty-four Tuscan cubits of finer Portuguese or Flemish cloth.

The town has judges and imams, but the people obey them only in matters of religious law or devotion; in secular matters whoever has more kinsfolk has the advantage. If someone kills another, the dead man's relatives may seek revenge if they wish. If they favour the killer, he stays in town; if not, he is exiled for seven years before paying a penalty to the relatives, as determined by the town's gentlemen, and so keeping the peace. Many Jewish craftsmen live in Tiout, paying a few small presents to the town's gentlemen as their only tribute.

2.1.2.3. Taroudant

Taroudant is a fairly grand little town comprising 3,000 homes, built by the ancient Africans four miles south of the Atlas mountains and thirty-five miles east of Tiout. Taroudant is like the latter in its customs and the fertility of its lands, though smaller and more cultured, for when the Marinids ruled Fez they also ruled Sous and used this town as the residence for the king's viceroy; even now there remains a ruined fortress built by those kings. After the dynasty lost the kingdom, the towns-folk regained their liberty.

The inhabitants wear fabrics and textiles; many are crafts-men, living in peace, and four of their gentlemen govern at a time, for six months each. Around the town, towards the Atlas, are many villages and hamlets. The plains to the south are pas-tures belonging to the Arabs, to whom the people of Taroudant pay considerable tribute for the fields, keeping the road secure for locals as is usual in Sous. In the author's day, the town rebelled against the Arabs and declared allegiance to Prince Sharif in AH 920 (AD 1514–15).

2.1.2.4. Gartguessen[20]

Gartguessen is a fortress commanding good fields at the very end of the Atlas mountains, where the river Sous enters the ocean. Twenty years ago, after it had been captured by the Portuguese, the people of Haha and Sous agreed to retake it together, and at their request many soldiers came to their aid from distant lands, choosing as general a *sharif*, that is a noble gentleman from the house of Muhammad. With this army he besieged the fortress for many days. Many of them were killed, so they left and most returned home, while a few remained with Sharif to keep waging war on the Christians. The people of Sous agreed to supply pro-visions for 500 cavalry; but, once he had received these payments and controlled trade in the region, he turned around and made himself prince. When the author left his court, Sharif had more than 3,000 cavalry, countless infantry and limitless money, as explained more fully in the *Epitome of the Muslim Chronicles*.

2.1.2.5. Tidsi

Tidsi is a large city of 4,000 homes, which the ancient Africans built thirty miles east of Taroudant, sixty miles from the ocean, and twenty from the Atlas mountains. The land is abundantly fertile, growing much grain, sugar cane and indigo. There one finds merchants from the south, that is the Land of the Blacks. The intelligent and upright people live in peace, and are governed by a changing group of elders, chosen every six months by casting lots. The Sous flows three miles from Tidsi. The town has many Jewish craftsmen, goldsmiths, blacksmiths and others. It has a splendid mosque furnished with imams and servants, and the community provides stipends for judges and legal scholars. On Mondays they hold a market where the local Arabs and mountainfolk gather. The author notes that in AH 920 (AD 1514–15) the town offered itself to Sharif, who set up his chancellor's court there.

2.1.2.6. Tagawst

Tagawst is a large city, in fact the largest in Sous, walled in rough stone, with 8,000 homes. It was built by the ancient Africans sixty miles from the ocean, fifty miles south of the Atlas mountains and twenty miles from the Sous. In the city centre are many squares, shops and craftsmen. The people are divided into three factions which are usually at war; sometimes one of the factions asks the Arabs for help against their opponents, and the Arabs accept pay from the faction that offers the most money, or that seems the most useful to them once they've won.[21]

The town is surrounded by fertile fields and flocks, and they sell their wool very cheaply. They make a good deal of cloth which they bring to Timbuktu, for the city's many merchants make an annual trip to Timbuktu and Walata in the Land of the Blacks. Twice a week the town holds a market. They are well clothed and the women are beautiful and graceful. Many people in the city are brown, born of white and black parents. Victory depends on them, for although they have no right to govern, nor even to take the rank of gentlemen, they favour the factions on the basis of money. In AH 919 (AD 1513–14) the author stayed there for thirteen days with Prince Sharif's chancellor, buying female slaves for the prince.

2.1.2.7. Mount Ankisa[22]

This mountain is the westernmost of the Atlas mountains, and extends east forty miles; in its foothills are Massa and the other regions of Sous. The inhabitants are such valiant warriors on foot that any one of them has enough courage to defend himself against two horsemen using only his customary spears. The mountain grows no wheat, though plenty of barley and honey. All year round the top of the mountain is snowy, but the cold does not seem to bother the people, who wear few clothes even in winter. Prince Sharif wanted them to offer him obedience and tribute, but they refused and waged constant war against him, having nearly achieved victory by the end of AH 919 (AD 1513–14), the year the author was there.

2.1.2.8. Mount Ilalen

This mountain begins in the west at the border of the previous, and goes east to the region of Guzula; to the south it borders the plains of Sous. The inhabitants are noble and brave, possessing lots of horses. They are always at war with one another over the vein of silver in the mountain; the victors can profit from it, but, when the factions are equal, none can use it.

This is the end of the second book, concerning the province of Sous; the next is the third book, dealing with the province of Marrakesh.

2.1.3.1. The province of Marrakesh

This region begins with Mount Nfifa to the west, and stretches east to Mount 'Adimmei; to the north it slopes down along the Tensift until that river joins the Assif Inwal where Haha begins to the east, forming a triangle. The region is marvellously fertile in wheat and other grains, with plenty of livestock, water, streams, fountains, fruits, dates, grapes, figs, and apples and pears of all kinds. The whole plain is similar to Lombardy in Italy, though the mountains are bitterly cold and dry, growing nothing but a little barley. The author will now describe the region's towns and mountains in turn, starting to the west.

2.1.3.2. Al-Jumu'ah,[23] Marrakesh

The town of al-Jumu'ah is seven miles from the Atlas mountains, in the plain next to a river called Chichaoua. It was built by the ancient Africans and later destroyed when the Almohad dynasty lost the kingdom; Arabs now possess its territory. When inhabited, this town comprised 6,000 households, yielding revenues of 10,000 ducats, but now only traces are left and the Arabs sow what fields they need and leave the rest. The author passed by the town and stayed with these Arabs, who were lively and generous despite being robbers and thieves.

2.1.3.3. Imejajen[24]

Imejajen is a fortress at the summit of one of the Atlas mountains, twenty-five miles south of the previous town; it has no walls, being protected well enough by its slopes. In times past the fortress housed certain nobles of the region, but then the heretic 'Umar as-Sayyaf[25] besieged it and took it by force, running the men through with spears and killing the women; those who were pregnant were ripped open and the infants killed at their breasts. This occurred in AH 900 (AD 1494–95), and the town lay uninhabited; when the author passed by in AH 920 (AD 1514–15), it was only a few months since people had begun to live there again. The mountain is farmed on all sides, but one cannot till or even cross the plains for fear of the Arabs and the Portuguese Christians.

2.1.3.4. Tenezza

Tenezza is a town on the slopes of the Atlas mountain known as Guadmioua. The Africans of old built it eight miles east of the river Assif Inwal. Below it lie many plains excellent for growing grain, but the inhabitants are unable to work the fields on account of the Arabs oppressing them; they sow only the slopes between their town and the river, for which they pay the Arabs a third.

2.1.3.5. New Jumu'ah

This town is a large fortress on a high mountain, surrounded by other high mountains. Just below it begins the river Assif el-Mal, which in the African language means 'the roaring river', for it plunges to dizzy depths, much like the Valle dell'Inferno in Tivoli near Rome. It was built by recent rulers, and the town now comprises 2,000 homes. A tyrant descended from the old Marrakesh kings holds the fortress with a good number of horsemen and infantry, taking a revenue of 10,000 ducats from the hamlets and villages of the Atlas mountains; he is an ally of the Arabs, sending them large gifts, and has sometimes made trouble for the ruler of Marrakesh. The inhabitants are clever and well dressed, many of them craftsmen, for they live fifty miles from Marrakesh. Between the mountains lie many gardens and orchards, which grow plenty of fruit, grain, flax and hemp, and they keep many goats. They have imams and judges, being upstanding, noble people, though coarse by nature and protective of their women. The author lodged there with one of his relatives, who had left Fez because he got into hot water over his alchemy; he struck up a friendship with the town's ruler and so became his secretary.

2.1.3.6. Amizmiz

The town of Amizmiz is quite large, built by the ancient Africans twenty-four miles west of the town just mentioned, on the slopes of a mountain in the Atlas. Below it lies a pass through the Atlas to the province of Guzula, called the Bou er-Rich, meaning 'feathery', for there is always a blizzard there, as if of white feathers.[26] Below the town stretch great plains, joining it to Marrakesh thirty miles away. The best wheat I have ever seen grows there, large and of a gorgeous colour, making excellent flour. However, the Arabs and the ruler of Marrakesh heavily tax the town, so most of the countryside is uninhabited and even the townsfolk are starting to abandon it. The remaining people have little money, despite plenty of grain and farms. The author never stayed in the town, but just outside in the tent of Sidi Kannoun, a hermit highly respected there.[27]

2.1.3.7. Tumeglast[28]

Tumeglast comprises three ksars in the plain fourteen miles north of the Atlas and thirty from Marrakesh. It is surrounded by date palms, vineyards and other fruit trees; its fields are excellent for grain, though most are uncultivated because of the ravages of the Arabs. The ksars are nearly uninhabited, except for twelve or fifteen families who are kin of the hermit just mentioned, and who by his favour may till a patch of land without paying the Arabs.

Meanwhile, the Arabs get along by staying in the houses of the hermit's kinsfolk. These houses are in bad shape, more like stables for donkeys; they are full of fleas and bedbugs, and the only water comes from a salty well outside. When the author was there, he lodged with Sidi Yahya (u-Ta'fuft), who came to collect tribute on behalf of the king of Portugal, having been made governor of the Safi region.[29]

2.1.3.8. Tesrast

Tesrast is a small town on the banks of the Assif el-Mal, fourteen miles west of Marrakesh and twenty miles from the Atlas mountains. Many gardens, date groves and fields of grain surround it; all the inhabitants work these groves though occasionally the river floods and washes away all the orchards. In summer the Arabs often come and eat everything they find. The author has passed through this town, stopping only long enough to fodder the horses; that was the day they escaped being robbed by some Arabs by a stroke of luck.

2.1.3.9. Marrakesh

Marrakesh is one of the grandest and greatest cities in the world. It is the noblest city of Africa, situated in a very large plain fourteen miles from the Atlas mountains. It was built by Yusuf ibn Tashfin, king of the Lamtuna, at the time he arrived in the area with his people. He set the seat of his kingdom off the road from Aghmat, which crosses the Atlas mountains down to the desert, and there settled his people. The city was built with the help of architects and ingenious builders; it was of great size, and when 'Ali ibn Yusuf ibn Tashfin was king of Marrakesh, it had 100,000 homes or more, with twenty-four gates, the whole city surrounded by very beautiful and strong walls of lime and earth.

Some six miles distant from Marrakesh is a mighty river called the Tensift. The city is supplied with mosques, colleges, hammams and inns of the sort customary in Africa. Some of the mosques were built by the Lamtuna kings, and others by their successors, the kings of al-Muwahhidun.[30] In the middle of the land is a splendid mosque built by 'Ali ibn Yusuf, the first king of Marrakesh, called 'The Mosque of 'Ali ibn Yusuf'. The successor to this kingdom, 'Abd al-Mu'min ibn 'Ali, demolished the mosque and rebuilt it anew to erase 'Ali's name and title, but this was a waste of effort, for the people still called it by its first name.[31]

Another mosque was built near the citadel by 'Abd al-Mu'min, who rebelled and succeeded to the kingdom.[32] His grandson (Yusuf Yaqub) al-Mansur enlarged it by fifty cubits on all sides, and had many columns brought for it from Spain. Under it he built a cistern as big as the mosque itself; sheets of lead covered the roof, with channels conveying every drop of rainwater into the cistern. He also had a minaret built of large, finished stones like those of the Colosseum of Rome; it is 100 Tuscan cubits around and taller than the Asinelli Tower in Bologna. Its highly polished ramp is nine palms wide and the outer wall is ten palms thick; the wall of the core of the tower is five palms thick. Within the tower are seven beautiful rooms, one above another, and a lovely light shines into the stairwell through the windows ingeniously made wider on the inside than the outside. When you come out on top of the tower, you find another turret with a tip like a spire, about twenty-five cubits around, just like the tower's core, the height of two spears and constructed in three levels. One goes from one level to another by three wooden ladders. At the top a finial is fixed deeply into the spire, and on it three silver balls are strung like beads, the largest one below, the middle next and the smallest at the top; the three together weigh ninety-three Italian weights. If you stand on the highest level and look down like someone in the lookout on a ship's mast, a person below will look as small as a one-year-old child. You can see the mountain of Safi 130 miles outside Marrakesh and the whole plain around for about fifty miles.[33]

The mosque is rather plain inside, with wooden roofs in as fine a style as those of many churches in Italy. It is one of the greatest mosques in the world, but it is now abandoned, because the people pray there only on Fridays, since the city lacks housing, especially in the surrounding areas, which are all ruined; it takes great effort to reach it through the houses fallen down on top of one another. As you know, its name comes from the streets of booksellers near the mosque;[34] for once you could find as many as 200 bookstalls under its porch, but nowadays there are none anywhere in Marrakesh.

Two-thirds of the city are nearly uninhabited, only one remaining; the derelict area is all planted with palms, vines and fruit trees, since those living in the city cannot protect their lands outside the walls from the ravages of the Arabs. It is true that the city has been worn down before its time, since only 500 years have passed since it was built by Yusuf ibn Tashfin in the year AH 424 (AD 1033–34).[35] After Yusuf's death his son 'Ali reigned; after 'Ali died, his son Ibrahim reigned. During Ibrahim's reign there was a rebellion, so that by great wars and changes of ruler the city was worn down over just a short time. The imam al-Mahdi,[36] who lived in the mountains, started a war with King Ibrahim, forcing him to leave his camp to defend himself; by a stroke of misfortune the king was wounded and could not get back to Marrakesh, so he fled eastward into the foothills of the Atlas mountains with those who escaped the mad rout. The leader of the imam's disciples, one 'Abd al-Mu'min, went with half the army to follow King Ibrahim. The king could not find refuge or protection until he reached Oran with the few remnants of his destroyed camp. 'Abd al-Mu'min set about besieging the king, who gave up when he realised that the townsfolk did not want to be harmed on his account. One night Ibrahim mounted his steed and, setting his wife on the rear of his saddle, left by a gate unrecognised. He made for the shore, and the horse, spurred on by the king, raced ahead and dashed them all to pieces on the rocks. In the morning they were found dead, and they were buried like wretches.

Victorious, 'Abd al-Mu'min returned at once to Marrakesh with his men, and on the very day his old imam died he was elected king and caliph by the forty disciples and ten ministers, according to a practice new to the law of Muhammad. After besieging Marrakesh for about a year, at last in AH 518 (AD 1124–25) he entered by force and seized King Ibrahim's son, killing him along with most of the soldiers, officers and the city's people.[37] The disciple's house ruled from AH 516 to 668 (AD 1122–1270). They were removed from the kingdom by the kings of the Marinid dynasty, who reigned until AH 785

(AD 1383–84). From then on the house lost its earlier power and Marrakesh was ruled by several lords from the Old Mountain near Marrakesh. You can see how many lords have changed Marrakesh. The most damage was done under the Marinid dynasty, for they installed a viceroy there after moving their palace and court to Fez, which they made the capital of the kingdom of Mauretania and the whole Maghrib. How many catastrophic wars were waged on the poor city on account of this change can be seen in the *Epitome of the Muslim Chronicles*.

We should now return to the city, which contains a citadel itself as large as a city, with thick, strong walls, splendid arches of travertine and gates all fashioned in iron.[38] In the middle of the citadel is a magnificent mosque with a very beautiful minaret topped with an iron finial on which are strung three balls of gold worth 13,000 African ducats, the largest ball at the bottom and the smallest at the top.[39] Many rulers have wanted to remove these balls to sell them, but each time misfortune has foiled them, so that it is now held to be bad luck to remove them. The common people say these balls were placed there under a specific planetary alignment so that they could never be taken down by mortal hands. Other stories say that whoever put them there enchanted them, appointing many spirits to guard them. In the author's time, the king of Marrakesh imagined he might remove them, giving as a reason the need for money to fight off the Portuguese Christians; but the people did not consent to give up their city's noble glory. The author has read in the histories that al-Mansur's wife, when she saw that her husband had finished building the mosque, begged him to have some things put there to remember her by when she was dead. Al-Mansur agreed, and she sold all the jewellery – gems, gold and silver – that he had given her when they married; with the money he had the balls made in her memory.

Also in that citadel is a very fine madrasa with around thirty rooms and a lower hall where they used to lecture a long time ago; every student with a room in the college had his expenses paid and was given clothes once a year. Some lecturers received 100 ducats, others 200, depending on their skill; but there was no student there who had not first earned a degree in the principles of the disciplines. The college is copiously adorned with mosaics; the inner walls are all faced with fine glazed tiles cut into delicate flowers and other kinds of work, especially the lecture hall and the covered porches, which are entirely faced with the glazed tiles we now call *ezzuleigie* (*zellij*), as are used these days in Spain. In the middle is a dazzling fountain of the whitest marble, deep like African fountains. But in the author's time the college had barely five students, and there was a lecturer, the most ignorant jurist, who knew nothing of the humanities nor of any other discipline. In the city lived a very rich old judge, a great historian, especially of the city itself, who knew little of the law; he was appointed judge for his experience, having been a notary and a favourite of the king for forty years. The author lodged with him because the other courtiers seemed like fools, as the author experienced outside the city when they were with the king in the countryside the first time he requested entry into the region of Marrakesh.

In addition to these, there are in the citadel around twelve very well-built and finely decorated buildings constructed by al-Mansur. The first you come across as you enter was built for the guard of Christian crossbowmen, who numbered around 500 and would march in front of the king. The next building along housed the guard of the archers, and a little way past this is the building of the scribes and secretaries, called in their language the House of Business. A little further on is the so-called Victory Building, where the arms and munitions are kept, and after that, slightly further away, the home of the king's stable master. Near this are three stables built in turn, each holding 200 horses, and two others, the first holding 100 mules, and the second mares and female mules for the use of the king and his concubines. Next to the stables were two double-storeyed granaries.[40] The first held straw in the lower level and barley for the horses in the upper one. The other could hold more than 30,000 bushels of grain in each level. It had holes in the roof and a smooth ramp next to it; laden animals went up onto the roof, where the grain was measured out and thrown down into the holes. When the grain was to be removed, there were other holes below which could be opened and shut without any difficulty.

A little further on is a fine little building that housed the school for the king's sons and the other young boys of the royal family. It contains a very beautiful square room with corridors around it, and gorgeous windows of multicoloured glass; around the inside of the room are cupboards made from carved pieces of wood and decorated with fine blue and gold. Beyond that is a building for the guard of the eunuchs and opposite is a grand building where the king holds general audience; next to this is the place where he meets ambassadors and his secretaries. Between these is the family house where the wives, concubines and slaves are kept. Near this building is another divided into many apartments for the sons of the sheikhs, that is, the nobles.

Further away, towards the citadel wall next to the country-side, is a very large and beautiful garden where there are all sorts of fruits and flowers and delights. In it is a squared-off pit, seven palms deep, paved and walled with marble; the edge is decorated with carved marble. In the middle is a column, at the top of which a marble lion spurts water through its mouth, and on each side is a leopard, made of a white marble with natural round, green blemishes, found only on the peak of a mountain in the Atlas range 250 miles from Marrakesh. On the other side next to the garden is a great enclosure where there were many wild and exotic animals, such as giraffes, elephants, lions, stags and goats, although the lions had separate rooms to themselves, so that even today this place is called the Lions' Den.

These remains of the citadel demonstrate the power and pomp that al-Mansur enjoyed in those days. But now it is unin-habited, except the rooms of the family and the building of the crossbowmen, where the porters and mule-drivers of the pres-ent king live.[41] The rest is occupied by pigeons, crows, owls, horned owls and similar birds. The garden is now a place to throw rubbish. The building where the library once was now contains roosters on one side, and in the library itself are domes-tic pigeons who make their nests in the old book cupboards. So it goes in the world, in which nothing is secure.

After all, al-Mansur ruled Africa from Massa to Tripoli in Barbary – a distance the author could not cross on horse in less than ninety days east to west, or fifteen days north to south – in other words, all the noblest part of Africa. He also ruled all of Baetica in Europe, from Tarifa to the region of Aragon, and size-able parts of Castile and Portugal. Not only al-Mansur, but also his grandfather 'Abd al-Mu'min, his father (Abu Yaqub) Yusuf and his son Muhammad an-Nasir, who was defeated in the king-dom of Valencia; at that battle he lost 60,000 of his soldiers, both cavalry and infantry, but he survived and returned to Marrakesh.[42] The Christians began to press their advantage in victory and within thirty years had recaptured Valencia, Dénia, Alicante, Mur-cia, Cartagena, Córdoba, Seville, Jaén and Úbeda; with such losses the royal houses of Marrakesh began to decline. Then Muham-mad died, leaving ten adult sons who were all kings and viceroys of the kingdom; each wanted to rule and so they started to kill each other. This was why the Marinids could invade and rule Fez and the surrounding areas; the people of 'Abd al-Haqq rose up and took power in Tlemcen, removing the Tunisian viceroy from their lands and appointing a king from among themselves. The house of al-Mansur survived only as long as his sons, who mur-dered each other until they lost their lives and their state to Yaqub ibn 'Abd al-Haqq, the first king of the Marinid dynasty. All this is described in the *Epitome of the Muslim Chronicles*.

In the end, then, the city was left with a poor reputation, con-stantly besieged by the Arabs whenever its citizens were unwilling to satisfy them. The author has narrated this little information about Marrakesh as he has seen it with his own eyes, and likewise he has read the chronicles of Marrakesh by Ibn 'Abd al-Malik (al-Marrakushi) in seven volumes. This matter can also be found in the *Epitome of the Muslim Chronicles*.

2.1.3.10. Aghmat

The city of Aghmat was built by the ancient Africans on the slopes of one of the Atlas mountains, twenty-four miles from Marrakesh. It has 6,000 homes and was very cultured in the days of the Almohads, like a second Marrakesh, encircled by gardens and vineyards along the mountainside and plain. Below it a beautiful river[43] flows down from the Atlas mountains, joining the Tensift. Between the two is a marvellous countryside of the most fertile fields, which the locals say can produce a fiftyfold harvest. The water is always crystal clear, just like the Umbrian rivers Narni and Nera. They also say that the river, which heads towards Marrakesh, has a source next to the city and flows through various subterranean canals, though these cannot be seen within Marrakesh. Many rulers have wanted to know the source of the water and so sent men into these canals with lights and lanterns, but inside they came up against a terrible wind, which extinguished the lights, putting them in great danger of losing the way out, for the path was broken up at various points where the water scattered out between great rocks. As there were many caverns, they doubted they would ever get back, once inside; one of them came straight back to where they were, so that only with the greatest of difficulty did they find the path, after having lost hope of ever finding a way to the surface; because of this, no one has wanted to try since. Some historians say that the ruler who founded Marrakesh learned from his astrologer that war would befall Marrakesh, against him and his house; when he made the canals he built them under a constellation so that no one would know where the water comes from, and no enemy could ever cut it off.

Below Aghmat, next to the river, is a pass through the Atlas mountains to the province of Guzula; now, though, all but the citadel is overrun by wolves and foxes, owls and crows. In the author's day, a hermit lived there with a hundred disciples, all with good horses, and they began to act like secular rulers, only without vassals. The author lodged at the hermit's home for eight days, for his brother was a marvellous friend – he had studied at the madrasa by the author's home in Fez, and they attended theology lectures together on the epistle of an-Nasafi.[44]

2.1.3.11. Animmei[45]

The small town of Animmei lies on a slope of the Atlas mountains facing the plain, at the pass to Fez forty miles east of Marrakesh. Those who would take the road along the mountainside and the river Aghmat pass fifteen miles from Animmei. The countryside between the river and Animmei, like that around Aghmat, is excellent for crops. The area from Marrakesh to the river was ruled by one of the town's young lords, a valiant youth who warred against Marrakesh and the Arabs, ruling many peoples of the Atlas mountains. He was generous and brave; at the age of twelve he killed his uncle and, after making himself ruler, he once repelled an invasion of many Arabs and 300 Portuguese Christian light cavalry. With 200 cavalry and a few Arabs of his own, the young lord put up a brave defence; he killed the enemy Arabs and wretched Portuguese in great swathes, leaving none alive to tell the tale back home, for the land was unfamiliar to them. This happened in AH 920 (AD 1514–15).

The king of Fez then came to demand tribute from the young lord, and when he refused, the scorned king sent a large army of cavalry and crossbowmen. Wanting to fight in person, the youth threw himself into battle and caught a gun bullet in the chest, instantly losing his life and rule. The king's general imposed a heavy penalty on the town and on the lord's wife, and brought many noble prisoners to Fez in chains, leaving behind a governor to rule Animmei. This was in AH 921 (AD 1515–16).

Having spoken of the region of Marrakesh and its plain, the author will now tell of the most prominent, famous mountains in the region.

2.1.3.12. Mount Nfifa

The region of Marrakesh begins on the west at Mount Nfifa, which divides it from Haha. The mountain is well inhabited and the peaks, even the snowy ones, are good for growing barley. The people are wild and rough, entirely uncultured, marvelling at burghers and their clothes. The author was there for two days; he wore a white cloak in the fashion of the students there, and it soon became stained, for all the gentlemen he talked to pawed it to get a better look, and within two days it was as filthy as a dishcloth. He had no choice but to trade his horse, worth ten ducats, for a sword worth barely one and a half in Fez, for the merchants never go without one on account of the many highwaymen all around. The mountainfolk have plenty of goats, millet and argan oil, for they have just started growing argan there.

2.1.3.13. Mount Semede

This mountain extends twenty miles east from the river Chichaoua, which marks the borders of Nfifa. The inhabitants are layabouts, coarse and poor. There are many springs and the mountain has snow throughout the year. The people will heed no legal judgement but that of a foreign traveller, at least one with a bit of knowledge. The author stayed for a night with a religious man honoured there, and had to eat a food they make with barley flour in boiling water,[46] with the meat of a billy goat more than seven years old. He had to sleep on the ground on a mat, enduring the night in the thought that he would leave first thing in the morning. Little did he know of their custom. On waking at dawn, the author looked around to see over fifty people waiting for him to decide their cases, demanding guidance on their disputes and differences. He answered that he knew nothing, but then three gentlemen came forward to say, 'You do not know our custom, sir; you cannot leave until we have dealt with everything.' They took away the author's horse and companions, ignoring their protests, and he was forced to stay to address their disputes. In fact, it was not enough to deliver judgements; he also had to write the documents out, since none of them could put two words together. He had to endure the bad food and rough bed for this!

The nuisance went on for nine days. When everything had been done, they promised that evening to present their gifts the next morning. The author spent the night wondering what they would be: perhaps a hundred ducats, maybe fifty, or at least thirty. When morning came, he was called after prayers and asked to sit under the colonnade of their mosque, and with lowered heads they came forward one by one, each with their gift. One brought a cock, another a nutshell; some gentlemen brought one, two, or three plaits of onions or garlic, while some brought goat bucks. At this sight, the author despaired of their gifts, which were useless to him since no one in the region had money to buy them. In the end, he had to leave everything with the man who had put him up, and rode on. Fifty people accompanied him for twenty miles, some on horse and some on foot, since the road was not safe.

2.1.3.14. Mount Chichaoua

This mountain, which has snow all year, follows the previous, and the river named after it begins there. The people are extremely brutish, always at war with the mountainfolk at their borders, using catapults[47] to throw stones. They live on barley, millet and goat meat, and among them are many Jews who are skilled with weapons and work as craftsmen, smiths and woodworkers, making shovels, scythes and horseshoes. Some are builders, though they have little to do: the walls are made of stone and clay, and the roofs are straw set across beams; they don't use lime, planks or bricks like those on all the other mountains. They have many good jurists who deliver guidance in some matters. The author recognised many of those who had studied in Fez; they gave him a warm welcome and company for the road.

2.1.3.15. Mount Seksiwa

This accursed mountain is high and cold, with woods and ceaseless snow covering its slopes and summit. The inhabitants wear soft white caps, and all over the mountain are springs from which the river Assif Inwal begins. The mountain has many wide, deep caves, where for three months of the year, from November to January, they keep their livestock, that is, cows, horses and goats, which are fed on hay and foliage from certain tall trees. All the provisions come from beyond the mountain, which grows nothing itself, though in spring and summer they have plenty of fresh cheese, butter and milk. The inhabitants are long-lived and strong in their old age, reaching eighty, ninety, or even a hundred years, and tending their herds to the ends of their days. They never see foreigners, and the only shoes they wear are a kind of sole under their feet with strips of cloth tied around their legs with cords, because of the snow.

2.1.3.16. The mountain and city Tin Mal

Tin Mal is an extremely high and cold mountain exactly like the previous but with a city at the top named after the mountain. It is well inhabited, with a lovely mosque; a river runs by it, and the preacher al-Mahdi is buried there with his disciple 'Abd al-Mu'min.[48] The inhabitants are a malicious people. They believe themselves learned, being devoted to the study of theology as taught by that preacher, whom others consider an evil heretic; whenever they see a foreigner they try to argue with him. The people are all badly dressed and live beastly lives, for their wickedness means no one comes to trade with them. The only governance they have is their imam's guidance. They eat barley and olive oil, with plenty of walnuts and pines.

2.1.3.17. Mount Guadmioua

This range borders Mount Semede to the west, going east twenty-five miles to Amizmiz. The inhabitants are poor, lowly subjects of the Arabs, for their dwellings are in the plains to the south, towards Tin Mal. The slopes grow plenty of olives and barley, and the peaks are tall with great forests and many springs. Besides the Arabs, the people are subject to the ruler of New Jumu'ah.

2.1.3.18. Mount Hintata

This is the highest mountain the author has ever seen with his own eyes. It borders Guadmioua to the west and extends east forty-five miles to Mount 'Adimmei. The inhabitants of this mountain are able and wealthy, having many horses. There is a citadel held by a ruler kin to the ruler of Marrakesh, though he is always making war on him via various villages and fields on their borders. Many Jews live on this mountain as craftsmen, paying tribute to the ruler; they belong to the Karaite sect, and are skilled warriors.

2.1.3.19. Mount 'Adimmei[49]

'Adimmei is a large, high mountain, bordering Mount Hintata and extending east to the river Teseut. The ruler of its town was killed in a war with the king of Fez. The mountain is well populated, with forests of walnuts, olives and quinces. The people, who were all subject to the dead ruler, are able and generous, with much livestock of all kinds, since their mountain has temperate air, good soil and plenty of springs as well as the two rivers, mentioned below in the section on rivers.

End of the third book, a brief account of the plains and mountains in the kingdom of Marrakesh. Now it remains to speak of the region of Guzula, which is across the mountains from the kingdom of Marrakesh; the Atlas mountains divide the two regions.

2.1.3.20. The Guzula region[50]

The Guzula region is a well-populated land; it borders the mountain in Sous mentioned above[51] to the west, the Atlas foothills to the north and the region of Marrakesh to the east. The inhabitants are brutish and have little money but plenty of livestock and barley. The region has many veins of copper and iron, and the people make copper vessels, bringing them to neighbouring regions to barter for textiles, medicines, horses and other things they need.

There are no cities or ksars in the region, but there are good and substantial villages of a thousand homes, give or take. They have no rulers, but govern themselves, and are always at war with one another, though in the author's day they kept a truce for three days a week when they could speak with friends or enemies and go from one town to the next – but on the other days they killed each other like dogs. The truce was arranged by a hermit they considered a saint, who only had one eye; he was a good man, wise and generous, and the author spoke with him and lodged in his home. He truly deserved the highest praise for his fairness, given the troubles and worries he endured to bring that people peace and quiet.

This people wear short, sleeveless woollen shirts with belts. They carry broad, curved daggers, sharp on both sides and narrowing towards the tip; they also carry swords like those of Haha. They hold a fair for two months of the year, where the people feed all the foreigners, even when 10,000 come over the whole season. Before the fair starts, they make a truce and select as guards a captain and 100 men from each faction; they patrol the fair and if anyone transgresses they publicly punish him accordingly, while thieves are swiftly run through with spears and their bodies left to the dogs. The fair takes place on a plain between the mountains, and the merchants keep their goods in tents and stick huts. The tents are sorted into areas, for example, one for sellers of cloth and fabrics, another for haberdashers, another for saddlers, another for coppersmiths, another for swordsmiths, so that every kind of good is kept separate. The livestock merchants stay outside the camp; among the tents are large stick huts to house gentlemen, and there they feed the foreigners.

As more foreigners arrive, some run to let the gentlemen know to lay on more food. The locals spend a lot, but they do a roaring trade and earn a lot more from their sales, since people come from every region, some even from the Land of the Blacks.

In fact, the people of Guzula are coarse and brutish, except for the way they manage this fair peaceably – in this they are the best in the world. The fair begins on Muhammad's birthday, 12 Rabi' (al-Awwal), the third month of the Arabic calendar. The author was at the fair for fifteen days with prince ash-Sharif,[52] who went to enjoy it in AH 920 (AD 1514–15).

2.1.4.1. The Doukkala region

The province of Doukkala has the river Tensift on the west and the ocean to the north; it borders the river Habid on the south, and the Oum Er-Rbia on the west. The province is three days' journey long and two across, and well populated, though the people are rude and wicked. They have a few walled towns, as one will see when taking each place in turn.

2.1.4.2. Safi

Safi is a city on the shores of the ocean, comprising 4,000 homes; it was built by the ancient Africans and is now filled with people of middling culture. It has many craftsmen, as well as perhaps a hundred Jewish households. The surrounding fields are excellent and fertile, though the inhabitants are ignorant, with barely ten vineyards and only a few small orchards.

After the kings of Marrakesh lost control, Safi was ruled by the Beni Farhun. In the author's day, it was in the hands of a powerful ruler by the name of 'Abd ar-Rahman ibn Farhun, who had killed his uncle for the kingdom[53] and so ruled the town in peace for many years. 'Abd ar-Rahman had an extremely beautiful daughter who secretly carried on an affair with a faction leader called 'Ali ibn Washman. She did this with the knowledge of her mother, as well as a slave-woman, who informed the father, using as evidence that she had given her bracelet, a gift from him, to her lover 'Ali. The father asked them about it, and on learning the truth threatened the mother and daughter with death. For a while he pretended not to think of the matter any longer. But the girl and her mother, who knew his wiles and did not trust him, sent word to 'Ali to avoid capture, for the ruler was only pretending to forget everything; 'Ali would have to find a way out or they would all be killed. On the alert, he went straight to a friend,[54] the head of another faction, and, on telling him what happened, the other agreed that he would not be safe from 'Abd ar-Rahman. Together they decided to kill the ruler, just as he planned to do to them.

It all happened one Friday, when the ruler had decided to invite these leaders for some entertainment. He sent them a message to join him for a ride at a certain time and place after prayers, having laid a plan to kill them there and then. Anticipating the plot, 'Ali hired a seaworthy and well-armed brigantine bound for Azemmour, thinking that if things went badly at least he would have a means to flee. He then found his friend and together they armed themselves with twenty brave companions, going to the palace for the ruler. There they learned he had gone to the mosque for prayers, so they pursued him and found him there, praying together with all the people of the city. The ruler himself was in the central aisle of the mosque, behind the imam where rulers usually are, with his guard around him. The two went up to the ruler; his guard, following his command, said nothing, so 'Ali came up behind and thrust a dagger through the ruler's back and out of his chest. As the body fell to the ground, his companion Yahya stabbed him in the groin, killing him.[55] The guards began to defend the ruler, but the twenty companions rushed in with swords drawn and the guards immediately suspected that the people favoured the traitors, so they fled and everyone left the mosque in shock. The author heard from 'Ali's own mouth that, before they decided to kill him, the ruler would not have been caught in the mosque had it not been for the two of them and their twenty companions. With the ruler dead, the two leaders went out into the square and gave the people their reason: that they had rebelled and killed him because he had sought to rule and was trying as hard as he could to kill them, and they did not want to wait for death at his hand. In any event, the two began to rule and govern.

For a while they ruled in harmony, but after several months they took sides against one another and a rift grew between them. In 'Abd ar-Rahman's day, many Portuguese merchants had been killed because they counselled their king to send an armada to invade Safi, while others had advised the opposite, arguing that the wise ruler would not allow himself to be defeated as they thought. But after 'Abd ar-Rahman was killed, the merchants unanimously advised the king to seize the town by an inexpensive ruse, exploiting the disunity between the ruling faction leaders. They approached one of the leaders[56] with presents and gifts, gaining his friendship to request one concession: they wanted to build a strong building by the sea where they could safely protect those goods that had not been sacked when the old ruler died. He agreed, though the other leader did not, guessing what would happen to the town. At last, whether out of friendship or obligation, the other gave in. The Portuguese constructed a very strong building, bringing in guns and arquebuses hidden in barrels of oil and bundles of merchandise; the townsfolk suspected nothing, taxing the barrels and bundles without further inspection. Once the Portuguese were well supplied with weapons, they began looking for an excuse to fight the Moors, until one day a servant of theirs argued with a butcher over some meat he was buying. The butcher hit the man, who in turn stabbed him to death and fled to the Portuguese building. The people got up in arms to sack it, but, when they approached, the Portuguese began to fire their guns, arquebuses and crossbows, and the Moors fell into disarray like sheep; 150 died, though the fighting continued for several days.

Then an armada arrived from Lisbon with supplies, munitions and weapons, including heavy cannons, 5,000 infantry and 200 cavalry.[57] At this sight, many Moors dropped everything and fled to the Beni Mager mountains, though the faction who had agreed to the Portuguese building nearly all stayed behind, albeit under the king's captain, who treated them well. But they had their chief Sidi Yahya brought to the king, who was kind enough to provide well for him and his ten servants, finally sending him back to Africa as governor in the city and its region, since the king's captain did not know the customs of that ignorant people. In the meantime, Safi remained nearly uninhabited and the countryside in ruins.

The author has related this history at some length only to show how one faction and one woman caused the downfall of the town and all of Doukkala and its people. When the author visited, he was a mere youth of twelve years, though fourteen years later he spoke with the governor just mentioned on behalf of both the king of Fez and ash-Sharif, prince of Sous and Haha.[58] At that time Yahya was near Marrakesh[59] with his camp, accompanied by 500 Portuguese cavalry and over 2,000 Arab cavalry, in order to attack the king of Marrakesh, collecting all the land's revenues on behalf of the king of Portugal. This was in AH 920 (AD 1514–15), as told at greater length in the *Chronicles*.[60]

2.1.4.3. Conte

The town of Conte is twenty miles from Safi, built by the Goths when they arrived on the coast. It is presently in ruins and its fields are controlled by Arabs of Doukkala.

2.1.4.4. Tit

The ancient city of Tit is twenty-four miles from Azemmour, built by the Africans on the ocean. It has good fields that grow excellent grain. The people, however, are coarse, keeping no gardens, orchards or fine things like that; but they are richly dressed, since Portuguese ships arrive there frequently. When Azemmour was taken by the Portuguese, Tit reached an agreement with their captain to pay tribute. When the author was there, the king of Fez came to offer aid to the people of Doukkala, which in fact caused the town's ruin: when he arrived, the people went out to meet him with presents and gifts, bringing with them their commissioner and treasurer, the one a Christian and the other a Jew. The king hanged both. He saw that he could not help the town and, since he didn't wish to abandon it to the Christians, he evacuated them to the region of Fez, giving them a small village twelve miles away, which had previously been uninhabited.

2.1.4.5. Al-Medina, Doukkala

Al-Medina is a leading city in the region of Doukkala. It is walled in a fashion typical of the area, but rougher and in poorer shape than elsewhere. The town was well populated by an ignorant people who wore clothes of the local wool, and whose women wore many ornaments of silver and carnelian. The men were brave and kept many horses.

They were brought to his domain by the king of Fez, who was suspicious of the Portuguese; he had found some of their officials with an old faction leader in the town who had advised them to pay tribute to the king of Portugal. The author saw the old man imprisoned, barefoot and in chains; he felt great compassion for him, since the man had only done what he had to, thinking it better to pay tribute than to lose life and property. But, because of evil tongues wagging at the king's court, the poor old man was treated badly. Several other good men serving the king, such as the chaplain and the judge, intervened on behalf of him and other prisoners, so the king sent them away on horse, though still in chains; they were all freed with a fine. The town was still uninhabited in AH 921 (AD 1515–16).

2.1.4.6. Hundred Wells, Doukkala[61]

The small town of Hundred Wells sits on a travertine hill full of pits for storing grain; the locals say these pits have kept grain for a century without spoiling or starting to smell. Outside town are many wells, which is why it is called 'Hundred Wells'. The people were base and had no craftsmen beyond some Jewish smiths. When the king arrived in al-Medina, he made its people attack Hundred Wells, but the locals fled immediately to Safi, not wishing to leave their homeland. The king then sacked the town, leaving only some grain, honey and heavy things.

2.1.4.7. As-Soubait

As-Soubait is a small town on the river Oum Er-Rbia, forty miles south of al-Medina. The town is ruled by the Arabs of Doukkala, and has plenty of excellent grain and millet, though out of ignorance the people have no orchards or vineyards. After Boulaouane was ruined, the king of Fez brought the people to his kingdom and gave them a small, uninhabited town on the outskirts of Fez. As-Soubait remains deserted.

2.1.4.8. Tamarrakesht

The small town of Tamarrakesht in Doukkala lies along the Oum Er-Rbia. It was built by the ruler who founded Marrakesh and is named after that city. It was well populated, comprising 400 homes, and was subject to the people of Azemmour, but after the Portuguese took that city Tamarrakesht was destroyed and its inhabitants fled to al-Medina.

2.1.4.9. Terga

Terga is a small town on the Oum Er-Rbia, thirty miles from Azemmour; it is well populated, with 300 homes. It was once subject to the Arabs of Doukkala, but, when Safi was captured, the same 'Ali who led the faction against the Portuguese[62] came to live here with many valiant men. He stayed until the king invited him and his family to live in Fez, leaving the town home only to owls and horned owls.

2.1.4.10. Boulaouane

This small town was built on the Oum Er-Rbia where it meets the road from Fez to Marrakesh. It comprises 500 homes and is inhabited by many noble, generous people. The people also set up a house with many rooms and a large stable, where travellers stay at the people's expense. They are rich in grain and livestock, each burgher having around ten oxen and so many fields that some of them collect two or three thousand loads a year, and the local Arabs buy from them sufficient grain for the whole year.

In AH 919 (AD 1513–14), the king of Fez sent his brother[63] to watch over the region of Doukkala. On approaching, he heard the news that the captain of Azemmour was coming to sack the town and take its inhabitants captive. To defend the town, the brother at once sent two captains with 2,000 cavalry and a third with 800 crossbowmen. When they arrived the next morning, they heard that the captain of Azemmour was stationed twelve miles away, so the three captains led their men out into the countryside to attack them. But the Portuguese had come with many armed cavalry and 2,000 Arab auxiliary cavalry; they defeated those from Fez, who fled, leaving the unlucky crossbowmen out in the open plain. All were killed, except eight who fled to the Arabs. Meanwhile, the Moorish cavalry returned to Fez, pursued by the Portuguese, who killed 150 of them. Soon after, the king's brother came to Doukkala collecting tribute with promises of protection; when he reached the heartland of the region, however, the Arabs turned on him and he swiftly fled, as if routed, back to the kingdom of Fez. The townsfolk, when they saw this brother collecting revenues without helping them, evacuated to the mountains of Tadla, in fear that they would be unable to pay the Portuguese levies and so be taken captive.

The author was there during the rout and saw the crossbowmen being killed, though he was a mile away, riding a mare that nothing in Africa could escape. He found himself there on his way to Marrakesh from the king's camp in Fez, to inform the ruler and Prince Sharif that the brother would shortly arrive in Doukkala, so that they could plan what they might need to prepare against the Portuguese.

2.1.4.11. Azemmour

The city of Azemmour was built by the Africans in Doukkala where the Oum Er-Rbia flows into the ocean, thirty miles south of al-Medina. It has many inhabitants, comprising 5,000 homes, and does a bustling trade with the Portuguese merchants, its people being very cultured and well dressed. The people are divided in two factions, though they always keep the peace.

The town grows abundant grain in the surrounding country-side, though it has no gardens or orchards beyond a few fig groves. The river produces revenues of six or seven thousand ducats in sardinella, which they fish in season from October through April. These fish have more fat than flesh, so when they want to fry it they first use a little oil; when heated, it drips out a pound and a half of fat, which they burn in lamps for light, since they don't produce oil locally. Every year, the Portuguese merchants come to buy vast quantities of these fish, paying such high duty that they advised their king to seize the city, and he sent a fleet of many ships. But their captain was so inexperienced and disorganised that they were routed in battle; those ships that reached the river were sunk and little of the armada escaped.

Two years later, the king of Portugal sent a vast fleet of 200 ships; the townsfolk were terrified at the sight and began to flee, the crowd trampling eighty people at the gates. One prince, even, who had come to the town's aid, was unable to escape through the gates and let his family over the walls with ropes. The people fled on horse and foot, and some later told the author what a piteous sight it was to see the children, women and old men running on bare, bloody feet. The Christians, the morning they planned to attack, looked for activity in the city, but saw none. Some thought this was a trick by the Moors, others dared approach with no need to doubt, since they heard no noise and only saw the Jews signalling for the Christians to enter. For the town's Jews, before the fleet had arrived, had sent for a safe-conduct from the king of Portugal, saying that, if he would keep them safe, he might take the town as he wished; he agreed and the Christians entered without trouble. Some of the townsfolk fled to Salé, others to Fez; they suffered this loss on account of their great vice of sodomy, which they carried on shamelessly, fathers seeking lovers for their sons, caressing them and making merry. The city was taken at last in AH 918,[64] while the author was in the Land of the Blacks.

2.1.4.12. M'Ramer

The town of M'Ramer was built by the Goths twenty-four miles inland from Safi. It has 400 homes and its land is fertile for grain and oil. It was subject to the ruler of Safi, but, after that city was taken by the Portuguese, M'Ramer's inhabitants fled and it lay uninhabited for a year, before they reached a treaty with the Portuguese and returned; to this day they pay tribute and live in peace. Even so, when the king of Fez came to Doukkala, the town's inhabitants went to Safi until he left, at which point they returned.

2.1.4.13. Mount Beni Mager

The mountain of Beni Mager, which is inhabited by many craftsmen, is twelve miles from Safi, where all the mountainfolk keep houses. It is especially abundant in grain and oil. When Safi was captured, its people had nowhere to seek refuge but here. The mountain had formerly been subject to the ruler of Safi, while paying tribute to the Portuguese king. But, when the king of Fez arrived in these lands, some went to Safi, while others were brought back by the king, for they did not wish to stay under the Christians; now they are returning to live here, as mentioned above.

2.1.4.14. Green Mountain[65]

Green Mountain is high and begins at the Oum Er-Rbia to the east, extending west to the hills of Haskoura which divide

Doukkala from Tadla. The mountain is harsh and wooded, growing plenty of acorns, pines and trees of what they call the 'African' fruit.[66] Many hermits dwell there, who live on nothing but the fruits of the trees, being twenty-five miles from the nearest settlement. There are many springs and Muslim shrines, and some ancient African buildings.

Below the mountain lies an exquisite lake similar to Lake Bolsena in the Papal States, full of excellent fish, including eel, sardinella, pike and others that the author has not seen in Italy, but no one fishes in it. When the king of Fez, Muhammad, came to Doukkala, he took the route past the lake and camped there for eight days. He saw people with shirts sewn at the neck and sleeves, fastened at the bottom to hoops of sticks, which they placed in the lake to catch fish in unimaginable quantities. For the fish had been stunned by the horses and camels wading into the lake for a mile around. There were perhaps 14,000 horses, most belonging to the Arabs who rode with the king, some as vassals and others as soldiers in his service. The Arabs all brought camels too, three times as many as the horses; there were another 5,000 camels in the train of the king and his brothers, for he had 14,000 men, half of them cavalry and the other half messengers, mule- and camel-drivers, water carriers, woodcutters, cooks – who are relieved of having to look after their own families – and the man in charge of fodder, as well as his secretaries and their assistants. The king provided for each of these officials, with the exception of the mercenaries[67] and the cavalry captains, who provided their own tents, camels and households. These are all noted in the *Epitome of the Muslim Chronicles* mentioned before; here we will note only what concerns the lake, so as to explain how the vast number of animals wading into it caused the fish to be caught; they disturbed the water so much that those wanting clean water had to go in up to their necks. The lake is surrounded by countless trees with foliage like pines, full of turtledove nests, each packed with chicks, for it was late May, the season when six chicks go for a *baiocco*.

After the king had rested three days, he went up the mountain and stopped with imams and courtiers at every shrine on it, crying out: 'God, you know I have come to this wild land with the sole intention of bringing aid to the people of Doukkala, to free them from the hands of the impious, rebellious Arabs and our enemies the Christians; if Your Majesty knows or sees otherwise, punish me alone, for my followers are blameless.' He stayed on the mountain the whole day, returning to his lodgings in the evening. The next morning, the king went hunting with hounds and falcons in the forest by the lake below the mountain; each caught as many wild geese, ducks, hens and other waterfowl as he could carry on his horse. The next day, he held another hunt with greyhounds, falcons and eagles, catching countless hares, deer, porcupines, goats, foxes, wolves, partridges and terns, since there had been no hunt on the mountain in two centuries.

Two days later the king rested, before setting off for al-Medina in Doukkala. Allowing the scholars and imams to return to Fez, he sent one group of them to Marrakesh for prayers, with whom the author had to go. This happened in AH 921 (AD 1515–16).

2.1.5.1. The region of Haskoura[68]

The region of Haskoura begins in the hills on Doukkala's border to the north. To the west, it borders the river Tensift below Mount 'Adimmei; the eastern border lies along the Oued el Abid or River of Slaves, which separates Haskoura from Tadla. Between Haskoura and the ocean lie the hills of Doukkala. The people are more cultured than those of Doukkala, since the land produces plenty of oil and Morocco leather; they are all tanners and raise large herds of goats. All the sheep nearby are tanned in town, where the people also weave much woollen fabric in the local fashion and make handsome horse saddles. The merchants of Fez do a roaring trade in the region, trading cloth for leather and saddles. The Arabs and settled folk of Doukkala spend all their money in Haskoura on oil and other necessary items.

2.1.5.2. Al-Medina, Haskoura[69]

The town of al-Medina is on the slopes of the Atlas, built by the Haskoura people ninety miles east of Marrakesh and ninety from al-Medina in Doukkala. It comprises 2,000 homes, well populated by tanners, saddlers and other craftsmen, with many Jewish merchants and craftsmen. The town is set within an olive grove and trellised vineyards where there are towering walnut trees. The town is divided into factions, hostile to each other and to a town four miles away.[70] Because of this hostility, no one can safely walk to his fields, except for slaves and women. Foreign merchants who want to go from one town to the other must be accompanied by free men. The people pay someone with a crossbow or gun a monthly salary of ten or twelve ducats in their coin, or sixteen Italian ducats.

The town has several legal scholars, among them judges and notaries. The town leaders collect tax from foreigners and spend it for the benefit of all, paying Arabs tribute for their fields on the plain, though they earn ten times what they pay.

The author was there on his return to Marrakesh and, together with nine companions and their servants, lodged at the house of a wealthy Granadan who had lived there for eighteen years as a crossbowman. They stayed with him at his expense three days before leaving, even though the townsfolk wanted them to move so they might host them; however, the author was the man's compatriot, so he would not let them lodge at the common expense. Even so, the community kept sending gifts of lambs, calves, chickens and other tokens of respect. Seeing an abundance of kid goats, the author and his fellows wondered why they received other things and not these, and asked a local, 'Why do the people never give a kid, given that there are so many?' He answered that they considered kids a poor present, preferring a nanny or a buck.

The women are lovely, white and friendly, and have time for a foreigner in private.

2.1.5.3. Alemdin[71]

Alemdin is a town of 1,000 homes four miles west of the previous one, built in a valley surrounded by four high mountains. It is freezing cold, inhabited by craftsmen, merchants and gentlemen, and they are forever at war with al-Medina. In the author's day, the king of Fez acquired the two towns by means of a merchant of Fez who had been wronged as follows. The merchant's father had betrothed him to a beautiful woman, and, when the day came to lead her to his home,[72] a town leader disrupted the wedding and made off with the young woman to marry her instead. Abandoned and insulted, the merchant made a show of leaving, demanding permission from the town leader to go. When he got it, he bought many fine things from the area and went to Fez, where he presented them to the king and requested a special favour: to borrow 200 crossbowmen, 300 cavalry and 400 soldiers at his own expense. He promised to seize the two towns in the king's name and pay 7,000 ducats a year out of the region's profits. In a gesture of munificence, the king said he wished him to pay for nothing but the crossbowmen, and dispatched a letter to the viceroy of Tadla to aid the merchant with a company of cavalry and soldiers led by two valiant captains. They formed an army and laid siege to the town for five days. The people wished to avoid harm, as well as the king's anger and displeasure, and, when the leader realised this, he disguised himself as a beggar and left town. However, he was recognised by one of the merchant's servants, caught and brought to a captain, whereupon the merchant clapped him in chains. On learning this, the people opened the town gates and many burghers flooded out, having decided to give him the city in the king's name. The merchant entered with his captains. The father brought out the kidnapped young woman, and all her relatives claimed that all along they had known and wanted the merchant as her true and legitimate husband, but they had been helpless against the town leader.

He wished to lead her home, but, because she was eight months pregnant, the law dictated that he wait until the birth before renewing the marriage. The jurists, when asked what legal

penalty the man deserved, said he should be stoned as a fornica-
tor and rapist. The very morning after the merchant brought the
young woman home, the wretched town leader was stoned.
Meanwhile, the merchant remained governor of both towns
and established peace between them, just as he had promised
the king. The author stayed in Alemdin and met the merchant;
after he was made governor, the author returned to Fez. This
was the year he left home for Constantinople.[73]

2.1.5.4. Tegodast[74]

The town of Tegodast is built on a lofty mountaintop, surrounded by four other mountains; there are delightful gardens
on its slopes, full of fruit trees of all kinds, where the author
saw apricots as large as bitter oranges. Above the trees are trellised vines with luscious grapes in every colour, as well as a
variety they call 'chicken egg' in their language, a name certainly warranted by their size. They also have plenty of oil and
excellent honey, white as milk and yellow as bright gold. In the
town are great springs of water, which they use to grind grain
in small mills on the mountain slopes. Craftsmen there supply
necessary items.

The people are somewhat cultured. The women are gorgeous
and wear silver jewellery, for the people do substantial trade in
oil, which they export to the towns bordering the desert south-
ward across the Atlas, and leather, which goes to Fez and
Meknes. The town is six miles from the plain where they pay
Arabs for fields of grain. Inside is a handsome mosque, and they
have some important imams and judges as well as many nobles.

When the author was there, the town was ruled by an old
gentleman who was completely blind, but whom everyone obeyed.
As a spirited youth he had killed two faction leaders who were a
threat to the people. After they were dead, the gentleman set about
bringing peace to the town, arranging an alliance of kinship
between the two factions; they governed themselves in freedom,
with his counsel and approval, as long as he lived. The author
stayed with the old man, who showed magnificent generosity in

putting him up with his companions and their eight horses, and feeding them all kinds of meat. They talked on and on all three nights they stayed, gossiping, telling tales and discussing how he had brought peace to the town. When they came to depart, the author and his companions tried to offer apologies and thanks for the bother they had caused, to which the old man replied: 'By God, gentlemen, of course I am a good servant to the king of Fez. However, you should know that I have not honoured you for his sake, but because we are noble; our ancestors bequeathed us the custom of feeding and caring for both acquaintances and strangers, for the love of God, who provides all things. This year we have harvested 7,000 bushels of wheat and barley from our fields, and there are not enough people to eat it all. I myself have more than 10,000 sheep and goats and profit only from their skins, leaving the cheese and milk to my herders; they give me a little butter, which cannot be sold in town since everyone has their own livestock. The skin, wool and oil we bring eight days' journey away to sell. If our king should return from Doukkala and pass our mountain, his men will recognise me as a good friend and the king himself will acknowledge me as his good servant.' And so the author and his companions departed, admiring and praising the old man for the rest of their journey.

2.1.5.5. Al-Jumu'ah, Haskoura[75]

The town of al-Jumu'ah is five miles from Tegodast, built in modern times on one of several high mountains. It has 500 homes, and in the nearby valleys are many springs and gardens of all kinds of fruit, especially imposing walnut trees. Throughout the surrounding hills are fields growing barley and countless olive trees. The town is well inhabited by craftsmen, especially tanners and saddlers, as well as smiths, since a vein of iron is nearby. The smiths make a great number of horseshoes, which they bring to lands lacking such goods, trading them for slaves and for animals only found in the desert, whose leather makes strong shields and other items. They bring these to Fez to barter for fabrics, textiles and other necessities.

The town is so far from the main road that when they see a foreigner arrive, the children run out to see him, especially when he is dressed in an unfamiliar way. The people of the town are governed by Tegodast, for al-Jumuʻah was built by that town's common folk when the harmony between its gentlemen began to fall apart; the commoners, not wanting to get between them, gathered to build al-Jumuʻah, leaving Tegodast to the gentlemen. To this day al-Jumuʻah has only commoners, while Tegodast is full of nobility and magnificence.

2.1.5.6. Bzou

Bzou is an old town built on a high mountain twenty miles west of al-Jumuʻah, and three miles below it flows the river Oued el Abid. The inhabitants are all wealthy, well-dressed merchants, who export oil, leather and cloth to the desert regions. Their mountains are fertile for oil, grain and all kinds of fine fruit, with raisins excellent in colour and taste; they have prodigious fig trees, thick and tall, with walnut trees of wondrous size, at the top of which kites make nests for their young, since no one dares to climb so high. All the slopes along the river are planted with charming gardens right up to the bank. The author was there in late May when the apricots and summer figs were ripe; he stayed with the town's imam next to a pretty mosque that had a stream flowing through it, out into the town square.

2.1.5.7. Mount Tin Wawaz[76]

Tin Wawaz is a mountain next to the Haskoura region, on the south side of the Atlas. It is densely populated by men skilled in arms on foot or on horse, and possessing many small horses. The mountain, which has snow all year round, grows much indigo; it produces no wheat, but much barley, which they live on. Among the people are many nobles and knights, one of whom serves as a prince or ruler over the region, taking a substantial revenue that he spends on war with the neighbouring mountain of Tensita. He maintains 100 soldiers with crossbows and guns, 1,000 cavalry of his own, and another thousand from the mountain's gentlemen and knights.

In the author's time, the ruler was lavishly generous, enjoying the gifts and praise he received, and giving what he had and what he did not. He took great pleasure in poems of excellent Arabic, and everyone marvelled at his imagination, because, although he did not understand a word, he delighted whenever some fine phrase was spoken in his praise. When the king of Fez sent the author's uncle to the king of Timbuktu as an ambassador, he passed the Draa region about 100 miles from Tin Wawaz. As soon as its ruler heard of his fame – for the author's uncle was a great, elegant poet – he wrote to the governor of Draa to send him this man, since he wished to meet him. The ambassador gave the excuse that he would have happily come, but it would not be right for a royal ambassador to make detours, leaving the king's subjects for rulers along the way. Instead, he would send his nephew to kiss his hand, namely the author, wishing only to please both his own ruler and that of Draa. And so the author went, bringing a pair of ornate stirrups finely worked in the Moorish style, worth twenty-five ducats; a pair of magnificent, decorated spurs worth fifteen ducats; a pair of silken cords, one purple and the other blue, woven with golden thread; a beautiful book, newly written and bound, of the lives of the African saints; a poem in praise of the ruler; and two horses from his uncle's stable. The author used the four days on the road to Tin Wawaz to write a poem himself.

On arriving, they found the ruler away from his palace on a hunt. At the news of their arrival, the ruler sent a horse for the author and asked how his uncle was. The answer was that he was well and at his excellency's disposal. The man then offered lodging, saying that he would be able to grant a better audience after the hunt. That evening, the ruler sent for the author, who greeted him by kissing his hand and presented his uncle's gifts. The ruler was delighted at the sight, and when he received the uncle's poem immediately had it read aloud; his advisers remarked that he did not understand Arabic but that he was always happy when it was recited. After the poem, the ruler went to the table to begin the meal, which comprised different roasted and boiled meats wrapped in a flatbread like sheets of lasagne but firmer and thicker. Then came couscous and *al-ftat*,[77] along with other kinds of foods which escape the author's memory.

At the end of the feast, the author got to his feet and explained that his uncle, being only a poor scholar, had sent his excellency only the smallest of presents, comprising a few words and some trinkets of no account, 'in order to be remembered by your lordship as a good servant'. Meanwhile the author, as a poor student with no possessions, had crafted a small gift of words, for he wanted to be counted among the ruler's servants; and so he began to recite his own poem. The ruler continually asked his ministers to explain what the reading meant, as he understood nothing, but he listened in wonder, for, although the author was only sixteen years old, his poem was just as elegant as his uncle's. Afterwards the ruler gave him permission to go straight to bed, for he was exhausted too.

In the morning, the ruler invited the author to dinner, informing him afterwards that his uncle needed to leave Draa swiftly and so had written to send him back in haste. Meanwhile, the ruler had arranged to present the uncle with 100 gold ducats, one horse, and three slaves to care for him on the way; the author with fifty gold ducats and a horse; and his companions with ten ducats each. He was to tell his uncle that these items were only for the poem, but the ruler would repay the rest when the uncle returned from Timbuktu, in the hope that he would pass this way. The ruler then commanded one of his ministers to show the route and, having planned a campaign against some enemies, extended his hand in farewell, giving permission to leave the next morning, which the author did.

The author has told this story at length only so the reader can understand that Africa indeed has great nobles like this ruler.

2.1.5.8. Mount Tensita

Tensita is one of the Atlas mountains, bordering Tin Wawaz to the west, Mount Dades to the east and the Draa desert to the south. The mountain is populous, with fifty ksars all walled in clay and rough stone, and little rain falls there, because it faces south. All the ksars are three or four miles from the river Draa. The area has a great ruler who keeps 1,500 cavalry and the same number of infantry, much like the ruler of Tin Wawaz; despite being close relatives they are mortal enemies, constantly at war with one another. There are many dates in the fields along the river below the mountains, and the inhabitants are farmers and merchants. Barley grows there, but very little wheat or meat, since they have little livestock; nevertheless, the ruler receives a revenue of 20,000 gold ducats, where one ducat weighs two thirds of an Italian ducat, or twelve carats.

The ruler is very friendly with the king of Fez, always sending him magnificent gifts; the king reciprocates with fine things, such as richly outfitted horses, scarlet fabrics, silken banners and handsome tents. In the author's day, the ruler sent an impressive gift of fifty male and fifty female black slaves, ten eunuchs, twelve riding camels, one giraffe, ten ostriches and eight civet cats, along with a pound each of fine musk, civet and ambergris, and also 600 hides of what they call the *lamt* (oryx), used to make fine shields worth eight ducats each in Fez. The male slaves were worth twenty ducats each, the female slaves twenty-five; the eunuchs forty, the camels fifty and the civet cats 200; the musk, civet and ambergris were each sixty ducats a pound. This is not counting all the sugared dates and Ethiopian peppers.[78] The author was with the king of Fez when this gift arrived, and the ambassador was a very black little man, fat and barbarous in his speech and habits. He bore a letter about the gift from the ruler, sewn into his clothing, and since he had sworn to his master that he would not touch the letter himself, he wanted the king to unstitch it. The king laughed heartily at this, and one of his ministers unstitched the letter, which was clumsily composed in the obscure style of ancient orators; the ambassador's elocution was even worse, so the king burst out laughing together with his brothers and courtiers, even as they honourably tried to hide it behind their hands or clothes. At the end of his speech, the king arranged a good lodging in the house of the great mosque's protector, paying the expenses for his twenty-four servants and companions until they departed.

2.1.5.9. Mount Ghojdama

The mountain of Ghojdama borders the previous one. It is only inhabited on the north side; no one lives on the south side, for when Ibrahim, king of Marrakesh, fled in defeat from the disciple of al-Mahdi,[79] the group living there showed the king great compassion in an effort to help him, even though fortune did not favour him. After the disciple had left the kingdom he sought vengeance against the mountainfolk, setting fire to their houses, ruining their fields and driving them all away. Now one part remains uninhabited, while the other part is inhabited by a lowly people who live off the sale of oil and are badly clothed, both women and men. Nothing grows there but olives and barley; they raise many goats and a few diminutive mules, since their horses are tiny. The people live in freedom thanks to their mountain.

2.1.5.10. Tasawin

Tasawin is a pair of mountains that border Ghojdama to the west and extend to the mountain of Tegodast. The area is inhabited by a poor folk who produce only barley and honey. Although each of the mountains is the source of a river that flows through a beautiful plain, the locals cannot do anything there because of the Arabs.

Here ends book five, on the region of Haskoura. Next is book six, on the region of Tadla.

2.1.6.1. The region of Tadla

Tadla is not a very large region; it stretches from the Oued el Abid west to the river Oum Er-Rbia, then extends south to the latter's source in the Atlas. To the north it is bounded where the two rivers meet, making the region triangular: the rivers begin in the Atlas, and as they stretch north they flow closer together until they eventually join.

2.1.6.2. Tafza

Tafza is the principal town of Tadla, built by the Africans on the slopes of the Atlas five miles from the plain, with walls of the travertine stone known in their language as 'tafza',[80] which explains the town's name. It is well populated with rich people, including many Jews, who have 200 houses there, all wealthy merchants and craftsmen. Foreign merchants swarm the city to buy a certain kind of black cloak that they weave in one piece together with its hood, many of which are made in the region. This cloak is called a 'burnous' in their language; a few are seen in Italy, but many in Spain. Most of the merchandise made in Fez is sold here: cloth, knives, swords, saddles, bits, caps, needles and all kinds of trinkets. If the merchants are willing to barter, they sooner find a home for their wares, for the locals have plenty of foreign and local goods, including slaves, horses, burnouses, indigo, leather and cordovan; if merchants want coin, they must sell at a very low price, though the locals will pay with unstruck gold, while silver coins have no currency there. The people are well dressed, with the women beautifully adorned and all friendly. The town has many mosques, imams and judges.

In the past, the town ruled itself in freedom, but then the people started to fight and kill one another, so much that, in the author's day, leaders of one faction arrived in Fez to ask the king of Fez a favour, to help set their town in order, even offering him the rule of the town. The king agreed and sent 1,000 light cavalry along with 500 crossbowmen and 200 gunmen on horse. The king then wrote to some vassal Arabs known as the Zaër for another 4,000 cavalry for his captains, should the need arise. He chose a truly valiant knight called az-Zarangi as general, who, when he arrived at the camp, besieged the town, since the opposing faction had entrenched itself inside. But they had called some neighbouring Arabs, the Beni Jabir, to help them, and, when the general saw the 5,000 cavalry coming, he stopped the siege to engage them in battle.

After three days, he had routed them and was again in control of the countryside, so the town, seeing their situation was hopeless, sent out ambassadors to negotiate a peace. They agreed to pay the king's expenses along with another 10,000 ducats per year, including the condition that the townsfolk outside could return without hindrance or regulation. When the general told those outside the news, they replied: 'My lord, we know our own people. Get us inside, and we promise to hand you 100,000 ducats twice over, without any injustice or pillaging any houses, but simply by making the other faction pay the profit our fields have yielded over the three years they occupied them; these profits are at least 30,000 ducats, which we would pay you willingly for everything you have spent for our sake. Then we will give you the town's revenues, at least 20,000 a year; we will also levy up to 10,000 ducats as one or two years' tribute from the Jews.' On hearing this, the general wrote to those in the town, saying that the king had given his word to help those outside in any way he could, preferring that 'the rule should be in their hands instead of yours, for many reasons'. He added that if they handed over the town to the king, there would be no charge against them, but if they stubbornly wanted to hold onto it, he was prepared, with God's help and the king's blessing, to make them pay everything.

At this news, the people were divided, some wanting to join the king and others preferring war, and finally they took up arms. A spy returned to inform the general, who had half of his men, including crossbowmen and gunmen, dismount and approach the town. After three hours, he entered the town without shedding any blood, for the faction now supporting the king had come together at one of the town's walled-up gates, and begun to open it from within; the general did the same from outside, for no one was there to stop him. He had no tools for the task, having come unprepared. Those inside kept fighting until the gate was open; they too were unprepared, having been forced to flee from the other faction, which was three times their number and pressing closely, but they realised that the only solution was to break down the gate, allowing them to flee to safety and letting the general in. But the king was lucky, and the general entered without any harm. Setting the king's banners over the walls and in the squares, he sent cavalry through the town to stop everyone from fleeing. The general proclaimed in the king's name that, on pain of death, no person, whether soldier or townsman, should pillage or kill.

The town submitted at once. All the enemy leaders were taken prisoner, and the general informed them that they would remain captive until the king had been wholly reimbursed for a month of keeping the cavalry, amounting to 12,000 ducats. The prisoners' wives and families quickly came up with the money. Then the king's faction came forward, wanting repayment of the profits from their fields and assets over the last three years, but the general answered with uncertainty, saying he was unsure and they should bring it before the judgement of the scholars, who might or might not offer a ruling; the other faction would remain in prison for the night. But then the prisoners said to the general: 'My lord, will you not keep your word? For you promised that we would be freed once the king was satisfied.' The general answered that he was keeping his word to the letter; they were now prisoners not on account of the king, but 'for the sake of those who have demanded their assets back from you'; they would do as the judges and scholars said, and perhaps that would be better for them.

The next morning the judges and scholars all assembled before the general. The prisoners' lawyer spoke first: 'My lords, although these people now hold the fields that belonged to their opponents, the latter's ancestors took them from the prisoners' ancestors over two decades ago.'

The other lawyer replied: 'My lords, he speaks of a matter that happened 150 years ago; there exists no witness or document to prove it.'

'It can easily be proved, for it is common knowledge.'

'But who knows how long those ancestors held the lands? And perhaps they had a good reason for seizing them, since it is also commonly said that the prisoners' ancestors were rebels against the crown of Fez, and these lands had belonged to the royal treasury.'

Then the general pretended to show compassion for the prisoners, saying to the lawyer, 'Don't blame these poor prisoners!'

The lawyer answered, 'Poor? General, see if each one cannot come up with 50,000 ducats! As soon as they escape these chains, whether or not you see them, they will drive you out; you have only caught them unprepared.'

On hearing this, the general became afraid and dismissed the assembly, gesturing for the prisoners to go through, be fed and then brought before him. He said to them, 'I want you to pay your opponents; otherwise, believe me, I will bring you to Fez, where you'll pay double.' The prisoners then sent for their wives and mothers, saying, 'Try to pay up, for we are accused of great wealth, though we have barely an eighth of what they say.' After eight days, in the general's presence, they brought their opponents 28,000 ducats' worth of rings, bracelets and other such jewellery, for the women cleverly wished to look like they had no money. Once this was paid, the general said: 'Gentlemen, I have written to the king about this matter, which I now regret, since I cannot let you go until I see his response. In any event, you will be freed, for you have paid everything, so keep your spirits up.'

That night, the general considered how he might extract more money from the traitors, without being blamed or disgraced among the people for breaking his word. The author, guessing his intention, said: 'Lord general, tomorrow morning pretend that you have received a message from the king, and that he commands you to cut off their heads. But then show pity on them, saying you do not wish to trouble yourself with their deaths, preferring to send them to Fez out of respect.' That morning we wrote a return letter from the king, and the general summoned all forty-two of the prisoners to tell them, with a great show of compassion: 'My dear gentlemen, we have received a letter from the king; it brings bad news, saying that his highness has been well informed of your deeds, that is, your rebellion against his crown, even as his vassals. For that reason he commands me to behead you all. This is deeply regrettable, for it will look to all as if I have broken my word; but I am his servant, and cannot disobey his command.'

The poor prisoners began to weep and implore the general, while he feigned tears together with them and said: 'The only solution I can think of is to send you to Fez, relieving me from blame on your part. Perhaps then the king will pardon you or do as seems right to him. I will send you straight away, with 200 cavalry.' At this they only cried louder, beseeching God and the general. Then a third man said to the general: 'Lord general, his majesty the king has sent you in his place, and you can do as seems best. Consider for a moment the possibility that these gentlemen pay a substantial amount to redeem themselves; you might explain to the king that you promised they would come to no harm, and ask his highness to pardon them for your sake. Then tell him how much they would pay, and the money might sway his judgement.'

The poor prisoners begged the general to do this, happily agreeing to pay whatever the king pleased and offering the general prodigious gifts. He feigned reluctance, asking what they could offer the king; some said 1,000 ducats, others 500, others 800. The general said: 'Send it, but I will not write to the king. Better that you go yourselves, and perhaps he will do as he said.' They again begged and beseeched him until he relented: 'You are forty-two very rich gentlemen, some with more than others, and if you promise me 2,000 ducats each I will write to the king in the hope of saving you; otherwise I will send you to Fez.' They agreed that each would pay as much as he could to come up with the whole amount. He replied: 'Do as seems right to you.'

They took eight days and he pretended to write to the king; after four more days he showed them a fake letter, pretending that the king had agreed to pardon them for his sake. Three days later, the prisoners' families had brought all the gold they had, 82,000 ducats. The captain had it weighed, astonished that only forty-two men from such a small town had so much gold. He then freed the prisoners and sent the king the excellent news of what had transpired, asking what his majesty wished to do with the money. The king sent two ministers with 200 cavalry to collect the money and take it back to Fez. The gentlemen then presented the general with a gift worth 2,000 ducats, including horses, slaves and musk, with the excuse that they had no more money, thanking him for having spared their lives. The region continued to belong to the king, under the rule of General az-Zarangi, until it was destroyed by the treachery of Tadla's Arabs. It brought the king 20,000 ducats a year.

The author has related this story at length only because he was there and took part in it, earning a few ducats as an interpreter, and because it was astounding to see so much gold in one place. Not even the king had ever seen so much at once; like his father, he was an impoverished king who barely collected 300,000 a year, and, from day to day, never had more than 10,000 on hand. This episode, which occurred in AH 915 (AD 1509–10), also shows the crafty plans and lengths people will go to for money. You might marvel even more at another Jew who, on his own, paid just over what all those gentlemen paid, for someone had spied on him and his wealth, and the king finally took the Jew and his money into custody. The Jews then paid a fine of 50,000 ducats because they had favoured the faction opposing the king. The author was with the commissioner who collected that money.

2.1.6.3. Efza

Efza is a small town of 600 homes, built in the Atlas foothills about two miles from Tafza. Its inhabitants, many of them Moors and Jews, are all craftsmen and farmers governed by the burghers of Tafza. The town produces a great many burnouses; the women are highly skilled in working wool, so they earn more than the men by making excellent burnouses and *al-kisa*.[81] A stream called the Darna runs between Tafza and Efza; it flows from a source in the Atlas between the hills and across the plain into the Oum Er-Rbia. Along the banks among the hills are beguiling gardens and orchards of every kind you can imagine. The inhabitants are so genial and generous that any foreign merchant can go into the groves and take as much fruit as he likes. These merchants are valued dearly, but the locals take a long time to pay their debts; merchants must pay for burnouses three months in advance, yet they can end up waiting a year.

The author was there when the king of Fez was encamped in Tadla. Efza straight away offered its allegiance and the second night he was there they brought his general fifteen horses, each led by a slave, 200 lambs and fifteen cattle. For this reason the general always remembered them as the king's faithful servants and friends.

2.1.6.4. Ait Attab

The town of Ait Attab was built by the Africans on a high mountain fifty miles west of Efza. It is inhabited by plenty of nobles, knights and commoners, most of them merchants, who make burnouses in quantity, for which throngs of foreign merchants keep coming. One can always see snow on the mountain. The whole valley around the town is full of vineyards, gardens and orchards, so abundant with fruit that it cannot be sold in town. The women are very pale and well dressed, decked out in silver jewellery, with jet black hair and dark eyes. The people are very haughty; when the king of Fez invaded Tadla, they never surrendered or submitted, and instead chose one of their gentlemen as captain, paying 1,000 light cavalry to guard their town and its environs. When the captain waged war, the king's general nearly lost the region; however, the king sent his brother with a powerful army, though to little avail, for the war lasted three years, until the king had a trusted Jew poison the town's captain. With their captain dead, the town agreed a treaty with the king's brother, in AH 921 (AD 1515–16).

2.1.6.5. Ait Ayad

Ait Ayad is quite small, a town of 300 homes built by the Africans on a smaller Atlas mountain, twelve miles from the previous. The side facing the mountain is walled, but the town is open towards the plain, where the slopes serve as walls. Within the town is a small, handsome mosque where a canal flows like a stream through its courtyard. It is well inhabited by knights, nobles, a good number of merchants, foreign and local, and many Jews; the craftsmen and merchants are wealthy. There are many fountains in town that flow down into a stream; plenty of orchards and gardens produce excellent grapes, figs and large walnut trees, and the mountainside is covered with olive groves. The women are beautiful and friendly, adorned with silver, rings, bracelets and other things in their style. The fertile soil of the plain produces grain of every sort, while the mountain soil is good for barley and keeping livestock, especially goats. In the author's day, the town was a refuge for the rebel Momun Bengui-hazzan[82] before he was killed. The author was there, lodging with an imam, in AH 921 (AD 1515–16).

2.1.6.6. Mount Seggelame

Mount Seggelame is famous in Tadla; it faces south, extending from the border of Mount Tasawin east to Mount Imghran, where the river Oum Er-Rbia begins, and then south to Mount Dades. The inhabitants are a tribe of the Zanaga people, strong and ready men who are skilled in arms, carrying spears and curved swords and daggers, and slinging stones with force. They are enemies of the people of Tadla, whose merchants can only pass through the region by acquiring a safe-conduct and paying a heavy toll. Their way of life is crude and their dwellings spread out, with one house here, another there, and occasionally three or four together. They have plenty of goats, and mules as small as donkeys, which graze in the mountain forests, though you should note that the lions eat their share of them. The inhabitants obey no ruler, since their mountain is so challenging that it can be easily defended. In the author's day, the general who took over Tadla wished to wage a campaign in the region, which their spies found out; they called up a fine company of valiant men, who hid in the bushes by a narrow path set into the mountainside, which the general's cavalry would have to take. When they saw the cavalry coming up the mountain, they launched their spears and large rocks. Unable to turn around on the narrow path, many cavalry leapt off the side and were dashed into a thousand pieces below. They hadn't considered which path to take, thinking they could proceed undetected until they reached the houses of the mountainfolk, and on the return would take the usual path; however, their enemies were better prepared. Valley, forest and man overcame them. The fleeing remnants of the campaign either broke their necks or were captured; for the latter it was a black day, for they were tied up and brought to the mountainfolk's homes, where the women cut them to pieces, since this people do not deign to kill prisoners themselves, but in contempt leave them to the women. After this, the general never again attacked these people, but they could no longer trade in Tadla for fear of him. To be sure, they have no need of Tadla, since the mountain grows plenty of barley and livestock and has more springs than houses; they are simply inconvenienced in what they buy and sell.

2.1.6.7. Mount Imghran

Mount Imghran is next, looking south to the land of Ferkla[83] on the desert border; the mountain extends east from the previous one and ends at the foot of Mount Dades. There is always snow on its summit. The inhabitants have so much livestock that they cannot stay in one place, so they make houses from strips of bark, which they fix to thin poles; the roof supports are arranged like the circular roofs of the baskets used for carrying women on mules, as used for journeys in Italy.[84] In this way, once the mountainfolk have finished pasturing their livestock in one place, they hoist their houses folded onto their mules and bring their family and herds to wherever they find grass. In winter, however, they stay put and construct a kind of low stable covered with sticks, where they keep the livestock at night. To warm the animals, they make a large fire very close to the stable; sometimes the wind rises and sets fire to the stables, though the animals then can get away swiftly. For this reason the mountainfolk build their stables without walls, supporting them only on forked branches. The wolves and lions eat as much as they like. The customs and dress of these mountainfolk are like those mentioned earlier, the only difference being that they live in these huts, whereas the others live in walled houses. The author passed this mountain on his return from Draa to Fez in AH 917 (AD 1511–12).

2.1.6.8. Mount Dades

Dades is a high, freezing mountain with many springs and forests. It begins at Imghran to the west and extends eighty miles to the borders of the Adekhsan mountains, bordering the plain of Todgha to the south. The traces of an ancient ruined city are still visible, including some walls of thick stones, a few of which are inscribed in an unknown alphabet. The stupid locals believe that this city was built by the Romans. The author has read no authority who mentions it, except Sharif as-Sacalli,[85] who notes a city called Tidsi on the border of Sijilmasa and Draa, but does not say that it is built on the mountain of Dades. Some from Africa say this is that city, for they can see no others in the area.

The inhabitants are shiftless; most live in damp caves, and they all eat barley bread and *asida* – barley flour boiled in water and salt, as described in the first book on Haha[86] – for nothing grows there but barley. They do have many goats and donkeys, and in the caves where they keep the goats are large amounts of saltpetre.[87] As you can imagine, if this mountain were near Italy it would bring in 25,000 ducats a year, but the mountainfolk don't know what saltpetre is.

The people are so badly clothed you can see most of their body. Their houses are ugly, stinking of the goats they keep inside. There is not a single ksar or walled town to be found on the entire mountain; instead, their settlements are divided between caves and some villages built of stones heaped up without lime, and faced with thin, black slabs like those sometimes used in the countryside of Assisi and Fabriano. The author never saw so many fleas in his life. The inhabitants are thieves, bandits and cut-throats, killing a man for a hair and quarrelling among themselves over the slightest thing. They have no judge, imam or anyone with skill, and, since they are lazy illiterates, they conduct no trade in the region. The land has been abandoned because it is infertile. Merchants with the bad luck to venture nearby are taxed a fifth of their wares – and only when the locals don't rob them, either because they don't want the goods or thanks to a safe-conduct granted by one of their leaders. The women are worse than the men, ugly and badly clothed, treated and used like donkeys, hauling on their backs water from the well and wood from the forest. Nowhere in Africa is less pleasant than this loutish place. In AH 918 (AD 1512–13) duty compelled the author to cross this mountain on the way from Marrakesh to Sijilmasa.

This ends the book on the region of Tadla; the next is on the kingdom of Fez.

BOOK 2.2.

KINGDOM OF FEZ

2.2.1.1. [Introduction]

The kingdom of Fez stretches from the river Oum Er-Rbia in
the west to the river Moulouya in the north-east, and it is also
bounded by the ocean and the Mediterranean. It is divided into
seven provinces: Tamasna, Fez, Azgar, al-Habat, er-Rif, Garet
and Al Haouz. Formerly, however, these provinces were each
ruled by one of their own, and Fez itself was not a royal seat.
Although it was founded by a schismatic[1] whose dynasty ruled
it for 150 years, it was the Marinids who, when they ruled this
region, gave Fez the title of kingdom and made their residence
and fortress there, for the reasons recounted in the *Chronicles
of the Muslims*. This will be seen as we go in turn through each
province and town in our usual order.

2.2.1.2. Tamasna province

The province of Tamasna stretches from the Oum Er-Rbia in
the west to the river Bou Regreg in the east, and from the Atlas
mountains in the south to the ocean in the north. It is quite flat,
measuring eighty miles west to east and sixty north to south.
This province was the flower of the region, for in it were forty
towns and 300 ksars, teeming with different Berber peoples
and nations. But in AH 323 (AD 935–36)[2] it was seduced by a
preacher called Ha-Mim ibn Mann Allah, who began to preach
against the rulers of Fez, saying they did not deserve tribute or
obedience, because of their injustice. Moreover, when the people

started to follow him, he claimed to be a prophet; the province was soon full of rebels and heretics and he was made the secular and spiritual ruler of all Tamasna. The rulers of Fez were just then occupied in a cruel war against the Zanata, so they had to make peace with the preacher, leaving him in this province without giving him trouble or bother, and receiving none in return. And so the preacher ruled for thirty-five years, and his sect lasted in the province for around a century.[3]

The Lamtuna invaded under Yusuf ibn Tashfin, and the moment they had finished building Marrakesh they sought to rule Tamasna and cure it of the heresy, sending many learned and orthodox men to convert the locals without war. As soon as they reached Tamasna, the people gathered in the city of Anfa with their prince, a grandson of the preacher, and decided to kill the poor ambassadors, which they did. The prince assembled an army of 50,000 men from his people, seeking to drive the Lamtuna out of Marrakesh and the whole region. Yusuf was most unhappy to learn of this; in his fury and anger he raced out of Marrakesh to attack the people of Tamasna and their prince, arriving within three days and crossing the Oum Er-Rbia.[4]

When the prince of Tamasna saw the size of Yusuf's army he and his men grew afraid. He escaped with his army, crossed the Bou Regreg towards Fez and abandoned Tamasna in flames. Yusuf sacked the cities and put all the people, even the suckling infants, to death, then he burned all the towns and ksars in the province. Within the eight months he spent in Tamasna he left it deserted and uninhabited, and to this day only traces of the towns remain. When the prince of Tamasna crossed the Bou Regreg, the ruler of Fez realised that the time had come to take revenge against him and his people. So the ruler made a truce with the Zanata and left Fez with a huge army, arriving at once before the army of the unlucky prince of Tamasna, which was feeble with hunger and need. Seeing the army of Fez, the prince was bewildered and went to cross back over the Bou Regreg, but the pass had been taken by the ruler of Fez. Out of desperation he tried to cross at a place where there was no ford but only woods and steep banks; in their haste the entire army of Tamasna was destroyed, some drowning in the river, others breaking their necks on the banks, while those who managed to cross fell into Yusuf's hands and were cut to pieces. In this way Tamasna lost its inhabitants and settlements within ten months; it is thought that a million men, women and children were killed. Yusuf returned to Marrakesh to raise a new army against the ruler of Fez, leaving Tamasna to the lions, wolves and owls.

The province remained uninhabited for eighty years, until al-Mansur returned from the kingdom of Tunis, bringing with him certain Arab peoples with their chiefs; he gave them Tamasna to live in and they remained there for fifty years. But then the house of al-Mansur lost the kingdom and the Arabs fell into misery and calamity, finally being driven out by the Marinid kings, who gave the province to the Zanata as a home in memory of their support against the kings, or rather caliphs, of Marrakesh. That people lived at liberty in the province, multiplying and growing wealthy, until in modern times, a century ago, they made the kings of Fez tremble, being estimated at more than 60,000 cavalry and 200,000 infantry. The author has visited and had dealings in this province countless times and will now mention a few towns he has seen.

2.2.1.3. Anfa[5]

Anfa is a large city built by the Romans on the shores of the ocean, sixty miles north of the Atlas mountains, eighty miles east of Azemmour, and forty miles west of Rabat. It was very cultured and fertile, for its territories are excellent for all sorts of grain and it has the best site of any city in Africa, surrounded by plains for eighty miles except to the north. There were many mosques and shops in the city, and tall, beautiful palaces, as can be seen from their traces today; around it were many gardens and vineyards bursting with fruit of all kinds, especially melons, watermelons and cucumbers, which begin to ripen in early April. The inhabitants would take fruit to Fez since it ripened later than that city's fruit. They were well clothed, for the town had much business with Portuguese and English merchants, and so it was very cultured in goods and learned men.

However, the people faced misfortune and ruin for two reasons: first, they wanted to live at liberty without any constraint, and, second, they kept foists in their little port, with which they did great damage to the island of Cadiz and the entire coast of Portugal, so the king of Portugal decided to destroy the town. He ordered a fleet of fifty ships full of soldiers and artillery; when they saw the fleet the townsfolk did not wait but at once gathered up their best possessions and abandoned the city, fleeing to Rabat and Salé. Upon arrival the captains got ready for battle, believing that there were still defenders in the town, but when they found nobody there they disembarked quickly and sacked all the goods left there within a day, emptying and burning the houses and knocking over the city walls.[6] After destroying the town, the captain returned to Portugal with his fleet and left the town to the wolves and owls.

The author has visited the town many times, and the sight made him weep despite himself, for most of the houses, shops and mosques are still in ruins. The vineyards and gardens have become forests, but still bear fruit. However, due to the impotence and other faults of the kings of Fez, the town will never be inhabited again.

2.2.1.4. Al-Mansor

Al-Mansor is a little town of 400 homes built by al-Mansur, king and caliph of Marrakesh, in a splendid plain two miles from the ocean, twenty-five miles from Rabat and the same from Anfa. Beside it flows a stream called the Guir, along which are many vineyards and gardens, although they are currently abandoned, for when Anfa was destroyed the inhabitants of al-Mansor, fearing that the Portuguese were coming, fled at once to Rabat. It was abandoned, but its walls all remain intact, albeit smashed in a few places by the Arabs of Tamasna.

The author has passed by many times and thought it a great pity that the town is not inhabited, for all that would be needed is to rebuild the houses and live there. But nobody can live there, due to the lawless violence of those malicious animals, the Arabs of Tamasna.

2.2.1.5. Nukhaila

Nukhaila is a little town in the middle of Tamasna, formerly very populous because in the time of the heretics all the people of the province held a great fair there once a year. The townsfolk were prosperous because they had forty miles of plains around them in every direction. One also reads in the histories that, in the time of the heretics, a camel load of good grain was not enough to buy a pair of shoes. When Yusuf ibn Tashfin arrived in Tamasna, the town was destroyed like the others, although there remain some vestiges of the walls, as well as a tower which was in the middle of the mosque. All the gardens and vineyards still remain, along with certain ancient trees that no longer produce any fruit. The Arabs of Tamasna, when they finish ploughing the land, leave all their tools and equipment around the tower, for they say a saint lies there, so nobody steals anyone else's tools for fear of him. The author has passed by countless times, for the town lies on the route from Rabat to Marrakesh.

2.2.1.6. Adendun[7]

Adendun was a little town built in the hills fifteen miles from the Atlas mountains and fifteen from Nukhaila. All the hills are good for sowing grain; beside the town is the source of a great river of clean water, and around it are many small palms that do not produce fruit. The river flows between rocks and valleys said to have been iron mines, and this must be true, for the rocks and valleys have that sort of colour and one can tell from the taste of the water. Only the smallest traces of this town remain, that is, foundations of walls and fallen columns, for it was destroyed in the war of the heretics like the other parts of the country.

2.2.1.7. Tegget

Tegget is a little town built by the Africans along the banks of the Oum Er-Rbia on the route from Tadla to Fez. The town was populous, cultured and very rich, for it is near the pass through the Atlas mountains to the desert, and those who lived on the borders of this part of the desert all went to the town to buy grain. But it too was destroyed in the wars of the heretics, although after a long time it was resettled, because some of the Arabs of Tamasna kept their grain there and the inhabitants guard it. No shops or craftsmen are found there, except a black-smith to maintain the ploughs and shoe the horses. The inhabitants are like their masters the Arabs in honouring every-one who passes through the town; merchants must pay a small toll of one *giulio*[8] per load of textile or valuable fabric, but noth-ing for the livestock and horses. The author often passed the town and it greatly displeased him, but the land is excellent, abundant with grain and livestock.

2.2.1.8. Ain el-Hallouf

This is a little town not far from al-Mansor, built in a plain where there are many forests of dogwood[9] and other, thorny trees that produce round fruit like jujubes, except yellow, with not much pulp but a stone larger than that of the olive.[10] Around the town are marshes crawling with turtles and fat toads, but the author has never heard that these toads hurt anyone. The historians make no mention of the town, and it seems to have been very small in ancient times, or more likely ruined. It also seems to contain nothing built by the Africans; rather, it was built by the Romans or some other people foreign to Africa.

2.2.1.9. Rabat

Rabat is a huge city on the ocean shores built in modern times by al-Mansur, the king and caliph of Marrakesh. The river Bou Regreg flows by it to the east and enters the sea; the citadel at its mouth has the river on one side and the sea on the other. The town is similar to Marrakesh in its walls and buildings, because al-Mansur deliberately made them alike, but it is smaller than Marrakesh. It was founded because the king, who ruled all of Baetica, realised that Marrakesh was very far away, and therefore that if Baetica faced any trouble from the Christians it would certainly be difficult to help. With his viziers, then, he decided to build a town by the shore where he could stay all summer with his army. Some advised him to stay in Ceuta, a city on the straits of Gibraltar, but he judged it too small to support a camp for three or four months, given the leanness of its fields, and he foresaw trouble for the townsfolk in putting up his soldiers and courtiers. So he decided to found a new city for the purpose; it was built within a few months, and he furnished it with mosques, madrasas and all sorts of other buildings, houses, shops, hammams and hospitals. Beyond the southern gate he erected a tower like that of Marrakesh, but with wider steps that three horses can climb side by side. There are no battlements at the top, from which, it is said, a fleet can be seen a long way off. The author thinks it marvellous in height.

Al-Mansur summoned many craftsmen, scholars and merchants and offered them a provision on top of the wages from their trade; when this news was heard, all the skilled men of every trade rushed to live there and it grew rich. The town was soon the most cultured and prosperous town in Africa, for its inhabitants made two salaries and traded with the king and his courtiers, especially during his residence from the beginning of April until the end of September. The town was built on a site lacking good water, for the sea penetrated ten miles up the river, filling the local wells with brackish water. So al-Mansur had water brought from a spring twelve miles away on an aqueduct supported on fine arched walls, like those seen in parts of Italy, especially Rome; it divides into many channels, some going to the mosques, others to madrasas and royal palaces, as well as the public fountains found throughout the town's quarters.

After al-Mansur's death, however, the town began to deteriorate, and barely a tenth remained; the aqueduct was ruined by the wars between his successors and the Marinid kings. The town is now worse than ever, and you would struggle to find four hundred inhabited houses, the rest being vineyards and farms. But two or three areas by the citadel have a few small shops; this district remains inhabited and still stands in danger of being captured by the Portuguese. All the past kings of Portugal have planned to do so, in the belief that, if they could, they would easily be able to take the entire kingdom of Fez. But the king has always given the town great provision and sustained it as best he can. The author has visited countless times, always feeling a deep melancholy for the vast difference between the life of the world when Rabat was founded, and its life today.

2.2.1.10. Chellah

Chellah is a little town built by the Romans beside the river Bou Regreg, two miles or so from the ocean and one mile from Rabat, which one passes on the way to the coast. It was ruined in the wars of the heretics. Al-Mansur later renovated the walls and built a very fine hospital, a magnificent block as barracks for his soldiers, and a splendid mosque with a hall adorned with inlaid marble mosaics and windows of multicoloured glass. On his deathbed he made a will that he should be buried in this room, and so his body was brought from Marrakesh and interred here, with two epitaphs on marble tablets at his head and feet, inscribed with copious verses by various great men expressing grief and lamentation for his passing. All the rulers of his house would have their bodies buried in this hall, and likewise the Marinid kings when their rule flourished.[11] The author has been there and seen there thirty or so tombs of great rulers, each with two epitaphs;[12] in AH 915 (AD 1509–10) he stayed in the town until he had written them all down.

2.2.1.11. Ma'aden Awwam

This town was founded in modern times by a treasurer of Caliph 'Abd al-Mu'min, who saw how much trade the nearby iron mines attracted and had the idea of building a little town there, on the banks of the river Bou Regreg ten miles from the Atlas mountains. Between the town and the Atlas are many dark woods with huge, terrifying lions and leopards. During the reign of the Almohads, the town was highly cultured and well populated, supplied with fine houses, mosques and inns. But it did not last long, for in the wars of the Marinid kings the town was ruined and the inhabitants were killed or fled to Salé. This happened because the people, thinking they would never receive help from Marrakesh, gave their town to one of the Marinid kings; unfortunately for them, the king of Marrakesh sent a general to protect the town and its people, and the moment they saw him they rebelled against the governor inside, who had to flee in haste.

Many months later, the Marinid king[13] passed the town in person with his camp on his way to Marrakesh. The moment he saw the king's army, the general abandoned the town and fled with his soldiers, and out of dire need the people surrendered to the king's mercy; but he showed little mercy, sacking their goods and cutting the men to pieces, except one who escaped in haste. It has never been inhabited since, but the town walls and the mosque's minaret remain. The author saw the town in AH 920 (AD 1514–15) when the king of Fez made peace with his cousin and went to take a vow to Taghia at the tomb of one of that town's saints, Sidi Bou 'Azza.[14]

2.2.1.12. Taghia

Taghia is an ancient little town built by the Africans in the Atlas mountains. Its environs are bitterly cold, with meagre, harsh fields and marvellous woods left to rabid lions; little grain grows there, but honey and goats are copious. The town has no culture and the houses are badly and illogically built. However, it does contain the tomb of a saint who lived in the reign of the caliph 'Abd al-Mu'min; they say he performed many miracles against the lions and had wondrous powers of divination. A scholar named at-Tadili[15] wrote a biography of him that relates his miracles in detail, and anyone who credits such things will greatly marvel at it. The author has seen the book, and would sooner believe that he performed these deeds either by a magical art or by some natural secret knowledge against the lions.

The town is much frequented for the sake of the tomb, and every year the people of Fez – men, women and children – go to visit it after Eid al-Fitr, bringing a tent to camp out and animals to carry the food. Groups of seventy or a hundred tents travel together, staying fifteen days before coming back, for it is 120 miles away. The author went there to visit the tomb with his father every year, and then by himself many times, often in great danger from the lions.

2.2.1.13. Zarfa

Zarfa was a city built by the Africans in a huge, splendid plain in Tamasna full of streams and springs. There are many fig trees dotted around the remnants of the town, and not far off is a forest of cherries and the fruit they call the 'marine cherry'[16] in Rome; there are also spiny trees with fruit called *nabiq*[17] in Arabic, smaller than cherries with about the taste of jujubes. There are also wild palm trees in the plains, though very small ones, and they produce a large fruit like a Spanish olive but with large stones and not much flesh, much like the sorb before it ripens.[18] In the time of the wars of the heretics, the city was ruined and most of its inhabitants were killed. At present the Arabs of Tamasna sow its fields and get marvellous results due to the soil's fertility, receiving a fiftyfold yield.

End of the book on Tamasna province; the book on the territory of Fez follows.

2.2.2.1. Territory of Fez

The territory of Fez stretches a hundred miles from the river Bou Regreg in the west to the river Inaouen in the east; to the north it is bounded by the river Sebou, and to the south by the Atlas foothills. It is marvellously fertile for grain, fruit and livestock. Its hills teem with villages as big as cities, but the plains are sparsely populated due to the past wars; the only inhabitants are base Arabs who are poor and powerless, maintaining the fields for either the burghers of Fez or the kings and their courtiers. Although certain noble and knightly Arabs sow the fields of Salé and Meknes, they are also subjects of the king. Now each town and place will be discussed in turn.

2.2.2.2. Salé

Salé is an ancient city built by the Romans and conquered by the Goths; when the Muslim armies invaded the region, the Goths gave it to their general Tariq (ibn Ziyad). When Fez was built, however, Salé became subject to its rulers in the wars. The town is located in a beautiful spot by the ocean a mile and a half from Rabat, with the river Bou Regreg in between. Its houses are built in an ancient style, much adorned with marble columns and mosaics; all its mosques are gorgeously decorated, and the shops likewise have been set into arcades, with arches that they say were fashioned to divide one trade from another. Thus the town had all the conditions of culture, especially in its port, which was much frequented by different families of Christian merchants – Genoese, Venetian, English and Flemish – for this is the port for the whole kingdom of Fez.

In AH 670 (AD 1271–72)[19] the city was assailed and captured by an armada of the king of Castile,[20] and the townsfolk fled in haste. The Christians stayed for about ten days, for Yaqub, the first Marinid king, prudently left his campaign against the king of Tlemcen and quickly returned to Salé with his army. On arriving, he immediately joined battle with the

Christians, who were unprepared because they had been such a short time in the city, and had not expected the king to return from his campaign; the king of Castile had counted on this when he ordered the armada. The town was finally recaptured by the king; any Christians found in the town were killed and the rest escaped in the armada. For this reason Yaqub was much loved by all the people of the region, as were all the kings of his house who reigned after him. But before it was recaptured the town lost a third of its population and two-thirds of its culture, and so there are now many empty houses throughout the city, especially near the walls, with beautiful columns and multi-coloured marble windows that the current inhabitants do not look after or even appreciate.

Around the town it is all sand and fields where little grain grows, but there are many gardens and rich cotton fields. Most of the townsfolk are weavers of fine cotton cloth, but they also make combs for sale throughout the towns of Fez, because nearby are many forests of boxwood and other woods that polish well.

There is still culture in the town now, and there are governors, judges and many other officers such as customs and tax officials. For many Genoese merchants come to town and trade a great deal there, and the king of Fez welcomes them warmly so as to maintain their custom, which brings in huge profits. Some of the merchants have lodgings in Fez, others in Salé, and each is as good as the other for selling goods. The author has conversed with the merchants of both cities, and all of them show a real nobility in their business, especially when it comes to exchanging merchandise. They spend a lot of money to acquire the friendship of the rulers and courtiers – not from a desire to get something from them, but to live honourably in foreign lands. In the author's time one Messer Tomaso Murino[21] lived in Fez, a good and wealthy man whom the king greatly esteemed and welcomed; he remained there for thirty-odd years, and when he died his body was brought back to Genoa, leaving many sons in Fez, all rich and honourable according to the rulers and their courtiers.

2.2.2.3. Fanzara

Fanzara is a town of middling size built by one of the Almohad kings in a splendid plain twenty miles from Salé. The entire plain is abundant in wheat and other grain, and by the walls outside town are many beautiful fountains built by the kings of Fez.[22]

The last Marinid king, Abu Sa'id,[23] faced a rebellion during his reign from one of his uncles named Sa'id, a prisoner in Granada. Because Abu Sa'id would not carry out a plan by Abu 'Abdullah, king of Granada,[24] the latter, out of spite, freed Abu Sa'id's uncle and sent him to Fez with a huge army and lots of money, joined by Arabs and mountainfolk. Fez was besieged for seven years, during which the Arabs did as they pleased, so all the nearby ksars and towns were ruined by the wicked conduct of the rebel lord and the Arabs.[25] After seven years a great plague afflicted the kingdom, and, worse, a famine; in AH 818 (AD 1415–16) the besieging ruler died of the plague, so Fez and its king could breathe again. But the ruined towns were never resettled, especially Fanzara, given as a home to Arab faction leaders who came to the rebel's help.

2.2.2.4. Ma'mura[26]

Ma'mura is a little town built by one of the Almohad kings at the mouth of the great river Sebou, although the town itself, surrounded by sandy plains, is a mile and a half from the sea, and a mile or so from Salé. It was founded to guard the river mouth against invasions from enemy fleets. Nearby is an expansive wood with towering oaks that produce acorns as large as damsons, but thinner and nicer-tasting than chestnuts. Some of the local Arabs earn a good living by taking these acorns in bulk on camels to sell in Fez, and mule-drivers also leave town and bring them back to Fez; but there is a great danger from the accursed lions, who are notorious for eating the pack animals, and sometimes the men too if they are inexperienced.

The town was ruined 120 years ago during Sa'id's war against the king of Fez, and all that remains are traces showing that it was not very big. In AH 921 (AD 1515–16) the king of Portugal sent a huge armada to build a fortress at the mouth of the river.[27] The moment they arrived they started building a very strong fortress, and in just a short time its entire perimeter with its bastions had been put up, and most of the armada had entered the river. But the king's brother[28] and his men repelled the Portuguese, routing them and killing all 3,000 in a stroke, due to the chaos of the invaders as they disembarked to capture the king's artillery. For they made a huge mistake in the numbers they brought against the king's soldiers – 5,000 infantry and 9,000 cavalry. The Portuguese assumed that they would reach the fortress before the king's camp heard the noise of their artillery, because it was two miles to the camp from the place where the artillery was kept; but the artillery was always guarded by six or seven thousand men. The Portuguese dragged the artillery almost a mile towards their fortress; the guards had fled, for they were badly armed, and most were lost, because the attack came before dawn so they had been asleep. So great was the noise, however, that the soldiers in the camp came running towards the Christians, and, although the latter showed great courage in defending themselves, when they saw huge numbers of cavalry coming straight for them and cutting them off from their fortress, they gave up hope and threw down their arms to surrender. Nevertheless, the brutish Moors did not spare them but cut them to pieces; only three or four escaped, whom the generals of the king's brother favoured.

The captain of the fortress therefore despaired, because the flower of his people had been killed. He sent a request for aid to the captain general, who was stationed outside the river mouth on a large ship with certain Portuguese lords and knights who had come to represent the armada. They wanted to help, but the fleets could not enter the river, because it was well guarded with artillery that sank vast numbers of ships. A few days later, news reached the Portuguese that the king of Spain[29] was dead, and all the ships and soldiers he had sent wanted to return; the captain of the fortress, lacking auxiliaries, had no choice but to abandon it. Not even the ships already on the river wanted to stay, but they lost two-thirds as they left, because in seeking to avoid the side where the enemy artillery lay, they ran aground on the sand where the water was shallow. The Moorish ships closed in on them, and those who could swim had to jump into the river and head for the large ships, but most were killed in the water before they reached them. The grounded ships were all burned by the Moors and all the artillery fell into the water. For three days the waves heaved with blood; it is said that 10,000 Christians were killed. Finally the king of Fez arrived and hauled 400 valuable bronze cannons out of the water.

This all happened on account of two mistakes. First, the Portuguese underestimated their enemies when they set out with such small numbers to capture the artillery, and so were routed. Second, the king could have sent an armada without the Castilians, because whenever two armies belonging to two different rulers fight the army of a single ruler, the two are defeated due to disagreements between the advisers and ministers. African rulers reckon it a sign of victory when they see the armies of two rulers against one. The author was present throughout this battle and afterwards left to travel to Constantinople.

2.2.2.5. Tefelfelt

Tefelfelt is a little town built in a sandy plain fifteen miles east of Ma'mura and twelve miles from the ocean. A small river flows nearby, and along its banks are forests of [. . .], where vicious lions can be found, worse even than those elsewhere in Africa and always wounding travellers, especially those who stay the night in the countryside. But on the main road to Fez outside town is an empty shack which serves as a lodging where mule-drivers and travellers shelter, barring the door with branches and thorns. It is said that the shack used to be an inn when the town was inhabited, but in Sa'id's war the town was abandoned and left on its own.

2.2.2.6. Meknes

Meknes is a great city named after the Miknasa people who built it. It is thirty miles from Fez, fifty from Salé and twenty-five from the Atlas mountains; it contains 6,000 homes and teems with people. Long ago its inhabitants lived amicably in the countryside, but then they divided into factions, one of which was more fortunate and defeated its opponents; the beaten factions got together and founded the city because they had lost their livestock and horses and could stay in the countryside no longer. It was built in a splendid plain near a river of middling size,[30] and around it for three miles are gardens bursting with excellent fruit, especially huge, fragrant quinces and pomegranates, wondrous in size and taste; they have no stones and are sold cheaply. Damsons and white plums are found in such abundance that one load goes for five or six *baiocchi*, and every year they pick large amounts of jujubes, which they dry for use in winter as well as taking them to sell in Fez. They also have a great quantity of figs and grapes grown on trellises, which they eat fresh because the figs become like bran when dried and the grapes, likewise, do not stay good as raisins. There are large nuts, and peaches which are thrown away because they are very poor and watery, almost green in colour, as well as infinite amounts of olives, one *cantar* of which – 200 Italian pounds – goes for a ducat and a half. The town's territory is very fruitful, often returning twenty-five times what is sown. Flax and hemp are harvested in vast quantities, most of which is sold in Fez and Salé.

The town itself is highly ornate and well ordered; it is provided with gorgeous mosques, three madrasas and ten or so large hammams. Every Monday there is a market by the walls outside, where a huge number of Arabs bring their cows, lambs and other livestock, as well as butter and wool, selling it all cheaply. In modern times the king gave the town to the prince,[31] and it is thought to produce a third of the fruit of the whole kingdom of Fez. But the town suffered enormous losses in the past wars between the rulers of this region, to the tune of thirty or forty thousand ducats, from all the many times it was besieged for five, six or seven years at a time.

When, in the author's time, the present king of Fez assumed the throne, one of his cousins rebelled against him, with the support of his people.[32] The king arrived with his camp and besieged the town for two months, but the citizens would not surrender, so to spite them the king cut down their fields, which, it is thought, sustained 25,000 ducats' worth of damage in a week. One can imagine how much worse the damage was when it was besieged for five, six or seven years. However, one faction friendly to the king opened a gate for him, battling the governor and the other faction all night until it was open. The governor withdrew into the citadel until he fell into the king's hands; he was put in prison, remaining there before finally escaping. After that there are long stories which have not been narrated in modern chronicles.

In summary, the town is handsome, fertile, well walled and fortified, and its streets are wide and cheerful. It gets excellent water, via an aqueduct, from a spot three miles away; this is parcelled out between the citadel, mosques, madrasas and hammams, but the mills are all two miles out of town. The inhabitants are skilled in armed combat, generous and reasonably cultured, but a little fatheaded, and all of them – gentlemen, merchants and craftsmen – trade in whey.[33] A citizen feels no shame in loading an animal with grain to take to work in the countryside. They hate the people of Fez for no reason known to either side. The gentlemen's wives do not leave the house except at night with their faces covered; they prefer not to be seen at all, covered or uncovered, and their husbands are dangerously jealous of them. The author has visited and done much business in the town; he was greatly displeased by the filth in the streets in wintertime.

2.2.2.7. Jami' al-Hammam[34]

This is an ancient town built on a plain near a spa fifteen miles south of Meknes, thirty miles west of Fez, and ten miles from the Atlas mountains; one passes it on the way from Fez to Tadla.

Arabs farm its fields because it was ruined in Sa'id's war, but the walls and many towers remain, and although the mosques have lost their roofs the walls remain standing.

2.2.2.8. Khamis Matghara

This is a little town built by the Africans in the countryside of the Zouagha fifteen miles west of Fez. Its territory is very fertile and for two miles all around are beautiful gardens of excellent grapes and figs, but these have been restored, for the town was ruined in Sa'id's war, and all the farms remained empty for 120 years. After some Granadans moved to Mauretania the town began to be settled again; a great number of white mulberry trees were planted because the Granadans traded in silk goods,[35] as well as sugar cane, albeit less good than that of Andalusia. The town was once well populated and highly cultured, but in modern times there is no culture at all, because its inhabitants are all farmers.

2.2.2.9. Beni Basil

Beni Basil is a little town built by the Africans on a stream in the middle of the Fez countryside, eighteen miles west of the city. The town itself has a huge countryside full of streams and large springs, and it is all farmed by Arabs, who sow barley and flax, although the grain they produce is not very good, because the soil is very wet and rough; the land all belongs to the chief mosque in Fez, bringing in 20,000 ducats a year. The town was once surrounded by gardens and vineyards, as can be seen from the surviving traces, but it was ruined in Sa'id's time and remained uninhabited for 120 years. After the king of Fez returned from Doukkala, he gave the town as a home to some of the people of Doukkala;[36] these new inhabitants have no culture at all, for they were forcibly relocated and live there against their will.

2.2.2.10. The great city of Fez,
capital of all Mauretania

Fez, the greatest of cities, was built by a schismatic's son during the reign of the caliph Harun (al-Rashid) in AH 185 (AD 801–02);[37] it was called Fez because on the first day the workers went to dig the foundations they found an axe, which in Arabic is *fez*. This is the true reason, but others say that the place where the town was built was named Fez after a river flowing there, for in the African language that river is called Ief, and the name was corrupted to Fez.

The schismatic, Idris (I), was a close relative of the caliph. By law and good reason, the caliphate should have passed to the schismatic instead. For, although Caliph Harun and Idris were both of Muhammad's house, Idris was so on both his mother's and his father's sides – being descended from Muhammad's cousin 'Ali, who married Muhammad's daughter Fatima[38] – but Harun was related to Muhammad only on one side, for he was descended from al-Abbas (ibn 'Abd al-Muttalib), Muhammad's uncle.[39] The house of Harun and his forebears possessed the caliphate by malicious means, for both houses were deprived of the caliphate for the reasons narrated in the chronicles. Harun's great-grandfather,[40] however, was a cunning and ingenious man who pretended to favour 'Ali's house in order to give them the title, but secretly sent ambassadors and preachers to every corner of the world, causing the house of Umayya to lose that title, which fell into the hands of 'Abdullah as-Saffah, the first caliph.[41]

When he[42] realised that that title could not be left in such a way, he revolted against the house of 'Ali and began to persecute them until their princes fled to Asia and India. One of them, 'Abdallah ibn al-Hasan, remained in Medina as an old religious man, and nobody gave him any trouble. When his two sons grew up and achieved great renown and status in Medina, Caliph 'Abdullah wanted to lay hands on them, and so both fled into Africa; one was captured and strangled,[43] while the other, Idris, escaped to Mauretania, where by good fortune he acquired great renown, reputed among the people as a ruler both spiritual and secular. He lived on Mount Zerhoun, thirty miles from where Fez is now, and all of Mauretania gave him tribute until he died, childless, although he left behind a pregnant slave-woman, a converted Goth.[44]

After Idris's death, she gave birth to a son named Idris after his father. The people all wanted him for their ruler, so he was well brought up and taught good manners by a general of his father named Rashid. When he was fifteen years old the boy began to do great deeds, acquiring many lands for his followers and armies to grow. Seeing that his father's homeland was not large enough, he decided to build a city, bringing together many architects and engineers and taking them around all the nearby plains. They advised him to build the city where Fez is now, for they knew it was a very suitable site, with many springs and a large river flowing among hills and valleys, and a great forest to the south. The river began not far away, flowing eight miles across a plain and down through the valley to the town.

Idris began building the town on the east bank of the river, and within a few months there was a citadel of 3,000 homes, well appointed with all the culture befitting its status.[45] After his death, one of his sons built another citadel on the opposite bank,[46] and little by little both parts grew into small districts, since each of the city's many rulers enlarged and improved it a good deal. Two hundred and eighty years after it was built, the townsfolk divided into factions; each had a leader and they fought many wars for a century or so. However, Yusuf ibn Tashfin, king of the Lamtuna, marched with his armies against the two rulers, whom he captured and put to a terrible death.[47] The people of Fez were almost entirely wiped out, for the city was sacked by the king and 30,000 were killed. The king decided to unify the two parts of the town, and so he smashed all the walls separating them and built many bridges over the river; the two towns became one city, and it was then divided into twelve districts.

Having described the foundation and original characteristics of the town, it remains to speak of Fez and its characteristics in modern times.

2.2.2.11. Fez

Fez is an enormous city with fine, high walls. The town is on a plain with mountains on all sides; the river is divided into two parts, one of which flows past New Fez[48] and also through the old city to the south, while the other enters from the west. Inside the town the river separates into many canals, most going to the houses of the burghers, courtiers and others; likewise every large and small mosque receives its share, as do all the inns, hospitals and madrasas. In the neighbourhood of the mosques there are lavatories in a square house, around which are little cubicles with porticos; inside, water comes out of a fountain in the wall and falls into a marble basin. When the river has a good current the water flows into the latrine and washes all the dirt into the river. In the middle of the house is a low fountain three cubits deep, four cubits wide and twelve long; water flows into the channels around it and underneath to the latrines, of which there are fifty or so.

The houses of the city are well built of brick and stone, and most are handsome, adorned with fine mosaics and brickwork; their porticos and courtyards have glazed tiles of various colours like those of glazed pots, all painted with pretty designs and precious colours like gold and blue. They have flat wooden roofs to make full use of the space; in the summer one can spread rugs over them and sleep up there. Almost all the houses are of two or three storeys, on each of which are corridors to go from one room to the next under the roof, for the middle of the house is uncovered, with the rooms on either side. The doors to the rooms are very tall and broad, but well made, and the rich have doors of mixed inlaid woods. To the sides of the rooms, all along the wall, are pretty, painted cupboards where they keep their favourite things; some of them are high, and others six palms deep to serve as beds, for they sleep on top. The porticos of the houses have columns faced with tiles, half of which are glazed, although others have marble columns; between each column is an arch faced with mosaic designs, while the beams between the columns holding up the floors are of wood inlaid with gorgeous designs and colours.

Many homes have rectangular cisterns six or seven cubits wide, a dozen cubits long and six or seven palms deep, all uncovered and faced with glazed tiles. At either end they put low, pretty fountains of the same coloured bricks, with round marble basins in the middle like the fountains in Europe. When the fountains are full, the water flows into the cisterns via finely decorated open channels, and when the tanks are full the water flows through pipes under the latrines into the river. They always keep the cisterns clean and polished, and they only use them in the summer, when the whole family bathes in them – men, women and children. On top of the houses are towers containing ornate chambers where the women relax when tired from work, for almost the whole town can be seen from them.

The city contains around 700 large and small mosques;[49] fifty of these are large, well built and adorned with marble columns and other ornaments. Each has beautiful fountains of marble and other stones unknown in Italy, under cupolas worked in mosaic or inlaid wood. The roofs of the mosques are all built like the churches in Europe, that is, covered with wooden beams, and the floors are all covered with fine mats, sewn together so closely that one cannot see the ground at all. The walls are all covered with the same mats, but only up to a man's height from the floor. Each mosque has a high minaret where they cry out to announce the times appointed for prayers. Each has a single imam, who recites the ordinary prayers and keeps account of the mosque's revenues, distributing them among the servants who light the lamps, open and close the doors, and climb the minarets at night. However, those who perform the call by day do not receive a salary, although they pay no tithe, ordinary or extraordinary payment, or tribute to any town official, on account of their service to the mosque.

There are two principal mosques in the city. The first, al-Qarawiyyin, is vast, around a mile and a half in circumference, with thirty-one wide, high doors. Its courtyard is around 150 Tuscan cubits long and eighty wide, with a very high minaret where they call for prayers; there are thirty-eight arches along its length and twenty along its width. To the east, west and north are certain colonnades, thirty cubits wide and forty long, and under these are storehouses for lamp oil, matting and other items the mosque needs. Each night 900 lamps are burned in the mosque, for each arch needs one, especially the aisle down the centre of the mosque, which alone holds around 150 lamps. Along the row are great bronze lanterns, each of which has enough oil for 500 lamps; these were made from bells acquired by the kings from Christian towns.

Around the walls inside the mosque are many pulpits,[50] where learned masters lecture on religious matters and sharia law every morning. They begin at dawn and finish an hour after sunrise; but in summer they only lecture from midnight to half past one in the morning. During these times they lecture on moral and spiritual matters according to Islam; those who lecture from books by the light of candles or lanterns are private citizens, but jurists lecture in the morning, though all are paid for their lectures.

The imam of the mosque has no duties except leading prayers, but he also takes care of the pupils' possessions, and organises the donations of money and other items for the pupils. Furthermore, he oversees the revenues of money and grain given as benefices to the needy; every feast day he dispenses these among all the poor of the city, each according to his means and household. But the man in charge of the mosque's revenues has his own position, and he receives a ducat per day for his wages. He has eight notaries, each earning six ducats a month; six people to collect the rent from houses, shops and farms, each taking five per cent; and around twenty administrators who go around paying the farmers, vineyard workers and gardeners, and who earn three ducats a month. A mile or so outside town are twenty lime kilns for repairing and rebuilding the mosque's properties, and other kilns for bricks. All in all, the mosque has an income of 200 ducats per day, around half of which is spent on the things just mentioned, and on providing for all the large and small mosques that lack their own income. The other half is spent on useful things for the community, because the community in this city has no income of its own. In modern times, however, the kings of Fez have borrowed a great deal of money from the protector of the mosque without repaying it.

In the city are eleven well-built madrasas, with much mosaic decoration and carved beams faced with marble and glazed bricks. Each madrasa has many study rooms; the larger ones have a hundred, others more or fewer. All of them were built by various Marinid kings; one built by King Abu 'Inan is especially amazing for its size, beauty and ornamentation.[51] It has a marble fountain huge enough to hold twenty-five bushels of grain, and through the madrasa flows a stream in a canal,[52] the bottom and sides of which are decorated with marble and glazed bricks. There are three covered porticos with vaults, the beauty and ornamentation of which must be seen to be believed.[53] Around them, fixed to the wall, are octagonal columns of different colours; between the capitals are mosaic arches adorned with fine gold and blue. The roof is made entirely of pretty, ornate mixed inlaid woods, and between the porticoes and the courtyard are certain fine [...],[54] so that from the courtyard you cannot see those in the rooms under the portico. The walls, from the floor as far up as a man can reach, are all covered with glazed bricks fashioned in pieces, and around them are verses containing the date of the madrasa's construction, and a passage from their scripture testifying that the madrasa is a good and holy work. There are also verses in praise of its founder Abu 'Inan written in letters of black glazed bricks on white, large enough that you can see them from far away. The main gates are of ornate, finely worked bronze, and the doors to the study rooms are of inlaid wood. In the large prayer hall is a pulpit with nine steps of [...],[55] a most wondrous thing to see.

The author has heard from many of his teachers, who in turn heard it from their teachers, that King Abu 'Inan, when he completed the madrasa, wished to see the account books, and, turning over a page or two from one of them, he discovered that he had spent 40,000 ducats. In astonishment, he ripped up all the books and threw them in the stream running through the madrasa, repeating a verse from the Arabic writers: *An expensive thing, when it is thought beautiful, is not expensive, and anything that delights the soul is priceless*. Ibn al-Hajj, a minister and treasurer of the king, was in charge of the building's expenses, which ran to 480,000 African ducats in all.

All the madrasas in Fez resemble this one. Each employs lecturers in various disciplines: some lecture in the morning, others in the evening, but all of them receive a good salary or benefice endowed by the madrasa's founders. Formerly, every student was given expenses and clothing for seven years, but today they get only their rooms, for in King Sa'id's time many properties, fields and gardens were destroyed by the war, and barely any income remains for the lecturers; some receive 100 ducats, others 200, others less or more. This is why excellence has almost disappeared from Fez, and not only from Fez but all the cities in Africa. Only foreign students live in these madrasas, subsisting on alms from the burghers and gentry of Fez; few local students live in them. During the lectures, a student reads out the text and the lecturer recites the commentary and exposition from memory; sometimes the students dispute with each other on the topics of their reading in front of the lecturer.

[2.2.2.11.2. Hospitals]

In the city are many hospitals[56] as beautiful as the madrasas, and travellers used to lodge there for three days. Outside the gates are many other hospitals like those inside, and all of them were once rich, but in the time of Sa'id and his accursed war the king of Fez was short of money, and certain scholars and judges at the time advised him to sell all the assets belonging to the hospitals. The people, however, would not consent to this. A spokesman for the king replied to them that the hospitals had been built with the alms of his forebears, and that he was now in danger of losing his kingdom: 'Wouldn't it be better to sell or mortgage these assets to see off his and our enemies? When the situation has been resolved, the king can easily buy them back.' So the people agreed, and the assets were sold to the burghers. The king did as best he could, but died before he could buy the assets back, and every year until the present the situation has only got worse. The hospitals have grown ever poorer and emptier; but they are often given to foreign scholars to live in, or to poor nobles to upkeep the buildings.

There is currently a poor hospital for sick foreigners, but it has no doctors or medicine; it only gives them expenses and rooms, looking after them until they die or recover.[57] In the hospital are rooms set aside to hold madmen who throw rocks and do other mischief, and who are kept locked and chained in the rooms. The walls of the rooms next to the corridors and courtyard are built like iron, but are in fact made of strong wooden beams. When he enters to give them food, the warden always carries a large staff, and if he sees anyone move he hits them with it and pursues them. Sometimes, when the madmen see a strange visitor, they call to him and one of them will complain that the officers are keeping him prisoner, because he has already been cured. When the visitor hears this he believes them and approaches to see them better, and then they grab his hand and drag him in by his clothes, taking their shit in their other hand and throwing it on him. For they leave their filthy mess in the middle of their rooms, and every day the warden has to clean it up. Currently the gates of the hospital are constantly guarded, and those who enter are warned not to bother the madmen lest they get any nastiness from them. The hospital has many officials: notaries, administrators, custodians, cooks and others who guard and look after the sick. In his youth the author served as a notary there for two years, as is customary for students, receiving three ducats a month from the burghers.

[2.2.2.11.3. Hammams (bathhouses)]

In the city are a hundred or so hammams, which are well built and ornate. Some are small, some large, but all have the same layout of four halls, around which are low-ceilinged colonnades up a flight of five or six steps; here men disrobe and leave their clothes, making use of fountains like large cisterns in the middle of the room. Through a door one enters the room which has a heater, although it is rather cool, and a fountain to cool the water when it gets too warm. The next door leads to a second, warmer room, where an attendant washes, cleans and perfumes the customers. The next room is very hot, with a walled furnace to heat the water, and here one sweats.[58] In the furnace is a hole, not too high to reach with the hands; from it the attendants take water to put in large wooden pails, giving every customer two jugs full, as they are obliged to do. Whoever needs more water or wants to be washed must give the attendant or servant a *baiocco* or more, for any smaller tip would be shameful. The owner of the hammam is paid only two *quattrini*. The water is warmed with a fire fuelled by animal dung; the managers keep servants and donkeys who go around the town stables asking if there is any dung, and clearing out the stalls where they find it. They carry it out of the town and heap it up in a circular mound, leaving it to dry for two or three months before bringing it back to burn and heat the water.

The women have hammams of their own. Others are operated for both women and men, for instance, with the men using it in the morning until three o'clock, and the women using it from three until midnight. But, when the women enter, they pass a curtain put up over the hammam door as a signal that no man can enter; if someone wants to say something to his wife, he has to call one of the black female attendants to take the message for him.

Inside the hammam, men and women eat and sing loudly. Common youths enter as naked as the day they were born, looking at each other without any embarrassment, while men of higher status wrap towels around themselves before they enter; they do not sit in the communal areas, but there are always little chambers around the rooms appointed for men of renown. When the attendants are going to wash a person they lay him down, sometimes rubbing him with oils and sometimes with tools resembling the scrapers used to clean dirt off leather clothes, but softer, thinner and attached to a piece of cork. Rulers, when they want to be washed, lie on a piece of felt with cushions of felt-covered wood under their heads. In all the hammams are barbers who pay rent to the proprietor to store their cases with their working instruments. Most of the hammams belong to mosques or madrasas, but a few belong to the burghers. They pay a huge rent: some 200 ducats, others fifty, others less or more, depending on their size and location.

Once a year the servants of the hammams hold a feast so they can carouse with their friends and leave town accompanied by trumpets and pipers. They pluck a lily bulb or squill and put it in a fine brass vase covered with brocade scarves, bringing it on someone's head, accompanied by music, back to the hammam. Then they put the bulb in a basket and hang it up over the door, declaring that it will bring profit, for the hammam will get lots of customers. But many think that this act is a sacrifice like those of the ancient African heathens. The custom has been preserved ever since, just as there are Christian ceremonies which are still observed today, although the reason for them has been lost. In every town they observe these festivals and customs left over from when the Christians ruled Africa. You will see the ceremonies of a few festivals when the subject comes up later.

2.2.2.12. The city's inns

There are 200 well-built inns in the city, some of them very large, especially those near the great mosque which are on three levels, one with 120 rooms, others more or fewer. In all of them are fountains and latrines with taps of the sort not found in Italy outside the Spanish College in Bologna and the Palazzo di San Giorgio[59] in Rome. The doors to the rooms lead out to the corridor. Beneath all the splendour the lodgings are poor; without beds or cots, each traveller gets only a mat and a blanket from his host, and has to buy his own food for the host to cook. It is not only foreigners who stay at these inns, but also widowers without homes or family, who keep rooms either alone or with a companion, providing their own beds and cooking for themselves. The worst of these lodgings are with a group called *al-hiwa*,[60] who wear women's clothes and adornments, shave their beards, speak like women and spin flax. Each of these accursed hosts takes a man in the manner of a husband, and they are said to use them like the prostitutes in European brothels. They are also permitted to keep and sell wine at their inns without any trouble from the court. For these reasons all disreputable men frequent these inns, for they can get drunk and go with whores – or worse – without danger from the court. The hosts have a consul and pay tribute to the castellan and governor of the city; because they are talented in the kitchen, they are also obliged to send a team with the camp of the king or prince to cook for the soldiers.

The author wanted to keep some of these things back, to speak vaguely, or to omit such a shameful defect in the city where he was raised and nurtured; but he has to tell the truth in every account, as it is everyone's duty to do. In his opinion, if the kingdom of Fez lacked this vice and this wicked group, its moral life would truly be the best in Africa. The group deals only with common idlers, for no literate man, merchant or wealthy crafts-man will ever talk with them; they cannot enter the mosques or even the merchants' square, nor the hammams or houses, nor can they keep inns near the mosque where important merchants lodge. The people all wish these gluttons[61] dead, but the rulers allow their presence so they can use them for camp duties.

[2.2.2.12.2. The Fez mills]

There are around 400 mills in the city, but there could be more than a thousand millstones, for each mill-house is a large hall in which are four, five or even six stones; part of the country-side does its grinding in the city. Flour-merchants rent mills, buy and grind wheat, and sell the flour in shops rented to the masters; they keep servants to sell the flour and make a profit on the merchandise. All the craftsmen who have neither the ability nor the means to supply their own grain stores buy flour from the shops and bake bread in their homes. Other wealthy men buy wheat and have it ground in mills set aside for the burghers; they pay two *baiocchi* per bushel, but the merchants' mills do not grind any wheat but their own. The mills mostly belong to mosques and madrasas, and only a few to the burgh-ers, who pay a high rent of two ducats per millstone.

[2.2.2.12.3. Fez shops and squares]

Each of the city's professions is in its own district, separate from the rest. The most prestigious ones, such as the notaries, can be found near the great mosque; of these there are eighty shops, some by the mosque walls, the others opposite, with two notaries in each. To the west are thirty booksellers and to the south fifty shoe shops, which buy shoes and buskins in bulk from the cobblers and sell them individually. Past these are around fifty cobblers who make children's shoes. On the eastern side of the mosque are copper and brass workers.[62] Opposite the main gate on the western side are fifty fruiterers, and beyond them are the wax workers, who fashion the most beautiful wax items in the world, working at home and bringing their torches and candles to their well-appointed shops. Past them are a few haberdashery shops, then the flower sellers, who also sell citrons and lemons. It is a fine thing to see all the flower arrangements in various colours as if they were painted, and there are around ten shops, for those who drink wine always want flowers around them.

Near the flower sellers are milk shops, furnished with glazed jugs. They buy from farmers with milking cows, who send the milk every morning in wooden jugs reinforced with iron, narrow at the mouth and wide at the bottom, and it is sold under the shops. The shopkeepers buy whatever is left over in the morning or evening and make butter from it; they make it sharp, both liquid and solid, and sell it to the people. All in all, twenty-five barrels of milk and butter are sold every day in the city.

Beyond this are thirty cotton shops, which card cotton and sell it spun. Near the milk shops to the north are the hemp dealers, selling ropes, halters, twine and all manner of cord. Next are those who make leather belts, slippers, and saddle furnishings like pouches; they fashion halters with silk embroidery on the leather. Then the scabbard makers, who also make knives and horses' harnesses, and salt merchants who buy in bulk and sell in small quantities. Then a hundred dealers in pots, which they buy in bulk from the kilns and sell individually; the pots are pretty and of an exquisite colour, but never in more than one or two shades. Then eighty shops selling second-hand horses' bits, bridles, belts, saddles and stirrups.

Next is the porters' office. There are 300 porters; they have a consul[63] and cannot work freelance, but must wait together at the office until one is needed. The consul has them draw lots to work on a given week or day; the money is put in a box locked with many keys kept by the senior staff, and at the end of the week it is shared among those who have worked. The porters have an excellent custom, like a fraternity; if one of them dies and leaves little children, they look after the girls until they marry, and support the boys until they are old enough to practise the trade. Whenever one of them marries or has a child, he holds a feast for the entire company, and each guest pays ten *baiocchi* to the married couple. Nobody can enter their trade until he has feasted the company, and if someone wants to work without doing so, he only earns half for his labour. By the grace of the rulers, they pay no fines, rent, ransom or tax at the gates, nor do they pay the ovens for baked bread, nor even, if one of them commits a crime, will he be punished and chastised in public. They all wear a short robe of the same colour when on duty, but when off duty they wear whatever they want. They lead honourable lives and are held in good repute.

Beyond the porters' office is a square where the chief consul[64] and judge of all the food markets works. In the middle of the square are rectangular enclosures of cane where carrots and swedes are sold; it is sort of official, for nobody can buy carrots or swedes from the gardeners except certain appointed men who pay the customs office a fee. Every day you'll see 500 or more loads of carrots, and the same again of swedes, sold in huge quantities at a very low price: one *baiocco* for thirty pounds, or twenty of the most expensive. When beans are in season, they are sold peeled in bulk for two *baiocchi* per *scorzo*.[65] Around the square are shops selling vermicelli, and others selling little balls of ground lean beef fried in oil with spices; each ball is the size of a fig, and a pound goes for six *quattrini*.

North of here is the square of the greengrocers, who sell cabbages, turnips and other produce from the countryside, forty shops in all. Beyond these is the square of smoke, where they sell bread fried in oil like the honeyed bread sold in Rome; these traders keep many tools and servants in their shops, for it is a complex operation. Every day they shift a huge amount of this bread, which is eaten at feasts, especially at weddings, and during Lent before daybreak. They eat it with roast meat or honey, or with a coarse, liquid soup made with cooked, ground meat and coloured with 'red earth'.[66] The meat is not roasted on a spit. Instead, they put one oven above another, setting a fire in the lower one until the upper one is hot; then they cook a whole lamb inside the oven, stopping up the mouth with clay but making a hole in the roof to put the animals in without burning their hands. The meat comes out browned and well done, and it is absolutely delicious because the smoke doesn't touch it. Rather, it is roasted by the heat alone, and they leave it cooking all night, before selling it in the morning, always in the bread. More than 200 ducats' worth of the roast meat is sold every day, for there are fifteen shops that sell nothing else. They also make fried meat and fish, and a flatbread only a little thicker than a sheet of lasagne; their dough is mixed with butter and they eat it with honey and butter. They also sell cooked heads and feet of animals. Those who till and labour in the countryside come here early in the morning to eat in the shops selling this sort of slop, then head off for work.

Beyond these are the shops selling oil, salted butter, honey, mature cheese, olives, lemons, carrots, pickled capers; they have glazed jars worth more than the merchandise, and also sell jars of butter and milk, measured by porters employed for that job. The porters also measure the oil when it is sold in bulk. The jars of butter each weigh fifty pounds, for the cowherds have to make them at that weight; the shepherds buy them in town, carry them out to fill them up and then return to town to sell them back. Next to these are forty butchers' shops, built tall like those of the other professions. Inside they cut the meat and weigh it on the scales, but they do not kill animals here, using instead a slaughterhouse by the river. They skin them and have the porters carry them to the butchers' shops, but the porters, before they arrive there, visit the chief consul's office for a document fixing the price at which the meat should be sold. The butcher hangs it up next to the meat so that everyone can see and read it.

Beyond the butchers is a square with a hundred shops selling large rolls of a local woollen fabric. Everyone who brings a roll for sale must give it to a crier, who carries it on his shoulders, hawking it from one shop to another; there are five dozen criers, who work from midday to the late evening and are paid two *baiocchi* per ducat sold. The merchants of this profession do a roaring trade. Next are those who polish and sell weapons: swords, daggers and spears. Beyond are those who fish in the town's river and the one outside,[67] selling good, plump fish very cheaply, around three *quattrini* a pound. During one season, from October to April, they catch a huge quantity of fish called *alaccia* (sardinella) in Rome, as you will see in the book on rivers.[68] Next are forty shops selling chicken cages made from cane, since all the burghers keep chickens to fatten and they don't want them to get loose and befoul their homes. For this reason they make many cages. Next are a few shops selling liquid soap, but these shops are scattered through the districts. The soap is not made in the city, but the inhabitants of nearby mountains and their mule-drivers bring it in to sell in the shops.[69] Next are the flour sellers and there are few shops together, for they are dispersed through every district. Next are those who sell excellent grain and beans to sow, and also grain for those who only want a small amount, such as a half or quarter bushel, since the burghers will not sell a tiny amount. In this square are grain porters who own mules and horses with packsaddles; they can carry a bushel and a half on each animal, in three sacks laid on top of each other, and fetch one *baiocco* per bushel. These are the porters who have to measure the grain. Next are twenty shops selling small quantities of straw.

Beyond these is the square where they sell flax and spun thread, and where the flax is prepared. The square is like a large house with four colonnades around it where the cloth merchants sit with the officials who weigh the spun thread. In other colonnades sit women with a huge amount of spun thread to sell; they give it to criers who hawk it around the merchants, and the market is open from midday to evening. Another square, separated from this on one side, is like a little house where they comb the flax, and on the other side are shops where they sell it. In the middle of the square are many mulberry trees planted to give shade. Sometimes a person who wants to go and see the market just for fun cannot get out without great difficulty due to the throng of men and women; sometimes the women quarrel, fight and insult each other, a sight at which one can't help laughing.

Returning west towards the mosque, as far as the gate to Meknes, and beyond the square of smoke by the main road, are twenty-four shops selling leather buckets to use in houses with wells. Next are thirty shops selling sieves for grain and flour, then fifty shops belonging to cobblers and shoesmiths who make shoes in bulk for the peasants and others. Then the makers of leather shields and bucklers in the African style, just as one sees in Europe. Next are the laundries run by men of humble status; these are shops with large fixed vats, to which the burghers and men without maids at home bring their shirts and sheets for these men to wash. After the items are washed the men stretch them out to dry on ropes tied high above, skilfully tossing the fabrics over the ropes with long canes; when they are dry they fold them up neatly and beat them with bundles of wood on benches fixed to the ground. The washed fabrics turn out so clean and neat that their owner can hardly recognise them. There are around twenty shops altogether, but those in other districts and squares number more than 200. They have a consul and leader.

Next are 300 extraordinary shops of various professions; then the shops selling wood for horses' saddles, and fine apothecary shops on the western side of the city, near the Bou Inania Madrasa. Next are forty shops selling ornaments for stirrups, spurs, harness clasps and bridles, all producing excellent work admired by everyone in Italy and the rest of Christendom. Then the smiths, who only make stirrups, bridles and iron trappings for horses. Next are a hundred shops of saddlers who work in leather, making three covers for each saddle, one on top of the other; the most beautiful is in the middle and the top one is less attractive, but all are of cordovan leather. They work to excellent standards, since examples of their work, that is, saddles for the jennets, are sought after in Italy. Next are those who sell spears, with long shops in which to make them. Next is the citadel on one side and a pathway extending as far as the western gate. On the other side, opposite the citadel, is a large palace where the king's sister or other kin lives.

[2.2.2.12.4. Fez merchants' square]

These shops begin at the great mosque, and to stick to the order the square of merchants has been left till last. That square is like a citadel with walls and two gates; each gate is chained to prevent horses and other animals from entering. The square is divided into five areas. In two of them are shoemakers for the burghers, and not for craftsmen, soldiers or courtiers, and in two others are the silk-weavers. Of the latter there are fifty shops selling ribbons for horses and other streamers and adornments, and another fifty selling coloured silk for shirts, pillows and other things. Next are those who make woollen belts for women, which are large, clumsy things. Others make similar items of plaited silk, as thick as two fingers so you could easily tie a boat with them.

Next to these are two other areas where merchants from Granada sell woollen fabrics from Europe, as well as silk curtains and caps, and raw silk. Then the makers of leather rugs, mattresses and cushions for summer. Then the tax collector's office, for in the square all the fabric is sold by the criers, who, after they pick it up, have it stamped and then hawk it among the merchants. There are five dozen criers here, and they are paid one *baiocco* per roll. Beyond the tax office are three areas for the tailors, and past them an area selling plaited cloth to wear on the head. Next are two other areas of cloth merchants selling women's shirts and fabrics, the richest merchants in the whole city, for they do the most business. Beyond these is another area where they make ornaments and tassels for the cloaks called burnouses.

Next is another area selling garments of European cloth;[70] every evening the criers hawk the fabrics brought for sale by the burghers when the material gets too old or for some other reason.

Then an area selling shirts, scarves, towels and all manner of second-hand items of cloth. Finally there are little colonnades where they hawk carpets and coverlets.

[2.2.2.12.5. The Kissaria]

All together, these areas are called the Kissaria, an ancient name derived from Caesar, the greatest ruler of Europe. For the coastal cities of Mauretania were ruled by the Romans and the Goths, and their merchant squares were called Kissaria because, as the African historians say, the Roman and Goth officials kept *funduqs* and storehouses throughout the cities. They also kept the city's tribute and profits here, and the people often ransacked them. One emperor ordered the square to be built like a citadel, with shops inside for the merchants to congregate with their goods. He also ordered his officials responsible for the city's profits and tribute to keep them in the *funduqs* of the citadel, reasoning that if the people wanted to ransack the empire's goods again, there would be no less danger to the merchants' and burghers' goods. Thus the rich townsfolk carefully watched their own goods, and under their protection the empire's goods were watched as well, because if the burghers allowed anyone else's goods to be ransacked, the people of the city would stop at nothing in their fury. This is sometimes observed in Italy, when soldiers enter a divided town to support one faction against the other; the soldiers start to sack the enemy side and, when they realise that those goods are not enough, turn on their allies' goods next.

[2.2.2.12.6. More shops]

By the citadel to the north are the apothecaries who own fifty shops along a straight road.[71] The road is closed at each end with large, fine, strong gates, and the apothecaries maintain paid guards to stay there at night with their lanterns, dogs and weapons. They sell the usual wares and medicinal items but cannot make syrups, cerates or electuaries.[72] Instead, doctors make these at home and bring them to their shops, where they have servants to hand them over after receiving them from the doctors; these shops are largely mingled with the apothecaries, and most people confuse the two since they have no idea what doctors or medicine are. The apothecaries have tall shops with such fine ceilings and cabinets that there cannot be any place like it in the whole world. It is true that there is a large apothecaries' square in Tabriz, a city in Persia, but the shops there are in rather dark, albeit well-built arcades of marble columns, and in the author's opinion they are dissimilar to Fez, because of the lack of light.

Beyond the apothecaries to the west are thirty shops selling combs of boxwood and other woods in large numbers. Next are the greengrocers, but they have already been mentioned. At the bottom of the apothecaries' square, by the apothecaries' college to the east, are fifty shops of craftsmen working with lapis.[73] Next are the lathe workers, although there are few shops together, being dispersed over lots of other districts. Next are many flour dealers and soap makers, around twenty shops at the edge of the square of spun thread we mentioned before, and there are broom dealers under the shops selling milk. Among the fruiterers and cotton merchants are those who make coverlets and canopy beds. Not too far from them are shops selling poultry and songbirds, only a few, but it is still called the fowlers' square. Most shops here in fact currently sell large and small cords and ropes of hemp. Beyond the bed sellers are those who make clogs for the citizens to wear in the muddy season, although they are made with hobnailed soles and pretty silk designs on the leather. Even the lowliest citizen will own a pair of these clogs; they are worth a ducat each, and many are worth two, ten or even twenty-five, for the work and the wood. They are mostly made of black and white mulberry wood, but others are of walnut, orange-wood or jujube; the latter are nicer and smoother, but those of mulberry are more durable.

Next are twenty shops selling countless crossbows, most of them run by Spanish Moors. Below these are fifty shops selling brooms made of wild palms like the ones in Rome brought over from Sicily. The dealers carry the brooms across town in large baskets, selling them for bran, cinders and broken shoes; they sell the bran on to the cowherds in the milk trade, the ashes to those who bleach thread and the broken shoes to cobblers. Next are the nail-makers. Then the makers of wooden vessels as large as barrels but shaped like buckets, who also make grain measures. Their consul certifies the measures, taking only a *quattrino* per load. Beyond these are the wool dealers, and others who buy skins from the butchers next door, have their servants wash them and shave off the wool, and tan the hides. They only tan sheep leather; cordovan and ox skins are tanned by a separate profession.

Further on are those who make ropes from hair, as well as the sort of horse tethers used in Africa, and next to them are the copper dealers. Beside the measure sellers are those who make combs for flax and wool, and then a long square of various trades and professions, including drill makers and those who file iron items, such as stirrups, spurs and the like, since the smiths don't file them. Next are the masters of woodwork for large items such as ship's wheels, ploughing tools, mill wheels and other tools. Then the dyers whose shops are on the river; they have a beautiful fountain where they wash silk, but they wash wool in the river. Behind the dyers are the makers of packsaddles in a broad square planted with mulberry trees, which in summer is the coolest and most pleasant square in the city. Next are the farriers who shoe horses and other animals, and then the workshops making iron horseshoes and steel parts for crossbows, and those who whiten coloured cloth with sticks and basins.

This square completes the list of squares in one part of the city, namely the western part, which was originally a city in its own right, built after the other city to the east.

[2.2.2.12.7. Madinat Fes]

The eastern city is cultured and boasts fine buildings, mosques and madrasas, but not as many as the other one, for there are only merchants or tailors who work with coarse fabrics, and only shoemakers who work in bulk. They do have a little square of apothecaries, but there are only thirty shops. Near the city walls are brickmakers and potteries, and below these is a large square where they sell white, that is, unglazed vessels such as bowls, dishes and cooking pots. Beyond that is another large square of shops and granaries. Then another fine square on a hill, well paved, opposite the doors to the great mosque;[74] here there are shops of various trades and professions. All the previously mentioned squares are organised by trade, but there are also dealers scattered across the districts of the town in a disorganised manner, except the fabric merchants and apothecaries, who are only found in their appointed places.

The city also contains 300 cloth-weaving workshops in sizeable buildings of many floors, with large halls each housing many weavers. The tools are not provided by the owners but supplied by the masters, who pay them nothing but the rent for the rooms. This is the greatest trade in Fez, said to employ 20,000, just the same as the mills. There are also fifty workshops where they whiten spun thread, built mostly beside the river and furnished with heaters and walled vats where they boil and lye the thread. There are large workshops throughout the city where they saw wood; poor Christian slaves do the work and their owners pocket the money and provide them with necessities, letting them rest only on Friday afternoons and on eight other days a year for the Moorish festivals.

Throughout the city are places like brothels where prostitutes earn money by permission of the police chief or town governor. Certain men in town are allowed to work as pimps without any trouble from the court; they keep women and wine in their homes, and those who want to can go there for a fee and enjoy those things safely. The pimps are always out for money: when a rich man visits they will welcome him into their home, then go to the court and tip them off. After he is arrested, the court gives the pimps a reward.

The city has 600 springs, that is, natural fountains in locked enclosures, each of which disperses into many parts that flow through underground canals into houses, mosques, madrasas and inns. Houses supplied by the springs are worth more than those supplied from the river, because the river is sometimes dry, especially in summer, when they have to drain it to clean the canals. In every area of the city are innumerable fountains fed from the springs, and these are used by all the people without water in their homes. In summer, the burghers whose houses are supplied from the river send for spring water, since it is fresher, and in winter the reverse happens. Most of the springs and fountains are in the west and south of the city, but the northern part is full of travertine mountains with huge, deep pits where they store grain for many years.[75] Some pits can hold 100 bushels of grain, and the locals all live off the rent from these pits, for they are all men of lowly status, and every year they are paid one bushel per hundred.

In the southern part of the city, which is almost uninhabited, are many gardens full of excellent trees and fruits, especially oranges, lemons and citrons. There are also other delights, such as jasmine, damask rose and broom, which are prized in Africa because they are not found in the native countryside but were originally imported from Europe. In the gardens are beautiful buildings, fountains and pools, over which hang trellises of jasmine and damask rose, with orange trees planted around the pools. In spring, anyone approaching will smell such sweet fragrances and odours from the blossoms of orange, lemon, citron and other fruit that it will truly seem a paradise on earth. The burghers go to live in these areas from the beginning of April until the end of September.

In the western part, which borders the royal city, is the citadel itself, which is as large as a city, built in the time of the Lamtuna kings; here the governors and rulers of Fez had their residence before it became a royal city. But, after New Fez was built by the Marinid kings,[76] this citadel was abandoned by the rulers, leaving it for the governor alone. In the citadel is a fine ancient mosque[77] built when it was well populated, but the public buildings have all been destroyed and flattened to make orchards and gardens. Through the citadel, and through the current home of the governor and his family, runs part of the river used for grinding. There are many colonnades and seats where the governor gives audience and holds conversations. There is also a prison constructed as a long, broad vaulted cellar supported by pillars; it can hold 3,000 people, and there are no separate rooms, let alone hidden ones, for nobody is kept secretly in prison in the city.

[2.2.2.12.8. Law and dress]

There are only a few legal positions in the city: the governor, who is in charge of civil and criminal law, the judge, who is in charge of canon law – that is, law derived from Muslim scripture – and the judge's deputy, who deals with marriage and divorce law, examines testimonies and passes judgements generally. The other official is the public defender, who gives legal advice and to whom appeals are made on the judges' decisions either when they are mistaken, or when they follow a scholar of lower rank.

The governor makes a large profit from fines and imprisonments. Almost all criminals are punished by being whipped in his presence: they are given one or two hundred lashes, then chained at the neck and led through the entire town by the executioner, naked but for a pair of trousers, accompanied by the police chief who has passed the judgement. Often several go chained together, and the executioner cries out their crimes in public; when they reach the top of the square they get dressed again and are put back in prison. The governor exacts a ducat and a quarter for each criminal and each prisoner. He also receives a certain fee from the city, one *baiocco* a month per shop from every craftsman, two per shop from the merchants, four from each hammam and mill, and one from each weaver. In addition to the profits from the town he owns a mountain where many people live, which brings in 7,000 ducats. But he is obliged to send 300 light cavalry when the king goes to war, and always keeps the horses and soldiers at his own expense.

The canon law judges get no wages, salary or remuneration, for it is forbidden in Muslim law for a judge to receive a salary, but they live on other salaries, either as lecturers in a madrasa, or imams in a mosque. It is the same for the public defender. The prosecutors are drawn from the summoners,[78] who are common and uneducated men. The judges have a prison for debtors and others jailed for minor misdeeds. There are four police chiefs, each with an office for his men, and they conduct searches from midnight until two in the morning. The chiefs and their men receive no salary except for the arrests, and some small fines that they keep, but they can all work as tavern keepers, brothel keepers and pimps. The governor has no auditors, judges or notaries of his own, but passes judgement according to his own whims, without learning or knowledge.

The city has only one official who runs both the customs office and the tax office, and he pays the king's treasury eighty ducats a day. He keeps guards and notaries at each gate; small items are taxed at the gate, but larger goods are brought from the gate to the customs office accompanied by one of the guards, who earns one *baiocco* per load, while the notary earns a *quattrino*. Sometimes the guards travel far out of town to meet the mule-drivers and bring them to the customs office so they cannot hide anything; those who cheat the office, if caught, have to pay double duty. The ordinary customs payment is two and a half per cent, except for carnelian, on which a quarter of the value is paid, but no tax is paid on wood, grain, cows and chickens. Likewise, the butchers pay no tax on their lambs at the gate, paying duty in the butchery instead, around eleven *baiocchi* per lamb. They pay another *baiocco* to the governor of the squares – that is, the chief consul[79] – who keeps a court of a dozen men and often goes around town on horseback to inspect the bread and other things for sale, weigh the bread and test the butchers' weights. If he discovers an underweight loaf he will tear it into pieces and have it sold for almost nothing, before beating the seller on the neck until he is puffed up. Likewise, if he should find a dealer's weights lighter than they should be, he beats him at once and parades him through the town. The king bestows this office on men chosen by the burghers; in the past it was usually a learned man, but now the rulers give it to common, ignorant men.

The inhabitants of the city, or at least the burghers, are very cultured. In winter the rich wear foreign wool fabrics: a tunic over the shirt with short, narrow sleeves, and over that a broad

jacket fastened in front, and over that a cloak called a burnous. They wear simple caps on their heads, like those worn in Italy at night but without covering the ears; over that they wind cloth fabrics twice around their head and beard. They do not wear long or short socks, but they do wear cloth trousers or breeches, except when they go on journeys, when they wear boots. Lower-class men wear tunics and burnouses without jackets, and no cloth on their heads but a wretched cap. The scholars and elder burghers wear jackets with wide sleeves like those worn by Venetian gentlemen who are officials. The common people, that is, the lowest class, wear clothes of coarse white local wool and burnouses of the same kind.

The women are well dressed, but in the warm season they wear only a blouse with a tight cloth around their forehead, and very awkward belts. In winter they wear ample dresses with wide sleeves, sewn in front like men's robes, but outdoors they wear long trousers covering the whole leg, and a cloth in the Syrian style that covers their whole clothing and person. They hide their faces with a piece of cloth, leaving only their eyes uncovered, but they wear large gold earrings with pretty gems, while those of a lower class wear silver without gems. They also wear a gold or silver bracelet on each wrist, each weighing a hundred ducats; others wear them on their ankles.

[2.2.2.12.9. Food]

As for food, the common people eat fresh meat two days a week, but the burghers eat well every day, depending on their means and appetite. They eat three meals a day, but breakfast is very light: just bread, fruit and a soup made with wheat flour and more liquid than that made elsewhere. In winter, instead of soup, they make liquid spelt cooked with salted meat. At midday they eat only light things like bread, salted meat, cheese or olives. In summer they eat a good meal during the day, and at night a very light supper, such as bread with melon, grapes or milk. In winter they have a good supper at night, namely, boiled meat with a kind of food called couscous; this is made of a confetti-like pasta, steamed in a pot with a perforated base above another pot,[80] then mixed with butter and soaked in broth. They do not eat roast meat. Couscous is the staple of the common people like the craftsmen and poorer burghers. But rich men, such as the elder burghers, the merchants and courtiers, live better, and the rulers live sumptuously.

By comparison to the rulers of Europe, however, life in Africa seems very lowly and wretched, not from a lack of goods but from a lack of manners. For they eat sitting on the ground from low tables without tablecloths; nobody uses a napkin, and they eat couscous or some other food from a communal dish. They eat with their hands, without spoons, putting the soup and meat together in a dish; each person takes a piece of meat and places it before him without cutting it, then picks it up with his hands and bites into it without using a knife. They eat very fast without drinking; only when they have had enough food do they take a cup or mug of water. This is the common practice, but learned and wealthy men are more refined; nevertheless, an Italian gentleman is more refined than any ruler of Africa.

[2.2.2.12.10. Wedding customs[81]]

When it comes to marriage, the people of Fez have a custom that when the bride's father promises his daughter to a man, the groom's father, if he has one, invites all his friends to the church,[82] bringing two notaries to draw up the contract for the dower[83] and gifts from the husband to the wife. The middling burghers will generally give thirty ducats in cash, a black slave-woman worth fifteen ducats, a piece of fabric made of multicoloured silk and linen like a bag,[84] and some other, smaller silk items to wear on the head. They will also give two pairs of well-decorated slippers, two pairs of handkerchiefs, silver mirrors and many other little trifles such as combs, perfumes and pretty fans. When the notaries have written up the contracts and both parties have agreed, the husband holds a feast for all the men in his house, giving them bread fried in oil with roast meat or honey. He also sends some of the food at home to the bride's house, and her father invites his friends to feast on the groom's gifts.

When the contracts have been inscribed in a document, the bride's father will splash out on clothes and adornments for her. Whatever he spends of his own money is out of kindness, for he doesn't have to spend anything but the money given to the husband; however, it is a great shame for a burgher to give his daughter nothing but the dowry and goods for her husband. The current custom is that someone who has set aside thirty ducats for his daughter's dowry should add 300 ducats of his own for clothes and household furnishings, though he will not give a house, vineyard or farm. To his daughter he will typically give: three outfits of fine fabric and another three of silk, taffeta, satin or damask, along with many elaborate blouses and cloaks with

strips of silk on either side, as well as embroidered pillows and cushions; eight mattresses, four for decoration on the cupboards at the sides of the rooms, two of coarse wool for the bed, and two of leather also for decoration; a coloured pile rug twenty cubits or so long, which they fold and put over the mattress; three wool-stuffed coverlets eight cubits in length, smooth on one side and rough on the other, one of which they fold on the bed, putting one part underneath and the other above; another three coverlets embroidered with silk on both sides and stuffed with cotton, which they keep as decoration in their rooms; a white coverlet stuffed with cotton used as a light cover in warm weather; and, finally, a pretty sheet of fine wool fashioned in patches worked in

flames and other designs, and furnished with fringes of gilded leather, over which hang silk tufts in various colours and silk buttons
to hang the sheet on the wall with nails. This is all to repay the
dower of thirty ducats and a slave-woman. But the larger the
dower the husband gives, the more the bride's father will owe in
return, and many burghers encounter difficulties on this account.
It is said in Italy that Muslims have the custom of the husband
giving his wife a dower, but they do not know just how much a
girl can ruin her father in any land.

When the husband wishes to take his bride home, she is carried in a sort of wooden box with eight sides, covered with
beautiful sheets of silk and embroidered cloth, and lifted on the
heads of bearers; they go accompanied by friends of her father
and of the groom, with an abundance of pipers and trumpets
and tambourines and torches. The groom's friends walk in
front with the torches and musicians, while the father's friends
walk behind; they proceed from the bride's house to the groom's
via the main square next to the mosque, and, when the bride
arrives at the square, the groom and two of his companions go
to greet her father and other family.

Then she is brought to his house, and he goes ahead into the
bedroom; when she enters the house, her father or brother or
uncle accompanies her to the bedroom door and delivers her
to the groom's mother. As the bride enters the room, the
groom puts his foot over hers and they close the door. Then the
other family members join the banquet, leaving only one spe-
cially selected woman; when the groom has deflowered his
wife, he brings her bloody underwear[85] out to the woman, who
inspects it and takes it away, calling and singing out and telling all the guests at the banquet that the bride has been
deflowered and showing them the blood. The groom's family
all tip the woman and leave, accompanied by other women or
effeminate men making music all the way home; then the
mother and sisters tip the woman and her companions. If it is
discovered that the bride is not a virgin, the husband will send
her back to his father's house and the wedding is ruined; the
guests leave without eating, and there is a great shame for the
bride's family.[86]

They hold three wedding banquets at the groom's house: the first on the night the bride is led forth, the second the evening after – but only for the women – and the third on the seventh day after the bride is led forth. The bride's father and mother attend this banquet, along with all her other family, and her father sends great gifts of sweets and whole roast lambs; the husband also provides a spread of his own and invites many guests, both women and men. He has not left the house since the day his bride was led forth, but today he leaves home and goes to the square to buy fish and bring it home; his mother or another woman throws the fish on the couple's feet as a good omen, according to the ancient custom.

The father of the bride holds two banquets. The first is on the day before they send away their daughter; in the evening the mother invites all her friends and dances all night. The next morning, certain women visit who are skilled in the art of adorning brides; some comb her hair, others braid it in a pretty way. They take a red pigment and darken her hands and feet with beautiful designs, but the colour does not last long. On that day they hold the banquet and have the bride stand up on a platform to be admired by all the women, who then tip those who have so expertly adorned her. Then she is brought to her husband in the box, as described above.

On the day the husband leads out his bride, all his close family and friends send large vessels of bread fried in oil, cheese bread with honey, and whole roast lambs. The groom sends for many guests and feasts them with these gifts. At the people's dance, the musicians and singers sit together and the singers sing and the musicians respond and the guests dance one by one; once each person has danced, he takes a coin worth a *baiocco* out of his mouth and throws it on the singers' carpet. A friend who wants to honour a dancer has him kneel down, setting many of these coins on his face, and the singers collect them. And so it goes, one after another, until the morning, for they stay up all night. The women do just the same, but they do not dance with the men, nor are their female singers and musicians permitted to be in the presence of men. This is the wedding custom when the bride goes to the groom's house a virgin.

If she is a widow she is led out with less fanfare; they provide boiled beef, lamb and chicken to eat, but mixed with various soups, and they put twelve bowls in a large wooden tureen for a dozen or so to eat together. This is the custom of the burghers and merchants. The poorer classes offer instead a stew made from a flatbread as thin as a sheet of lasagne soaked in a meat broth, into which they put a lot of hot butter and meat cut into large chunks; ten or so people eat with their hands without spoons, from a single dish, so there is less ceremony and expense.

They also hold banquets when they have a son, especially on the seventh day. When they circumcise him, the father calls the barber and feasts his friends, and at the end of the meal each friend gives the barber money: some a ducat, others a half or a quarter, according to their means. The money is not paid together but individually; they place the coins on the face of a boy that the barber keeps by him, and, while each is giving the money, one of the barber's servants or someone else loudly calls out the giver's name and thanks him. When each person has finished, he gives the crier two or three coins and the next begins; so it goes with each in turn until everyone is done. Then the barber gets up, collects his money and circumcises the son. They hold a dance for the men and another for the women, as above. For daughters there is less to be cheerful about.

[2.2.2.12.11. Feasts, customs and funerals]

A few traces of the Christian holidays remain in the city, on which days the townsfolk have certain practices that they themselves do not understand. On the first day of the Christian year the young boys put on masks and go around the burghers' houses, asking for fruit and singing songs. That night they cook all their beans together – fava beans, chickpeas, lentils, as well as grain – and eat it instead of confectionery. On Christmas Eve they eat a soup made of seven kinds of vegetables, such as cabbage, turnips, carrots and other greens. On the feast of St John[87] they buy straw and build bonfires in every district, both day and night. When a boy starts teething, his family holds a banquet for the other children, and they call this ceremony *tiendentilla*, a Latin word.[88] They have many other customs and omens that the author has seen in Italy, especially Rome, and their feasts are set down and required by law, as seen in the present work below on 'The Laws and Religion of Muhammad'.

When one of their husbands or family members dies, the women get together, take off their clothes and put on sacks, rubbing their faces with mud or cooking grease or swamp dirt. They summon those accursed men who wear women's clothing to beat large drums and sing improvised verses on the dead man's life and virtues. At the end of each verse, the man's family wail in a loud voice, beating their chests and cheeks until blood gushes out, and pulling their hair out. This lasts for seven days, and then they stop for forty days before renewing their lamentations for another three days. Such is the custom among the rulers and men of high rank. But the burghers lament honourably without beating themselves; their friends all go to comfort them and the close family sends gifts of food, for there is no cooking in the dead man's house. It is not the custom there for women to accompany the dead man, even if it is their father or brother. The offices and ceremonies performed in washing and burying the dead bodies are discussed below in 'The Laws of Muhammad'.

[2.2.2.12.12. Pigeons]

In the city are certain vain men who keep pigeons in cages like apothecaries' cabinets, each in its own compartment, on the roofs of their homes; they open the cages once in the morning and once in the evening, and the pigeons fly about, mingling with those belonging to others. The luckier owners manage to catch pigeons coming over from their neighbours; they don't keep them to breed, but only to enjoy them. The birds that fly more are worth more, and some are worth a ducat or more, and their owners know it. These men have many disputes out of love for the pigeons. In the middle of the charcoal-merchants' square are seven or eight shops selling these pigeons. Those who keep them at home have little nets fastened to rings made of thin sticks which they tie to long canes; they stand up on their roofs enjoying their pigeons with these nets in their hands, and, when they see a neighbour's pigeon pass by, they grab it with the net if they can. Most of the rulers keep these pigeons, but also men of lower classes.

[2.2.2.12.13. Games and fighting]

Respectable men in the city do not indulge in games except chess, according to the old custom. There are games of other kinds, but they are idle things only enjoyed by the lower classes. Sometimes the youths gather in the evening and duel with sticks, and the youths of one district will duel with the others, provoking heated arguments until they bring weapons to stab and kill each other, especially on feast days when they duel outside town. Late at night, they throw rocks, and the police chief and court come to separate them but never can; if they catch one they jail and beat him, and parade him through the town. The gangs congregate at night, crossing the gardens and farms outside town, and when those from one district encounter others they get into armed fights and kill each other, so there is always a wild, thoughtless hatred between them. If one is arrested by the court he will suffer an unimaginable punishment.

[2.2.2.12.14. Poetry]

The city is home to many poets who compose in the common tongue; their poems are on various subjects, but especially on love, and, just as they sing of their love for women, so also they describe their love for boys, publicly and without shame, some-times even mentioning the boys by name. Every year on Muhammad's birthday,[89] each of them composes a song in praise of Muhammad, and they gather from morning to evening in the chief consul's square, getting up on the consul's seat and reciting their songs in turn before a crowd of people. When they have finished they judge who has recited best, and the winner they make chief poet for that year.

But it was all a more splendid affair in the time of the Marinids.[90] The king would hold a banquet in a great hall for all the scholars and men of letters, drawing up a list of all the elegant poets in his kingdom; each poet would get up on a stage before the king and all his guests and recite a song of 100 or 150 verses in praise of Muhammad and of the king. The best poet, in the judgement of those present, received a hundred ducats, a horse, a slave-woman and a robe of the king's livery; the others received fifty ducats each. However, due to the kingdom's decline, it has been fifty years since they stopped holding this event.

[2.2.2.12.15. Schools]

In the city are around 200 schools for boys, each of which is a large hall with steps around it for the boys to sit on. The master teaches them to read and write, using tablets instead of books, and each day they learn a short section of the Qur'an. When they have finished the Qur'an, in two or three years, they go over it again so that, by the end of his seven years at school, a boy has learned the whole book by heart. Then the master teaches them a little spelling, though spelling and grammar are also studied in the madrasas along with the other arts.

The masters receive a miserable salary of around two *baiocchi* a month per student, but when a student reaches a certain part of the Qur'an his father has to give the master a large gift. When he has finished the entire Qur'an, the father holds a banquet for all the students of the school, and the son is dressed in princely clothes and rides a valuable horse, both lent out by the castellan of the royal city. All the schoolboys accompany the student on horseback to his house, and when they are inside they sing many songs in praise of God and his prophet Muhammad; then a dinner is held for the boys and all the father's friends, and each gives the schoolmaster something, and the father gives him new clothes. This is the custom of wealthy men, but the less well-off have a smaller ceremony.

The students hold a feast on Muhammad's birthday, and their fathers are obliged to give the school torches, so at dawn each boy brings a torch weighing thirty pounds, or more or less according to the father's means. The torches are well crafted and adorned with pretty flowers and waxen fruit, and they are kept burning until sunrise, while the schoolmaster brings in singers to recite in praise of Muhammad's birth. When the sun has risen, everyone returns home and the torches stay with the master, except the flowers, which he gives to the students and singers. This feast maintains the schoolmasters, for each torch is worth a fair amount, and each may be sold for the wax for a hundred ducats, or more or less depending on the student and the district. No master pays rent to the school, for the rooms are supplied by alms from various people for the sake of their souls. The students of the schools and madrasas take two days off a week, when they do not read, let alone study.

[2.2.2.12.16. Tanneries and fortune-tellers]

There are many leather tanneries in the city, but there is one larger than the others, where skins are sold at the door.[91] The customs officer has a station and office on the door to the tannery, taking four *baiocchi* for every ox skin and two for every ram skin. Inside are several fountains fed from a spring, and many workshops for the different masters, who pay a high rent for them, so the tannery can bring in 2,000 ducats profit. There are many other tanneries elsewhere, but none as rich as this one.

There are around 200 barbershops for trimming one's beard and shaving the sides of one's head, but they do not wash the head. Although they let blood, pull teeth and circumcise boys, they cannot dress wounds or the like.

There are also many fortune-tellers, who are of three kinds. The first tell fortunes by the art of geomancy. They keep rooms where the men and women who need their services go to find them; the fortune-tellers then make each person a drawing and they pay a certain amount for each figure. The second kind put water in a glass bowl with a drop of oil. The oil lingers like a mirror into which the fortune-tellers look, where they see demons gathering together as if in a camp. They say they see the demons behaving like men who, when they want to set up camp, put down tents and go for water and firewood. When the fortune-teller sees that the demons no longer have anything to do, he starts asking what he wants to know for his divination, and the demons answer him by gesturing with their hands and eyes. Then he weighs up just how gullible the customer is, and how much he can take them for. Some take a basin or jar and put a little oil on the hand of some boy or girl of around eight years old, and ask the children if they have seen the army of demons, and they answer, as children do, yes! Then the fortune-tellers ask them, one after another, if they have seen such and such, and they always say they have. But they never let the children say anything on their own. The crazy people who go to consult these fortune-tellers believe them and pay them good money.

The third kind are women who lead people to believe that they have red demons as lovers; some are called white demons and others black. Each of these women, when she wants to tell someone's fortune, puts on certain perfumes and the demon – that is, she says, her lover – enters into her and she changes her voice, pretending it is the spirit speaking. The customers then address the spirit with reverence and humility: 'O Sir So-and-So, I beg you to tell me what will happen regarding such and such!' The spirit gives the answer it pleases, and the questioner leaves a gift for it. But these women, in the view of good and learned people, are *suhaqiyat* or lesbians, who engage in the wicked practice of fucking each other.[92] When one of them is visited by a beauty and likes what she sees, she asks her to fuck, not in her own persona, but in that of the spirit. The woman agrees, thinking that the one fucking her is the demon lover, and that the fortune-teller is only there between them making it happen.

The women who desire this sort of thing first pretend to be ill, falling to the ground, so that their cuckold husbands call on the fortune-tellers for a cure for their wives. When they meet, the sick woman secretly offers herself to the fortune-teller who wants her to join her gathering. The fortune-teller leads the husband to believe that his wife has been possessed by a demon who wants her for a lover, and that, if he wants her cured, he should let her freely go and make merry with the fortune-teller. So the husband prepares a feast and gathers all these false women, inviting some Ethiopian musicians; when everyone has eaten, they begin to dance – not as women, but as demons, each changing her voice. Some wild women there jealously believe that the others have entered into the demons' good graces. After the feast, the woman goes as she pleases to tell fortunes for money like the others, and her husband consents to it all, being either taken for a fool or a poor man who agrees for the money, letting his wife earn as best she can. A decent man will not let himself be tricked; when his wife starts saying she is possessed by spirits or demons, he at once whips and beats her so soundly that neither spirits nor demons ever come back. Other men pretend that they are possessed by the demons' wives, merely for the excuse to have at it with the fortune-tellers, who join them in the guise of the male demons with whom they associate; others join the female demons who accompany the men.

[2.2.2.12.17. Exorcism and *za'irja*]

There is another group called *al-muʿazzimin*, that is, the enchanters; these are held to be able to free a person from spirits with their enchantments, or by giving him certain inscribed pages, or circles that they paint on paper and bid him wear against the spirits. Sometimes, if they are advanced in their wisdom and learning, they confront the demon, but, when they do not, they make the excuse that it is faithless or one of the celestial spirits. A better trick of theirs is to make remedies against the demons: they take braziers and write certain characters on them, drawing circles on the hand or forehead of the possessed, and perfuming them with many scents. Then they conjure the spirit to speak and to tell them where it has entered the person, and what its name and origin is; when the demon has replied, they conjure it to leave the body, and the spirit departs.

Another group of diviners are those who study the rule called *za'irja*[93] or kabbalah – not a scriptural but a natural sort of kabbalah, by which the diviners know the secret and future things that are asked of them. But the rule is very difficult, for whoever would trouble himself with the art will have to be an excellent reckoner and astrologer.

The author has watched them draw up a figure, which takes a whole summer's day. When they make these figures, they first draw a series of circles one within the other. In the first they draw a cross, marking at the edges the four sides of the universe: east, west, north and south. Inside the cross, that is, where its lines intersect, they mark the two poles, and outside the circle they mark the four elements. They divide the circle into four quadrants, the next circle also into four quadrants, and the next into seven parts, marking in each segment one of the twenty-eight Arabic letters, that is, seven per element. In the next circle they mark the seven planets, in the next the twelve zodiac signs, in the next the twelve months of the Latin year, in the next the twenty-eight lunar mansions, and in the last the 365 days of the year. Outside this they mark the four principal winds. They take only one letter from the thing asked about, which they multiply with all the things listed here. When they find out what number the letter signifies, they divide it into parts depending on what the letter is and in what element it lies, so that one number is left. After the multiplication, division and result, they see what letter agrees with the number left over, and they mark this resulting letter outside, performing the same operation on this discovered letter that they performed on the first one. They keep going, step by step, until they have generated twenty-eight positions or letters; then they combine these into words, and the words into sentences, that is, replies to the questioner. The answers are always given in verse in the first Arabic metre, called *at-Tawil*, which contains eight pegs and twelve cords according to the rules of metre, as will be seen in the *Arabic Grammar* in the final part of that work.[94] The true response to what was asked will be found in the generated verse, and then the answer on what will come is issued. They are never deceived in their divination – such an extraordinary thing that the author has never seen anything so far beyond nature as this.

He once saw a figure made in the courtyard of the Bou Inania Madrasa in Fez, which is paved with a fine, polished white marble. The space is fifty cubits square and two thirds of it were taken up by the things the figure required; three people made the figure, each in charge of one part of it, but it still took an entire day. Another he saw made by an accomplished master in Tunis, whose father had originated the rule in two volumes. Those who know the rule are very rare, so the author has only met three masters in his life, two in Fez and the one in Tunis, as well as two commentaries on the rule. One is by al-Marjani,[95] the father of the master I met in Tunis, the other by the chronicler Ibn Khaldun. If your lordships – or any other readers – would see the rule with its commentaries, it will set you back at least fifty ducats, for the book is in Tunis near Italy. The author has been too lazy to learn the rule, even though he has had plenty of time and a master who agreed to teach him for free; he refused because it is forbidden by the Muslim theologians as a dishonourable science. It is almost a heresy, for their scriptures are full of passages warning that all divination from texts is vain and that nobody knows future and secret things but God alone. Sometimes their inquisitors jail and persecute those who trouble themselves with this science.[96]

[2.2.2.12.18. Sufism]

There is a group of people in the city called the Sufi, meaning the wise and moral teachers.[97] These men observe certain rules over and beyond the majority commanded by Muslim law, and they are reputed to be orthodox by some theologians, while others grant them little credit; the common people, however, hold them to be saints, even though they treat certain things as licit which are prohibited by Muslim law. For instance, singing love songs with the musical rule is forbidden in Muslim law, but the Sufis treat it as licit.

They adhere to various orders, some stricter than others, each with a sheikh[98] of its own; they also have scholars who defend the orders with many works on the spiritual life. This sect began eighty or so years after Muhammad, and the first and most famous member was al-Hasan ibn Abi al-Hasan of Basra,[99] who gave his disciples rules but wrote nothing down. A century later there was a most talented master named Harith ibn Asad[100] of Baghdad, who wrote a fine work for all his disciples. The sect was subsequently attacked and banned by jurists close to the caliphs, and all those in it were threatened with punishment if they were found to be observing the rule.

After eighty years there arose another talented man belonging to the sect, followed by many disciples; he began to preach publicly and was therefore accosted with his disciples by the caliph's jurists. The jurists all ruled against them, sentencing them to execution by beheading, and the caliph confirmed the judgement. When the preacher heard the news, he sent one of his own thumbs, begging the caliph's grace to hold an assembly of the jurists and order a disputation between them in his presence; if he should lose, he would willingly die, but if he should win it would not be honourable for the caliph to order so many killed. The caliph agreed to the request. When they disputed together, the jurists were defeated by the preacher, who at once began to declaim against them, adducing many passages of their scripture, until with a great cry the caliph converted to the sect and the preacher and his disciples were freed.

After this the sect grew and the caliph had many monasteries and madrasas built for their successors; they remained in favour for a century until Malik Shah (I), an emperor of the Seljuk Turks who was hostile to the sect, invaded from Asia Minor. He immediately expelled many Sufi scholars; some went to Cairo, others to Arabia, and they remained in exile for twenty years until the reign of Caselsah, Malik Shah's grandson, who appointed a grand vizier named Nizam al-Mulk, a member of this sect.[101] Then he wrote to all the exiles that they should soon return, and when they did the vizier had an enormous madrasa built, with many study rooms for the law students, and another just as large as this for the Sufis. He sent to Asia Major for talented lecturers, among whom was al-Ghazali,[102] an expert in law, Sufism and all the other disciplines. On the vizier's request and of his own goodwill, al-Ghazali wrote a very influential work of five large volumes reconciling the laws with Sufism;[103] he showed it to the vizier, who immediately commanded it to be read publicly in the presence of many jurists and Sufis, and none of the jurists dared criticise anything. The vizier held a huge banquet and invited the lecturers, scholars and students of either side, making them all dine together; then he delivered an excellent speech advocating peace between the two sides, and all agreed, so they drew up contracts and legal articles and became brothers. The jurists were given the title of *erectors* and *upholders* of the Prophet's law, while the Sufis received the title of *interpreters* and *authors* of the Prophet's law and religion. The peace lasted until Baghdad was ruined by the Tartars[104] in AH 656 (AD 1258–59), but this did not harm the sect at all, for by then they were spread out all over the world, that is, across Africa and Asia.

Back then, nobody entered the sect but very capable men who had studied every subject, especially scripture, to practise defending the opposite side in debate. For the past century, by contrast, the sect has been full of ignorant fools. They say no learning or knowledge is needed to join the sect, since the Holy Spirit directs those with a pure heart and a good will; they adduce weak reasons for this, abandoning all the necessary and important commandments of the Sufi rule. They worship just like the jurists, but take great pleasure in things permitted by the law: they hold banquets and sing beautiful love songs and poems, dancing together at the banquet. Some of these boors tear their clothes in accordance with the verses they sing and the violent movements of their hearts. They say that those who wail and tear their garments do it under the influence of the gifts of divine love, and under this pretext they often fall to the ground when they dance. As far as the author is concerned, he does not believe a word of this feeble excuse, for he has often found himself at such feasts and never seen one of them with any trace of divine love. They all eat for three and are notorious gluttons.

When they are to marry, good men – that is, the educated and honourable burghers – hold a banquet for a sheikh and his disciples out of their good faith. At first the Sufis will play the wise man, reciting prayers and divine songs until they have eaten, when they start to wail and lament, tearing their clothes; they pretend to do this out of divine love, but in the author's judgement they do it for the love of the beardless youths who follow them in the hopes of joining their disciples. The sheikh and senior disciples are served by them when they eat, and if a disciple falls during the dance, the young men will pick him up and wipe the sweat from his face, and sometimes kiss him. As far as it is possible to judge, they do such things for the love of these little boys, and there is a proverb in Fez that testifies to their vice: 'like the hermits' banquet, when twenty are turned into ten', since at night after the dance, when they want to sleep, each of the disciples knows another's touch. They are reputed to be hermits, for they neither take wives nor practise any trade, leaving everything to chance. A thousand particulars are narrated in the commentary on the story of al-Hariri,[105] but for many reasons it would be dishonourable to repeat them in this work.

[2.2.2.12.19. Sufism continued]

Sufis adhere to some tenets held to be heretical by the rule of the theologians and jurists, for they differ from the others not only in legal matters but also in religion, holding that a man can become like the angels by good works, fasting and abstinence. By such manifest acts his intellect and heart will be so purified that he cannot sin even if he wants to, but only once he has climbed fifty steps of learning; even if he sinned before climbing the fifty steps, God will not hold it for a sin. The Sufis also have strange fasts, at the start of which they indulge in all the world's pleasures. They have a strict rule set out in a work of four volumes by a master of eloquence, as-Suhrawardi[106] of Suhraward, a city in Khorasan. Another of their scholars, Ibn al-Farid, put all their learning into exquisite allegorical verses that seem to be entirely about love, but al-Fargani's commentary finds in them the rule and the steps one should climb.[107] The poet was so talented that all the Sufis sing his verses at their banquets, and in 300 years there has never been an elegance like his.

The sect holds that the spheres, firmament, elements, planets and stars are God, and that no religion or faith is mistaken, for all people in their soul and mind seek to adore that which deserves adoration. They also hold that knowledge of God is restricted to the *qutb*, a man chosen and directed by God; in his knowledge he is like God. There are in the sect forty men of lesser rank and knowledge called *al-watad* or 'pillar'; when the *qutb* dies, another comes from the forty. There are seventy men of lesser rank again, and when one of the forty dies another comes from the seventy. And there are a further 765 men with a title the author has forgotten, but when one of the seventy dies another comes from the 765, although they are all unknown.

It is held in the rule that each of this number should live in the world incognito, or like a madman, a great sinner or a pimp. Under the protection of this rule, many crooks in Africa go around naked, showing off their privates and having their way with women, in the middle of the square in public like animals, without any fear; they too are thought saints by the common people. A large number of these people are found in Tunis and Egypt, especially Cairo. In the Bain al-Qasrayn square in Cairo, the author saw one grab a beauty leaving the hammam, lay her down in the middle of the square and have it off with her in full view of the people – he even saw the semen spurt from his prick. They prayed to God to grant this saint grace and blessing, that he might father some perfect creature for the world, and some said he only pretended to commit the crime but didn't actually do so. The moment he left the woman, everyone ran to touch her clothes in their devotion, because she had been touched by a saint. Some went to give the husband the good news and congratulate him, and so the next day the fool held a great banquet for many sheikhs of various orders, and did this as great alms, thanking God for such a blessing. The judges and scholars wanted to keep this saint in prison to interrogate and punish him, but the people rose up and the officials were in danger of being killed, because the crooks have great credit among the masses, who bestow great gifts on them. The author has seen particular things that, being a modest person, he will pass over and not mention at all.

[2.2.2.12.20. Kabbalah]

Among the Sufis is a still worse group or order resembling kabbalists; they keep strange fasts, eat no meat, and their food, clothing and bedding are determined for them. For each hour of the day or night they have particular prayers depending on the day and month, and they seem to select the prayers by means of number. They carry about their person certain square tablets painted with characters or carved numbers, and they say that good spirits appear to them and speak with them, imparting knowledge about the whole universe. There was a very capable scholar among them called al-Buni, who established the prayers and the rule for how they should make these tablets.[108] The author has seen several of his works, of which there are eight in total, and which they hold to be closer to magic than to kabbalah. The most famous is called *al-Lumaʿ al-nūrāniyya*, that is, *The Illumination of the Light*, where the prayers and fasts are established. Another is *Shams al-Maʿarif*, that is, *The Sun of the Sciences*, which contains the directions for making the squares and their uses. A third is *Sharh al-Asma al-Husna*, that is, *The Power of the Ninety-Nine Names of God*, which the author once saw in Rome in the hands of a Venetian Jew.[109]

Another order of that sect is the *suwwah* or hermits, who live alone in the woods or mountains, usually living on wild fruit and vegetables; nobody can understand the particulars of their existence, because they live like wild animals and want nothing to do with mankind.

Having spent a little more time discussing this sect, it will now be fitting to return to the topic of the work. The subject is better treated in the works of a scholar named al-Akfani,[110] who described all the different sects that come from the Muslim religion; there have been seventy-two principal sects, each holding itself to be the good and true one by which a person can be saved. But today there are only two: that of al-Ashʿari, which extends all over Africa, Egypt, Syria, Arabia and all of Turkey, and that of Imamia, which extends over Persia and some towns in Khorasan ruled by the Sophy, king of Persia.[111]

Almost all of Asia has been destroyed by the latter sect, for although those lands used to follow al-Ash'ari the Sophy sought to establish his own sect there by force of arms. Other sects can be found in the world, but none compares to these two.

[2.2.2.12.21. Treasure seekers]

There are certain men in Fez called *al-kennazin*,[112] who spend their time seeking treasure in the foundations of ancient buildings. They also leave the city to explore many caves and caverns in search of treasure, in the belief that when the Romans lost control of Africa and fled to Baetica, they could not gather up all their goods or money and so buried their valuables. For this reason these lunatics go looking for enchantments for the treasure, for, although they all boast of seeing ducats and silver in the caves, the fools say they have been unable to reach them because they lack scents or enchantments. They cause much damage in the night: sometimes they dig up the foundations of property or tombs, suspecting them to be places of treasure, and they have books that name mountains, caves and ruins containing treasure, according to their fantasy. They sometimes journey from Fez for ten or twelve days to find these treasures.

When the author left Fez they appointed a consul and made their trade public; if they wanted to dig up some place, they would first go and ask for permission from the owner, and afterwards account for all the damage they had done. The author had some dealings with these people, and especially with their consul; he found them a truly foolish and ignorant bunch, for their minds were filled with impossible things, and he often accompanied them to see their folly and misjudgement for himself.

[2.2.2.12.22. Alchemists]

There are many alchemists in Fez, constantly at work on that vain folly of theirs and always going around filthy and unclean, smelling of sulphur and other horrible odours. Every evening they gather in the great mosque, secretly discussing their empty fantasies among themselves; they have many works on that art written by eloquent men who can make the false true with their tongue. The first is by Jabir,[113] who lived a century after Muhammad and was said to be a Greek convert; his works are widely read, but only as allegories. Another who wrote a great work was at-Tughrai, the minister of one of the sultans of Baghdad, as is discussed above in more detail in *The Lives of the Arabic Philosophers*. They have another work in verse on the articles of the art by a master from Baetica named al-Mugairibi;[114] a commentary was written on this by a mamluk from Damascus who was a scholar of that art, but it is harder to understand than the text itself.

The city's alchemists are divided into two groups: the first seek the *elixir*, that is, the matter contained in every metal and mine, and the second seek the multiplication of metals by mixing one metal with another. In the end, however, they all become coiners of false money. How many there are in this city with only one hand! For when they are discovered to be counterfeiters, the law at once cuts off their hand.

[2.2.2.12.23. Mountebanks]

Then there are the mountebanks,[115] who go around singing the histories of battles and other subjects with their instruments: harps, viols and drums that are round like baskets. When they hear of a wedding in town, they show up uninvited to sing. When they sing in the squares, they often sell prescriptions against this or that disease, but all fake.

The basest, idlest fellows are a family who wander through the city with snakes in their hands, making monkeys dance, showing them off and reading women's palms; some make geomantic figures. They keep stallions that they take to the market outside town, and all the locals who want to impregnate their mares seek out and pay them; they set about at once to make the stallion erect, then manually put its cock in the mare. The stallions are amazing, sometimes worked eight or ten times a day; it is said they put certain herbs with this property in their fodder.

The people of Fez are mostly coarse, unfriendly and very rude. They do not talk to foreigners or even do them any kindness, although there is a good reason for this: there are few foreigners in the city, for it is 100 miles from the sea along a harsh and inconvenient route. There are some locals who are honourable and friendly, but not many. The rulers and their officials are even more proud and brutish, so they cannot criticise anyone on this front. The scholars and judges, to maintain their reputation, are very aloof: they have no dealings or conversation with the common people, nor with the rulers, to whom they will not condescend to speak, preferring their adversaries to look up to them. If any of them should interact with the rulers or receive gifts from them, they will lose all their honour and esteem in the eyes of the people.

In itself the city is very beautiful and well ordered, but in the rainy season there is so much mud that everyone has to wear clogs. They open certain channels of the canals that run through the districts and wash them clean, and in those areas without a canal their solution is to collect the mud on animals and take it to the river.

2.2.2.13. The suburbs of Fez

Having described many things inside the city, it now remains to discuss the things outside.

Outside the city to the west is a suburb of 500 homes, but these are primitive buildings crowded with a base sort of people: camel-herders, water carriers and woodcutters who accompany the king's camp. The suburb is very rough and dirty but well supplied with workshops for every kind of craftsman. All the mounte-banks and worthless musicians with their ridiculous instruments live here, and there are many public prostitutes, but they are crude and disgusting. Throughout the suburb are many large pits dug with iron tools, because it is in the travertine region where the pits were dug for the ruler's grain; at that time the only locals were there to guard the grain. After the wars died down they built granaries in New Fez, abandoning those outside the city; nevertheless, they are marvellous in size, and even the smallest holds 1,000 bushels of grain. There are around 150 pits, lying along the main road of the suburb. They are still uncovered today, and people have often fallen in, but recently walls have been built around the edges. The castellan of Fez, when he secretly executes criminals, throws their bodies in the pits, since there is a hidden door in the citadel that leads to the suburb.

There is a gambling den here, but they only play dice. Wine is openly sold and all the drunkards and criminals go there, since the mule-drivers for the king and rulers all live in the suburb and they are legally permitted prostitutes, gambling and wine, so the locals are free to give themselves a good time. After ten o'clock at night nobody is found in the shops, for they've all gone to dance and get drunk late into the evening.

Outside the city, to the north, is another suburb, where the lepers live; it has 200 homes, and the lepers have their elders and consuls who collect revenue from them. Many rulers and burghers, who have donated their property to support these lepers, no longer give anything or trouble themselves about their lives. The consuls and elders have the authority, when someone in Fez contracts the disease, to have them brought by force to live in the suburb, and, when one of them dies, half their possessions are given to the community of the suburb, and the other half to the dead man's creditors. If they have children, however, all the possessions go to them. They have certain laws and statutes beyond the usual ones. Those with morphoea, that is, white spots on their body, are also forced to live with the lepers, and if they have healthy children, the children can choose whether to live with their family in the suburb or to live in the city.

A quarter of a mile further is another suburb, inhabited by many mule-drivers, potters, brickmakers, woodcutters and those who work outdoors, but it has only fifty or so homes and the buildings are poor.

To the west, on the main road, is a large suburb of 400 homes also in crumbling buildings, all inhabited by poor peasants who will not or cannot live in the country. The nearby countryside stretches from the suburb two miles or so to the river, and three miles to the west; they hold a market here every Thursday, to which a huge number of men come with their livestock. The entire neighbourhood goes to spend money among the crafts-men and merchants of the city, all of whom arrive here with their goods and tents on market day. In the other part of the countryside, near the river and hospital, they sell goods from abroad, as well as livestock and horses. On that day it is a cus-tom among the burghers that three or four agree to buy a lamb between them, have it killed by a butcher, and divide it among themselves, paying the butcher with the head, offal or trotters, and selling the skin to the wool merchants next door. Little duty is paid on the goods sold in the market: one *baiocco* per ducat for horses; one *baiocco* for a hundred or more cattle, but noth-ing for fewer than a hundred; one *baiocco* per two ducats for camels; one *baiocco* per person for the merchants, craftsmen, cooks, greengrocers, fruiterers and mountebanks; and one *quat-trino* per jug or bottle of butter, honey or other liquid. The author has never seen a market in Africa, Asia or Italy thronged with so many people and goods, a quite unfathomable thing.

Outside the city, around a vast pit two miles wide, there are high cliffs from which they cut rocks to make lime. Inside the pit are many huge kilns where they heat the lime; one can hold 6,000 bushels, others more or less. This trade is run by rich burghers, but not nobles. To the west are a hundred huts next to each other on the banks of the river, owned by craftsmen who whiten cloth. They collect it in bulk from the merchants or weav-ers, and during periods of fine weather throughout the year they wash the cloth, laying it out on a meadow near the huts. When it is dry they use leather buckets with wooden handles to carry water from the river, or from little canals, and throw it over the cloth; in the evening they take the loads home to the city or leave them at the nearby hospital. The meadow where they spread out the cloth is verdant all year, and from a distance the lines of white cloth against the green of the meadow, and the clear blue of the river, make an exquisite sight. Many poets in Fez have written an epigram on the beauty of this charming greenery, truly demonstrating their great and noble wits and spirits.

[2.2.2.13.1. Common tombs]

Outside the city there are many fields where the dead are buried, donated by various burghers for the love of God. Each person is buried by himself, and over the grave they place a long, thin triangular stone, made by the masters appointed to dig and build the tombs, which is an art in its own right. Some notables receive marble tablets well fixed in the ground at their head and feet, and containing a few moral sayings along with verses of comfort and consolation for the hard and bitter stroke of death. Under these they put the dead man's name and family, and the date of his death. In his youth the author diligently noted down all the verses and sayings he could find on the epitaphs, and not only those of Fez but of all the others throughout the towns of Barbary he visited; he put them all in a work of many chapters on the grief, sadness and bitter fear of death, and gave it to the brother of the present king of Fez when their father the old king died.[116] Some of these verses are apt to give cheer and consolation for death, others to bring on melancholy and sadness, but one is bound to suffer either one or the other.

[2.2.2.13.2. Royal tombs]

Outside the city to the north is a beautiful building on a high hill where there are many tombs of the Marinid kings, fashioned of fine marble with gorgeous decorations; the epitaphs are written and engraved in marble, adorned with rich colours that amaze all who see them.

[2.2.2.13.3. Gardens and orchards]

To the north, east and south of the city are vast numbers of gardens of every sort of fruit; the trees are fat and tall, and streams from the river flow between them. The gardens are as dense as woods and their fields are not farmed, although they are irrigated in May so as to produce large numbers of succulent fruit, except the peaches, which are poor in colour and flavour. During the fruit season they are said to sell 500 loads a day, not counting the grapes, and the loads all go to a place in the city where they are taxed and sold at the fruiterers next door. In the same square they sell black slaves, and tax is also paid on them.

To the west of the city is a territory fifteen miles wide and thirty long, full of fountains and streams; it belongs to the great mosque, which rents it to gardeners to grow a great quantity of flax, melons, gourds, cucumbers, carrots, rapeseed, radishes, white cabbage and other crops. Every summer, it is estimated, 5,000 loads of fruit are gleaned from this territory, and the same amount again in the winter. But it is unhealthy in the summer, for all the gardeners and farmers have a sickly colour, and every year they contract fever and die in droves.

2.2.2.14. New Fez (Fes Jdid)

New Fez is a city surrounded by two very fine, high, strong walls, built in a splendid plain next to a river, around a mile west and a little south of Old Fez. Part of the river flows under the two walls, to the north near the mills, and the other part divides into two branches; one passes between New and Old Fez by the citadel, then through certain valleys and gardens by the old city until it reaches Old Fez in the south, while the other branch flows into the new city and beyond it through the Bou Inania Madrasa.

The builder of the city was Yaqub ibn 'Abd al-Haqq, the first king of the Marinid house; it was Yaqub who acquired the kingdom of Marrakesh and drove out its former kings. While he was at war with the king of Marrakesh,[117] the king of Tlemcen[118] gave him great trouble, pleasing the king of Marrakesh and preventing the Marinid house from rising any higher. Yaqub, after he had expedited the war of Marrakesh, planned revenge against the king of Tlemcen. But judging Marrakesh, where the royal fortress was, very far from Tlemcen, he decided to transfer the royal seat to Fez to be closer to his enemy, and so he caused the entire court of Marrakesh to depart, bringing with him many builders and architects. When they arrived, they at once began to build and to put walls up; he named it 'The White City',[119] but the common people called it New Fez. Once he had made the perimeter of the walls, he divided the city into three separate parts. In the first is the royal palace, along with the palaces of the king's sons and brothers with their gardens, and next to this a dazzling mosque, highly ornate and well planned. In the second part he built a huge stable for his horses, and many buildings for his generals and chief courtiers; in the district between the west and east gates he planned and built the town square which stretches for a mile and a half, where the shops of merchants and craftsmen of all kinds are. By the western gate of the inner wall is a huge colonnade and many smaller ones where the city guard and its soldiers live. Nearby are two impressive stables in which there are always 300 horses for the guard of the king's home. The third part of the city was set aside for the barracks of the king's personal guard of well-paid oriental archers, for there were no crossbows or guns back then.

In the town square are many beautiful mosques and hammams built at great expense. By the king's palace is the mint where they coin his money, laid out in a square around which are many little colonnades with the masters' cases and tools, and in the middle a large colonnade where the consul of the mint sits with his notaries. The mint is an office made for the king; he pays the masters, but the capital and earnings belong to him. Next to the mint is another square, like the one above, with the goldsmiths' workshops. It is their consul who keeps the stamp and form of the coins, and of all silver and gold items, for in Fez one cannot make rings or anything else from these metals without stamping them; if it is stamped it can be spent like money, that is, exchanged for its value, but if not, the money is wasted. Most of the goldsmiths are Jews who work in New Fez and take their wares to sell in their appointed square near the apothecaries in Old Fez. But one may not beat gold in Old Fez, or even find a Muslim to make such items for sale, because they say it is usury to sell things of silver or gold for more than their weight, although the rulers allow the Jews to do it. It is true that Muslim goldsmiths can be found, but they do not make goods for open sale, rather they work for the burghers and are paid for the manufacture.

The Jews currently inhabit the old quarter of the archers' guard,[120] since recent kings no longer maintain that guard. The Jews used to live in the old city, but they were badly treated by the Moors, who would rob and assault them whenever a king died, so King Abu Sa'id[121] made them move from the old city to the new with the agreement to double their tribute.[122] They have lived there with all their property ever since, endowed with a very long and wide square for all their merchants and trades, as well as many synagogues. The Jews in Fez have multiplied beyond number, especially after they were ruined and expelled by the king of Spain. They are held in contempt; they cannot wear shoes, but only slippers made from spiny rushes, and on their head they wear black turbans, while those who wear caps must also wear a piece of red cloth attached to the cap as a sign. They pay 400 ducats a month in total to the king of Fez.

In the space of forty years the city was furnished with strong walls and fine buildings and mosques, as well as a madrasa; some were built by the founder, others by his successors, and by his sons and grandsons, such that it is commonly believed that more was spent on the founding of the city than on the main walls. Over the river outside the city they have built huge wheels that lift the water over the walls, where it is conducted by canals to the buildings, gardens and mosques. The wheels are modern, put up only a century ago, but before that the water came to the city on an aqueduct, supported on beautifully worked arches, from a spring ten miles away. It is said that the aqueduct was built by a Genoese master who at that time was the king's favourite merchant,[123] and that the wheels were built by a Spanish master; they are truly marvellous things, especially the largest, which turns twenty-four times a day, receiving such speed from the water.

Not many noblemen live in the city, except the family of the rulers and certain courtiers. The rest are common and base officials, for the burghers and good people of Fez do not deign to be court officials or soldiers; they will not even give their daughters to those of the king's house.

2.2.2.15. The way of life in the court of the king of Fez

Of all the rulers in Africa, not one has ever been elected by the people, nor even called to the throne by a province or city; in fact, no secular ruler is legitimate in the law of Muhammad, except the caliph. After the power of the caliphs declined, all the chiefs of the desert peoples began to attack the inhabited lands and establish rule there by force of arms, against the law of their prophet Muhammad and their caliphs; just as in the Levant the Turks, Kurds, Tartars and Oghuz came from the east and took power, so the Zanata ruled in the Maghrib, then the Lamtuna, then the Preachers,[124] then the Marinids. It is true that the Lamtuna went to help the western peoples and free them from the heretics, assuming control as if to please the people; but all their rulers then became tyrants who displeased and scorned the people. For this reason, rulers today are not produced by a line of succession, nor elected by a general; instead, the ruling tyrant, on his deathbed, will make his generals and chief courtiers swear, almost by force, to appoint one of his sons or brothers their ruler, and they swear it either on their own free will or by force. When a ruler dies the chief courtiers sometimes choose the one he wanted, and sometimes the one who seems best to them, but, of course, they usually pick the most honourable, favoured, just and generous man. In these instances they choose the ruler neither according to the oaths sworn nor by recommendation, and the king of Fez is of this number.

When someone becomes king, he immediately appoints one

of his nobles as his chief vizier, to whom a third of the kingdom's revenue falls; then he appoints a minister who also serves as treasurer and major domo; then he appoints generals from the royal cavalry, who most often live in the countryside with their horses on guard. The king also appoints governors for each town, who collect all the profits and revenues but are obliged to keep a certain number of horsemen at the king's command at their own expense; in other words, every time the king wants to go with the camp, all the town governors go or send their cavalry and soldiers with him. Then the king appoints commissioners and administrators over the people living in the mountains, and also over the Arabs subject to them; these officials are entrusted with passing judgements according to the people's laws, while the administrators also have the job of collecting the revenues and keeping account of the ordinary and extraordinary payments.

The king keeps barons called 'guards' in their language, who each own a ksar or village or two, from which they collect revenues to support themselves and maintain their ability to accompany the king's army. He also keeps light cavalry whose expenses he pays directly while he is in the camp; when he is at home he gives out grain, butter and meat as a salary throughout the year, but very little money. On the other hand, he gives them clothing once a year, and they need not worry about their horses in the city, for the king provides them with everything. All the stable hands are Christian slaves with huge chains on their feet, but when the camp goes out the Christians ride the pack camels. Next, the king keeps a commissioner for his camels. This official gives deliveries to the shepherds and distributes the countryside among them; he also provides a number of necessities on behalf of the rulers, such as packsaddles for the camel-drivers. Every camel-driver keeps two pack camels in his charge, following his superiors' orders. The king also keeps a provisioner in charge of furnishing, guarding and dispensing food to the king and his army; he maintains ten or twelve large tents to store the goods, and continually arranges the camels in herds for carrying the supplies, so there is nothing lacking from the camp. Under the provisioner are the kitchen ministers and guards of the goods.

The king also keeps a stable master to provision and look after the horses, mules, stable hands and mule-drivers. He also keeps a commissioner for the fodder, in charge of furnishing all the king's horses and those of his soldiers; he orders the camel-drivers to bring barley when he sees that it is needed, and retains scribes and notaries to keep track of the dispensed fodder, passing on the accounts to the king's major domo.

The king also keeps a captain of fifty cavalry who serve as messengers to relay commands from the king's commissioner or secretary, on behalf of the king himself. He also keeps a very honourable general who serves as the captain of his private guard, and who commands officers on the king's behalf to carry out executions and confiscations, and to pass justice and arrest important men on the king's orders, imprisoning them and putting them to death. The king also keeps a faithful scribe at hand who holds his seal, writing and sealing letters without the king's involvement. The king keeps a large number of grooms, with a captain who hires and fires them, distributing the revenues and provisions among them according to their competence and service. Whenever the king gives audience the captain is present, ordering the grooms who are present to carry messages; he also serves in place of a magistrate and head servant.

The king also keeps a captain whose job it is to transport the king's private and communal tents, as well as those in which the king's light cavalry sleep; the royal tents are carried by mules, and those of the soldiers by camels. The king also keeps a troop of ensigns who carry his standards folded up and wrapped on journeys, with one going ahead of the whole army to carry a standard unfurled; it is the ensigns who know the routes, river crossings and forest passes.

The king also keeps a huge retinue of drummers, whose drums are wide above and narrow below, like a large copper pot with a skin stretched across the top. Because the drums are heavy they carry them on saddled horses with counterweights on the other side, using powerful coursers that can flee quickly if needed, since it is the worst disgrace for a ruler or general to lose a drum. The drums are played loud enough to be heard from a distance, and struck with bull pizzles, which they tan in such a way as to make a noise that frightens men and horses. The king does not keep trumpeters at his own expense, but those remaining in the city on the king's salary all year are obliged to send a number. The trumpeters sound at night when the king eats, and, likewise, when the army goes to war, they play at certain moments, sounding particular signals with which they communicate the general's intention to the soldiers.

The king keeps a master of ceremonies who, when the king holds a council or gives audience, is always standing by to maintain order and make each person speak in turn, according to their rank and title. The servants of the king, including the domestics, are mostly black slaves. He also keeps white women as wives, and white Christian slave-women, either Spanish or Portuguese, and all these women are under the guard of the eunuchs, who are also black slaves.

The king has a large kingdom but receives little revenue from it, scarcely amounting to 300,000 ducats, and he does not retain even a fifth of that, instead handing it all over to his generals, cavalry, city governors and other guards and retinue. Almost half of his revenues come in grain, livestock, oil and butter, and they are collected in different ways: some places pay a ducat and a quarter for each field large enough to be ploughed by two oxen, other councils and places, especially in the mountains, pay a ducat a year per home, other places pay a ducat and a quarter a year for each person of fifteen years old or more, other places pay both. There is no other tax except that paid in the large cities.

It should be noted that, according to the Muslims, no ordinary revenues or payments to secular rulers are licit on any account,[125] except the duty ordained by Muhammad of two and a half ducats per hundred earned by each person.[126] Whoever harvests ten bushels of grain from his fields has to give a tithe – a tax and duty sent directly to the caliph, who distributes it for the common good, providing for the poor, sick and widowed, and spending it in wars against their enemies.[127] But after the caliphate declined in power, the secular rulers and tyrants began to distribute these revenues according to their own whims and desires; and they did not stop there, but established further tributes and payments, with the result that there are few country dwellers in Africa who can even clothe themselves and their family. Because of this injustice and injury, no good man or scholar or man of conscience will ever have dealings with the secular rulers, or eat at their table, or even accept their presents and gifts, for all legal experts hold that the rulers' possessions are as good as stolen.

The king of Fez always keeps at his command 6,000 paid cavalry, 500 crossbowmen and 500 gunmen on horseback. In times of peace they are kept separate from him, but thousands always remain with him when he stays out in the country, likewise 100 crossbowmen and 100 gunmen, although he doesn't worry about a guard when in Fez. When he goes to war with the Arabs and his other enemies, his 6,000 cavalry are not enough, so he brings a large number of his Arab subjects at their own expense, and they have more experience in combat than the king's own cavalry. The king rarely does anything with pomp and ceremony, and then unwillingly, but on feast days or at great parades he has no choice.

When he wishes to ride, the master of ceremonies first communicates it, via the king's messengers, to his family, generals, guards and other cavalry, and they all gather in the square in front of his palace, spilling out into the nearby areas. When he leaves the palace, the messengers first dictate the riding order: in front go the flagbearers, then the drummers, then the stable master with his ministers, then the guards, then the master of ceremonies, then the king's ministers, the treasurer, the master of the mint, the judge and the general, then the king himself with his grand vizier and some princes. Ahead of the king's person are certain officers on horseback, one carrying his sword, another his shield and another his crossbow. Around him are grooms, one carrying his spear, another the saddle cover, halter and other coverings which, like the halter, are beautiful; when the king dismounts, they cover the saddle and put the halter over the horse's bridle to hold it. Another groom carries his shield and another his rapier, along with the king's clogs for ceremonies. Behind the king rides the captain of the grooms, then the eunuchs, then the house servants, then the captains of the company, then the light cavalry, then the crossbowmen and gunmen.

The king is moderate and honourable in his dress; those who do not recognise him will not believe he is the king, for those around him dress ostentatiously. None of the Muslim kings or rulers wears a crown or anything similar, for it is prohibited in Muslim law. When the king is in the country, he first has the great tent put down in the middle. This is a square with sides fifty cubits long resembling the walls of a castle with their battlements; at each corner is a cloth turret with painted battlements and a roof threaded with pretty golden balls.[128] The great tent has four gates, each with a guard of eunuchs, and in the middle are smaller tents, and the wooden chamber where the king sleeps, which is designed to be put together and taken apart. Around the great tent are the lodgings of the officers and favourite courtiers, and around them in turn are the guards' tents, made of goatskin like those of the Arabs. In the midst of these are the pantry, kitchen and mess, which are all very large tents, and nearby are the tents for the light cavalry, who eat wretchedly in the royal mess. A little way off are the king's stables, uncovered courtyards where the horses are kept tethered in neat rows. The royal mule-drivers stay beyond the perimeter of the tents, and they serve as the camp's butchers, grocers and haberdashers. The merchants and craftsmen travelling with the camp all lodge next to the mule-drivers. The king's lodgings therefore resemble a city, with the guards' tents serving as walls, since they are fixed together; if someone wanted to enter the enclosure he could do so only at the appointed places.

At night, a great guard is set up around the king's tent, but they are base men and none of them carries a single weapon; likewise, there is another guard around the stables, but often the guards fall asleep and the horses are stolen. Men have often been arrested inside the king's tent who, knowing his guards' idleness, came to kill him at the behest of his enemies. The king will be found in the countryside for almost the whole year, looking after his kingdom and keeping his Arab subjects at peace; he spends all day playing chess or hunting in the country with his hounds, hawks and eagles.

The author has certainly been a little long-winded in order to discuss Fez fully; it must not be thought that he meant to bore his readers, but he found it appropriate to use this method to discuss all the culture and elegance of Barbary and all of Africa.

2.2.2.16. Maqarmada

Maqarmada is a city forty miles east of Fez, built by Zanata rulers on the banks of a stream in a splendid plain. In ancient times it had a sizeable countryside and was highly cultured, with a sweep of gardens and vineyards along the stream. The king of Fez would give the city as a provision to his commissioners of the camels, but it was sacked and abandoned in the war of Prince Sa'id, and today there is nothing left but the walls. Its territory was and still is rented out by the burghers of Fez and by peasants.

2.2.2.17. Al-'Ubbad, Fez

Al-'Ubbad is a ksar situated on the side of a high mountain six or so miles from Fez. The whole city of Fez and its countryside can be seen from this ksar, which was founded by a hermit reputed to be a saint by the people of Fez. But the ksar has little habitable territory, and what it has belongs to the great mosque in the city; all the houses are ruined, except the walls and the mosque. The author spent around four summers in the ksar for the good air and a secluded place to study, since for many years his father held the land on trust from the mosque.

2.2.2.18. Zawiya[129]

Zawiya is a little town around twenty-four miles from Fez, built by Yusuf, the second Marinid king, who put up a great hospice and ordered that he be buried there. Fortune, however, did not favour this, for the king was killed outside the city of Tlemcen while besieging it.[130] Zawiya was not cared for, so it was soon abandoned and ruined, and all that now remains are the walls of the hospital; the revenues were given to the great mosque. The land is farmed by certain Arabs who are practically countryfolk of the city of Fez.

2.2.2.19. Khoulan[131]

Khoulan is an ancient ksar built on the river Sebou, around eight miles south of Fez. Outside the ksar is a spa with very hot water, over which Abu al-Hasan, the fourth Marinid king, built a handsome edifice, to which the burghers of Fez would flock every April for four or five days of pleasure. But it has no culture, and its inhabitants are base and greedy because the city is so near.

2.2.2.20. Mount Zalagh

Zalagh is a mountain that stretches fourteen miles west from the river Sebou; its highest peak is around seven miles north of Fez. The southern slopes are entirely uninhabited, but the northern slopes are all lush hills with innumerable villages and ksars. Most of the farms are vineyards whose grapes are the sweetest and best one can find; likewise, the olives and all the other fruit are excellent because the fields are dry. The inhabitants are rich countryfolk: you won't find a single one without a house or two in the city, and all the burghers of Fez keep vineyards on the mountainside.

All along the northern foothills of the mountain are excellent plains which are good for grain fields and orchards, since the river Sebou flows through the countryside to the south, and the ingenious gardeners have built wheels to raise the river water and irrigate the fields. The countryside is broad and expansive, so large it would take 200 pairs of oxen to plough it in a day; it is owned by the king's master of ceremonies for his own provision, but it does not bring in more than 500 ducats a year in rent, and a tithe goes to the royal treasury, amounting to 3,000 bushels of grain.

2.2.2.21. Mount Zerhoun

Mount Zerhoun begins in the plains of Saïs, ten miles from Fez, and extends thirty miles west, ten miles in breadth. It seems entirely wooded from a distance, but all the trees are olive trees. It is home to fifty villages and ksars, whose inhabitants are very rich because the mountain lies between two large cities, Fez to the east and Meknes to the west. Their women work, making and weaving beautiful woollen fabrics in the local manner, and they go around decked out in silver rings and bracelets. The men are hardy and brave; some catch lions in the woods and present them to the king of Fez.

The king holds another hunt in his citadel, in a large court full of little ditches with ramps. In each ditch is an armed man. They let the lion into the court, and those in the ditches raise their ramps on each side; the lion rushes at one, and the moment he sees it approach he lowers his ramp to enrage the lion. Then they let a bull into the court with the lion, and they start to fight. If the bull kills the lion, they hold a great feast, but if the lion kills the bull, the men in the ditches have to go out and fight the lion with iron spears a cubit-and-a-half long. There are twelve men, and if they defeat the lion the king reduces their number, but if the lion triumphs the king and his courtiers shoot it with crossbows from the gallery where they are watching. Most often, the lion doesn't die before it has killed one man and wounded others. The king gives each warrior ten ducats and new clothes; only the bravest enter, and they all hail from Mount Zalagh, while those who hunt in the countryside are from Mount Zerhoun.

2.2.2.22. Walili,[132] a city on Mount Zerhoun

Walili is a city built at the summit of the mountain by the Romans when they ruled Baetica. It is almost six miles in circumference, walled with large, polished stones and huge, tall gates. However, it was ruined by the Africans in ancient times, and when the schismatic Idris arrived in the region he began at once to remake the city, living there himself. It soon grew in culture and population, but after his death his son abandoned it and built the city of Fez instead. The father was buried in Walili, and his tomb is visited and venerated by all the people of Mauretania, for he was a caliph of Muhammad's family. At present only two or three households inhabit the city, that is, the custodians and servants of the tomb. But the entire area is well farmed and there are beautiful gardens and groves, for two springs emerge from the city and flow outside among the hills where the farms are.

2.2.2.23. Ksar Faraoun

Ksar Faraoun is a small town built by the ancient Romans at the summit of a low mountain eight miles from Walili. The locals, as well as some historians, believe that Pharaoh, the king of Egypt in the time of Moses, ruled the whole world, and that it was he who built this town on the mountain. But according to other historians this is a lie, for there is no evidence that the Egyptians ruled so many lands. The falsehood derives from a treatise on Muhammad's sayings[133] by the writer Ibn al-Kalbi, according to whom Muhammad said that there were two faithful kings and two faithless ones who ruled the world: Alexander the Great and Solomon ben David, and Nimrod and the Pharaoh of Moses.[134] The mistaken ones, then, have a justification from the words of their prophet. Nevertheless, the style of the buildings and the letters on the walls are Latin. Two streams flow around the town, one on each side, and all the nearby valleys and hills are full of olive groves. In the neighbourhood is a huge wood in which many lions and leopards are found.

2.2.2.24. Red Rock[135]

Red Rock is a small town built by the Romans on the mountainside very near the woods, so in the daytime lions come up to the city gates; but the inhabitants have so much experience with them that even women and children are not afraid. The towering walls are made of large, rough stones, but most are destroyed and the town is now like a village, although very rich in olive groves and grain fields, for it is near the plains of Azgar.

2.2.2.25. Douar Mghila

Mghila is a small town built by the ancient Romans, situated on a point of the mountain facing Fez. It has a fine countryside; there are olive groves on the mountain, and a splendid region in the plain full of beautiful springs where they grow much hemp and flax.

2.2.2.26. The Ksar of Shame[136]

This ksar was built long ago at the foot of the mountain by the main road from Fez to Meknes, and was called the Ksar of Shame because its inhabitants were very greedy, as is usual in the lands in that place. A king once passed by, and, when the inhabitants invited him to eat with them, he agreed. Then the people begged him to relieve the place of its ugly name by proclamations and decrees with threat of punishment, and again the king agreed. So they got together to slaughter lambs and prepare some dishes, ordering that large vessels should be filled with milk that night to drink according to their custom. When night came, it occurred to each person that, since the vessels were large, if their own share were to be partly of water it would not be evident in so much milk. But everyone thought the same, and so in the dark each of them brought one jug of water and another of milk to put in the vessels, thinking that the two would be mixed together.

Early the next morning the king wanted to ride, and first he wanted breakfast. The village elders came to furnish the table and they found all the vessels full of water. The king laughed as soon as the news reached him, telling the inhabitants that they

would have to put up with the name of the ksar, since no king
or ruler could remove something bestowed by nature. Now it is
ruined and abandoned, and poor Arabs work the fields.

2.2.2.27. Beni Wariten

This is an area around eighteen miles east of Fez, consisting
entirely of good fields and hills where much grain grows, and
countryside with fine pastures for livestock. It is home to 200
poorly built villages, and the peasants are base and feckless; no
vineyards, gardens or fruit trees are to be found here. The king
of Fez would distribute the area among his younger brothers
and sisters. The peasants are rich in grain and wool, but because
they are badly clothed and ride donkeys they are scorned by
their neighbours in the country.

2.2.2.28. Saïs

Saïs is an area twenty miles west of Fez, nothing but plains,
where, it is said, there once were many ksars and villages; but
now there is no trace or sign of any building, only the names of
ancient places no longer seen. The plains extend eighteen miles
west by twenty miles south, and the fields are very good, although
they produce a small, black grain, and there are few wells. It has
always been inhabited by Arabs who are like peasants, and the
rulers of Fez would give it to the city's castellan and governor.

2.2.2.29. Mount Tghat

Tghat is a mountain around seven miles west of Fez; it is very
high but not broad, extending fifteen miles east to the river of
Bou Nasr.[137] The whole side of the mountain towards Fez is full
of vineyards, as is the summit, while the side towards Ain Essikh
is full of grain fields. At the summit are many underground
caves and caverns; those who search them for treasure think

they lead to places under the mountain where the Romans left treasure when they left the region. Throughout the winter, when the vineyards are untended, these treasure hunters constantly explore the caves with their tools, digging up the earth and turning over large rocks, but it has never been said that they found anything. The fruits of the mountain are poor, as is the colour of its grapes, but they ripen earlier than elsewhere.

2.2.2.30. Tigrigra

Tigrigra is a mountain near the Atlas around forty miles from Fez, and from it arises a river that flows west into the river Baht. It lies between huge plains: one leads to Fez – that is, Saïs mentioned above – and the other, called Adekhsan, stretches to the south with rich, beautiful fields for growing grain and pasturing livestock. The latter plain is inhabited by the Zaër Arabs who are vassals of the king, but he has given the entire plain to one of his brothers, and it brings in around 10,000 ducats. These Arabs are much troubled by others called al-Husein, who live in the desert but come here in summer; however, the king of Fez provides the Zaër with camels and crossbows to guard the countryside from the desert Arabs. Throughout the plain are springs, streams and woods full of peaceful lions; a man or woman can go right up to one with a stick and chase it off.

End of the book on the territory of Fez; there follows the book on Azgar, a region of the kingdom of Fez.

2.2.3.1. Azgar

Azgar is a province bounded by the ocean to the north, by the river Bou Regreg to the west, by the Ghomara, Zerhoun and Zalagh mountains to the east, and by the river Bou Nasr to the south. It consists entirely of plains full of excellent fields, and once teemed with people throughout its many cities and ksars; however, an ancient war ruined all the towns, and there remains no trace or sign today but a few little towns which are still inhabited. The province extends eighty miles in length and sixty miles in width, and the river Sebou flows through the middle. The inhabitants are all Arabs called al-Khlot[138] by the ruler of the al-Muntafiq; they are subjects of the king of Fez when he wages important wars, and their province supplies food, livestock and horses to all the Ghomara mountains, as well as the city of Fez. The king stays here all winter and spring, for the land is healthy and abounds with deer and hares to hunt, although there are few woods.

2.2.3.2. Al-Gumha

Al-Gumha is a little town built in the modern era by the Africans on a stream in a plain, thirty miles into the province going from Fez to Larache. It was once well populated and cultured, but in the war of Sa'id it was ruined completely, and at present there are only pits in which the nearby Arabs keep their grain, and the tents of the Arabs who guard them. Outside are some mills in which they grind the grain from the nearby fields.

2.2.3.3. Larache

Larache is a city built by the ancient Africans where the river Loukkos enters the ocean; it is situated on the riverbanks, with the ocean on the other side. While Asilah and Tangier belonged to the Moors it was well populated and cultured, but it was abandoned when these two towns fell to the Christians, and remained uninhabited for twenty years. Then a son of the king of Fez – now the king himself – had the idea of resettling the city, and ever since then he has made great improvements to the town's fortifications and increased its abundance. He also supplied it with soldiers and munitions, for it was continually in danger and he worried that the Portuguese would capture it. However, he maintained a well-defended port at the river mouth, as well as a strong citadel occupied by a general with 200 crossbowmen, 100 gunmen and 300 light cavalry.

All around the town are many marshes and meadows where eels and waterfowl are caught in great numbers, and there are deep woods along the riverbanks with many lions and other animals. The townsfolk used to make a lot of charcoal to ship to Asilah and Tangier, so there was a proverb in Mauretania for a show-off: 'like the boat from Larache, with sails of cotton but a hold full of charcoal', for in the town's countryside they make a lot of cotton.

2.2.3.4. Ksar el-Kebir, that is, the Greater Palace

This is a large city, built by the decree of al-Mansur, king and caliph of Marrakesh. For he was once out hunting in this area, on a day of downpour and heavy clouds, when he got lost and had to stay in the countryside overnight. He stopped at a place where he feared he would drown in the marshes, for it was night and he could see no lights. Lost in thought, he came upon a fisherman catching eels in the marshes, and, when al-Mansur asked him directions to the king's encampment, the fisherman replied that it was ten miles away. The king asked him to show the way, but the fisherman answered, 'By my faith, if you were al-Mansur himself I would not lead you at this hour, for we would both be in danger of drowning in the marsh at night.'

'What does it matter to you if al-Mansur drowns?'

'By my faith, I care about al-Mansur's person no less than my own.'

'Have you by any chance received some great benefit from him?'

'What greater benefit than his justice and the care he has for his people? I can fish until midnight and return to my hut in this valley, and nobody will give me any trouble.' The fisherman added: 'Good sir, come stay with me tonight and I'll take you to the king's camp in the morning.'

Al-Mansur agreed, and accompanied him to his hut; the fisherman fed his horse and roasted many slices of eel for al-Mansur. But the king said: 'I'd prefer a little meat, and I'll pay you for it.'

'Good sir, I have a she-goat and a kid whose milk I enjoy; but blessed be the kid with which I may honour one such as yourself.' So he slaughtered the kid and his wife prepared the meat; al-Mansur had his supper and slept till morning. The fisherman woke him up and led him out of the marshes, where they found many people searching for him on horseback; when they saw him everyone rejoiced and did him great honour. The fisherman was amazed, and al-Mansur told him, 'Fisherman, for the love you have shown al-Mansur – for I am he – you will want for nothing.'

He told his generals what had befallen him, and each of them kissed the fisherman and gave him a garment or horse. While he stayed in that region al-Mansur had many grand buildings and homes built, but before leaving he gave them all to the fisherman to repay his generosity. The fisherman said: 'If your lordship wishes to complete the gift, he will put walls up around the buildings.' And so it was soon done, and the fisherman became the ruler of the town, every day increasing his number and putting up many other buildings, so that in just a short time, due to the fertility of the land, the town had 400 homes. The king would stay there every summer, which helped improve the town.

Beside it flows the river Loukkos, which sometimes floods and enters the city gates. Plenty of craftsmen and merchants live there, and it has many mosques, as well as a madrasa and a hospital; there are cisterns but no fountains or wells. The townsfolk are good and generous men, though a bit simple, and they are well dressed, wrapped in cotton sheets like cloaks. Outside the city are many gardens and groves of excellent fruit, but the grapes are poor because the fields are meadows. On Mondays they hold a market outside town, at which gather many Arabs living in the nearby countryside. In May the citizens go out to catch turtle doves, and capture a great quantity; the author once bought six for a *baiocco*. The fields are very fruitful, often producing a thirtyfold yield. However, the inhabitants cannot farm all of it, only six miles around, for the Portuguese trouble the town with violent attacks, because it is only twenty-eight miles from Asilah. The town's general has given the Portuguese inhabitants of Asilah much harm and trouble, for he is in charge of 300 cavalry, with whom he campaigns against Asilah.

2.2.4.1. The region of al-Habat

This region is bounded by the river Ouergha to the south, the ocean to the north, the Azgar marshes to the west, and the mountains facing the Pillars of Hercules to the east; it is eighty miles in width and a hundred in length. The region is marvellously fertile, consisting mostly of plains full of rivers. It was more cultured and renowned among the ancients – Ptolemy called it Mauretania – for it contained many ancient cities, some built by the Romans, some by the Africans and some by the Goths; after Fez was built, however, the region was reduced to a poor state. When Idris, the founder of Fez, died, he left ten sons; the eldest[139] reigned and divided the kingdom into several parts, giving this region to the next brother. Then many heretics and rulers rebelled, although their allegiances varied, some following the rulers of Baetica, others the rulers of Kairouan. The caliph of Kairouan, who was also a heretic, came and conquered the region immediately, bringing all the rebels and leaders with him to the east, and leaving behind viceroys. When he had returned, the great chancellor of the caliph of Córdoba at once sent a huge army to drive out all the viceroys, ruling the whole region as far as Zab. Fifty years later, Yusuf ibn Tashfin, the first king of the Lamtuna, arrived and drove out the Baeticans, and ever since the area has remained under the control of the king of Fez.

2.2.4.2. Asjen

Asjen is an ancient town built by the Africans on the side of a mountain ten miles or so from the river Ouergha; these ten miles are all plains with the town's fields and gardens, and there are more fields on the other side of the mountain. The town is seventy miles from Fez and has 500 homes, having under its power a huge countryside, both plain and mountain, that brings in 10,000 ducats. Its viceroy is obliged by the king to keep 500 cavalry as a guard, for the Portuguese often attack these lands from forty or fifty miles away.

The town has little culture, but at least there are craftsmen of the necessary arts; on the other hand it is beautiful and has many fountains. The inhabitants are prosperous, but few of them dress like burghers. They all drink wine, having statutes from former kings of Fez that they will not receive any trouble for it; wine is prohibited according to Sharia law, but they still drink it following their ancient practice.

2.2.4.3. Beni Taouda

This is an ancient city built by the Africans in a splendid plain on the river Ouergha, forty-five miles from Fez. It formerly had 8,000 homes, but during the war of the caliphs of Kairouan its people fought against the caliphs, so they were badly treated and the town was destroyed; little can be seen today but the walls. The author has visited this town and seen many noblemen's tombs, and a few other vestiges, especially the enclosed stone fountains, which are marvellous things. The town is around four miles from the Ghomara mountains, and its fields are very fertile and flat.

2.2.4.4. Amergu

Amergu is a town at the summit of a mountain ten miles from Beni Taouda; it is said to have been built by the Romans, for there are ancient walls on which Latin verses are found. The town is ancient and currently abandoned, but there is another, well-populated little town on the mountainside,[140] with many weavers of thick cloth, and around it is a spacious countryside of good fields. From the town can be seen two large rivers, each five or so miles away – the Sebou to the south, and the Ouergha, along with much else, to the north. The townsfolk call themselves burghers, but they are very greedy, ignorant and coarse, without any virtues at all.

2.2.4.5. Tamsor

Tamsor is a town of 300 homes on a hill ten miles from Amergu. There are very few craftsmen, and the inhabitants are extremely ignorant; lacking vineyards or orchards, they only sow grain, and they have a good quantity of livestock. The town lies on the middle of the route from Fez to the Ghomara mountains; for this reason its people are very greedy and cruel, in the manner of peasants and people without judgement.

2.2.4.6. Agla

Agla is an ancient town built by the Africans on the river Ouergha, with excellent fields around it that the Arabs farm. For the town was ruined by the aforementioned wars, although you can still see the walls intact and wells inside the town. In the countryside they hold a fine weekly market where many local Arabs and countryfolk gather, and many merchants come from Fez to buy wax, ox leather and wool, which are found in abundance. There are also tame lions who are afraid of humans, so there is a proverb in Fez for a coward who pretends to be brave: 'like the lion of Agla, whose tail is eaten by calves'.

2.2.4.7. Naranja

Naranja is a ksar built by the Africans on a mountain by the river Loukkos. It is ten miles from Asjen and surrounded by excellent, albeit hilly fields. On the riverbanks are deep woods with many wild fruits, especially the African or marine cherry.[141] The ksar was destroyed along with all its inhabitants by the Portuguese in AH 895 (AD 1489–90), remaining uninhabited and deserted ever since.

2.2.4.8. Al-Zezira[142]

Al-Zezira is an island in the mouth of the river Loukkos, ten miles from where it meets the ocean; on it was a little ancient town,[143] 100 miles from Fez, which was abandoned at the beginning of the war with the Portuguese. Along the river are many woods but little arable land. In AH 894 (AD 1488–89) the king of Portugal sent a huge army and it entered the river; the captain started to build a new fortress[144] on the island in the belief that taking it would allow them to attack and occupy the entire neighbouring countryside. Upon hearing this news, the king of Fez – father of the present king – was seized with such fright that he assembled his army, together with all the people of Fez, and marched against the captain. The moment he arrived he wanted to join battle with the Portuguese, but he could not, because of the river, and because the endless cruel artillery of the Portuguese prevented his army from getting within two miles. The king and his people despaired. But to his good fortune he was advised to build a dam with sticks in the middle of the river, and fill it up with rocks. The people at once obtained these sticks and planted them in the river two miles or so below the island; they cut down almost the entire forest and tossed the large trees in the river among the sticks, blocking it off. When the Portuguese realised this, they despaired of ever being able to get off the island with their fleets; the people of Fez then decided to strike, for their victory was secure. But the king, realising that more than half of his people and army would die before they won, reached an agreement with the Portuguese captain: the latter would offer a large sum, the king would free the king's daughters and generals imprisoned in Portugal, and a truce would be made with the whole city of Fez.[145] The captain had no choice but to confirm these articles to save his sovereign's army and fleet, so they returned to Portugal and the king confirmed the articles required by his captain, for they were kinsmen.

2.2.4.9. Basra

Basra is a middling town of 2,000 homes; it was built by Muhammad, the son of Idris, the founder of Fez, in a plain between two mountains eighty miles from Fez and twenty miles south of Ksar el-Kebir. He gave it the name Basra in memory of the city in Arabia Felix where 'Ali, the fourth caliph after Muhammad and Idris's ancestor, was killed.[146] This town was fortified with very strong and fine walls, and during the reign of the Idrisids it was highly cultured; the founder's successors would go stay there in summer, for it has a splendid countryside of mountains and plains full of fields and gardens of succulent fruit and excellent grain. There are beautiful orchards in every season, for the river Loukkos flows through the plains by the town. It was well populated and supplied with mosques, and the townsfolk were men of gentle spirits. But after the house of Idris fell its enemies ruined the town, which has remained in ruins ever since. Its walls are intact at the base, as are the wild gardens, which still produce fruit since the fields are no longer farmed.

2.2.4.10. Al-Homar

Al-Homar is a town built by 'Ali, son of the aforementioned Muhammad, on a hill overlooking a stream. It is fourteen miles north of Ksar el-Kebir, and ten miles south of Asilah. It was not large, but handsome and well fortified, with gorgeous plains full of good fields on every side; all around the edge of town were many vineyards and gardens producing grapes and good fruit. The inhabitants were almost all cloth-weavers, for they harvested much flax in their fields. However, it was abandoned when Asilah was captured by the Portuguese.

2.2.4.11. Asilah

Asilah, called Azella by the Africans, is a large city built by the Romans on the ocean seventy miles from the Pillars of Hercules, and forty from Fez. It was controlled by the ruler of Ceuta, who paid tribute to the Romans; then it was occupied by the Goths, who allowed the rulers of Ceuta to keep governing. It was then occupied by the Muslims in AH 94 (AD 713–14), remaining under their control for 220 years until it was assailed by the English[147] with a huge fleet; they had arrived by request of a Gothic king who believed that, if Asilah should be captured, the Muslim armies would return to Africa at once, until they had caught their breath and completed their plan. So he requested the help of the English, even though they were also the enemies of the Goths, for the English were idolaters and the Goths Christians. The English, realising that it was a good idea to impede the Muslims by forcing them to leave Europe, did even worse than the Muslims did, filling the town with blood and fire, and not a soul escaped alive.[148] After they returned home, the town lay ruined and uninhabited for ten years. When the caliphs of Córdoba began to rule Mauretania, they rebuilt the city better than before in its culture and fortifications; the inhabitants were men of good standing, rich, literate and well versed in arms.

The city's countryside is marvellous in its abundance of grain and fruit. Because it is ten miles from the mountains there is hardly any wood, but the inhabitants burn charcoal, which arrives from Larache in great quantities. In AH 882 (AD 1477–78)[149] it was attacked and occupied by the Portuguese, and its inhabitants were all taken as captives to Portugal. Among them was Muhammad, the current king of Fez, with one of his sisters – then children of seven years old – for their father, the former king, was a rebel in the province of al-Habat[150] and lived in Asilah. 'Abd al-Haqq (II), the last Marinid king of Fez, was killed by his people, led by ash-Sharif, a great nobleman of Fez and a member of the league of the founders of Fez,[151] whom the people subsequently elected as their ruler and prince. Al-Sheikh,[152] who controlled a powerful faction in Fez, was sure he could acquire the kingdom; summoned by his faction, he entered Fez twice, but both times he was driven out by ash-Sharif, thanks to the foresight of one of his grand viziers, who was al-Sheikh's fraternal cousin. But ash-Sharif imprudently sent his vizier out to gather the people of Tamasna and convince them to side with him against al-Sheikh; meanwhile al-Sheikh assembled all the Arabs of Azgar and marched with 8,000 cavalry, besieging ash-Sharif in New Fez for a year. Because ash-Sharif's vizier was delayed in Tamasna trying to entreat its people, the soldiers and townsfolk of New Fez started to starve, so they betrayed ash-Sharif; al-Sheikh entered New Fez and proclaimed himself king, exiling ash-Sharif and his father, along with their entire family, to the kingdom of Tunis.

While al-Sheikh was besieging ash-Sharif, the king of Portugal sent his fleet to occupy Asilah. Al-Sheikh, seeing that he stood to lose both towns, could not come to its rescue, so his son, the present king, was taken to Portugal. He remained there for seven years, learning good Portuguese with financial help from his father, and for this reason the Africans call him Muhammad the Portuguese king (al-Burtuqali). He frequently sought to drive the Portuguese out of Asilah in revenge, marching on the city with his army three or four times in an effort to capture it. The first time he attacked it with his entire army and the people of Fez without warning, demolishing one side of the walls and freeing all the Moorish slaves in the city.[153] But the Christians retreated into the fortress and sent word to the king of Fez, promising him the castle; they held out for two days, until Pedro Navarro arrived with a host of armed fleets and started pounding the city with his artillery, killing many both inside and out. The king and his army therefore had to abandon their campaign, and Asilah was then provisioned and fortified by the king of Portugal. Two or three times the king returned with his army, trying to recapture it, but this just showed his madness, for it was not possible, nor would ever be, to take that town by force.

The author himself was present each time the king of Fez marched on Asilah; each attack left 500 or more dead. The king warred with Asilah between AH 914 and 922 (AD 1508–1517).

2.2.4.12. Tanja (Tangier)

Tangier, which the Portuguese call Tangiara, is a large ancient city, built, according to the foolish opinion of some historians, by Shaddad ibn 'Ad, who ruled the entire world and wished to found a city that would imitate paradise on earth.[154] They say he fashioned the walls from bronze and the roofs of the houses from gold and silver, sending commissioners all over the world to collect a special tribute; Tangier was one of the towns that paid its share of the tribute. But, according to the most reliable historians, the Romans built the town while they occupied Baetica, by the ocean thirty miles from the Pillars of Hercules and fifty from Fez. When the Goths conquered Baetica the town was subject to the rule of Ceuta, until it was conquered by the Muslims along with Asilah.

The town was always cultured, noble and well populated, and there were beautiful public buildings, both ancient and modern. Although there are few good fields in its environs, there are nearby valleys full of springs and gardens of oranges, lemons and other fruit. Outside town there are also some vineyards, but the fields are sandy. The people of the city lived in great splendour until Asilah was occupied; on the day they heard the news from Asilah they abandoned their costly possessions and fled to Fez. Tangier remained empty for three days, but, when this came to the attention of the king of Portugal and his general, they at once sent a viceroy with a large number of people to claim the town for the king. Later the king sent a nobleman from his own family to serve as a general, for the city was of great importance, being near the mountains of the Ghomara, who are enemies of the Christians. However, twenty-five years before the city belonged to the Portuguese, the king of Portugal at the time sent a fleet to capture the city,[155] landing with his armed men and other soldiers. In his estimation, the city would receive no help from Fez, because the king[156] was at war with an adversary who had captured Meknes. But, when he heard that the Christians were besieging Tangier, the king of Fez made a pact with the rebels against the Portuguese and they arrived to fight them. In his disarray the Portuguese general was soon routed and killed along with most of his army, and the fleet departed and returned to Portugal. The grand vizier of the king carried the general's body in a box, which he hung over the gates of New Fez until it was taken down by ash-Sharif, prince of Fez, by request of the king of Portugal.

A few months after the war,[157] the king sent another fleet to attack the town unannounced by night. The Portuguese climbed the walls in the dead of night and were discovered by the guards; the people roused themselves to arms and killed a large number of the invaders on the walls. The fleet returned to Portugal. After these defeats which fortune served up to the king, the city was taken without a single drop of blood.

Recently the present king of Fez, Muhammad, went with a great army and a large artillery force against the Portuguese in Tangier, thinking that because it was less well fortified than Asilah, he could easily recover it in a surprise attack. The moment he arrived his artillery opened fire, but the Portuguese were defended by brave men, and, although the king did great damage to the town walls and destroyed many buildings, he could not capture or even approach the town. The author was present at this battle in AH 917 (AD 1511–12).

2.2.4.13. Ksar es-Seghir, that is, the Lesser Palace

This very small town was founded by al-Mansur, king and caliph of Marrakesh, on the ocean twelve miles from Tangier. Every year his army, en route to Baetica, found it hard to cross the mountains; he therefore built the town on this pass so that his army, having left Marrakesh, would no longer have to cross any mountains. It is situated in a splendid plain from which the whole nearby coast of Baetica can be seen. It was highly cultured and the inhabitants were almost all sailors who provided transport from Barbary to Europe; others were cloth-weavers, but there were also many rich merchants and brave warriors. However, the king of Portugal attacked and occupied it unexpectedly with a large fleet, and the inhabitants fled to the nearby mountains.[158] The king of Fez[159] at once sent one of his viziers with a great army and most of the people of Fez; in AH 863 (AD 1458–59) they besieged it for two months but did no harm at all, for it was winter and the snow fell around the camp without helping the army in any way.

2.2.4.14. Sabta (Ceuta)

Ceuta is a huge city, called Civitas[160] in Latin and Seupta by the Portuguese; it was built, in truth, by the Romans at the mouth of the straits of the Pillars of Hercules, and was the capital of all Mauretania, for it was the home of the Roman viceroy and was highly cultured and populated. It was later occupied by the Goths, who sent a noble ruler there, and his house ruled the city until the Muslims invaded Mauretania. At that time Julian, the count of Ceuta, suffered an insult from Roderic,[161] king of the Goths and all of Spain, so in his scorn he gave orders to the Muslim armies to cross over to Baetica, which caused the ruin of Roderic and his kingdom, while Julian maintained his position with the Muslims until his death.

Then, in AH 92 (AD 711–12), the Muslims took over Ceuta on behalf of their caliph, al-Walid ibn 'Abd al-Malik, who was based in Damascus. From then on the city grew in size and culture until it was the finest and most populous town of Mauretania, with many mosques and madrasas, as well as many craftsmen and talented men of letters. The inhabitants were men of gentle spirits and great ingenuity, especially the coppersmiths, who fashioned marvellous engraved pots, ornaments such as shells, and vessels, candlesticks, lanterns and inkwells, which they sold for more than if they had been silver. Such items, when they turn up in Italy, are believed to be Damascene work, and a few of them may be; nonetheless the Ceuta items are prettier and better made than those of Damascus.

Outside the city are fine farms and houses, especially in a place called Vignones,[162] where there were and still are excellent vineyards, but the city's territory is harsh and meagre, which is why there is always a dearth of grain in the city. From both outside and inside Ceuta one can see the coastline of Baetica along the strait, and one can even make out the animals, for it is only twelve miles across. In the recent past the town received its share of damage, having held out against the caliph and king 'Abd al-Mu'min before he took it by force, imprisoning most of its nobles and destroying their homes. Another time it was similarly assaulted by the king of Granada, who occupied it and did the same, removing the nobles and wealthy men and relocating them to Granada.

Then in AH 818 (AD 1415–16) the king of Portugal[163] attacked it with a large fleet, and the moment the townsfolk saw the fleet in the distance they abandoned their possessions and fled; the Christians entered without any difficulty and stayed for three weeks, thinking that the king of Fez[164] would come to the city's aid. But, by the grace of God, when the king heard the news he was holding a banquet with dancing and music, and he was so unwise and incompetent that he did not move or change a thing, but kept dancing as if the news were nothing. As his sins grew, so did the hatred of his people and his courtiers, until one night he and his seven sons were killed by a minister and general who wanted the king to stop sleeping with his wives.[165] The king Abu Sa'id was killed in AH 824 (AD 1421–22), and the kingdom of Fez remained widowed for eight years, until it was claimed by a son he had with a Christian woman, who had escaped to Tunis that night with her son 'Abd al-Haqq, the last king of the Marinids, who was also killed by the people of Fez, as recounted above.[166]

2.2.4.15. Tetouan

This is a small town built by the ancient Africans eighteen miles from the straits of Gibraltar and six from the Mediterranean, occupied by the Muslims when they wrested Ceuta from the Goths. When the Goths acquired the town they gave it to a countess with only one eye, who would go there every Sunday to collect the profits, and so it was called Tetouan, which means 'eye' in the

African language.[167] It was always under the control of the ruler and governor of Ceuta until that town was captured by the Portuguese; the inhabitants of Tetouan then fled and abandoned it, and it remained uninhabited for ninety-five years.

It was subsequently rebuilt and resettled by a Granadan general[168] who accompanied his king to Fez after Granada was captured by King Ferdinand of Spain. The general, known to the Portuguese as Almandarim, had repeatedly proved his courage in the war of Granada, so he requested Tetouan for his home. The king was especially pleased with him, so to help him he had him collect tithes from the nearby mountains hostile to the Portuguese of Ceuta, and the general had soon rebuilt all the walls and put up a formidable citadel surrounded by vast ditches. The general was constantly in conflict with the Portuguese, and caused huge damage to Ceuta, Ksar es-Seghir and Tangier, which he continually attacked, taking many Christians captive. He retained 300 cavalry, all excellent Granadans well versed in arms and experienced in war. The captive Christians were put to work on the town's fortifications, and very badly treated; the author has seen more than 3,000 of them there, dressed in cloth sacks and sleeping in heavy chains in underground pits. But the general was a generous man: he hosted every foreigner who came to town in his citadel, taking care of their expenses for the entire duration of their visit. He died in recent years after going blind; he had been stabbed in one eye, in which he remained blind, and then ten years later, in his old age, he lost sight in the other as well. The kingdom passed to his nephew, who was also a courageous man.

Having discussed the towns of al-Habat, we will now treat of the mountains, which are full of people. There are eight mountains more famous than the others and inhabited by the Ghomara, who mostly lead the same lives with the same customs; they all belong to the Muslim faith, but most of them, contrary to their religion, drink wine. They are all hardy men, enduring fatigue and exertion, but badly clothed: they are subject to the king of Fez and pay such heavy tribute that few have enough left over to clothe themselves well. There are some exceptions, as will be detailed below.

2.2.4.16. Mount Rhouna

Rhouna is a mountain near Asjen, measuring thirty miles by twelve and abundant with oil, honey and vineyards. The locals manufacture a great quantity of soap, purify wax, and harvest many vines because they all drink wine. The mountain brings in 3,000 ducats a year, collected by the general and governor of Asjen to maintain 400 cavalry.

2.2.4.17. Mount Beni Fenzekkar

This mountain, which measures twenty-five miles by eight, borders the last and is more highly populated. The locals polish cow leather and weave coarse cloth; they also collect a lot of wax and on Saturdays hold a great market where all kinds of merchants and merchandise can be found. Even Genoese merchants go there to buy wax and raw oxhide and import it to Genoa or Portugal. The mountain brings in 6,000 ducats, half of which goes to the general of Asjen and half to the king's treasury.

2.2.4.18. Mount Beni Arous

This mountain is eight miles or so north of Ksar el-Kebir, extending ten miles to the west, and six miles north. It was inhabited by noble knights and was well populated and fertile; but the people found the nobles so tyrannical and unjust that they abandoned the mountain after the Portuguese captured Asilah, except for certain villages on the summit very close to Ksar el-Kebir. These are still inhabited and once furnished the general of that town with 3,000 ducats.

2.2.4.19. Mount Habib

This mountain was once inhabited by an honourable people in six or seven rather cultured ksars, for when Tangier was captured by the Portuguese many of its citizens came to live here, being only twenty-five miles away. But they had a lot of trouble and bother from the Portuguese. Since Tangier was captured, half the mountain has been ruined and ravaged, because it is thirty miles from the captain of the guard's barracks, and whenever the Portuguese attack the mountain the locals receive no help from him.

2.2.4.20. Mount Beni Hassane

This soaring mountain was once inhabited by valiant men, and it remains very hard for its enemies to capture. The people were in conflict with certain noble tyrants, so they rose up against the tyrants and thrashed them as they pleased. One young man among these tyrants, disdainful of being subject to their former subjects, left and went to Granada, where he fought in the army against the Christians. After a few years he returned to a mountain near this one, where his faction was living; when he arrived he began gathering many cavalry to repel the Portuguese, who were at the time causing much damage at the mountain borders. He acquired great renown in this endeavour, and his cavalry and revenues increased daily, so much so that the king of Fez, seeing that he personally engaged in combat, marched with fifty mounted crossbowmen to the mountain against his enemies; they were victorious and freed the young man's kinsfolk from the subjection of the enemy tyrants. Then the man began to collect the revenues from the mountain, which were intended for the royal treasury, and so the king went against him with a great army.

When he saw the king's army, he repented and begged forgiveness; the king graciously pardoned him, establishing him as ruler of Chefchaouen and all its territory.[169] Then the tyrant became the legitimate ruler, making the people pay for all the damage on behalf of the king and the kingdom. He was descended from Muhammad, of the same line as Idris, the founder of Fez; when he became ruler he was well known by the Portuguese, who called him by his name and house, that is, 'Ali ben Ras.[170]

2.2.4.21. Mount Anjera

This mountain is around eight miles south of Ksar es-Seghir, extending ten miles in length and three in breadth. It has excellent fields, for they were cleared by the inhabitants, who cut down the trees to make ships in Ksar es-Seghir, where the shipyard was. They sowed a large amount of flax, and worked as sailors and cloth-weavers. But when the town was captured by the Portuguese, the people abandoned the mountain, and today all its buildings and farms remain as they were when inhabited and worked.

2.2.4.22. Wad Ras

This lofty mountain between Ceuta and Tetouan is full of men who proved their valour and expertise in the war between the Granadans and the Spaniards, for they went to Baetica as soldiers of fortune, although they were worth more than the rest of the king's men. From this mountain came Hellul,[171] a man who fought in great battles against brave Spanish soldiers, and the people of Africa and Baetica recorded his exploits in histories written in mixed verse and prose, just like the deeds of Orlando among the Latins.[172] Hellul was killed in combat by the Spaniards when Yusuf an-Nasir, king and caliph of Marrakesh, was routed near a castle in Catalonia that the Moors call the Castle of the Eagle.[173] Sixty thousand fighters were killed in the defeat of the Moors, and nobody escaped but the king and a few of his family. This was in AH 609, which ought to be 1160 in the Christian date.[174] From that day on, the Christians pursued victory in Baetica, reclaiming all the towns occupied by the Moors until Granada was captured by King Ferdinand of Spain, 285 Arabic years after the first one; step by step they took back Baetica and some towns in Castile.

2.2.4.23. Beni Wagarfet

This well-populated mountain near Tetouan does not extend far; its valiant inhabitants have enough skill to serve under the afore-mentioned general of Tetouan, who greatly welcomes them. They would accompany him on campaigns to the towns captured by Christians, and for this reason they pay no tax or anything but levies on their fields. They make a lot of money from the mountain with its boxwood forests, from which the comb dealers of Fez and other towns import rough-hewn planks.[175]

End of the treatise on the region of al-Habat; there briefly fol-lows the treatise on the region of er-Rif, which is likewise a province of the kingdom of Fez.

2.2.5.1. Er-Rif

Er-Rif is a province or region that borders the strait of the Pil-lars of Hercules to the west and extends 140 miles east to the river Nekor. Its first part is bounded to the north by the Medi-terranean, and it stretches forty miles south to the mountains near the river Ouergha in the territory of Fez. It is a very harsh land, nothing but frozen mountains covered with forests of beautiful straight wood; not much grain grows, but there are many vineyards, figs, olives and almonds. Its inhabitants are all hardy men, but they are dreadful drunkards and are poorly clothed. Few animals are found in the mountains except goats, donkeys and apes in large numbers. There are few cities, but many villages, consisting of poor buildings of a single storey like country stables; as for the roofs, some are covered with straw and others with black branches arranged like planks. All the women and men of the mountain have fat goitres. All are brutish and ignorant.

2.2.5.2. Targha

Targha is a little town on the Mediterranean eighty miles from the straits, built, according to some, by the Goths. It contains 500 homes, all made in a poor style, and its walls are weak; the inhabitants are almost all fishermen, making great quantities of salted fish which the mountainfolk buy and transport a hundred miles south inland. The town was once very cultured, but it began to decline in population and culture when the Portuguese captured the towns mentioned above. Around it are the forests of the harsh, cold mountains, where the little barley does not suffice the inhabitants for even half the year. They are courageous men, but brutish, ignorant and badly clothed, and almost all of them are happy to get drunk.

2.2.5.3. Badis

Badis, which the Spanish call Vélez de la Gomera, is a town of 600 homes on the Mediterranean, built in a mediocre style. Some historians say it was founded by the Africans, others by the Goths. It lies between two high mountains, and next to it is a valley which, when full, becomes a great river. There is a square in town with many shops and an adequate mosque. But the town has no drinking water, and, although there is a well half a mile away by the tomb of one of their saints,[176] it is dangerous to draw water from it at night because it contains many leeches.

The inhabitants are divided into two groups: the fishermen, and the corsairs who travel in foists throughout Christendom. Beyond the town are high, harsh mountains with forests of excellent wood for foists, boats and galleys, and all the mountainfolk make their living by exporting this wood. Not much wheat grows there, so in the town they eat barley bread, along with sardines and other fish. Because the fishermen catch huge hauls every morning they need help in pulling up the nets, so all the poor of the town go each morning to help them. They put the sardines to one side, and divide the other fish between themselves and the poor who help them; they also give them to anybody present, rich or poor. The sardines they salt and export to the mountains.

In the town is a fine, extensive quarter where the Jews live. They sell wine, which almost all the inhabitants drink, and give them a good time: every evening, in fine weather, they all get into their boats with their wine, singing and drinking all night. The town has a beautiful citadel in which the ruler lives, though it is not all that strong. However, the ruler has another palace outside town with a gorgeous garden, and by the shore is a little shipyard where they are always building some foist, galley or boat. The ruler and burghers of the town often send armed foists to pillage Christian lands, and they are constantly causing great damage. In response, Ferdinand of Spain sent a fleet to capture an island a mile from the town, where he built a fortress on the rocks.[177] The fleet arrived at the island with plenty of food, along with artillery, which they fired at the town, giving the inhabitants great difficulty until they could no longer resist with either foist or boat, nor leave the port due to the artillery's devastation. The Spanish kept shooting at the town, killing the men in the streets and mosque like dogs.

The ruler finally requested help from the king of Fez, who sent some infantry. As soon as they arrived they climbed onto the island, precipitating a huge, bloody battle with the Christians; most of the Moors were killed or wounded, others were captured, so the king's camp returned without achieving anything. The Christians held the island for eleven years until the king of Fez sent another army, but still it could not prevail against the island. There was one Spanish soldier, however, who had received a great offence from his general on account of his wife, and so he killed the general and allowed the Moors inside; they slaughtered all the Christians except the soldier and his wife, who were welcomed and rewarded by the ruler of Badis and the king of Fez in AD 1520.

The author heard this story in Naples from some men who were present at the capture of the island, but when it was taken by the Christians the author was in Fez; the ruler of Badis has held [the island] with a great guard until the present, and the king of Fez helps him because it is the nearest port on the Mediterranean to Fez, around twenty miles away. To this port the Venetian galleys are accustomed to come once or twice a year with their merchandise. They do good business with the king of Fez, bartering goods and selling them for gold coins; they bring Moorish merchandise from the port to Tunis, or even as far as Venice, and sometimes to Alexandria and Beirut.

2.2.5.4. Jellich[178]

Jellich is a little town on the Mediterranean six miles from Badis; it has a good little port where ships stay en route to Badis when the sea is rough. There are many mountains nearby with vast pine forests. In modern times the town was abandoned because of the Spanish corsairs, and has remained uninhabited except for a few little fishermen's huts; they are constantly on the alert, and whenever they see foists they signal with fire to the nearby mountainfolk, who come at once in large numbers to help.

2.2.5.5. Taghassa

Taghassa is a small, well-populated town on a river two miles from the Mediterranean. It contains 500 homes, but the buildings are poor. The inhabitants are all fishermen and boatmen who go out to bring food back, for the town's land is nothing but mountains and forests where no grain can grow, although there are many vineyards and fruit farms. There is no culture in the town at all; the men and women are badly clothed and live only on barley bread, sardines and onions. When the author was there for three days, the walls and streets seemed to stink of sardines, and three days felt like three months because of the squalor and dirt of the town and its people.

2.2.5.6. El Jebha

El Jebha is a well-walled town built by the Africans on the Mediterranean twenty-four miles from Badis; it is inhabited off and on, depending on the provision that reaches its captains of the guard. The land surrounding the town is harsh, but there are many springs, forests, vineyards and fruit farms. Except for the walls, there aren't any attractive buildings or structures in town.

2.2.5.7. Al-Mazamma[179]

This is a large town on a mountain by the Mediterranean, on the borders of the province of Garet. Below the town to the south is a large plain ten miles by twenty-eight, through the middle of which runs the river Nekor, dividing er-Rif and Garet. In the plain live certain Arabs who work its fields and harvest a large amount of grain, giving 5,000 bushels a year to the ruler of Badis. In ancient times the town was highly cultured and contained the lodgings of the province's ruler, but it was ruined three times. The first time was when the caliph of Kairouan[180] demanded tribute from the ruler, who replied with brazen contempt; the wrathful caliph sent his army to capture and kill the ruler, whose head was sent to Kairouan on the end of a spear. The town was sacked and burned in AH 318 (AD 930–31), and then remained uninhabited for fifteen years.

It was later resettled by other rulers under the protection of the caliph of Kairouan. But then the caliph of Córdoba[181] sought to acquire it out of jealousy because it was only eighty miles from his own borders – that is, the breadth of the sea between it and Málaga in Baetica. So he demanded tribute from the ruler, who refused to give it and requested aid from Kairouan. But before the news reached Kairouan, 1,300 miles away, the caliph of Córdoba's fleet arrived from Málaga, seizing and sacking the town and taking its ruler as a prisoner back to Córdoba, where he remained until his death. The town has remained in ruins ever since, but the walls are all still intact. The final destruction was in AH 872 (AD 1467–68).

End of er-Rif, now on the mountains, and first the most famous.

2.2.5.8. Mount Beni Grir

This mountain, inhabited by a Ghomara tribe, is near Targha and extends ten miles in length and four in width, with many forests, vineyards and olive groves. The inhabitants, both men and women, are impoverished and badly clothed, and keep few animals, but they harvest a lot of wine and cooked must from their vineyards. A tiny amount of grain grows there.

2.2.5.9. Mount Beni Mansur

This mountain extends five miles by one mile, and is full of woods and springs. The inhabitants are healthy but poor, for nothing grows on the mountain but grapes, and they keep a few goats. They hold a weekly market at which the author has seen only onions, garlic, raisins and salted sardines, and a little grain or panicum that they make bread with. Both this and the previous mountain are on the sea coast and subject to the ruler of Badis.

2.2.5.10. Mount Bokoya

This mountain extends twenty-four by eight miles. Its inhabitants are richer than the others, dressing well and owning many horses, for the mountain has good fields around it and they pay little tax, because the saint buried outside Badis was from this mountain.

2.2.5.11. Mount Beni Khaled

Those who travel from Badis to Fez will pass this frozen mountain with its wild forests and icy springs where no grain grows, although there are many vineyards. The inhabitants are also subjects of the rulers of Badis, but, because of their poverty and the heavy tax they owe their rulers, they have turned to brigandage.

2.2.5.12. Mount Beni Mansur

This mountain extends eight miles and is just as far from the sea as the last two; its inhabitants are hale and hearty but they are great drunkards. They harvest much wine but little grain. Their women are unafraid of the goats in the forests while they pasture their flocks, and during this time they spin thread, like the women of the other mountains mentioned here.[182]

2.2.5.13. Mount Beni Yusuf

This is a mountain twelve by eight miles across, whose inhabitants are very poor and badly clothed. For nothing of value grows there but a tiny amount of panicum, which they mix with the grape seeds to make a very poor, rough black bread. They eat plenty of onions and drink from muddy springs; they also keep many goats, whose milk they hold to be a precious food.

2.2.5.14. Mount Beni Zarwil

This is a mountain with plenty of vineyards, good fields and many groves of olives and other fruit, but the inhabitants are destitute because they are subjects of the ruler of Chefchaouen and taxed heavily, and so have little left over from the profits of their wine. They hold a market once a week where lots of figs, raisins and oil can be found, and they slaughter many old goats and rams who are no longer good for breeding.

2.2.5.15. Mount Beni Razin

This is a mountain near the Mediterranean on the borders of Targha; its inhabitants prosper because the mountain is well defended, so they pay no tax to any ruler. It is fertile, full of grain, olives and vineyards; there are many forests but also good fields on the mountainside. Their women are also goat-herds and farmers.

2.2.5.16. Mount Chefchaouen

This mountain is more cultured than the other mountains of Africa, and hosts a little town full of craftsmen and merchants; this is because it is home to Sidi 'Ali ibn Rashid, the ruler of many mountains who first brought culture there, and who rebelled against the king of Fez and waged perpetual war on the Portuguese. The inhabitants of the town and villages on the mountain pay their ruler no tax, for they are almost all soldiers, both cavalry and infantry. On the mountain little grain grows, but much flax and fodder, and there are extensive forests and countless springs throughout. The inhabitants are well clothed and refined.

2.2.5.17. Mount Beni Jebara[183]

This mountain is high and harsh; a few streams flow below it, and it has many vineyards and fig groves, but not a single ear of wheat. The inhabitants are impoverished and badly clothed, but they have plenty of goats and small cows that many take for eight-month-old calves. They hold a market every week, albeit one with almost no goods; however, there are traders from Fez and mule-drivers who bring the goods and fruits to

Fez. The mountain belonged to a kinsman of the king of Fez, and it brought in around 2,000 ducats a year.

2.2.5.18. Mount Beni Yarzou

This mountain was once much inhabited, and had a madrasa for students of law, on account of which its inhabitants were free from tyranny. Recently, however, a tyrant demanded tribute from its people, for he saw that they were prospering and he was envious. But the instructors rose up against him, so with the consent of the king of Fez he went with an army and besieged the mountain; he took it by force, and had many renowned men killed, sacking the madrasa and its library, whose books were worth 4,000 ducats. This happened in AH 918 (AD 1512–13).

2.2.5.19. Mount Tizirane

Tizirane is a mountain near the previous one. It has many springs and forests and vineyards, and its inhabitants are very ignorant and poor due to heavy taxation; on the mountain are many ancient buildings like temples, which in the author's judgement are of Roman origin, and throughout them are found many madmen who go digging up the foundations for treasure.

2.2.5.20. Mount Beni Bou Chibet

This mountain is harsh and frozen, and no grain grows there, nor can they even keep livestock, because it is so cold and dry. Its forests, dense with tall trees, cannot be used for pasturing goats. But they have many nuts, supplying Fez and all the neighbouring towns, and black grapes with which they make a fine, thick, sweet *zebibi* as well as cooked must and terrible wine.[184] The inhabitants all wear woollen sacks,[185] like the poor blankets that Italian merchants put their fabrics in when carrying them from place to place; these sacks are trimmed in black and white, with hoods for the head, and whoever sees the locals in the woods will sooner take them for animals than men. All the mule-drivers of Fez visit the mountain in winter to bring back the nuts and black *zebibi*, but travellers like these will hardly ever find wheat bread or meat, for the mountainfolk are accustomed to barley bread, onions and salted sardines, which are much in favour there. They also eat a lot of cooked must with bread and bean soup, which they think is the best food imaginable.

2.2.5.21. Mount Beni Walid, er-Rif

This is a very high and challenging mountain, and its inhabitants are wealthy, for they own many vineyards of black grapes for *zebibi*, and farms of almonds, figs and olives; moreover, they are free and pay the king of Fez no tribute but a quarter of a ducat or so per village. They are therefore able to sell their goods at the markets in Fez and in the plain. If one of them should commit a crime in Fez and return home, the first person from Fez to find him on the mountain will arrest him until he makes amends for the harm he did in the city. The inhabitants, both men and women, are so well clothed and adorned that, in the author's estimation, if the mountain were controlled by the king of Fez it would bring in more than 6,000 ducats, for there are eighty villages, all of them prosperous. All the criminals and exiles from Fez can live safely on the mountain at the communal expense, because the mountainfolk are noble and very generous.

2.2.5.22. Mount Marnisa

This mountain borders the last and belongs to roughly the same tribe. Its inhabitants are just as rich, free and noble, but they have the wicked custom that if a man should beat his wife, she will at once flee to another mountain, take another husband and abandon her children. For this reason the mountainfolk are constantly arguing with each other, and if they would ever make peace the new husband must return the wife to her first husband, along with the expenses for their wedding. They are constantly suing each other and the judges bleed the litigants dry.

2.2.5.23. Mount Hagustum[186]

This is a very high, cold mountain, with many springs, vineyards of black grapes, good figs, fat, fine and fragrant quinces, and citrons in the plain below the mountain. They have many olive groves, from which they extract plenty of oil. The inhabitants are free, but out of courtesy they send large gifts to the king of Fez every year; he is very welcoming to them, so they are safe to sell goods and buy grain, wool and cloth throughout his domain. They dress like burghers, especially those of the chief village where the craftsmen, merchants and many nobles are.

2.2.5.24. Mount Beni Ider

This mountain is huge and well populated, but nothing grows there except black grapes for making *zebibi* and wine. They had nothing else but their liberty, so that in their great poverty they became rogues and brigands on the paths, and they were continually in disputes and fights with the people of the neighbouring mountains. The ruler of Badis therefore allied with their enemies and deprived them of liberty, exacting tribute from them. But, although there are fifty large villages on the mountain, they bring in barely 400 ducats between them.

2.2.5.25. Mount Lokay

This mountain is very high and challenging, and its inhabitants are very rich, for it overflows with *zebibi* grapes, figs, almonds, oil, quinces and citrons, and, since it is only thirty-five miles to Fez, all their goods are sold there. The people are generous, proud nobles and knights, never paying tribute from their mountain to any ruler. All the exiles of Fez can live there safe from the court because the mountainfolk take them in, except when they know that a person has been exiled for fornicating with married women; in this case they welcome him for three days and then free him to leave the mountain, for they are zealous and just men. Their chiefs never leave the mountain for the plains, for fear of falling into the hands of the king of Fez, who wants to put them to death, although he lets everyone trade on the mountain because his city's merchants need it.

2.2.5.26. Mount Beni Wazarwal

This range extends thirty miles in length and fifteen in width, and contains three mountains with streams between them. The inhabitants are hale and hearty, but they are heavily taxed by the king of Fez, paying his captain of the guard 8,000 ducats a year. The mountains are very fertile with grapes, olives, figs and flax, so they make a great deal of wine, cooked must, oil and thick cloth, and earn money on these goods to pay the captain, who keeps commissioners and administrators to gouge the mountainfolk for money.

There are countless villages and hamlets on the mountain – or 120 to be more precise – some of 100 homes, some 200, others more or less, from which come 25,000 warriors. They are always at war with their neighbours, killing each other like dogs, and the king likes to fine them for the men killed on either side, so the war works for him. There is a highly cultured town on the mountain with many craftsmen and noblemen, and surrounded by groves of grapes, quinces and fat citrons, which they bring to Fez. They also make plenty of cloth. Judges and lawyers live here, and for this reason many mountainfolk can be found in town on market day.

In a valley in the mountains is a hole like a cave breathing fire; as the author can attest, the travellers come to marvel at it, throwing bundles of sticks inside to see the great speed with which they burn up in the flames. It is one of the most remarkable things ever seen in nature. But the locals believe it is the gate to Hell.

2.2.5.27. Mount Beni Ouriaghel

This mountain borders the previous one, but the people are enemies and always at war. Below it are plains bordering the territory of Fez and the river Ouergha flows through them. The inhabitants harvest large amounts of oil, grain and flax, and make much cloth, but the good king steals all their goods; they would be richer than the other mountain peoples, but due to the rulers' injustice and cruelty they are indigent beggars. They are naturally valiant and hardy men, numbering 12,000 warriors from sixty large villages.

2.2.5.28. Mount Beni Ahmed

This mountain measures eighteen miles in length and seven in width, and is quite harsh. It has many forests, vineyards, olives and figs, but few fields for grain, and the king of Fez taxes them very heavily. There are streams and springs all over the mountain and below it, but the water is very dirty and full of chalk. Many inhabitants have large goitres. The men, women and children all drink unmixed wine, which the locals store and preserve for fifteen or twenty years, fermenting a little of it, but also preparing it without fermentation. They make a lot of cooked must, which they keep in vessels narrow at the bottom and wide at the mouth.

They hold a weekly market selling infinite quantities of wine, oil and red *zebibi*, for the mountain people make half *zebibi* and half wine and cooked must from the fruit of their vines. Because of their deep poverty, they are badly clothed. They are divided into factions, and one village often quarrels with another for some ancient reason. Their two noble houses are always stirring up war among the people.

2.2.5.29. Mount Beni Yanfen

This mountain borders the last and extends for ten miles, but a stream divides them. The inhabitants get drunk all the time, but they are strong and sturdy. They harvest no grain but make lots of wine, and they keep many goats in the woods, hardly eating any meat but mutton, as on the previous mountains. The author has spent a good part of his life talking with these mountain people, for his father kept farms here, but he struggled to collect any profit from them, for none of the farmers of the fields or vineyards, or in fact any of the mountainfolk, can be trusted to pay what they owe.

2.2.5.30. Mount Beni Mesguilda

This mountain borders the last and the river Ouergha. Its inhabitants are all soap-makers, for the mountain is full of olives for making oil, but they do not know how to make hard soap, only liquid. Below the mountain are wide plains farmed by Arabs; the mountainfolk often have disputes with them, and the king of Fez always blames them and fines them heavily. Among the mountainfolk are many learned jurists, and they attract crowds of students who cause enormous damage throughout the mountains, especially in the places where they are not welcome. The jurists secretly drink wine, even though they lead the people to understand that it is forbidden, but few obey them. The inhabitants of the mountain are not heavily taxed, because they maintain the students and instructors.

2.2.5.31. Mount Beni Wamoud

This mountain borders the territory of Fez, but the river divides the two; it has twenty-five towns and all the inhabitants are soap-makers, from whom the king extracts 6,000 ducats a year. All the slopes of the mountain have good fields, but there is hardly any water. The inhabitants keep livestock and bees, and they are very rich, for the mountain is very fertile and they go every market day to Fez, ten miles away, to sell their goods. In a few of the villages there is some culture that produces the necessities of life.

End of the tract on the most famous mountains of er-Rif province; there follows Garet, the sixth province of Fez.

2.2.6.1. The province of Garet

The province of Garet stretches from the river Nekor in the west to the river Moulouya in the east; to the south it is bounded by the mountains and deserts bordering Numidia, and to the north by the Mediterranean. Its width along the sea runs from the Nekor to the Moulouya; to the south, one part ends at the river Mouloula and runs west by the mountains of Al Haouz, descending towards the sea along the Nekor. The province is fifty miles long and forty miles wide, and is barren and arid like the deserts of Numidia. It is almost uninhabited, especially since the Spanish captured its two principal towns, as will be seen below, going through each area in turn.

2.2.6.2. Melilla

This is a great, ancient city of 2,000 homes, built by the Africans at the tip of a gulf in the Mediterranean. It used to be very cultured, being the capital of the province. It had a great countryside that produced a large amount of iron and honey, and for this reason it was called Melilla, which in the African language means honey.[187] In the port they once fished for shells containing pearls. The town was once subject to the Goths, but the Muslim armies captured the town in the early years of their invasion of Africa, and the guard of the Goths fled to Baetica a hundred miles away across the sea. In modern times it was attacked by a Spanish fleet, but the inhabitants were forewarned and sent for

help to the king of Fez. At that time he was much occupied with
his war against the people of Tamasna,[188] but he sent one of his
generals with a light army. When he arrived the people realised
they had no chance, for they had already been informed of the
size of the Spanish fleet, so they abandoned their goods at once
and fled to the Bou Touya mountains. The general, on witnessing
this, began to destroy and burn the town to spite both the inhabitants and the Christians, who were en route, so it was soon in
ruins. This occurred in AH 896 (AD 1490–91).[189] Then the Spanish armada arrived and found the town abandoned, so they
landed, fortified the citadel and began rebuilding the town walls,
remaining there ever since.

2.2.6.3. Cazaza

This town is twenty miles from Melilla; it is well fortified with
strong walls, and has a good harbour, where Venetian galleys
once went every year and did a roaring trade with the people of
Fez. The current king of Fez took a large amount of money
from them, but unfortunately for him he was forced into a war
at the start of his rule with a neighbour and cousin of his. King
Ferdinand of Spain sent an army to attack the town, and when
the general and governor of the people informed the king of
this fleet, the reply was, 'Do the best you can.' In despair, the
people fled, abandoning their goods to fortune, but the general,
a valiant former captain of 500 cavalry under the king of Granada, remained with his fifty cavalry until he saw them arrive at
the port, then straight away he rode off with his men, returned
to Fez and made his apologies.[190]

2.2.6.4. Tazouta

This is a town in Garet five miles inland from Cazaza; it was
built on a lofty tuff with a little path that winds around the rock.
There is no water in the town except a single cistern, because
the fortress was built by the Marinids for their grain and goods

before they were rulers. They had travelled the deserts, because there were no Arabs in Garet or the deserts that bordered it; but, once they had taken control of the region, their chiefs went to govern the most important provinces, giving this domain of Garet to their old friends and neighbours in the desert. They were given this province because they were kinsmen of the Marinids, and as a reward for their favours and help, and it remained in their hands until Yusuf ibn Yaqub, the second Marinid king, marched with his armies against the king of Tlemcen. While he was occupied with the siege of Tlemcen, the ruler of Tazouta and all of Garet rebelled against him, and the king got an army to send with his brother against the rebels. They headed for Tazouta and besieged it for two months, after which they stormed it, destroying it on the king's orders.[191]

It remained in ruins until Cazaza was captured by the Spanish.[192] Then the king of Fez was asked by his Granadan general if he could resettle and rebuild Tazouta; the king permitted him the state and profits from Cazaza, and with the king's favour the general began to rebuild Tazouta with the help of the neighbouring people, who had been hassled by Christians from Cazaza and Melilla. It was soon finished, and has remained inhabited ever since. The general constantly attacks the Christians of Cazaza, and the Christians likewise attack him; sometimes the one wins, sometimes the other.

2.2.6.5. Amejjaou

Amejjaou is a little town on a high mountain ten miles west of Tazouta; it was built by the Africans six miles south of the Mediterranean, and its inhabitants are noble and generous. Below the mountain is a fine plain for sowing grain, and there are veins of iron in all the neighbouring mountains, which contain many villages and hamlets for the miners.

The town is under the control of a brave, noble knight who is of royal Almohad origin, though he was born to a destitute cloth-weaver who taught him the trade. When he was old enough to learn of his nobility, and that his ancestors were not weavers, he grew very sad that he could not remedy his low estate, and left Fez in desperation, heading to Badis to join the ruler's light cavalry. But the ruler accepted him as a servant, not only as a soldier but also as a lutenist, because he had a talent for it. The general of Tazouta, wishing to attack the Portuguese, sent to the ruler of Badis to beg the aid of some cavalry, and the latter out of goodwill sent a hundred men, one of whom was this poor nobleman. The attack went ahead, and the Portuguese cavalry came out and fought the Moors, but were defeated by the good man, who showed his courage. On that day he came into the people's good favour, as he did in every subsequent campaign, so the general of Tazouta and the ruler of Badis were envious of his deeds, discharging him from their army and confiscating his salary.

The ruler of Badis desired him to stay on as a musician only, but scorning the idea he left the city with some of his friends in the cavalry from Garet, who supported him both personally and materially. They installed him in the fortress of Amejjaou and stayed there with him, fifty brave horsemen in all. He then began to collect revenues from those among the mountain people who were well disposed to him. The ruler of Badis sent 300 cavalry and 1,000 infantry against him, but the young man was victorious despite having so few men, and, from that day on, his fame grew so great that the present king of Fez sent a privilege to confirm his rule. The king also gave him the revenues from the royal treasury formerly allotted to the rulers of Badis for defending the king against the Spanish, for he now saw the uselessness of those rulers. The young man's income from the king has since doubled, so he can afford to maintain 200 cavalry at his own expense – but his 200 are worth more than 2,000 belonging to the neighbouring generals and rulers.

2.2.6.6. Mount Ikebdanen[193]

This mountain extends east from Cazaza to the river Moulouya, and south from the Mediterranean to the desert of Garet. The inhabitants were healthy and rich, for there is a great abundance of honey and barley, and a huge quantity of livestock since it is full of good fields, and all around it inland are countless pastures for the animals. But when Cazaza was captured by the Spanish they could not support themselves on the mountain, for they all lived in villages far apart from each other. So they abandoned their goods, burned down their houses with their own hands, and went to live on other mountains.

2.2.6.7. Mount Beni Sa'id

This mountain near Cazaza extends west as far as the river Nekor twenty-four miles away; it is divided among many peoples, all rich, healthy and so generous that merchants and travellers spend nothing when they stay there to conclude their trade, that is, in iron and other goods with the locals. They extract a large quantity of iron and barley from the area, and keep much livestock because they have a considerable share of the plains. Their blacksmiths are at liberty, and the people pay no tribute except on the fields. The veins of iron are all in the plain, where there is plenty of water, and each smith keeps his own forge by his house and livestock, extracting and refining the iron. They sell whatever they can in pellets to the merchants of Fez, for they do not use it themselves, and they cannot make it in rods; the rest they make into tools – hoes, needles, axes, ploughshares, saws and simple weapons – for they cannot get steel from it.

2.2.6.8. Mount Segangan

This mountain borders Cazaza to the south, and was once well populated, with many villages and small towns. It was full of rich and healthy men, for like the previous ones it is fertile, but with the added advantage that its foothills meet the desert of Garet, whose inhabitants all trade with the mountainfolk. However, it too was abandoned after the capture of Cazaza.

2.2.6.9. Mount Beni Tuzin

This mountain borders the last to the south, and extends over ten miles from the desert of Garet to the river Nekor. On one side are many plains, which the mountain people farm without paying anything to either the general of Tazouta or the ruler of Badis,[194] for they have twice as many cavalry as those two men, and, moreover, they have sided with the ruler of Amejjaou, often doing great damage to the vassals of the ruler of Badis. But the king of Fez welcomes them, for they were old friends of his family before it became royal, and also because one of the mountainfolk, a great, learned lawyer in Fez and a royal favourite, always praised his people to the kings, reminding them of the ancient friendship between their ancestors, until the current king granted the mountain its liberty. The mountainfolk enjoyed the most favour of all when the Marinids were in power, because the mother of Abu Sa'id,[195] the third Marinid king, was a great noblewoman from the mountain. By their good fortune they have maintained their reputation for a long time.

2.2.6.10. Mount Ouardan

This mountain borders the last to the north and extends twelve miles to the Mediterranean and eight to the river Nekor. Its inhabitants are rich and courageous soldiers, and enjoy a great abundance like those mentioned above. Every Saturday they hold an excellent market by a brook in a plain where most of the mountainfolk of Garet gather, as well as a huge crowd of merchants from Fez, who do good business there, trading horse trappings, oil and other wares for iron, since not many olives grow in the region of Garet. Nor do they cultivate vineyards, and nobody has any wine or will allow anyone else to have it, being neighbours of the drunken mountainfolk of er-Rif.

The inhabitants were once vassals of the ruler of Badis, who mistreated them. But among them was a learned preacher, who accomplished so much with his tongue and by his honourable life that the king let them decide how much tribute to send to his treasury. So every year they give the king fine gifts of horses, slaves and much money; by their generosity the gifts they make for their freedom are worth more than double what they paid when subject to the ruler of Badis.

2.2.6.11. The desert of Garet

This region of Garet is divided into three parts: one part is the city and its territory, the second is the mountains, where the Bou Touya live as mentioned above, and the third part is the desert, which stretches from the Mediterranean in the north to the Al Haouz desert in the south; it borders the mountains to the west and the river Moulouya to the east, extending sixty miles in length and thirty in width. It is arid and harsh, with no water but the Moulouya. There are many of the same animals as are found in the Libyan desert bordering Numidia. For half the year, that is, during the hot season, many Arabs are found in the desert who spend all summer by the Moulouya, and a hardy tribe of shepherds called al-Batalisa,[196] who keep a large amount of livestock – horses, sheep and camels – and are always quarrelling with their Arab neighbours.

End of Garet, the sixth region of Fez; the region of Al Haouz follows.

2.2.7.1. Al Haouz

Al Haouz is a region of Fez believed to occupy a third of the kingdom, for it extends west from the river Za to the end of the river Tigrigra, a distance of 180 miles. In width it is seventy miles or more, spanning the whole range of the Atlas facing Mauretania and a good part of the plains and mountains bordering Libya. When 'Abd al-Haqq, the first prince of the Marinids, invaded and acquired Mauretania and the other regions around it, he shared it out among the tribes of his people and his four sons: Abu Bakr,

Abu Yahya, Abu Sa'id and Yaqub.[197] The last was made king because he drove out and ruined the Almohad dynasty, the kings of Marrakesh. His three predecessors died before they acquired Marrakesh, so they were not given the title of king. The four sons were each given one area by their father, and the three other areas were divided into six parts, that is, one for each of the four Marinid tribes, and two for other tribes who were neighbours and kinsfolk of the Marinids. As a result, the region was believed to contain three domains, there being ten parties who shared the kingdom, and seven areas.[198] Prince 'Abd al-Haqq was the first who divided the regions into parts, making Al Haouz the largest part, as will be seen in considering each town, mountain and place in turn.

2.2.7.2. Taourirt

This ancient city was built by the Africans on a high hill by the river Za. Around it are good fields but they do not extend far, for they border the harsh, arid desert. It adjoins the Garet desert to the north, the Draa desert to the south, the Angad desert at the edge of the kingdom of Tlemcen to the east, and the Tafrata desert by the city of Taza to the west. Taourirt was once well populated and cultured, with 3,000 homes, and its buildings and mosques all walled in travertine. But, after the Marinids came to power in the west, they quarrelled over this town, among other things, for they wanted it to belong to the domain of Fez, while the Zayyanid rulers of Tlemcen wanted it for their own domain.

In the end it was occupied by the Marinids, who, when they invaded, ruined a good part that stood against them. Subsequently, as they began to involve themselves in the wars of Marrakesh, a matter of great importance, they lost interest in Taourirt, so the king of Tlemcen reconquered it, ruining and sacking the opposing part. When Yaqub, the Marinid king, acquired Marrakesh,[199] he returned at once to take Taourirt, so that in the space of fifty years it changed rulers ten times, owned by the king of Fez one day and the king of Tlemcen the next.

The town was ruined and abandoned in the last war in AH 780 (AD 1378–79), after Abu 'l-Abbas Ahmad (al-Mustansir), the eleventh Marinid king of Fez, gave it to an Arab chief for his provision. When its few inhabitants saw that they were now condemned to Arab rule and governance, after being ruined by so many wars, they decided to abandon the town in desperation. So one night they fled to Nedroma, a town belonging to the king of Tlemcen, and Taourirt has remained eerily deserted ever since; the walls, towers and houses are still intact today, but the roofs have fallen down.[200]

2.2.7.3. Al-'Addaja[201]

This is a little town built by the Africans like an island, because the Mouloula flows by it into the river Moulouya. The town was formerly well populated and cultured, but it began to decline when the Arabs invaded to the west, for it borders the Draa deserts inhabited by wicked Arab tribes. It was completely ruined along with Taourirt, except the walls, which can still be seen today.

2.2.7.4. Guercif

Guercif is an ancient ksar built on a cliff beside the river Moulouya five miles from Taourirt; it was used by the Marinids as a fortress to store their grain while they were in the desert, then it was commanded by Abu 'Inan Faris, the fifth Marinid king. In the plains around it are very few fields. There are little gardens of grapes, peaches and flowers, but because the ksar is surrounded by desert, the gardens here seem an earthly paradise. The inhabitants are base men with no culture; all they do is guard their Arab masters' grain and goods. From the outside the ksar looks squalid, resembling a burned hut, because it has black, broken walls, like the buildings inside, which are all covered with slabs of black stone from Tlemcen.

2.2.7.5. Debdou

Debdou is an ancient city built by the Africans on the side of a very high mountain; it is very well fortified, and inhabited by a Zanata tribe. Many springs flow down from the peak into the town, which is five miles from the plain; from below it looks only a mile and a half away, but the path is lengthened by its windings around the mountain. All the town's farms are at the summit, for the plain is barren, although there are some gardens along the banks of a stream flowing under the mountain. The farms on the mountain are not enough to support the town for a month, but they import grain from the territory of Taza. For Debdou was built as a fortress by a Marinid tribe when they divided the western regions, and the region of Debdou belonged to a house named Beni Ourtajjin, which has held it until the present. When the Marinids lost the kingdom of Fez, the house of Beni Ourtajjin remained, attaching itself to the fortress with the favour of the house, or rather of the mountain. The nearby Arabs sought to drive them out of town, because their kinsfolk had mistreated the Arabs when they reigned in Fez, but when they lost their protection they were forced into a siege until the town came to be ruled by a valiant man of that house named Musa ibn Hammu. He fought and led campaigns against the Arabs until he had driven them from the mountain, returning to enjoy the same income that his predecessors had made. The Arabs had to make a truce with him so that they could do business in the town.

After he died, he was succeeded by one of his sons, named Ahmad, who resembled his father in all his ways, and maintained the domain in peace until his death. Then Ahmad's son Muhammad succeeded him, a very able man who had acquired many towns and ksars in the Atlas foothills on the borders of Numidia to the south. It was he who restored culture to the town, having it build a mosque, a hammam and many shops for the merchants and craftsmen; he was so generous that every traveller – whether merchants or mule-drivers, poor men or nobles – stayed in his court at his expense until they had finished their business. He gave them rooms and expenses according to their means, so he enjoyed the goodwill of all and an excellent reputation.

Many advised and encouraged Muhammad to attack the city of Taza and its territory, in order to lift it from the subjugation of the king of Fez. So he arranged with some mountainfolk near the city to travel there quickly, joining them himself in the guise of a mountain dweller going to market. Once they reached it, they attacked the captain of the city's horse guards, killing some and putting others to flight.[202] Part of the city favoured Muhammad, but the ruse was discovered by Sheikh[203] – the first Wattasid king of Fez and father of the present king – who decided to ruin the ruler of Debdou. So the king gathered a large army from the biggest and best part of Fez along with many Arabs, and marched on Taza. Because he wanted to punish the mountainfolk first, he ordered his men into battle when he reached the foot of the mountain, burning their houses and killing the inhabitants.[204] But the mountainfolk, who numbered 6,000 or so, were cruel and cunning, allowing part of the king's army to climb up by very steep, narrow paths. Exhausted and dishevelled, the soldiers were then attacked by the locals, who were fresh and hardy. They wanted to retreat from their opponents' fury, but more than a thousand of them broke their necks and a further 3,000 were killed, because the paths were blocked by others who had climbed up.

There was no honour or consolation for the king in this skirmish, so he retreated from the mountain in confusion, pursuing his campaign against the ruler of Debdou. He first made provision of 500 crossbowmen and 300 gunmen. When he arrived at the foot of the mountain of Debdou he wanted to join battle, but Muhammad, seeing that he could not defend himself in any way, surrendered to the king. He came down on foot in the guise of an envoy with letters in his own handwriting, and asked the guard for permission to speak to the king because he was bearing letters from the ruler of Debdou. The king bade him enter, and once inside the royal tent he handed over the letters, which the king at once had his minister read out. Then the king said to the incognito ruler, 'What's your view of this foolish ruler of yours?'

Muhammad replied: 'He seems quite mad to me. But the devil has the power to deceive the great as well as the small.'

'By my faith, if I got my hands on him I'd skin him alive.'

'Your lordship, if he should seek clemency and beg your forgiveness, coming to Your Highness on foot as a humble person, how would your lordship treat him?'

'By my faith, and on my father's life, I would confirm his rule and give him my two daughters for his sons, along with fields and ksars in the territory of Fez, to show him my mercy and compassion out of love of our respective ancestors, who were kith and kin. But I don't believe that this fool could act in such a manner.'

'I truly believe he would, if your lordship can promise this before your chief courtiers.'

'Are these four not enough? This is my chief minister, this is the captain general of my cavalry, this is my father-in-law, and this good old man is the chief justice and imam of Fez.'

The ruler asked the four men if they were who the king said they were, and they replied that they were. Then he abased himself humbly, crying out and kissing the king's feet, saying: 'My lord, I am that sinner, and have no refuge or defence but your compassion.'

The king was astonished, like the rest of his courtiers, and said, 'By God, then you aren't the fool I thought.' He embraced and kissed the ruler and called his chief courtiers at once; within an hour they had become family, and Muhammad brought countless presents along with his two sons, so that night they all dined together. In the morning, the king got up with his camp and returned to Fez with his two new sons-in-law. But the people of Fez suffered immeasurable loss on that journey, for it was during June and July when the land is hot and arid. It being eighty miles from Debdou to Taza, with no water except in three camps, they were forced to walk quickly and a good number died in the heat, both on the outward journey and on the return. This occurred in AH 904 (AD 1498–99).

The old ruler lived until AH 921 (AD 1515–16), a year when the author himself left Fez and stayed at his home, receiving a great welcome thanks to letters of recommendation by the king and his brother, who married Muhammad's daughter. The author stayed for two days, and was asked in detail about the court of the king of Fez and his brothers.

2.2.7.6. Taza

Taza is a large, noble, well-fortified, fertile and abundant city, built by the ancient Africans on a high mountain nine miles from the Atlas range, fifty from Fez, thirty from the ocean, and seven from the Mediterranean through the Garet desert towards Cazaza. The city has 5,000 homes, but the buildings are not very fine except the palaces of the nobles, the mosques and the madrasas, which are well constructed. A stream flows down from the Atlas through the town and even inside the great mosque, but it is controlled by the rebel mountainfolk. When they are at war with the citizens, they divert the river, causing great harm to the townsfolk, who cannot work their mills, nor access drinking water except from the cisterns, which do not have good water.

Taza is the third city[205] in rank and dignity, and likewise in culture. It has a huge mosque, bigger even than that of Fez, three madrasas and many hammams and inns. Its squares are ordered like those of Fez, and its inhabitants are hardier and more generous. Among them are many learned, wealthy gentlemen, for the city has the best fields, often producing a thirtyfold yield, and around it are valleys along streams, covered with gardens of excellent, plentiful fruit. There are also many vineyards of white, black and red grapes, but they all use trellises; the town's Jews, who number 500 households, make a large amount of wine from them, which they claim is the best in the region.

Within the town is a large, handsome citadel where the viceroy or city governor lives. The modern kings of Fez give this city to the second-born son, but it really ought to be the royal seat for its good air in both winter and summer; many Marinid rulers used to stay here in summer, not only for the air, but also to guard these lands from the desert Arabs, who travel every year to buy food and bring dates from Sijilmasa to barter for grain. The burghers make all their money from selling grain to the Arabs, which is why their city and its inhabitants are so excellent, except that in winter one cannot move for the mud.

The author has visited countless times and conversed with many of its nobles, in particular one old man held to be a saint by the people; he was very rich from his fruit and fields, and from the offerings of the townsfolk and people of Fez. The burghers of Fez would travel fifty miles to meet him. The author was among those who doubted his deeds, and after they met he seemed just like any other, but his doings are of the sort that deceive the common people.

The city has a vast territory, with many well-populated mountains – Mount Matghara, Mount Ghiata, Mount Mgassa, Mount al-Baranis, Mount Beni Ourtenaj, Mount Bou Iblan and Mount Selelgo. Having everything it needed on these mountains, the town could support its inhabitants for ten years under siege. There are also two springs, each the source of a river.

2.2.7.7. Mount Matghara

This mountain is very high and difficult to climb because it has dense woods and very narrow paths. At its summit are excellent fields and springs. The mountain is five miles from Taza; its inhabitants are free and harvest grain, oil and flax, also keeping a great quantity of livestock, especially goats, and so they hold the rulers in low esteem. It was they who defeated the army of their master, the king of Fez,[206] and ever since they have not been on friendly terms with him or trusted him. For this reason they abandoned many of their fields in the plains, leaving them uncultivated, lest any of them should fall into the king's hands.[207] The mountain has 7,000 warriors and fifty large villages.

2.2.7.8. Mount Ghiata

This mountain is as difficult to scale as the last; it lies five miles west of Taza and has good fields on both its slopes and summit, where much barley and flax grows. It extends eight miles from east to west and five miles in width. On it are many valleys and forests full of apes and leopards. Its inhabitants are cloth-weavers; they are valiant, generous and spirited, but cannot do business in the plains, because they once disobeyed the king of Fez, proudly refusing to pay him tribute.

2.2.7.9. Mount Mgassa

Mgassa is a harsh, difficult mountain full of forests; very little grain grows there, but a lot of oil. Its inhabitants are all cloth-weavers, for they have plenty of flax. They are hale and hardy men on both foot and horseback, and they are very pale because the mountain is high and cold. They are also free, so they can welcome exiles from Fez and Taza. They have many gardens and vineyards, but none of them drink wine. The mountain has 6,000 warriors and forty large villages.

2.2.7.10. Mount al-Baranis

This mountain is five miles north of Taza; it is inhabited by a rich, sturdy people, who are free and have many horses. A lot of grain grows on their mountain, and they have many gardens and vineyards of black grapes, from which they make not wine but *sapa*.[208] The women are very pale and voluptuous, wearing many silver ornaments, for they are very rich. They are a scornful, spirited and generous people, and they too will favour exiles, but woe to anyone who gets involved with their women.

2.2.7.11. Mount Beni Ourtenaj

This mountain, which is thirty miles from the city of Taza, is high and difficult because of its cliffs and forests. Grain, flax, olives, citrons and excellent, fragrant quinces all grow there. There is much livestock, except horses and cows, which are rare.

The inhabitants are valiant, liberal and refined like burghers, but there are thirty-five villages on the mountain, with 3,000 brave and well-equipped warriors.

2.2.7.12. Mount Bou Iblan

This frozen mountain is very high and broad; it extends sixty miles in length by fifteen in width, bordering the mountains of Debdou to the east and Mount Beni Yazgha to the west, while Taza is fifty miles north. One sees snow all year round on its peak, which was once inhabited by a great people, valiant, rich and always free. But they sought to become tyrants; the peoples of the mountains mentioned above united against them, killing the men and burning their villages, and so the mountain has been uninhabited ever since. But one family of Mount Bou Iblan, when they saw that their kinsmen aspired to tyranny, divided up their goods and households and went to live at the summit like hermits. When the other mountainfolk were destroyed, God miraculously pardoned and liberated this family; their descendants have been honoured ever since for living well and studiously, and the king of Fez, like his predecessors, holds them in high regard.

In the author's time there was a good and learned old man of this family, who was pressed into service by the king of Fez whenever he would make a truce or peace with some Arab tribe. For the Arabs had little trust in their rulers, but when they saw someone like the old man they trusted him, because they knew that the king could not go back on his word when it was conveyed by such a person. The courtiers or officials that the king persecuted often fled to this mountain so that one of the hermits could intercede on their behalf.

2.2.7.13. Mount Beni Iesseten

This mountain is subject to the ruler of Debdou, its neighbour. It is inhabited by a lowly people who are always badly clothed and barefoot, although they make a sort of sandal[209] from spiny rushes; when one is to embark on a journey in their region and has put on his shoes, he will first go pluck the rushes, and plait a new pair on his way. But the ones on his feet will scarcely last until the new ones are finished. The rest of their lives can be judged from that! On their mountain nothing grows but panicum, from which they make bread and other foods, although in the foothills there are many gardens of grapes, dates and peaches. They take the stones out of the last and cut them into four parts, drying them in the sun to preserve all year as precious food. The dates they eat in season, but they go bad if one tries to preserve them.

On the slopes are many veins of iron, which they are always mining. They make pieces a pound in mass, enough to shoe a horse, and these can be spent instead of money, because there is little or no silver. But they also sell the iron for a lot of money, because the desert Arabs, their neighbours, spend a lot to shoe their camels and horses. They also make daggers from it, but these cannot even cut a gourd. Their women wear iron rings on their fingers and in their ears, and they are very badly clothed; they also go into the forests to cut wood and pasture the goats. There is no culture on the mountain, nor anyone who can read, for they are like animals with no intelligence or judgement.

[In Debdou the royal chancellor told me a delightful tale that reveals the nature of these people. The ruler, he said, sent a deputy to the mountain, a man of great ingenuity. He took a fancy to one of the women of the mountain, but did not know how to achieve his desire, for she was married and her husband never left her alone. One day he saw the couple go to the forest with an animal to carry wood; when they arrived, the husband tied the beast to a branch, and both of them started cutting wood a little way off. On seeing this, the deputy, who had kept behind them, went to the tree and untied the animal, which slowly wandered off in search of grass. When the husband had cut a lot of sticks, he went back for the animal, leaving his wife to wait for him; not finding it where he had tied it, he walked a long way before he eventually came across it.

Meanwhile, the deputy, who had been lurking in the branches

nearby watching this result, revealed himself to the woman, and, without much of a struggle, had his way with her. Scarcely had he concluded this amorous pursuit when the husband appeared with the recovered animal, hot and panting from the exertion, but the deputy ran off so quickly that he was not seen. The husband was carrying the wood, and when he arrived he wanted to sleep, lying down by his wife in the shade of a tree. Fondling her, as he often did, one of his hands happened to touch her best asset, and found it still soft and moist. 'What is the meaning of this, woman?' he asked. 'Why are you wet?' She cunningly replied, 'I was lamenting that you would never return, thinking the animal lost, and my sister, thinking the same, began to weep out of compassion for me.' The idiot believed her, and told her to take comfort and cry no more.][210]

2.2.7.14. Mount Selelgo[211]

Selelgo is a mountain full of towering pine forests and great springs. Its inhabitants do not have walled houses but make homes from a matting of spiny rushes which they can move from place to place, since in winter they have to leave the mountain and go down into the plains. When the Arabs return from the desert at the end of May, the inhabitants of the mountain kill two birds with one stone, fleeing the Arabs and going somewhere cooler for the benefit of both the people and their animals, for they keep lots of sheep and goats. When winter comes, the Arabs return to the warmth of the desert, for the camels cannot live long in cold regions. On the mountain are many lions, leopards and apes. One huge spring of water gushes out so fast that the author has seen someone throw a hundred-pound rock into its mouth and have it thrown out again by the water's velocity. From it comes the Sebou, the largest river in Mauretania.

2.2.7.15. Mount Beni Yazgha

The people of this mountain are rich and honourable in their way of life. It lies next to the previous mountain where the river begins, which flows between them under high cliffs. They have made a marvellous bridge to cross it, planting two thick stakes on either side, to which are attached two pulleys, with large ropes of spiny rushes passing through them from one side to another. To the ropes is attached a large, thick, strong basket in which ten people can stand, and when someone wants to cross he gets into the basket and starts pulling the ropes on either side. The ropes are easily drawn through the pulleys and the basket glides across, and the person can cross in this manner. When someone wants to cross and finds the basket on the other side, he just pulls the ropes and the basket comes straight back, so that anyone can cross.

It was once reported to the author – though it has happened more often – that more people climbed into the basket than it could carry, causing it to give way. Those inside all fell down into the river, while the others clung to the ropes and were freed only with great difficulty, for they did not realise what later became clear, namely, that because they were stuck and tangled in both ropes, those who wanted to pull could not do so. When the author heard of this disaster, his flesh crawled with horror at the thought that the drop was at least fifty cubits, especially as the stakes are fixed at the summits of two high mountains and the river flows between them. Anyone would chicken out after seeing the basket's height above the river.

The denizens of the mountain keep a lot of livestock, for there aren't many forests. The animals' wool is very fine, and the women make fabric blankets from it that seem like silk; they also cut it to make their clothes. The blankets are sold in Fez for a good price; some three, others four or even ten ducats apiece. They also grow a lot of oil on the mountain, but the inhabitants are subjects of the king of Fez, and their revenues, which come to 8,000 ducats, are claimed by the castellan of Old Fez.

2.2.7.16. Mount Azgan

This mountain borders Selelgo to the east, Mount Sefrou to the west, the mountains over the river Moulouya to the south, and the plains of Fez to the north. It is forty miles in length and fifteen in width; it is very high, and so cold that nobody can live there except on the side facing Fez, which is all settled and planted with olives and other fruit. Many streams have their sources on this side, descending through the plains full of good fields for sowing barley, flax and hemp, which grow in great quantities. In modern times many white mulberry trees have been planted in the plain for the silkworms.[212] For five months of the year the inhabitants of the mountain cannot stay, but go live in huts on the plain. The water is so cold in summer that nobody will dare put his hand in it for longer than he can count to ten. The author has seen a person drink a cup of it for a dare. He was sick in bed for three months.

2.2.7.17. Sefrou

This is a little town in the Atlas foothills five miles south of Fez, by the pass to Numidia. It was built by the Africans between two rivers, surrounded by groves of grapes and other fruit. There are olive groves throughout the plains five miles around the town. Sefrou's fields are so meagre that they sow them with flax, hemp and barley. The inhabitants are rich, but they all wear ragged clothes stained with oil, for all year round they grind olives in large enough quantities to keep and export to Fez.

The town does not have very fine houses, nor any other fine building except the mosque, through which a pretty spring flows. There is also a pretty fountain beside the entrance to the mosque. But the town was almost ruined by the wicked behaviour of a brother of the present king of Fez, who rules the town.

2.2.7.18. Mezdgha

Mezdgha is a little town in the Atlas foothills eight miles west of Sefrou; it is well walled but inside are rough buildings. Each house has a fountain inside, like Sefrou. The inhabitants are almost all potters, making their pots from a good local pozzolan[213] to sell in Fez, only two miles to the north. The town's land is good for barley, flax and hemp, and it also has many olives, figs and other fruit. In the forests near Mezdgha and Sefrou are many lions, but they are not dangerous; although they hunt sheep, they will flee if anyone runs at them with a weapon in his hand.

2.2.7.19. Beni Bhalil

This is a little town built on the side of the Atlas mountains facing Fez, around two miles from the city, beside another pass towards Numidia. On the mountain overhead are many springs, some of which flow through the town, and the countryside around it resembles that of Mezdgha. To the south, however, is nothing but forests, and almost all the townsfolk are woodcutters, some of them felling and chopping the trees, others taking the wood to sell in Fez. They are heavily burdened by their rulers, so they struggle to get by and the town has no culture.

2.2.7.20. Ain al-Asnam

This town was built by the ancient Africans in a plain surrounded by mountains on the pass from Sefrou to Numidia. Its name, Ain al-Asnam, means 'the fountain of idols', because in ancient times, when the Africans worshipped idols, they maintained a temple in the plain by the town where all the mountain people gathered once a year. They made sacrifices in the temple, and held ceremonies at night; when these were finished they extinguished the lights, and all the men and women remained there together, doing whatever they wished. In the morning, every woman found in the temple overnight was forbidden to marry for a year, and all the sons they bore during that time were appointed priests of the idol on the mountain.

When the Muslims invaded the region, they destroyed the temple and town, so that at present only traces of a building can be seen. But even today the spring spreads out like a lake over the meadows, extending here and there to make the entire area marshy.

2.2.7.21. Al-Mahdia[214]

This is a city in the Atlas mountains among forests and springs, in a plain ten miles from Ain al-Asnam. It was built when the Zanata ruled Fez, by a mountain-dwelling preacher[215] who just about led to their downfall. He ruled almost the whole of this part of the Atlas near Fez, but when the Lamtuna invaded under King Yusuf the town was ruined and then sacked. All that remains are the walls and the mosque in the middle of town, for it was well constructed and the enemies did not want to destroy it. Since then, the mountainfolk have all become lowly subjects of the king of Fez, but they were once fierce and free. The city was ruined in AH 515 (AD 1121–22).

2.2.7.22. Sahab al-Marga, which means the Plain of the Brave

This is a plain thirty miles in width by forty in length, situated in a part of the Atlas mountains; it is surrounded by forests of tall trees, in which can be found the charcoal-makers' huts. They live like hermits, being so far from any settlement, and each has his own hut far away from the others. Their large furnaces can hold a hundred loads at once. Some go there with donkeys and mules to buy the charcoal from the locals and take it back to Fez to sell. But the forests are full of lions, which often eat the charcoal-makers; if one should have some task to do at night outside his hut, he goes out and the lions at once drag him off and eat him. They also make fine beams and planks on the mountain, which they export to Fez. But the whole plain is barren, littered with black rocks like flat, thin tablets,[216] and nothing at all grows there.

2.2.7.23. Azgar Igmaren

This is another plain surrounded by wooded mountains. It resembles a meadow where grass grows all year round, and for this reason many shepherds from the mountains gather in the plain during the summer. But at night they stand guard, hanging tall branches all around them and keeping watch lest they be caught unawares by lions.

2.2.7.24. The Mountain of a Hundred Wells[217]

This is the highest of the mountains, and at the summit are some ancient buildings; there is no record of what they were. Next to them is a very deep well, and many madmen come here in search of treasure,[218] bringing countless ropes to climb down with lanterns. They say the well has many levels, that is, one finds several broad spaces as one goes down into it. At the lowest level they find a large room dug out with iron tools, built on bases like columns, and apparently walled around. In the walls are four low openings that lead straight to other chambers with wells of fresh water. Dead bodies are often found beside the well, because people go down the well with lanterns and once inside they encounter a terrible wind that puts out their light; the man inside cannot find his way back to the mouth, so he remains inside and dies.

The author has personally heard the story from an impoverished nobleman of Fez who enjoyed hunting for treasure. The man once left Fez for the well with ten companions, and when they reached it they drew lots to see who would have to go down. Three were chosen, and the other seven were to stay up above to keep a lookout and hold the rope to let the hunters up and down. The author's friend was one of the three; he fastened himself with a very long rope and was the first to descend, arriving at the bottom with his lantern attached. Then the other two descended with their lanterns, and when they were all together they each decided to take one of the four openings. But the one who related the story was more shrewd, and winked at another to go with him; so one took one path and the other two took another, and when they had gone a quarter of a mile on the narrow path they encountered large bats that hurtled past them and struck the lanterns, putting one light out. They finally arrived at the last room where the spring of living water was, and beside it the bones of dead men, along with five very old but intact lanterns. When they looked into the well they found it full of water. Then they started to head back, but when they were halfway along the other light died in a gust of wind; then, unable to go forward or back, they were lost and swallowed up by the caverns, remaining there underground for over six hours. They grew desperate and worn out, because they sometimes had to go long distances bent over and exhausted, until they no longer knew what to do. Eventually they lay down together on the floor, wailing and vowing never to go underground again if they could only escape.

Luckily for them, the seven companions outside suspected that the three men underground had found no treasure and they had all been deceived. Five of them climbed down with lit lanterns and fire strikers, and when they arrived below they began shouting loudly and exploring. They left a large lantern under the shaft of the well, and after half an hour the two lost ones heard them and called out in reply, so the five found them with some difficulty. They were moaning and worn out, their clothes torn and their flesh all scratched from clambering through narrow holes and rough rocks. Their companions led them back to the shaft of the well where they had left the lantern, then returned to look for the third man, staying more than three hours to search for him, but never found him. Then they climbed back up one by one, until they had all emerged except the one, returning unhappily without him and anxious that they would be arrested by the court if his wife should publicly accuse them.

But, after three days, whom should they see but the tenth companion? By a stroke of luck he reappeared, saying that he too had got lost. After midnight he had heard a cry, the young of some animal that had lost its children in the cave going deep under the earth: it was a *dabuh* (hyena), an animal much bigger than a wolf. He walked towards the sound until he reached it with great effort, finding these baby animals without their mother. He stepped over them into a high cave. At length the mother returned and remained with them for a long time, though she was very suspicious of the smell. He did nothing but wait till morning when the mother left, and then he followed her, slowly but surely; before long he saw the light coming in through the hole where the animal had entered, and he emerged at the foot of the mountain. Thanking God, he went up to the summit for his companions but found nobody there; fearful and astonished, and half-dead from hunger, he came straight back down until he reached the hut of a charcoal-maker, who gave him something to eat. He related his story and the man laughed uproariously, thinking them very foolish and saying: 'You'd be better off staying with me to make charcoal and earn money than looking underground for things neither you nor your father put there.' He left, arriving at Fez three days after his companions, and they were all relieved to have escaped such danger. The author said to the survivor who told him the story: 'When you were lost you vowed never to go underground again.'

With a laugh the other replied: 'Actually, I've realised that my vow doesn't count, because I have to go underground when I die: my vow will be broken no matter what.'

'Well, go wherever you please!'

'These days I come prepared: I take the fire striker whenever I go underground.'

Since the author heard this tale, it was discovered that the building on the mountain had been built as a fortress by certain potentates. The well had been dug out until level with the plain, allowing water in from the valley around the mountain, and the four paths inside leading to the wells connected to the foot of the mountain on all sides. The one who escaped must have stumbled on some hole that led him out of the caves.

2.2.7.25. The Mountain and Pass of the Crows, Kheneg al-Gherben[219]

This mountain, which is near the last, contains many forests and lions. There aren't any towns or villages; it is completely uninhabited because of the cold. A stream flows through the pass, and the mountain crags on either side are very high. Many carrion crows live there, for which reason it is called the Pass of the Crows. Having crossed the pass you'll reach the top of the mountain, where many travellers from Numidia to Fez die when the north wind blows in the snowy season. But in summer the Beni Hussein Arabs go there for its fresh water and shade. Throughout the mountain are fierce leopards and lions.

2.2.7.26. Tezerghe

Tezerghe is a little town almost like a fortress, built by the Africans on a little river that flows between valleys by the foot of the mountain. Its people are ugly and its buildings have no culture or decoration. There are few fields between the valleys, and all that grows is a little barley and a few peach trees. The inhabitants are subject to the Dhawi Hussein Arabs.

2.2.7.27. Oum Jeniba

This was an ancient town destroyed by the Arabs, twelve miles from Tezerghe beside a pass on the southern side of the Atlas mountains. The pass is notorious for Arab brigands and thieves, for there is a large plain in the town and the Arabs who live there do not fear the king. Beside the town is a rise where, when a caravan passes, everyone in it has to dance, for the ancient inhabitants of the land say that whoever crosses the rise without dancing will contract quartan fever. For this reason the author has seen every traveller dance in fear.

2.2.7.28. Mount Beni Merasen

This mountain is very high and cold, but well populated by tribes who do not care about the cold. They keep great numbers of horses and large donkeys, and from them they breed mules like the pack donkeys, with light harnesses but no bridles or saddles. They do not have walled houses, but only huts of matting, for they constantly travel to pasture their horses and mules. They pay no tax to the king of Fez, for the mountain is difficult to attack, and so they are quite rich.

2.2.7.29. Mount Mestasa

This mountain extends thirty miles east to west, and twelve miles in width. To the west it borders the plains of Adekhsan, which in turn border Tamasna. The mountain is very cold, but it is inhabited by a noble and wealthy tribe who keep many horses and mules. Many of them work as scholars in Fez, but one can also find lots of scribes on the mountain; they write fine letters and copy books, sending them to be sold in Fez. The inhabitants are practically free, for they pay no tax at all to the king of Fez, only sending him a few gifts.

2.2.7.30. The Ziz mountains

These mountains are named after the river Ziz, which springs up in them. To the east they border Mount Mestasa, to the west Tadla and Mount Dades; to the south they face Sijilmasa in Numidia, and to the north the plains of Adekhsan and Tigrigra. All in all they extend 100 miles in length and forty in width. There are five mountains, all of them cold and barren, and many rivers begin there. All of them are inhabited by a fearsome Zanaga tribe who take no heed of the cold, in the snowy season wearing only a wool tunic with a cloak over it, and some rags around their legs and feet, but nothing on their heads. They keep many sheep, mules and donkeys, for the mountains have few forests. They are the worst brigands in the world, attacking the caravans that come and go from Numidia and killing people for little reason. There is a great enmity between them and the Arabs, whom they attack at night on foot, carrying off their camels and throwing them off high rocks; the camels hit the bottom in a thousand pieces. Sometimes they do this in a place where the Arabs who own the camels can see but not do anything, for they make every effort to disrespect the Arabs.

In the mountains is something almost miraculous, namely a huge number of large, tame snakes. They wander through the homes as if they were cats; when the mountainfolk want to eat, all the snakes in the house gather round, eating all the dry crusts of bread and other food, and never biting or hurting anyone except in retaliation. When a foreigner arrives on the mountain, the locals warn him not to hurt any of the snakes; but travellers have nothing to do with those accursed tribes, with a few exceptions. The inhabitants themselves hold the snakes to be benign spirits.

Some of the mountainfolk live in ugly walled villages, with buildings of clay-covered beams and roofs thatched with straw from the grain that grows plentifully on the mountain, from which they also make bread. Others, who live in huts of matting, have more livestock. Their shepherds make two journeys a year to Sijilmasa in Numidia, their closest neighbour, bringing their cattle, as well as wool and butter, and selling them for a high price in both cash and goods; but they travel only during the period when the Arabs are living in the desert, and the Arabs sometimes come to attack them with a huge cavalcade, killing them and stealing their goods. But the mountainfolk are valiant foot soldiers, each carrying up to six or seven little spears in their hands, as well as a sword and dagger. One of them can easily defend himself against two Arabs on horseback, for when he throws a spear at a man or horse he never misses; they will not lose them unless a large band of cavalry should arrive, and then they will fight to the death, never letting themselves be taken alive. But in modern times they send for safe-conducts from the Arabs and pay a certain amount of tribute per load or per animal. So the Arabs leave them to do as they please in safety.

The mountainfolk also give safe-conducts to merchant caravans, but the poor merchants have to pay each tribe in the mountains a separate tax, with safe-conducts for each mountain, or they are in danger of being waylaid for the tax by an unpaid faction, for the mountainfolk are all in cahoots with each other.

2.2.7.31. Gerseluin

Gerseluin is an ancient city built by the Africans at the foot of the mountains by the river Ziz. It has fine, strong walls constructed by the Marinid kings, and seems very splendid from outside, but inside it is hideous, with wretched homes and few inhabitants. For, after the Marinids fell, the town was freely ruled by the Dhawi Hussein, an Arab tribe who mistreated its denizens, so for a while it lacked any culture. It already belonged to the Arabs during the rule of the Marinids, but under their protection the Arabs could not do so much harm, for it was then more inhabited and cultured. Not a penny in revenue can be extracted from the city, since the inhabitants are destitute, having only a few fields in the north to sow, the other sides all being barren, because they are really the foothills of the mountains.

On the banks of the river, by contrast, are many mills and countless gardens of grapes and peaches, which they dry in the sun and preserve all year; in particular, they cook them mixed in with the wretched food they live on. They keep such a tiny amount of livestock that they all lead miserable lives, for the city was built in ancient times by the Zanata as a fortress to hold the pass to Numidia, fearing the Lamtuna would cross it – just as they did in fact cross another pass, as said above, and ruined the city. The Marinids later rebuilt it to house the mountainfolk, but their intended plan failed. This city too has a multitude of snakes; they slither around in the houses, and, whenever someone wants to eat, a large number of the snakes can be seen around them.

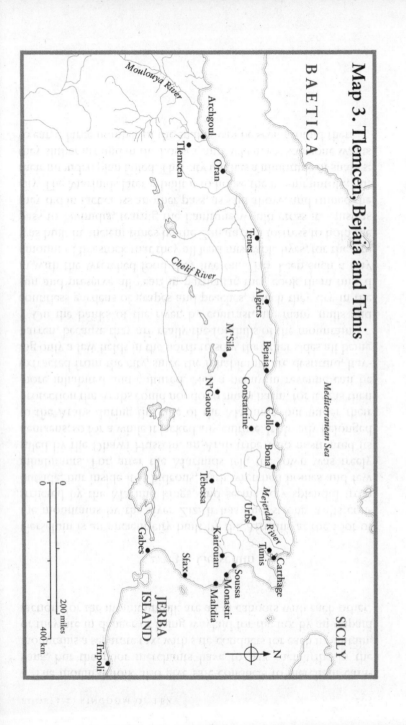

Map 3. Tlemcen, Bejaia and Tunis

BAETICA

SICILY

Moulouya River

Archgoul

Tlemcen

Oran

Tenes

Chelif River

Algiers

M'Sila

Bejaia

Constantine

Collo

N'Gaous

Bona

Mediterranean Sea

Tebessa

Urbs

Mejerda River

Tunis

Carthage

Gabes

Karouan

Soussa

Monastir

Mahdia

Sfax

JERBA ISLAND

Tripoli

0

200 miles

400 km

N

BOOK 2.3.

KINGDOM OF TLEMCEN

2.3.1. [Introduction]

The kingdom of Tlemcen is bounded by the rivers Za and Mou-louya to the west, the Greater River to the east, the Numidian desert to the south, and the Mediterranean to the north. The kingdom was called Caesarea in Latin, and was once ruled by the Romans, though after they left Africa it returned to its former rulers, the Beni 'Abd al-Wad, a tribe of the Maghrawa. The Beni 'Abd al-Wad ruled for 300 years, until the reign of the great prince Yaghmurasen ibn Zyan. The kingdom remained in Ghamrazen's direct lineage, and the dynasty changed its name from Beni 'Abd al-Wad to Beni Zayyan, or sons of Zayyan ibn Ghamrazen, a dynasty lasting 380 years. The dynasty was much beleaguered by the Marinid kings of Fez, and according to the histories around ten of them invaded Tlemcen with their armies; the Zayyanid kings were killed, some captured, and some driven to the desert with their Arab neighbours. From time to time, the kings of Tunis drove out and dethroned the Zayyanids, though the latter returned to their domains and lived in peace for ten years, untroubled by other rulers. But Abu Faris, king of Tunis, and his son 'Uthman[1] brought their armies several times to besiege the city of Tlemcen, until its king agreed to pay them a large tribute. The city's kings gave tribute for some time, until 'Uthman died in AH [. . .].[2]

The kingdom of Tlemcen is 380 miles from east to west, though very narrow from north to south; here the deserts of Numidia are only twenty-five miles from the Mediterranean. For this reason, the nearby Arabs are always causing the kingdom trouble and damage, so the kings have always agreed to pay them large sums and gifts. Since they cannot satisfy them all, rarely can one journey safely through the kingdom, for fear of Arab bandits. Nevertheless, Tlemcen does considerable trade, being next to Numidia and a stop on the way to the Land of the Blacks. It has two renowned ports, at Oran and Mers el-Kebir, where many Genoese and Venetian merchants do good business, bartering with the locals for their wares. However, these ports and towns were taken by the Christians during the reign of Ferdinand, the Catholic king of Spain, and for this reason the kingdom of Tlemcen fell into such poverty and confusion that the people seized the king Abu Hammu (III) and replaced him with his uncle Abu Zayyan, whom Abu Hammu and his father Abu 'Abdallah had kept in prison.[3] Once freed and enthroned, he had little time to rejoice, for he was then challenged by the Turk Barbarossa,[4] who had him killed by treachery. Barbarossa made himself king of Tlemcen, but then Abu Hammu, whom the people had exiled, went to the city of Oran and from there to Spain, to beseech his majesty the Emperor Charles (V) with humble devotion, pleading for aid against the people and the Turk Barbarossa. On hearing this, the Emperor, showing a mercy and pity rarely equalled among his ancestors, sent a great army with the king to enter the kingdom and slaughter Barbarossa and many of his family. Abu Hammu had many city leaders killed, in a single stroke taking revenge on the people of Tlemcen and reclaiming his throne. He at once repaid the Spanish who had come with him and sent an ambassador to the Emperor with the gifts and tribute he owed.

Abu Hammu lived several months before he died. His brother 'Abdallah[5] then came to the throne and withdrew his loyalty and the treaties his brother had made with the Emperor, instead declaring his allegiance to Suleiman, Emperor of the Turks, though he did not benefit from the arrangement in any way; he remains there even now.[6]

Most of the kingdom is dry, harsh land, especially to the south, though the plains along the coast are quite fertile. The area around Tlemcen is full of deserts, while the western coastal part is mountainous. Likewise, there are lots of mountains in the region of Tenes and above Algiers, though they are all fertile. The few cities and ksars there are profitable and fertile, as will be seen by taking each place and town in turn.

2.3.2. The Angad desert

The kingdom begins to the west in a flat, harsh and dry desert, without water or trees, stretching eighty miles long and fifty miles wide. It has great numbers of goats, deer and ostriches, and since the desert is the route from Fez to Tlemcen it swarms with Arab bandits. The poor merchants can rarely avoid them, especially in winter when the Arabs who are paid off go to Numidia while the others stay behind with their horses to rob people. Many shepherds are found there in winter, along with many rabid lions that ravage the flocks and people.

2.3.3. Timzizdegt

The ksar Timzizdegt sits on the border between the desert and Tlemcen, built by the ancient Africans on an outcrop. The kings of Tlemcen kept the ksar well fortified, to hold the pass against the king of Fez, since it is near the main road to Fez and below it flows the river Tesme. Around it are several good patches of land that grow enough to sustain the ksar. It was once under Tlemcen's rule and very cultured, but now it is ruled by the Arabs and has become a kind of stable for camel-drivers, since they only maintain it to store grain and packsaddles for their camels. The inhabitants have all fled the wicked behaviour of the Arabs.

2.3.4. Isly

Isly is an ancient ksar built by the Africans on a plain bordering the desert, surrounded by a few fields of barley and millet. The ksar had good walls in ancient times, but after the wars they were destroyed and the ksar was deserted for several years before being resettled by some men feigning piety, honoured by the kings of Tlemcen and Arabs alike, who harboured anyone, whether traveller or Arab, giving them food, drink and a bed for three days, and longer for acquaintances and those who come with recommendations. The ksar's buildings are squat, with bad clay walls and straw roofs. A spring outside is used to water the fields, for the weather is hot and they cannot grow anything without irrigation.

2.3.5. Oujda

Oujda is an ancient city built by the Africans in a great plain, forty miles south of the Mediterranean and forty miles from Tlemcen, with the desert of Angad to the south and west. All the fields around it are abundantly fertile, with many gardens, especially of grapes and figs. A spring flows through it, used for drinking and other necessities. The town's walls were strong and high, and likewise the houses and shops were finely built. The inhabitants were rich, cultured and healthy. However, in the wars between the kings of Fez and Tlemcen, the town preserved its allegiance to the latter, for which reason it was sacked and its walls entirely destroyed. The houses were left in ruins and empty for many years, until the rage of the king of Fez had subsided; the city was then resettled and its walls pieced together with some simple materials. But they have dug good, deep ditches all around the walls, and built many new houses, albeit cheap ones of a single storey; the shops were rebuilt in the same way in a square near the mosque. The rest of the town is nearly empty, with only 500 homes; the inhabitants have been impoverished by the tribute they pay the king of Tlemcen and their Arab neighbours in the desert of Angad. They all dress like countryfolk in short, coarse clothes, and they raise large, handsome donkeys for breeding large, handsome mules, selling them for a good price in Tlemcen. The inhabitants all still use the old African language, and only a few speak poor Arabic, in the manner of the burghers.

2.3.6. Nedroma

This city was built in antiquity by the Romans when they ruled the region; it occupies a large area on a plain about two miles from the mountains. Next to the town flows a modest river, and the historians say that the Romans built the city on a site like that of Rome, and in the same fashion. This is why it was called 'Ned Roma', for in the African language *ned* means 'similar or 'equal' – that is, to Rome.[7] The town walls are intact, though the houses inside were all razed to the ground, and those newly built are of poor quality. There are also other Roman remains in the town. The countryside is fertile and includes many gardens and farms. They grow large numbers of trees bearing a fruit known in Italy as the *carrobe* (carob), which they eat throughout the region. They also harvest honey and use it in their dishes.

Even today, the town is quite cultured and full of craftsmen, many of whom are weavers of cloth and cotton, growing plenty of the latter. The people live in freedom, with the support of all the mountainfolk nearby, so the king of Tlemcen cannot extract a penny of revenue from them. The inhabitants often send to the king for governors and judges, though whenever they dislike the justice and rulings they send them back to Tlemcen without complaint. Some inhabitants request the king's permission to trade in the city, for they often do business in Fez and Tlemcen.

2.3.7. Tabahrit

Tabahrit is a small town built by the Africans on the Mediterranean, on a cliff about two miles from Nedroma, near two high, harsh mountains that are well populated. The townsfolk are all cloth-weavers and have many carob groves and plenty of honey. The town lives in constant fear of night attacks by the Christians, so, being too poor to support soldiers, they themselves stand guard at night. The fields around the town are meagre and hard, barely able to grow any barley and millet; the inhabitants are poorly clothed and, being a coarse people, have little culture.

2.3.8. Honaine

Honaine is a small town, very refined and cultured, built long ago by the Africans. It has a little port with two towers, one on each side, and the town is surrounded by handsome walls that are high and strong, particularly those facing the sea. Every year, Venetian galleys use the port and conduct a lively trade with the merchants of Tlemcen fourteen miles away. When the Christians took Oran, the Venetians stopped coming to Tlemcen, for there was nobody there but Spanish soldiers, and the merchants of Tlemcen told them to go to Honaine instead.

The inhabitants were noble and cultured, all working in cotton and cloth; the houses are splendidly decorated with colourful bricks and ornate mosaic ceilings, and each has a well of fresh water and trellised vines in the courtyard. But the day the news arrived of Oran's capture by the Christians, the inhabitants left in a hurry, some fleeing to the mountains and others to Tlemcen. Today the town remains uninhabited but for a castellan and a few infantry, stationed in its citadel by the king of Tlemcen only to send word when merchant ships arrive. The town's fields still grow in abundance, supplying cherries, apricots, apples, pears, peaches, and countless figs and olives, though there is no one to harvest them. These fields lie on the banks of a river near the town, where there were once grain mills. The author felt great compassion for this town when he was there with a minister of the king of Tlemcen; they were there to collect tax from a Genoese ship with enough European merchandise to supply Tlemcen for seven years. The ship owed the king a tenth, and even that, according to the minister, amounted to 15,000 gold ducats.

2.3.9. Archgoul[8]

Archgoul was a large city of old, built by the Africans on a rock surrounded on all sides by the Mediterranean, with only a narrow road leading south to the mainland. It is about four miles north of Tlemcen. It had a large, highly cultured populace, who chose as ruler a brother of Idris, the father of the Idris who founded Fez; his family ruled the city for a century. After the kings and caliphs of Kairouan arrived, the city was ruined and its people oppressed and crushed, leaving it uninhabited for a decade, before being resettled by a people from Baetica with the army of Almanzor, an adviser to the caliph of Córdoba.[9] He rebuilt and resettled the city to meet the needs of the army he sent to Africa. After he and his son al-Muzaffar died, their armies were expelled by the Sanhaja and Maghrawa. The town was again ruined around AH 410 (AD 1019–20).

2.3.10. Tlemcen

The great city of Tlemcen is a royal seat. The histories do not say who built it, only that it was a small town, but it began to grow after the first ruin of Archgoul, especially once the armies of Almanzor had been driven away. The house of 'Abd al-Wad then began to reign and considerably enlarged the town's boundaries, so that it had 16,000 homes by the reign of King Abu Tashufin,[10] when it was highly cultured. However, the kings of Fez gave them considerable trouble, for Yusuf, the second king of the Marinids,[11] came with a vast army and built a small town two miles east. He besieged Tlemcen for seven years, driving the price of a bushel of grain up to thirty ducats, a *scorzo*[12] of salt to three, and a pound of meat to a third of a ducat, leaving the people and soldiers half dead with hunger. Eventually, the people gathered before the king to bemoan the pain and hunger they suffered for his sake. He answered, weeping, 'My people, if I had meat enough to feed you, I would divide it up and give it to you, but it would hardly be enough.' So he called five or six of the people's leaders and brought them into his kitchens, saying, 'Look in the pot, where you'll find dinner for me and my family.' They opened it and found a ten-pound chunk of horse meat, mixed with barley and the leaves of orange, olive and other trees to make it go further.

Faced with the king's own sufferings, the men began to weep and said, 'Your lordship needs our help more than we need his.'

He replied, 'Now that my shame is out in the open, all that is left for me is to die like a nobleman.' He called his sons and grandsons and told them, 'Whoever wants to die nobly, come with me; let those who would die like cowards stay!' And they answered with one voice: 'We shall die like noblemen.'

Having sent off their daughters, wives and sisters to monasteries and such places, they armed themselves, intending to go out and fight to the bitter end, be it death or escape to the desert. But the king's luck had not yet run out, for as he was arming himself, his enemy Yusuf was killed by a eunuch over an insult. The people of Tlemcen saw the enemy fleeing in every direction, and the king rushed out with his people, despoiling most of Yusuf's army and sacking the town it had built. That afternoon, the same *scorzo* of salt worth three ducats in the morning now went for two *baiocchi*, and likewise the rest; they found huge stores of food and livestock belonging to the army, an unexpected joy after all the suffering.

The city had been greatly damaged in the war, losing both homes and culture. Forty years later, Abu al-Hasan, the fourth Marinid king of Fez,[13] arrived at Tlemcen with his army and set about building a city two miles to the west, where he settled and besieged Tlemcen for thirty months. Each day he battled fiercely and constantly built strong bastions ever closer to the city walls; each night he built a new bastion, a new rampart, until he reached the walls and forced his way inside. The town was sacked and the king brought captive before the king of Fez, who had the wretch butchered and tossed on a dung heap. After the king of Fez rebuilt some destroyed buildings for the burghers, he moved on to the kingdom of Tunis, leaving his son Abu 'Inan in Tlemcen as viceroy. This was the second catastrophe to befall the city.

After the Marinids lost power, the town grew again in size and culture until it had 12,000 homes. The craftsmen and merchants are separated into different squares and districts, as in Fez, though the houses are built more cheaply. The city has fine mosques, well run and supplied with imams and preachers, as well as five beautiful madrasas, built well and adorned with mosaics and other handiwork; some of these were built by the

kings of Tlemcen and others by the kings of Fez. Throughout
the city there are also many well-run hammans both large and
small, though they have less water than those in Fez. There are
many inns in the African style, two of them especially beautiful
and large, where the Genoese and Venetian merchants lodge.
One large district has 500 Jewish families, who are all very
wealthy and wear yellow turbans to show that they are Jews.
At the death of Abu 'Abdallah V in AH 923 (AD 1517), they
were sacked and some of them killed; since then they have
become beggars.

The city has many fountains, though their sources are outside the city and have sometimes been captured by enemies in
times of war. The walls are high and strong, and the five town
gates, strengthened with iron, have rooms below porticoes
where tax officials and guards are stationed all day. The royal
palace is in the south of the city, encircled by very high walls
like a fortress; inside are many other mansions and courts, as
well as gardens, fountains and orchards of a splendid design,
with walls and decorations of great skill and expense. It has
two gates: one towards the countryside, facing the mountains,
while the other, where the captain of the guard is stationed,
leads into the city.

All around the city are delightful farms and buildings where the
burghers stay in summer, among the bubbling fountains and the
wells of cool water. Every farm has trellised vines, growing fat,
delicious grapes in every colour. They grow fruit in abundance:
more cherries than seen in Tlemcen, and of every kind and colour;
many figs, especially fat, long and black ones, sweet and tasty,
which are dried for the winter; and an infinite quantity of other
fruit, including melons and cucumbers, which they sell for a good
price. About three miles east of the city, along the river Sefsif, are
many grain mills; there are others nearer the city to the south, on
the side of the mountain al-Qal'a.

In the town are judges, lawyers and many notaries, as well as
many students and scholars of law and the natural sciences. The
madrasas have regular lecturers, provided for by the scholars
belonging to each madrasa. The townsfolk are divided into four
groups, namely merchants, craftsmen, soldiers and students. The

merchants are all upright and honest in their dealings, and like to trade in the Lands of the Blacks, bringing back goods to Tlemcen; among them are merchants of great wealth with plenty of cash on hand. The craftsmen are a talented lot, and they are always ready to have a good time and make merry. The king's soldiers are all paid according to their ability and rank, starting at three ducats a month – about three-and-a-half Italian ducats – which pays for a man and his horse, since a soldier in Africa means a light cavalry-man. The students are the poorest, staying cheaply in the madrasas until they have finished their studies, and then they can be lecturers, notaries or imams. The burghers and merchants dress well and honourably, sometimes better than those of Fez; they can be more reasonable and more generous too. The craftsmen also dress well, though their clothes are short. Few wear turbans, instead having caps without folds, as well as tall boots that come halfway up their legs. The soldiers dress worst of all, wearing only a loose smock with wide sleeves and a loose sheet of cotton that they wrap around themselves in summer; in winter they wear pelts fashioned into shirts, without a cloth lining. The richer soldiers likewise wear layers of clothing over their smocks, and hooded cloaks like the robes that travellers once used in Italy, with wide sleeves; they also wear hoods to cover their heads when it rains. The students dress according to their means, with some from the mountains dressed like mountainfolk, while those from Arab and noble families wear their usual clothing; others, on entering the madrasa, put aside their usual outfit and don instead the garb of a noble student. The judges, lecturers, imams and other officials dress more formally.

[2.3.10.1. Customs and duties at the king's court]

The king enjoys great splendour and renown. He does not let himself be seen, nor even does he give audience to any but his chief courtiers and officials, who perform their duties according to the hierarchy of the court. He has many officials. First, his lieutenant, who assigns the provisions and salaries to each person as he wishes, and keeps the armies supplied and ready for battle against any rebel or enemy; sometimes he goes with the army in person, acting with the authority of the king himself.

The second official is the first minister, who writes letters and responses according to the will of the king or his lieutenant.

The third official is the treasurer, who collects the revenue monies and rents from the king's officers, the tax collectors and customs men, and keeps it all at the king's disposal.

The fourth official is the bursar, who signs the orders for the royal treasury to pay the household officials what they need to furnish the household and stables.

The fifth official is the captain of the palace gates, who serves as a castellan over the palace guard and as a bodyguard for the king when he gives audience. There are other officials of a lesser rank, such as the stable master, the captain of the grooms, the chaplain and the chamberlain. The latter only serves when the king gives audience, since in his private quarters the king is served by slaves, his wife and Christian slave-women, and he keeps many eunuchs to guard and serve the women.

The king wears beautiful, modest clothing, whereas his horse is furnished magnificently; when he goes riding, there is not much pomp and ceremony, for the current king keeps no more than a thousand horses, and instead pays Arabs and other nearby tribes in times of war. Likewise, when he goes into the country-side with his army, he does not bring a great train or splendid tents, but rides like a private captain, albeit with a company of guards and officials, at little expense. The king has large ducats minted from impure gold, similar to the *bislacchi*[14] of Italy, weighing one and a quarter Italian ducats. He also mints coins in various sizes from low-grade silver, a quarter of which is copper, to be spent like *baiocchi* or *quattrini*. One hundred of these *baiocchi* make a ducat.

Even though the present king has little land, and what little he has is sparsely populated, it still supplies plentiful duties and taxes, for his domain is the gateway between Europe and Ethiopia, where one is taxed for entering or leaving. This was especially so after the Christians took Oran, when the king[15] imposed heavy taxes and duties on those who had been free under his predecessors; as a result, the people hated him his whole life. His son[16] then took the throne, planning to impose the same measures, so he was driven out of the kingdom until his majesty the Emperor helped him, as related earlier.[17] For the many years he ruled Oran, the kingdom yielded 300,000 or even 400,000 ducats annually; but more than half is spent supporting the Arabs and maintaining the kingdom, while the rest goes to soldiers' salaries and the upkeep of captains and chief courtiers. The king also spends lavishly on his household, conducting his affairs in great splendour on a grand scale.

This clearly shows how the people live in the city, and the king in his court. The author had business there on several occasions and stayed many months at different times. He has left out the customs and precise order of things, since they are like Fez and he didn't want to grow too long and tedious, having spent his time on other things.

2.3.11 Al-'Ubbad, Tlemcen

Al-'Ubbad is a small suburb in the mountains, a mile and a half south of Tlemcen. It is well populated, cultured, with many craftsmen and especially dyers. In one mosque, many steps lead down into a large, famous holy sepulchre; the saint, to whom many offerings and alms are given, was named Sidi Bu Madyan.[18] There is also a madrasa, and a hospital where foreigners may lodge for three days. The mosque, madrasa and hospital were all built by the Marinid king of Fez, as can be seen by the names inscribed on marble tablets.

2.3.12. Tafesra

Tafesra is a small town on a plain five miles from Tlemcen. It has many ironworkers, being next to mines. The fields around the town are excellent for grain. The inhabitants have little culture, for they do not apply themselves to anything but working iron and exporting it to Tlemcen.

2.3.13. Tessala

Tessala is a very ancient city built by the Africans on a great plain, twenty miles across, where they grow grain of the highest quality in colour and height, which they supply to Tlemcen. The farmers live in tents and pay tribute to the king and the Arabs. The city, ruined long ago, gave its name to the plain.

2.3.14. The province of Beni Rachid

This province spans fifty miles east to west, and is twenty-five miles wide. The south of the province is a plain, while the north is nearly all hills, though the fields are good throughout. The inhabitants are divided into two groups: one dwells in the hills, in walled houses, working the fields and vineyards and doing the necessary crafts; the other is nobler, living in tents in the countryside, raising livestock and keeping camels and horses as the Arabs do. They are well clothed, in their own way, even though they pay tribute to the king of Tlemcen.

The first group inhabit countless villages, two of which are more famous than the rest. One is Qal'at Hawwara, which has forty houses and many merchants and craftsmen; it is built like a fortress on a mountain slope among valleys. The other village is al-Mascara, where the king's lieutenant and his cavalry are based. On Thursdays it holds a weekly market, which attracts crowds of people with livestock, grain, *zebibi*, figs, butter, honey and local cloth; all kinds of haberdashers, saddlers and bridle makers sell their wares there.

The market is infested with cutpurses. When the author was in the region, he went to buy what he needed for a journey to Tunis, stopping on horseback. He was buying tent ropes, and, having agreed the price, swung his left leg over the horse's neck to count his money on his lap, letting go of the reins to pay. Turning back, he replaced his foot in the stirrup, and reached for the reins – but they were gone! Looking around, he called his servant to lead the horse to his lodgings. Then two of the lieutenant's grooms turned up, holding out his bridle. 'Sir,' they said, 'your bridle was stolen by some of the lieutenant's mule-drivers, who did not know you were staying with us. We saw this happen and seized it from them. Check to see that they haven't stolen anything else.' And so the author bought what he needed, returned to his lodgings, and at dinner that night recounted the tale to the lieutenant, who nearly died of laughter, and said: 'You should not be surprised; these are such low, menial tasks that we can hardly find men to do them. On top of that, we do not pay them enough, so they turn to theft; as a result, no matter how much they earn, working for us or someone else, they are accustomed to thieving. Since all the mule-drivers here are used to this from childhood, we allow them to steal, which is bad luck for those who don't keep an eye out.' The province brings the king of Tlemcen 25,000 ducats a year, and provides about the same number of warriors, both infantry and cavalry.

2.3.15. Al-Batha

This large, cultured and well-inhabited city was recently built by the Africans on a plain where plenty of grain grows, earning 20,000 ducats a year for the king of Tlemcen. However, it was ruined in the wars between him and his kinsmen living in the Ouarsenis mountains. These always had the help of the king of Fez and seized a good part of the king of Tlemcen's kingdom, destroying the towns they could not keep under their control. Al-Batha was destroyed so thoroughly that only traces of its old foundations can be seen today.

Alongside it flowed a modest river with banks full of gardens, farms and mills; even today one can see many trees left over from those farms. The entire plain around the city was abandoned, though recently a hermit has come to live there in the manner of the locals. He enjoyed great renown as a saint among the people, and many labourers joined him, working the land and raising many animals, horses and cattle for him – so many, in fact, that even he could not count them all, for, due to his reputation as a saint, neither he nor his comrades paid the king or the

Arabs any tax. The author heard from many of his disciples that a mere tenth of the land produces 8,000 bushels of grain for the hermit, and he has 500 horses, male and female, 10,000 sheep, 2,000 cattle, and a yearly income of four or five thousand ducats in offerings from those coming to see him from east and west, for his fame has spread all over Africa and Asia, and he has as many disciples as can be imagined. Around 500 men live in his household; all eat at his expense while helping in some capacity in the hermitage. His disciples have come from throughout the Muslim world, and he neither gives them penance nor requires anything more of them than regular prayers; however, he does present them with certain divine names and commands them to invoke God with these names so many times a day. As a result, there are always hundreds of men who come to be his disciples, but all return home after he gives them their orders. He kept about a hundred tents: some for visitors, some for the shepherds and farmers, and some for his own family, since this good hermit had four wives and several slave-women who gave him a good many male and female children, who all wore noble clothing. His sons also had wives and children, so that his family all together numbered around fifty.

Even today the hermit is much honoured by the Arabs, which makes the king of Tlemcen tremble. The author stayed three nights in a row at the hermitage; each evening he ate with the hermit in his private rooms and saw many of his books on magic and alchemy. The hermit argued that magic was a true science, and the author suspected that he was a magician, if only because he had seen him so highly honoured without doing or saying or using anything but his invocation of the divine names.

2.3.16. Oran

Oran is a large city of 6,000 homes, built by the ancient Africans on the Mediterranean forty miles from Tlemcen. It is highly cultured, furnished with all the buildings and other things of culture, including mosques with madrasas, hospitals, hammams and inns. Fine high walls surround the town, which is built partly on the plain and partly higher up. Nearly all the inhabitants are craftsmen, most of them cloth-weavers; once, many burghers lived on the revenues they collected. The town is not very fertile, so they eat barley bread for their meals, but the people are all friendly and good company, and they warmly welcome foreigners. The town used to be much frequented by Genoese and Catalan merchants, and even now there is a quarter named after the Genoese Loggia where they stayed.

However, the townsfolk have always harboured a grudge against the king of Tlemcen and constantly rebel; they never wanted his governors or judges, though they did accept his treasurer and an official who collected the port revenues. The people used to choose a leader of the council, to govern and provide legal judgements in civil matters, and they treated him as a ruler. He took for himself much of the port revenues, since he also held the office of port admiral.

The burghers and merchants also kept armed foists and brigantines, which they sent out as corsairs, doing great damage in Catalonia and the islands of Ibiza, Mallorca and Minorca, until the town was full of Christian slaves. The Catholic king, Ferdinand of Spain, then sent a great armada to seize the city's fleet and quell the trouble, but the fleet's officers and captains caused so much chaos that the people of Oran routed and killed most of the Spanish, and the survivors returned to Spain. Within a few months, the king, with the help of several bishops, archbishops and the Spanish cardinal,[19] gathered a huge sum of money to send another armada even larger than the last, with many infantry and light cavalry. The first day the Christians arrived, they took the city, for the savage Moors fell into confusion when they saw the Christians disembark and prepare for battle; sounding their trumpets, they picked up their weapons and rushed out to meet the Christians, leaving the city empty. Meanwhile, the Christians prudently sent one party around another side of the city, out of sight of the Moors, and found only women on the walls; they broke open the gate and entered, planting the Spanish king's standard on the walls. Seeing this, the Moorish brutes scrambled back into the city, aiming to drive off the enemy, but the army outside followed, trapping them in between. In barely three hours, the whole population of the city was captured – men, women and children. A few escaped the Christian cavalry surrounding the town, while they were distracted fighting the Moorish cavalry who had come to help from Tlemcen and the regions near Oran. The city was taken by the Christians in AH 916 (AD 1510–11).[20]

2.3.17. Mers el-Kebir

This small town was recently built by the kings of Tlemcen on the Mediterranean a few miles from Oran. Its name means 'The Great Port', for the town has a port without equal in the world, which can accommodate hundreds of ships and galleys – a safe haven in any storm. All the large ships and galleys of Venice come to this port when transporting merchandise to Oran; when the weather clears up, they proceed to the shore of Oran. The same events that befell Oran happened to this town, for the Spanish took it by force of arms a few months earlier.

2.3.18. Mazagran

Mazagran is a small town built by the Africans on the Mediterranean near the mouth of the river Chelif. The town is cultured and well inhabited by many craftsmen. They live with continual disruption from the neighbouring Arabs, but the town's governor can do nothing outside the walls, and little inside them.

2.3.19. Mostaganem

This city was built by the Africans on the Mediterranean about three miles east of Mazagran, on the other side of the river. In ancient times, the town was well inhabited and cultured, but, after the decline of the king of Tlemcen, it was greatly oppressed by the Arabs, so that it has lost more than two-thirds of its people; today, however, about 500 inhabited homes remain, with a beautiful mosque and many craftsmen and weavers. They have fine buildings and many fountains, for a stream passes through the town, along which are plenty of mills. Outside the town are a great many fields and gardens, with plenty of fruit, though most of them are abandoned, for there are more fields than inhabitants. Large, good plains of excellent soil surround it, so the people have plenty of bread. The town has a small port where European ships often come to do business, though they can do very little with the townsfolk, who are very poor and wretched.

2.3.20. Brashk

This is an ancient town built by the Romans on the Mediterranean many miles from Mostaganem. It is well inhabited by a coarse people, all badly clothed weavers, though the men are valiant and fierce as lions. All the men tattoo a black cross on their cheeks, with another on the back of their hands below the fingers, in the manner of mountainfolk in Algeria and Bejaia; the Arabic historians say that the countless lands, rivers and mountains here were once ruled by the Goths, and many of the mountainfolk became Christians. The Gothic kings ordered their governors and officials to collect no tribute from Christians, but the officials, not knowing the local language or customs, could not tell who was or was not a Christian, particularly since, when payment was due, non-Christians pretended they were, so as not to pay tribute. The officials and their king then decided that each man should mark his cheek with a cross; those who were baptised and thus marked themselves as Christians would be free of tribute, while those who refused would have to pay, even if they were Christians. This was the original reason for the mark, which is a little larger on the hand than on the cheek. After the Goths lost control, the Muslims took over these lands and all the people converted while still being marked with crosses. Now men and women both wear the mark, without knowing why.[21] Likewise, it is customary for both rulers and commoners in Mauretania to put a tiny black cross on their cheek with an iron point; the custom is ancient and can also be seen in Europe, where there are people from those lands.

The town overflows with fruit, especially figs, and the surrounding countryside grows plenty of flax and barley. The townsfolk have an alliance with the nearby mountainfolk, who support them, so that for a century the town lived in freedom, until they were saddled with the Turk Barbarossa. Many of the people used to trade by sea, making a good living by bringing figs and flax to the cities of Algiers, Bejaia and Tunis. Even today, there are many traces of Roman buildings in the town, especially its walls.

2.3.21. Cherchell

This is a very ancient city, built by the Romans on the Mediterranean, then taken by the Goths and later by the Muslims, who hold it now. It is surrounded by eight miles of very high walls of large, dressed stones. The side towards the sea has a large, tall temple built by the Romans; even today, its interior is faced with marble. All around the city are large, beautiful fields of good soil, and there was a large citadel on the sea, set on the promontory of a large rock. The city was devastated by the Goths, but under Muslim rule one part was resettled, and it remained well populated and cultured for 500 years. In the wars between the kings of Tunis and Tlemcen the city was abandoned, and it remained so for 300 years, until Granada was taken by the Christians. Then some Granadans came and began to resettle and rebuild the part where the citadel was, putting up many houses, farming all the fields and constructing ships for sea trade. They took up the silk trade, for they found many black and white mulberry trees.[22] The number of Granadans kept growing until there were 200 households, between them and the neighbours who came to live with them. They lived in freedom for many years, until the Turk Barbarossa came to power. Although they were his subjects, he gave them little trouble, barely collecting 300 ducats a year.

2.3.22. Miliana

Miliana is a large ancient town built by the Romans, who called it Magnana, though the name was corrupted by the Arabs. It is on a mountain peak forty miles from Cherchell on the Mediterranean. The mountain is so full of springs and walnut forests that anyone who wants to can go and pick them, and nobody buys or sells nuts during the harvest season. High, ancient walls surround the city; on one side a steep slope leads down to a deep valley, while the other side reaches the edge of the peak, like in Narni near Rome. The buildings all have beautiful fountains inside, in pleasing shapes that the author has seen elsewhere. The inhabitants are almost all craftsmen, weavers and wood-turners who make vessels; there are also farmers and some burghers. For a long time the town remained free, until Barbarossa ruled the region and it too fell under his reign.

2.3.23. Tenes

This is a very ancient city, built by the Africans on the side of a mountain a short distance from the Mediterranean. It is walled all around and inhabited by a numerous and coarse people. It had always been subject to the king of Tlemcen, but Muhammad, the grandfather of the current king, left three sons at his death; the eldest Abu 'Abdallah, and his brothers Abu Zayyan and Yahya.[23] Abu 'Abdallah took his father's place, and Abu Zayyan and Yahya supported him, who likewise loved and provided for them. After a while, however, they and certain burghers plotted to betray the brother; but the treachery was found out, and Abu Zayyan was arrested and imprisoned until the people of Tlemcen freed him. After Abu 'Abdallah died and his son[24] had been driven out, Abu Zayyan was king until Barbarossa killed him, as recounted above.[25]

The other brother, Yahya, fled to Fez, where he was warmly welcomed by the king. He stayed several years, until called back by the people of Tenes and by a group of knights who lived in the mountains nearby. So he went, with the help and blessing of the king of Fez, and when he arrived he was received like a king, acclaimed as such by the people. He reigned for several years, and when he died the throne passed to his son, guided by his uncle on his mother's side, since he was very young. After Barbarossa came to power, the poor ruler lost his kingdom and had to go to Spain to seek out his imperial majesty Charles V, then only king of Spain, who had promised to help him. This promise took so long to fulfil that the ruler of Tenes and his younger brother were both baptised while in Spain and remained there at the Emperor's expense, even as Tenes remained in the hands of Barbarossa's brother.

The city produces very little, for it has no port, nor is it even a town on a pass. It has no culture, beyond a few craftsmen of rough items. However, the city bears some fruit, gathering plenty of grain and honey from the region.

2.3.24. Mazouna

Mazouna is an ancient city forty miles from the Mediterranean, built according to some by the Romans. It covers a large area and has strong walls, though the buildings are poor, except one large mosque with a few smaller ones. It was once highly cultured, but then it was sacked many times by both the king of Tlemcen and the rebels opposing him. After that, it was ruled by the Arabs and ruined worse than ever, leaving few inhabitants, almost all weavers and farmers who are destitute because of their Arab oppressors. Nevertheless, the fields are excellent and abundant. There are many ruined Roman towns nearby; their names are unknown to us, but it is clear they are Roman from the lettering found on marble slabs, and from the fact that the African historians have not mentioned them.

2.3.25. Al-Jaza'ir (Algiers)

Al-Jaza'ir means 'the islands', so called from being next to the three islands of Mallorca, Minorca and Ibiza; the Spanish call it Alger. A large, ancient city of 4,000 homes, it was built by the African people known by the ancients as Mezghenna. Strong, beautiful walls of large stones surround it; inside there are handsome buildings and charming squares, ordered by district, each craft to itself. There are many inns and hammams, and a large, elegant mosque by the sea. In front of the mosque is a splendid path along the city walls, beaten by the waves. Around the city lie beautiful gardens and fruit farms, and along the eastern side, by the mills, flows a stream from which the townsfolk drink. Gorgeous plains sprawl all around, notably Mitija, which is forty-five miles long and thirty wide, and overflows with excellent grain.[26]

The city was mostly under the dominion of Tlemcen, but later aligned itself with the new kingdom in Bejaia; being closer to Bejaia, the people realised that its king was a threat, while the king of Tlemcen could be of no help, so they offered it their allegiance and tribute, thereby gaining a sort of freedom. The burghers and their leaders would build and outfit foists to attack the islands mentioned above, as well as the Spanish mainland. For this reason, the Catholic king Ferdinand sent a grand armada with the orders that, if they could not seize the city, the captains should at least fortify the island at the entrance to its port. To do this, they built a strong, handsome fortress from which even a gunshot could reach beyond the city walls, so one can imagine what artillery would do. Terrified and desperate, the people could think only to send an ambassador to the Catholic king, negotiating a ten-year treaty that obliged them to pay a certain tribute. The king agreed to everything, the ambassador returned and they were at peace for many months.

But then Barbarossa came to besiege Bejaia, capturing a fortress built by the Spanish, in the hope of taking back the other fortress and the kingdom of Bejaia. However, Barbarossa's hopes were soon dashed, since the mountainfolk supporting him left without leave to plant their crops; the Turkish soldiers with them left too, and Barbarossa hastily fled, personally burning his twelve foists behind him in the Greater River three miles outside Bejaia. Together with forty Turks, their families and their slaves, Barbarossa went to the ksar of Jijel, seventy miles from Bejaia, where he stayed for many months, until he was summoned by the people of Algiers when they wanted to break their treaty with the Spanish. For the Catholic king had died, and the people considered Barbarossa a man able to fight the Christians, thinking he might drive them from the citadel. The people made him general as soon as he arrived, and he attacked the citadel, though without doing any damage. After a few days, he killed the town's ruler, who had been a prince among the Arabs living on the plain of Mitija. His name was Salim at-Toumi, from the Thaaliba tribe, a branch of the Maqil people as noted above;[27] he was made ruler in Bejaia after it was captured by the Spanish. He had ruled for several years when Barbarossa came and killed him underhandedly in a hammam; Barbarossa was a proud, savage man, who wanted no thought of the ruler, and each of them scorned the other until Salim's death. Barbarossa then began to mint coins in his own name and proclaimed himself king, while all the neighbouring peoples sent him their allegiance and tribute. This is how his reign began.

The author was there in person for most of this history, since he was then travelling from Fez to Tunis, and he took shelter in the house of the ambassador to Spain; this man had returned from there carrying 3,000 Arabic books that he had bought in Xàtiva, a city in the kingdom of Valencia. From Algiers, the author went to Bejaia, where he found Barbarossa besieging the fortress. There he remained, witnessing all of Barbarossa's struggles until his flight to Jijel, when the author departed for Tunis by way of Constantine. After Barbarossa was killed in Tlemcen, his brother Hayreddin became ruler of Algiers, and still rules today. The king of Spain, that is the Emperor, planned to take Algiers and sent armadas in two different years. The first was interrupted by a sea storm and most of its ships sank off the shores of Algiers, while the second made it to land and besieged the city for three days, but in the end was routed by

Barbarossa; many Christians were killed and captured, and few escaped. This was in AH 922 (AD 1516–17).

2.3.26. Tagdemt

Tagdemt is a very ancient city, which some say was built by the Romans; its name means 'ancient' in the African language.[28] The city is about ten miles around, and one can see many walls and traces of foundations. When the Muslim armies invaded, it was populated and cultured, full of craftsmen, and the people worshipped idols in temples. Later, when ruled by the Muslims, it had many scholars and poets, for it was ruled by an uncle of Idris, the founder of Fez. His dynasty retained control of the city for fifty years, before it was destroyed in the wars with the heretical caliph of Kairouan in AH 365 (AD 975–76). Currently, nothing is there but remnants of foundations.

2.3.27. Medea

This city was built by the ancient Africans on the borders of Numidia, eighty miles from the Mediterranean, on a splendid, bountiful plain, among many springs and gardens. The inhabitants are prosperous and have fine clothes and buildings, for they trade a great deal in Numidia. But the city is also harassed and afflicted by the Arabs; the king cannot help, as it is 100 miles from Tlemcen. Formerly, the city was governed by the ruler of Tenes, and latterly by Barbarossa and his brother. The author stayed there around two months, and had a marvellous time, being honoured even more highly than the city's ruler; when a foreigner with a modicum of learning visits, the inhabitants fall upon him with such warm greetings and so many demands that he has to decide their lawsuits, write out their briefs and offer counsel in their affairs. In two months, the author earned several dozen ducats' worth of possessions, money and livestock. In fact, he planned to stay, but love and duty towards his master obliged him to move on.

2.3.28. Tamentfoust

Tamentfoust is an ancient city that the Africans built on the Mediterranean about two miles from Algiers, which it serves as a port, since Algiers itself has only a beach. The city was destroyed by the Goths, and now only traces of the walls remain; nearly all the walls of Algiers were built from stones taken from the walls of this city.

2.3.29. Dellys

Dellys is an ancient city built by the Africans on the Mediterranean thirty miles from Algiers. It has strong, ancient walls. The inhabitants are all craftsmen, especially dyers, since many fountains and springs flow through the town. They are all cheerful and know how to have a good time, and most play lutes[29] and harps and are well clothed, like the burghers of Algiers. Many fruit farms and grain fields surround the city. The townsfolk use nets to catch plenty of excellent fish, though they end up with so many that they don't buy or sell them in the city.

Here ends the discussion of the cities of the kingdom of Tlemcen; next follows the mountains.

2.3.30. Beni Iznassen

The mountain of Beni Iznassen is fifty miles west of Tlemcen, with the deserts of Garet and Angad on either side. This high, harsh and difficult range is fifteen miles long and five wide, and in its many forests one can find numerous carob trees, the long, thick and sweet fruit of which the inhabitants eat in large numbers, making up for the fact that they grow little barley. There are many villages on the mountain, inhabited by a valiant, hardy and spirited folk. There is a strong fortress on the cliffs at the summit, though the buildings are in a poor state; inside lives a clan whom the mountainfolk think of as princes. But they often betray and kill one another over control of the mountain. The author was there to do business with these rulers, for they had many kin who had been exiled to Fez; the king welcomed them at court, providing their necessities since they were brave and noble. The mountain can summon 10,000 warriors.

2.3.31. Matghara

This mountain is very high, extremely cold and well populated, ten miles from the city of Nedroma. The inhabitants are all valiant, despite being poor, since the mountain grows nothing beyond a little barley and plenty of carob. The people of Nedroma are allied with them, helping one another against the king of Tlemcen.

2.3.32. Walhasa

This high mountain neighbours the town of Honaine. It is well inhabited by a valiant though rustic people, who are often at war with the town, which they have sacked two or three times. Little grain grows on the mountain, but plenty of carob.

2.3.33. Aghbal

This mountain is well inhabited by a lowly people subject to Oran; they are all farmers and woodcutters who bring wood to the city. While Oran belonged to the Moors, the mountainfolk earned a good deal of money; after the Christians took the city, the mountainfolk were destitute and dispirited, enduring great affliction at Christian hands.

2.3.34. Beni Ournid

This mountain is three miles from Tlemcen, well populated and fertile, particularly for figs and cherries. The inhabitants are charcoal-makers and woodcutters, and some are farmers; the mountain produces 2,000 ducats a year, as the author heard from the minister of the king of Tlemcen.

2.3.35. Maghrawa

The mountain extends forty miles along the Mediterranean, next to the town of Mostaganem mentioned earlier. The inhabitants are noble, valiant and generous, keeping good fields on their mountain.

2.3.36. Beni Bou Sa'id

This mountain is near Tenes, well populated by a brave people who are very savage. They have great amounts of honey, barley and many goats, and they bring wax and leather to the shores of Tenes, to be sold to European merchants. They paid some tribute to the king of Tenes when he was a kinsman to the king of Tlemcen.

2.3.37. Ouarsenis

This lofty mountain is inhabited by a noble people who once waged war against the king of Tlemcen, since they were kin. When the Marinids first ruled Fez, they made an alliance with the mountain rulers against the kings of Tlemcen; the king of Fez provided the rulers with cavalry and weapons, so the war lasted eighty years. The mountain is very fertile, full of fountains and good fields, and the summit is very dry, with considerable quantities of tutty.[30] The people can come up with 10,000 warriors, of which 2,500 are cavalry. They supported Yahya, the ruler who was made king of Tenes.[31] After Tenes changed rulers, the mountain cavalry constantly raided these lands.

2.3.38. The mountains of Algiers

East and south of the plains of Algiers are countless mountains, inhabited by many peoples; these are all valiant men who live in freedom, being prosperous, generous, and possessing excellent fields, plenty of livestock and vast numbers of horses. They are so often at war with each other that the region is impassable, even by a foreigner, unless accompanied by one of their religious men. They hold many fairs and markets, though nothing is found there but livestock, wool, grain and what little merchandise comes from nearby cities.

End of the section on the kingdom of Tlemcen; next, the kingdom of Bejaia and Tunis.

BOOK 2.4.

KINGDOMS OF BEJAIA AND TUNIS

2.4.1. [Introduction]

Before the author had divided the kingdoms of Barbary, he promised to treat Bejaia as a kingdom of its own;[1] but later that approach seemed unsuitable, since Bejaia was not a royal city for long, and there is every good reason to think it properly belongs to the king of Tunis, even though many kings of Tlemcen have occupied it by force.

Abu 'Inan Faris, the king of Tunis,[2] supposing himself stronger than the king of Tlemcen, set out west with his army and drove off the cavalry under the generals guarding Bejaia; then he went to Tlemcen, gaining victory and tribute from the king. When he arrived at Bejaia, he left his son with a court to secure the region from the king of Tlemcen, since it was better to have a prince in place than a governor. To forestall any conflict over who would rule after his death, he divided the kingdom between his three sons: Bejaia went to 'Abd al-Aziz, Tunis to (Abu 'Amr) 'Uthman, who reigned there for forty years, and the Land of Dates to 'Amar. The last of these rebelled against his brother 'Uthman, who pursued and besieged him in the city of Sfax until he got him in his grasp, forcing him to choose between being beheaded or having his eyes gouged out. 'Amar chose the latter and was brought to Tunis, where he lived blind for many years. The other son, the prince of Bejaia, remained faithful to his brother and the kingdom stayed in his line for many years, until it was decisively overthrown by Count Pedro Navarro on behalf of the Catholic king Ferdinand.

2.4.1.2. The great city of Bejaia

This ancient city lies on the side of a very high mountain on the Mediterranean, surrounded by high, splendid, ancient walls; some say it was built by the Romans. The inhabited part comprises 8,000 homes but if the whole were inhabited it would be more than 24,000, for the city is spread over a marvellous distance towards the mountain. It has impressive buildings, such as the mosques and many madrasas thronged with students and teachers of law and natural sciences; the monasteries for religious men; and the hammams and inns, all beautifully built. The squares are well organised, as in the other great cities, but it is hilly, so the walker is always going up and down. Towards the mountain is a great fortress with good walls, where the nobles have magnificent palaces with walls marvellously adorned with mosaics, carved plaster and inlaid wood; the ornamentation is worth more than the structures themselves. The burghers were very wealthy, with plenty of fields and money, and they did a lively trade by land and sea. They used to send many armed foists to go raiding in Spain, which ultimately brought about the city's ruin. The other townsfolk led miserable lives, for all the fields around are meagre and harsh, good for fruit but bad for grain, which they perpetually lack. There are plenty of fruit gardens around the city, especially outside the eastern gate. The countryside and lands are rugged mountains, covered with woods, where apes and leopards live.

The city's inhabitants are all cheerful and pass the time making merry, all delighting in dancing and making music, especially the rulers, who, being of little account, are never at war. They showed what sort of people they are, or rather were, when Count Pedro Navarro arrived with his fourteen boats; the king and his people, without so much as unsheathing their swords, all fled to the nearby mountains, leaving their town full of grain and possessions. Navarro set his men to pillaging the city and, having sized up the situation, the Christians built a fortress on the beach while fortifying another old citadel by the sea, next to the arsenal.

The Spanish took Bejaia in AH 917 (AD 1511–12).[3] Six years later, the Turk Barbarossa came to retake it from the Christians and attacked with 10,000 Turkish fighters. Storming the Christians in the ancient citadel, they captured and fortified it; even though it was ruined, Barbarossa went to stay there. The people came from the neighbouring mountains to help him against the fortress still standing, but they never took it, for the Turks lost 100 valiant men in their first attack, while the mountainfolk lost 400. Therefore Barbarossa swiftly escaped, as has been already described.[4]

2.4.1.3. Jijel

This is an ancient ksar, built by the Africans on the Mediterranean, on a high cliff seventy miles from Bejaia. Its 500 homes are not very well built. The inhabitants are valiant, generous and faithful, despite all being farmers. The fields are very hard, good for barley, flax and hemp, which they grow in great quantity. They also have a large number of walnuts and figs that they ship to Tunis, having a few small boats for travel.[5] The town lived free from the kings of Bejaia and Tunis, since it is hard to besiege. But they willingly gave their allegiance to Barbarossa, who exercised restraint by not taxing them, except for the legal and customary tithe on grain and fruit; he installed no one there but a single commissioner.

2.4.1.4. M'sila

This is a very ancient town built by the Romans on the borders of the Numidian deserts, forty miles inland from Bejaia. It has ancient walls, and its houses and mosque are ugly. The inhabitants are all craftsmen and farmers, badly clothed and very poor due to the neighbouring Arabs, who demand half of their produce; likewise, the king of Bejaia wanted some for himself, so there was hardly enough left over to eat. After Bejaia was taken by the Christians, the Arabs took the king's revenues in addition to their own half. When the author passed through the town, he was shocked by the poverty, which was so severe that he could scarcely find fodder for two horses for the night; if he had stayed another night they would never have found enough, so great is the catastrophic misery afflicting the city.

2.4.1.5. Setif

Setif is a city built by the Romans sixty miles south of Bejaia, in a beautiful plain beyond the region's mountains, with walls of large, beautiful stones, dressed and squared. It was once very cultured and well inhabited, but after being seized by the Muslims it declined considerably, especially after the Arabs invaded Africa. It was nearly ruined and most of its walls smashed; barely a hundred houses are still inhabited, as the author once saw on his journey from Fez to Tunis.

2.4.1.6. N'Gaous

N'Gaous is a city on the border of Numidia, built by the Romans eighty miles from the Mediterranean and 180 miles from M'sila. All the walls are strong and ancient. Nearby flows a stream, where there are plentiful fields of figs and nuts; the town's figs are widely considered better than those of Tunis, and they export them to Constantine eighty miles away. In the plains surrounding the town are fields of excellent grain. The inhabitants are very wealthy, for they are not taxed heavily by the Arabs, and they only give the kings what they please. They are good, generous men, beautifully clothed like the burghers of Bejaia. The community maintains a house furnished like a hospital where they take in all foreigners. They keep a madrasa at their own expense, furnishing the students with garments. They also have a large, cheerful mosque, supplied with imams and servants. The men and women are pale and comely, nearly all with lustrous black hair which they wash at the hammams. Almost every house has a single storey, but they are charming and pleasant, for they keep little gardens in the middle of the courtyards, growing all kinds of flowers, such as roses, damask roses, myrtles, violets, camomiles, carnations and fine trees. Nearly every courtyard has either a fountain or a well, and trellised vines along one side to shade the house. Anyone who enters one of these homes, or the city as a whole, will be reluctant to leave, because of its pleasures and the conversation of its people.

2.4.1.7. Collo

Collo is a large town built by the Romans on the Mediterranean below a soaring mountain. It has no walls, since they were destroyed by the Goths. Then the Muslims ruled and left it as they found it. The town is quite cultured and filled with craftsmen; its fields are fertile, though they are in the mountains. The inhabitants are talented and generous traders, for they collect an abundance of wax and leather from their mountains and barter with the Genoese ships that regularly trade at the town's port, earning a good living. They live in freedom, as do the neighbouring mountainfolk, with whom the citizens are allied against the king of Tunis and his prince or viceroy in Constantine. These two are always trying to subjugate the town, but have never succeeded, because the mountains are very high and their inhabitants are brave. It is ten miles from Constantine to Collo, half of which is mountains controlled by neither king nor prince. As a result, no town on the coast of Tunis is as rich; first they make four times as much when they trade with the Genoese, and then they earn an astonishing amount by selling the Genoese wares to their neighbours.

2.4.1.8. Skikda

This is a very ancient town built by the Romans on the Mediterranean, thirty-five miles from Constantine. It was ruined in ancient times by the Goths and only a few traces remain, though the ruler of Constantine desired the port and erected some buildings and storehouses for the Genoese who traded there; he also had a village built at the summit of a neighbouring mountain, with a guard who notifies Constantine when the ships arrive. The mountainfolk of Constantine do good business with the Genoese, trading grain for European cloth and wares. From the port to Constantine there is a road of black stone like those of Italy, especially in Rome, which is an excellent sign that the town was built by the Romans.

2.4.1.9. Constantine

This city was built by the Romans, a fact impossible to deny; it is very large, with high, thick ancient walls of black, dressed stone. It is on a very high mountain; the southern side sits on high cliffs over the river Suf-Jimar.[6] Across the river are more cliffs just as high, and between them is a deep chasm more useful than any defensive ditch. The north side of the city has a high, strong wall around it, beyond which rises the mountain summit. There are only two routes into the city, on the east and west, where there are splendid, large, iron-bound gates. The city has 8,000 homes and is full of culture and abundance; there are beautiful houses and buildings, such as the principal mosque, two madrasas and three or four monasteries. The city squares are well planned and each craft is separate from the others. The inhabitants are able and talented, the craftsmen in particular, and there are many merchants who deal in woollen cloth made locally, in the city. Others conduct trade with Numidia, exporting oil, silk and cloth and bartering them for slaves and dates. For this reason no town in Barbary has such a good market for dates, since eight or ten pounds of them go for three *baiocchi* here.

Nevertheless, compared to citizens elsewhere, the inhabitants are badly clothed, haughty, savage and thick-headed, having a better quality of life than other cities in Barbary, yet without the culture of the others.[7] The kings of Tunis used to give Constantine to the prince, their firstborn son, but the present king has given it to one and then to others at various points. First he gave it to the prince, who had grown powerful and decided to fight the Arabs, but was killed on his first campaign and his army destroyed. Then he gave it to another son, 'Abd al-'Aziz, an unjust and brutal youth who was always drunk, dying of a tumour that ate away his sides. Then he gave it to another son, a callow wastrel, a vicious drunk and a sodomite; the people rebelled against him and besieged his citadel until his father sent officials to bring him back to Tunis in chains, where he was imprisoned and fined 50,000 *duppuli*. Then Constantine was sent a viceroy, a good man, son of Farah, a high officer of the king who had renounced Christianity and whom the king always used in the most important matters of service and governance. This viceroy satisfied the people, for he was a worthy man who ruled with moderation.

On the western side of the city is a large and strong citadel. Built when the city was founded, it was enlarged by the present king's viceroy, al-Qa'id Nabil,[8] a Christian convert from the province, though very ingenious. He held a firm rein over the people and tormented them as he pleased, and did the same to the neighbouring Arabs, powerfully curbing them even though they are the noblest, bravest Arabs in Africa. He once imprisoned their leader, who could command 5,000 cavalry, including his sons, nephews and brothers; Nabil did not release the man until he agreed to leave three sons in the citadel. Then the viceroy became so arrogant that he began to mint coins in his own name. This money was of better quality than the king's, who heard of it and sent for Nabil. But the viceroy, who was unwilling to go, sent the king a large sum of money and a substantial gift; there was nothing the king could do, so he said nothing. Meanwhile, after all the violence Nabil had inflicted on the people, they rebelled while he was away in Numidia, besieging the city of Biskra. Hearing the news, he immediately returned to Constantine but, unable to enter, he had no choice but to go to Tunis for the king's aid. As soon as he arrived, the king threw him in a harsh prison and fined him 100,000 ducats; upon his release, the king helped him to besiege Constantine for several days, eventually entering it by ingenuity and force. They then killed many of the city leaders, so the people again rebelled and in turn besieged the viceroy in the citadel. Day after day he fought, but so many of his own family died that in a few days he succumbed to grief and melancholy. Those defending the citadel surrendered to the people, who flooded in and sacked the viceroy's palace for valuable goods, 12,000 bushels of grain and 300 fine horses. The king then sent a messenger to convey that his majesty had pardoned the people for their wrongs. They accepted this, but insisted he send no more viceroys. This is the reason the king began to send his sons, one by one, as mentioned earlier.

The fields around the city are excellent and fertile, often returning a thirtyfold yield so there is plenty to go around. Outside, the river flows into the plain, where there are many gardens and orchards, which, since their owners know little of gardening, are not very fruitful. The vines are all trellised. There are many ancient, impressive buildings outside the city, especially one a mile-and-a-half away, which was actually built as a triumphal arch, like those in Rome. However, the foolish folk believe that the building once belonged to demons, who fled the divine power of the Muslims when they arrived.

One can reach the stream below the cliffs by steps that have been dug out with iron tools; there, next to the river, one finds a large portico with many pillars fashioned into vaults, also cut with iron tools, so that the pillars, roof and floor are all of a piece. The women wash laundry there. A stone's throw from the city is a spa, a hot spring that emerges from between large rocks. Lots of turtles are there, which the women consider spirits. When they see something bad they think it has come from the spirits, so they kill a white chicken, and put it unplucked in a pot surrounded by small wax candles; then they take the whole thing and leave it next to the spring. When the sly rogues in town see a woman going to the spring, they follow her and grab the chicken after she's gone, cooking and eating it at the foolish woman's expense.

East of the city is a marble fountain, with carved figures near it like those found in Europe. The stupid townsfolk believe that this marble building was once a school, and that God turned it and the master into marble.[9]

Twice a year the burghers send a caravan with a good deal of merchandise, such as local woollen cloth and something called *hashish*. For fear of the Arabs, they always set out accompanied by Turkish gunmen, who, for each camel load, get twice the load of a horse or mule. The Turks shoot and kill the Arab raiders and their horses, driving them off, as the author has seen with his own eyes. The merchants of Constantine pay no tax or customs to enter Tunis, though they do pay half a per cent when they leave Constantine. However, they are ruined once they've seen and tasted life in Tunis, and use up most of their wares enjoying the prostitutes.

2.4.1.10. Mila

Mila is an ancient town built by the Romans two miles from Constantine. It is surrounded by ancient walls and comprises 3,000 homes, though today it is not well populated, because of the injustice of its rulers. There are several shops of craftsmen, especially weavers of woollen blankets to cover beds. There is a pretty fountain in the square, used by the people and townsfolk. The inhabitants are valiant but thick-headed, and could live better if they knew how. People around the town can live very well, for they have many orchards of fruit, especially pears and apples; the town was named 'Mela' after the apples, having no other noteworthy characteristics.[10] Since the fields are very fertile, there is plenty of meat and bread. The viceroy of Constantine sends a governor to dispense justice and collect profits from the town. In the author's opinion, they could provide 4,000 ducats a year, but the people are dangerous, having killed several governors. Those caught in the act flee to the surrounding mountains, where justice cannot be delivered.

2.4.1.11. Bona[11]

Bona is an ancient city built by the Romans ten miles west of the Mediterranean. The ancient name Orpona was corrupted to Bona. The town was ruled by the Goths, but 'Uthman, the third caliph after Muhammad, sent a great army of valiant men, of his family and disciples of Muhammad, to lay siege to it. Taking it by force, they sacked and set it aflame, so the ancient city was ruined and abandoned. After many years, a town was rebuilt about two miles away, using stone from the ancient city, so the new city was named Bona like the old one. However, many people, especially common folk, called it Bilad al-'Unnab, or 'City of Jujubes', since there are many fields of these fruit nearby which the inhabitants eat in quantity and dry for winter. The city has about 300 inhabited homes, though few are finely built; there is one elegant structure, a mosque on the coast. Some of the pleasant inhabitants are merchants and craftsmen, and many weavers, since the merchants go in droves to towns in Numidia and bring back cloth to sell. But the people are brutal and savagely oppose the unjust governors, often killing them; the king of Tunis has no choice but to show them favour, since they will often threaten to give the town to the Christians if he doesn't send good and just governors. The city is cultured, furnished with every craft, each distinguished from the others. There is no fountain or fresh well, but only a reservoir for rainwater. The inhabitants are simple men, with great faith in those who carry on like fools, believing them to be saints and showing them great honour. On the east side of town the modern kings of Tunis have built a citadel that is not so large but very strong, with high, thick walls of large stones; this is the residence of the king's viceroy or the town governor.

Outside the city a flat, sweeping countryside spreads forty miles east to west and fifteen miles north to south, all good fields for growing fine, fat grain. This area is inhabited by the Mirdas,[12] an Arab people who farm the fields and keep many cows and bulls, as well as sheep that give them a lot of butter, which they bring to Bona in such quantities that, as with the grain, hardly any money is made on it. But each year many ships come from Tunis and its entire coastline, from Jerba and from Genoa, to load up with grain and butter. The burghers of Bona are kind and courteous to the merchants and try to please all foreigners; every Friday, from dawn to dusk, they hold a market outside the city walls that attracts many Arabs and mountainfolk looking for grain, animals, wool and butter. Nearby is a seashore where plenty of coral is found, though the people do not know how to gather it. The king of Tunis used to rent out the shore to the Genoese for a substantial fee so they could gather the coral, but they could not stay, because the savage Moorish corsairs were a great nuisance. As a result, they asked the king for permission to build a fortress to protect themselves and their merchants from the corsairs. The king agreed, but the people of Bona did not, for they understood that the Genoese had planned this as a ploy for gaining power; the town had once, long ago, been besieged and sacked by the Genoese, before a king of Tunis won it back.

2.4.1.12. Tiffech

Tiffech is a town built by the ancient Africans on the slopes of a mountain fifty miles south of Bona. It was once cultured and populous, with good walls and buildings. After it was ruined and sacked when the Arabs invaded Africa, it was resettled and left untroubled for several months. It was then given to some Arabs by the treasury of Tunis, and again ruined, remaining deserted for many years. Then an African people used it to store grain and anything else they did not need in the countryside; they also kept gardens there. The people who occupy it now are called the Hawwara; their current prince, Nasr, defended them with a large number of cavalry so that, in spite of the Arabs, they now dare to remain in the countryside. It was he who killed the prince of Constantine known as an-Nasir, son of the king of Tunis. The king himself returned from Numidia by way of Tiffech, pillaging it and destroying what remained.[13]

2.4.1.13. Tebessa

Tebessa is an ancient city built by the Romans on the borders of Numidia, a hundred miles south of the Mediterranean. Its walls are high and strong, made of large, dressed stones like those of the Colosseum in Rome, and the author has never seen such city walls in Africa or Europe. Inside, however, the houses are low and shabby, because they are new. Nearby is a fairly large river that flows through some parts of the town. In the town square, as well as on the outer wall of the town, are many Roman remains, such as inscribed epitaphs, a square structure on square marble columns supporting a marble platform, and other marvellous things. The countryside is fertile, though the fields are not very rich. From four or five miles away, the town looks like it is situated in the middle of a forest, though the trees are all large walnut trees that produce excellent nuts. The inhabitants are rascals, greedy, proud and poor, devoid of any virtue; very few of them are craftsmen. Nearby is a great mountain where caverns have been dug out with iron tools; some fools in Africa think that giants lived in them, but sensible folk think that these were the caves from which the stones of the city walls were dug. Indeed, the stones for milling grain are still carved out of them. The people are not happy to see foreigners and never welcome them, so when al-Dabbagh, a modern poet from Málaga, passed through, he was not shown the esteem and honour he had enjoyed elsewhere. He then wrote two verses insulting Tebessa and its people, which are known throughout the world and always will be, for the way they ridicule the town. They go like this:

> There's nothing to praise in Tebessa but nuts –
> Forgive me, Lord, also the river and walls.
> A city devoid of knowledge and science,
> It's hell, for the people who live there are swine.[14]

These lines may not be elegant and pleasing here, but in Arabic they are, because of the exceptions made and the phrase 'Forgive me, Lord', which is used when one has made a mistake or forgotten something. The poet al-Dabbagh wrote wonderfully elegant invective, and was known for it throughout his homeland of Baetica and all of Africa. He wrote a lament on the names of all the cities he had been in, cursing and skewering every town and its inhabitants in prose and verse; this work was a large volume and the author remembers some of it well, such as the verses above, but will omit the rest as irrelevant here. Al-Dabbagh's text was also inserted into a work by the

Granadan writer Ibn al-Khatib, when he wrote praise on each city, following it with verse and prose invective, in a work nearly twice the length of al-Dabbagh's.[15]

The inhabitants of Tebessa were constantly rebelling against the kings of Tunis, killing the governors and commissioners they sent, to the point that the present king, on his last journey to Numidia, took a route through this town and when near sent scouts to check if it survived. They answered that 'the red wall survives', referring to the town wall. The king became furious and attacked, entering by force, hanging over a hundred men, slitting the throats of a hundred more and pillaging the town. It remained almost wholly deserted in AH 915 (AD 1509–10).

2.4.1.14. Urbs (Laribus)[16]

As its name suggests, Urbs is an ancient city built by the Romans.[17] It lies in a gorgeous plain in the flower of Africa's provinces, where the fields are very rich, flat and well watered. The countryside supplies wheat and barley to all of Tunis, fifty miles north. The city has many Roman ruins, such as marble statues, epitaphs and inscribed tablets over the gate, and many walls of large, dressed stones. However, the city was ruined long ago by the Goths, with the help of the Africans, leaving only a citadel; this had been where the wealthy Roman nobles lived in Africa. After the Muslim armies conquered the region, the town began to be resettled as if it were a village, beginning with the citadel, and then two villages were built nearby within the old city. A good spring flows between the citadel and the two villages, from a hill half a mile away; the water moves through a canal of white stones that gleam like silver, where they grind grain. Today there is little culture, for the inhabitants are either farmers or cloth-weavers. The king of Tunis imposes heavy taxes. To tell the truth, if the kings of Tunis knew the town as they should – as it actually is, with good air and overflowing with grain, livestock and water – they would abandon Tunis to live there. The Arabs are more shrewd, for they live happily in the countryside all summer, fattening their horses and filling their sacks with grain for winter in the desert, without spending a penny.

2.4.1.15. Beja

Beja is an ancient city built by the Romans on a hillside fifteen miles from the Mediterranean and thirty west of Tunis, along the main road from Constantine. There was an ancient town already on the site when the Romans began to build, so it was called 'Vechia' (old). Although the name has been corrupted to 'Begia', the change from V to B is not so great, for in the Terra di Lavoro and Calabria they say *bino* for *vino* and *bechio* for *vechio*.[18] The city has ancient walls, and the inhabitants are very cultured, well organised and supplied with all the crafts, especially cloth-weavers. There are also a great many farmers, for the town has an extremely large countryside of good fields. There are not enough inhabitants to work even a third of the land; but, although plenty is left unworked, the Arabs farm enough that the townsfolk can sell 20,000 bushels of grain a year. In Tunis they have a saying: 'If there were two Bejas, grain would be worth less than sand in Tunis.' The king taxes them so heavily that the city will lose its population and culture.

2.4.1.16. Ain Zammit

This is a modern town, built by the kings of Tunis thirty miles from Beja; the king, seeing the abandoned fields, built the town so that he could reclaim and use them. But the settlement lasted only a short while, for the Arabs conquered it with the king's consent. Soon the town was ruined and abandoned, and, although the houses and towers still stand, their roofs are missing.

2.4.1.17. Kasbah[19]

This is a small ancient town built by the Romans fourteen miles from Tunis, in the middle of a vast plain which stretches for two miles all around.[20] The base of the walls remains, made of large, dressed stones, but some time ago the town was ruined by the Arabs, so the whole area is no longer farmed. It says something about the insignificance of the rulers, and the ignorance of the townsfolk, that they were left to die of hunger within two miles of such fields.

2.4.1.18. Al-Choros[21]

This is a ksar built in the modern era by the Africans on the river Mejerda eight miles from Tunis. It is surrounded by excellent countryside with good fields and a great forest of olives nearby. However, the ksar was ruined and abandoned by the Beni Heli Arabs, who are always rebelling against the king of Tunis and who live by highway robbery and by oppressing the poor locals with extraordinarily high levies.

2.4.1.19. Bizerte

Bizerte is an ancient town built by the Africans on the Mediterranean thirty-five miles from Tunis. It is small and sparsely inhabited by a destitute, miserable folk. A narrow inlet leads south from the sea past the town, becoming a large lake. Around the lake are many villages where fishermen and farmers live, for nearby to the west is the great plain of Mater, which is very fertile but heavily taxed by the king and the Arabs. They catch fish, especially large sea bream, weighing five or six pounds.[22] After October, they catch large numbers of a fish the Africans call *jarrafa*,[23] quite similar to what is called *alaccia* (sardinella) in Rome; the rain freshens the water at the inlet, so the fish enter the freshwater lake to be caught in quantity in the shallow water. This continues until the beginning of May, when, like those caught in the river of Fez, the fish thin out.

2.4.1.20. The great city of Carthage

Some say this ancient city was founded by a people from Assyria, others by a people originally from Armenia, who crossed the sea of Morea,[24] settled there and built the city. The chronicler Ibn ar-Raqiq[25] said it was built by a people from Barca, driven out of their kingdom by the Egyptian king; the Africans say that no authority knows the truth of the matter. The African historians and cosmographers such as Ibn ar-Raqiq and ash-Sharif[26] mention the city only after Rome lost its empire. The viceroys and deputies who then were in Africa continued to rule on their own, until deposed by the Goths. When the Muslims came to Africa and seized Tripoli and Gabes, all the inhabitants of those two cities fled to Carthage, where the nobles of the Romans and Goths had gathered; they all agreed to resist the Muslim armies together, fighting great battles until they fled to Bona, abandoning Carthage to sack and ruin. It remained uninhabited until the rule of al-Mahdi, the heretical caliph,[27] who resettled the town, albeit only a twentieth part of it.

The town has many walls still intact, and there is still a very large and deep cistern or reservoir; likewise, there is still an aqueduct bringing water to Carthage from a mountain thirty miles away, as high as that leading to the Palazzo Maggiore in Rome.[28] The author saw the water's source, where the aqueduct is quite low for a mile, due to the height of the ground near the mountain; the further it gets the lower the ground and the higher the aqueduct, until it reaches Carthage. There are many other ancient buildings in and out of the city.

Surrounding the city, especially to the west and south, there are a great many gardens and groves, the fruit of which is astonishing in size and quality, especially the peaches, pomegranates, figs and olives, which supply Tunis. The fields in the countryside have good soil, but the region is narrow due to the mountain to the north, with the sea and the lake of La Goletta[29] to the east and south; it also borders the plains of Bizerte, which once all belonged to this city.

At present, the city is reduced to wretched misery. It has no culture beyond twenty or twenty-five shops and 500 ugly houses, though there is an agreeable mosque of recent construction and a madrasa, the revenues of which go to the king's treasury, since it has no students.[30] The inhabitants all would like to be renowned as burghers, but they are poor and base. They try to be devout, and most of them are gardeners and farmers, none with ten ducats to his name, due to the injustice of the current king, who, when he left, as everybody knows.[31]

2.4.1.21. The great city of Tunis

Tunis is called 'Tunus' by the Arabs, who consider it a corrupt Latin or African name, since it means nothing in Arabic; the ancients called it Tarshish, like the other town in Asia. It was very small, built by the ancient Africans on the lake that emerges from La Goletta, about two miles from the Mediterranean. After Carthage was ruined, the population of Tunis began to grow, for the armies that had taken Carthage could not stay there for fear of attacks from Europe, so they fled to Tunis and settled there. Then 'Uqba, the viceroy leading the armies of the fourth caliph 'Uthman, arrived with the order that his armies should not stop or stay in towns by or even near the sea; so the viceroy built the town of Kairouan thirty-six miles from the sea and 100 from Tunis. The army stationed in Tunis then headed to the new town, while a new people took their place in the old one.

After 350 years Kairouan was ruined by the Arabs in the rebellion of the viceroy that caliph al-Qa'im had left in Africa, events already described in the section on the Arab invasion.[32] Since Kairouan was ruined, the viceroy and his household fled west to rule in Bejaia and its environs, leaving a household of their kin to govern in Tunis. About a decade later Yusuf ibn Tashfin, the king of Marrakesh, came to Bejaia and drove out its rulers, who then gave him their allegiance and service, and remained so as long as his house was in power. When this dynasty lost the kingdom to the Almohads, that is 'the preachers', the rulers renewed their allegiance and service to the caliph 'Abd al-Mu'min, king of Marrakesh; but, after he went to help Mahdia when it had been taken by the Christians, he returned by way of Tunis and overthrew its poor rulers, having their leaders butchered, placing his own viceroy in their stead and returning to Marrakesh. Tunis remained at peace under the rule of Marrakesh all the days of 'Abd al-Mu'min and his sons Yusuf and Yaqub al-Mansur; the latter took his armies to Tunis twice, not to attack it but to put down rebellions in a Numidian town 300 miles away.

After al-Mansur died, his son Muhammad an-Nasir[33] headed for Spain to attack the Christians with a large army, which was routed by the king of Spain; Muhammad escaped to Marrakesh with a few people, as told in the *Muslim Chronicles*.[34] He only lived a few months after that. His brother Yusuf,[35] who was chosen as his successor, was eventually killed by some cavalry of the king of Tlemcen. In the period between his father's rout and death and Yusuf's own death, the Arabs rampaged around the region of Tunis and often besieged its viceroy, who wrote to Marrakesh demanding help or he would give it to the Arabs. The king and caliph of Marrakesh together with his court, thinking they needed a great man for such an undertaking, chose a viceroy from Seville in Baetica by the name of 'Abd al-Wahid;[36] the king supplied him with papers giving him the authority of the king himself. And so 'Abd al-Wahid set off with his household and possessions, accompanied by ten great ships, and, when he arrived, found Tunis half-ruined by the Arabs. With prudence and eloquence, he put the city in order and brought peace to the region, collecting all the local revenues.

After 'Abd al-Wahid died, his son Abu Zakariya took his place.[37] Wiser and more learned than his father, he built a great citadel on the west side of Tunis, the highest part of the city, where there are beautiful buildings and a splendid mosque, with a lofty, elegant minaret.[38] Abu Zakariya went to Tripoli and returned through the southern part of the countryside, collecting the land's profits as he went, so he left a huge treasure upon his death. The young son who succeeded him was proud and disdained being subject to the rulers of Marrakesh, for their power had declined; the Marinids had begun to rule around Fez and the Zayyanid dynasty was already ruling in Tlemcen, while Baetica rebelled against the king of Marrakesh and drove out his governors. Moreover, all of these were fighting and jostling over control – nephews and uncles, fathers and sons. The ruler of Tunis, thinking himself stronger, went to Tlemcen with his army and exacted tribute from that king. Then the Marinid king, on campaign against Marrakesh, sent the ruler of Tunis gifts and ambassadors as a tribute; the ruler accepted him as a friend but an inferior one, and returned home in great honour and triumph, declaring himself king of Africa. He deserved the title, for nowhere in Africa was there a greater ruler. So he set up a royal court, with secretaries, viziers and generals, and adopted the royal ceremonies of Marrakesh.

From that day on, Tunis has only grown, excelling all other cities in Africa in culture. After the ruler's death, during his son's reign, four suburbs were built around the city. There is one of 300 homes outside the Bab Menara gate, and another of 1,000 homes outside the Bab Souika gate. These two suburbs are bustling with culture, with countless craftsmen, food shops, apothecaries and other livelihoods. In the second suburb is a neighbourhood like a little suburb all its own, home to the Christians who work for the ruler's guard and perform other duties not done by the Moors. Another suburb is outside the Bab el-Bahr, the sea gate about half a mile from the lake of La Goletta; this is inhabited by the foreign Christian merchants, such as the Genoese, Venetians and Catalans, and another group who keep their *funduqs* and inns separate from the Moors. Between the Christians and Moors, this district comprises 300 homes, though they are small buildings. The walled city and its suburbs in total comprise nine or ten thousand homes.

Tunis is magnificent and well organised, with each craft separated from the others. It teems with people, mostly weavers who make huge amounts of a fine and durable cloth sold throughout Africa for a high price. The women spin it to perfection: they sit in a high part of the house and drop the spindle down through a window onto the courtyard, or through a hole in the floor between storeys, and the thread is thoroughly stretched and twisted by the weight of the spindle. There is a square where the big cloth merchants, who are considered among the city's richest, keep many stalls, along with many other merchants, craftsmen like apothecaries who sell syrups and infusions, perfumers, silk-dealers, tailors, saddlers, furriers, fruiterers, grocers, milk-sellers, shops that make bread fried in oil, sausage sellers and butchers, who slaughter lambs more than anything else, especially in spring and summer. There are countless others whom it would be tedious to name one by one.

The people are respectable; all the craftsmen and merchants are well dressed in beautiful clothes, and the imams, teachers and officials all wear large turbans, which they cover with a long veil. The turbans of the king's courtiers and soldiers are also large, but uncovered. There are few rich men, on account of the scarcity of grain, since the common price is three *duppuli* a load, or four Italian ducats; usually the price is higher, and it rarely falls, for the townsfolk cannot work the fields around the city, because of the oppression of the Arabs. So all the grain comes from Urbs, Bejaia and Bona. Some burghers own walled patches of land near the city, where they grow a little barley and wheat; because these fields need to be irrigated, every farm has a well, from which they get water using wheels turned by a donkey, mule or camel, and surrounded by canals with floors to water the crops. Given such mechanisms and labour, one can only imagine how little grain these walled farms produce; it is barely enough for half the year.

They make a delicious white bread, baked in all kinds of shapes. It is not made of flour but bran, and the bakers toil to make the dough, using large pestles similar to the sticks used to beat barley and flax in Egypt – a gruelling task. During the day, the burghers, craftsmen and merchants eat a crude food made of barley flour moistened with water until it sticks together, adding a little oil and lemon or orange juice, and mixing it together. They eat it little by little, boiled or as raw chunks swallowed without mixing or chewing, truly barbarous to watch. They call this dish *bsisa*. There is a square where craftsmen keep shops and earn their living by buying barley, having it milled and refined, and selling the flour to the townsfolk. They make another dish that is better than what was just mentioned, taking a light dough and boiling it in water, and then putting it in another pot to mix and beat it with a large ladle. They put it in a pot and make a little indentation which they fill with oil or a meat broth, soaking pieces of the food and swallowing them without chewing. Besides this dish, called *bazin*, they have other tasty, refined dishes.

Around Tunis are no watermills, but only mills turned by animals, so it takes a day and a night for one mill to grind barely two loads of grain. There are no fountains, rivers or wells of fresh water, only cisterns of rainwater. One very deep well outside town has fresh water that tastes of salt, and the water carriers go there with animals and waterskins, bringing it back to sell in the city; nearly everyone drinks it, because it is healthier than the cistern water. There are several other wells with excellent water, but they are on the farms of the ruler or his courtiers.

There is a magnificent grand mosque, with revenues to support its appointed imams; beautiful and well-furnished smaller mosques are found throughout the city and the suburbs. There are many madrasas, though they only provide for the lecturers, while the students only have rooms. Other colleges are styled like monasteries, where religious folk live with a prior; despite small revenues they live well, for the people give them many gifts and alms, the stupid city folk being ready to believe that any fool who throws rocks and goes about naked is a saint. These days one Sidi al-Dahi, who wears only a sack, with bare head and feet, wanders the town yelling like a madman and throwing rocks, and because of this he is widely credited a saint; in the end, the king built him a handsome monastery, with a rich endowment, gifting it to this saint and his family as long as they last.

Most of the houses are well built of dressed stone, adorned inside with mosaics and carved plaster on the ceilings. Wooden planks are rare in Tunis, so the beams they use for the roofs are ugly; after making the vault of the roof they cover it with plaster, cut with marvellous, elegant designs and finely coloured in blues, reds and greens, in the most beautiful fashion. They also pave their rooms with glazed tiles and the courtyards of their houses with well-dressed, square stones. Most houses have one storey, and one enters by a pretty vestibule between two doors, one opening onto the street and the other leading to the rooms inside. These entrances have high steps decorated with glazed tiles, and their roofs are more beautiful than the rest of the house, for the burghers pass time there conversing with their friends and servants.

Tunis has many hammams, better arranged and maintained than those of Fez; despite being less beautiful and having less water, they are set out better and more convenient for bathing. Outside the city are splendid farms that produce excellent crops, albeit in small quantities and therefore expensive. Likewise the many gardens are well designed with fine buildings, planted with oranges, lemons, roses and other delicate flowers, especially in the area known as Bardo, where one finds the king's gardens and lavish apartments; those built by the present king are marvels of gracefully carved ornament in elegant colours. For five or six miles all around the city the countryside is full of olive groves, producing enough oil to supply the whole town and export to Egypt. The olive trees also provide wood for charcoal, used in the city for cooking and for their hearths; nowhere in the world has so little wood as Tunis.

Because the people are so poor, there are many prostitutes and, still worse, young boys of the wicked sort. A foreigner there will find many opportunities to marry, for a father is only too happy to get rid of his daughter and have her off his back.

The people eat a substance called *hashish*, which is very pricey; when someone consumes an ounce of it, he is immediately happy and starts laughing worse than a drunk, and it excites his stomach, making him hungrier than three men, inflames his desires and puts him to sleep. It is astonishing, but makes those who try it become fearful.

The women are well dressed and adorned, though outside the home they cover their faces like the women of Fez. One will be frightened the first time he sees a woman of Tunis out and about. For they wear a certain kind of wide ornament on their foreheads, about half a palm high, and when outside they cover everything, including their headgear, with a cloth called a *sefsari*, making their heads seem as huge as a giant's. They adorn and perfume themselves with great care, so the perfumers there do more business than all the other craftsmen; they are the first to open their shops in the morning, and the last to close at night, when everyone goes to sleep.

2.4.1.22. The king's court, arrangement, ceremonies and best-known officials

The king of Tunis is crowned on the basis of heredity and his father's choice, following the practice of his predecessors, with the sworn support of leading generals, officers and official scholars, such as the imams, judges and lecturers. When a king dies, these leaders install the prince on his throne and offer their allegiance. He then appoints a top official called *al-munaffid*, who acts as deputy to govern the kingdom and collect its revenues; this deputy appoints other officials, signs orders to provide for soldiers, with the king's consent and approval, and gives an account of everything that passes through his hands.

The second official in rank and title, called the *mizwar*, is like a general with authority over the soldiers and the king's guard. He receives and reviews the letters from those Arabs the king supplies, signing orders for their provision; he employs and fires soldiers as he pleases. He leads the army against rebels, or to collect revenues from lands without governors or viceroys, though recently the king has to do this himself.

The third official is the castellan, who maintains the citadel's soldiers and their provision, maintaining it and the king's rooms; he also oversees those imprisoned in the citadel for matters of great importance. The castellan has the authority to dispense justice to petitioners, and he commands the police chief and other officials as if he were the king himself.

The fourth official is the city governor, whose palace is in the city; he dispenses justice in criminal matters, pursuing and prosecuting criminals, punishing them, and taking ordinary and extraordinary fines.

The fifth official is the head secretary, who writes letters and replies to officials and others. He has the authority to open letters addressed to the king, with the exception of those from the principal officials like those mentioned above.

The sixth official is the chamberlain, who by day advises on the arrangement of rooms, the tapestries and fabric wall ornaments, positions people according to their status, and directs the king's runners to carry messages to and from his council. He also commands the guard to arrest any important man whom the king wishes to imprison. He enjoys great intimacy with the king, able to speak with him as he pleases.

The seventh official is the treasurer, who takes the money from the officials and entrusts it to those keeping the accounts; he oversees the money, ensuring it has the correct weight, exchanging it for ducats with the money changers, and dispensing it on larger official orders, with the king's signature.

The eighth official is the tax collector, who taxes goods that go by land and exacts levies on foreign merchants, half a per cent annually. His police are a team of ruffians who, when they find a foreigner with an air of wealth, bring him to the authorities or clap him in prison until the official returns, forcing him to pay the levy on his money or goods. If he claims not to have brought anything, the official makes him swear to it, roughing him up a little and seizing whatever money he has anyway.

The ninth is the customs official, who collects the customs on goods exported and imported by sea. He keeps an office on the lake of La Goletta near the town, as well as another commissioner in La Goletta itself, by the sea, to examine the goods unloaded from ships and provide him with a manifest of their number and weight. This office is usually held by wealthy Jews.

The tenth official is the bursar, like a household steward, who oversees the furnishing of the house with all its daily needs. He sees to the clothes of the closest household members, such as the king's women and girls, as well as the eunuchs and black slaves who serve in the chambers of the king and his wives. He manages the expenses for the king's young children and their nurses, and allots tasks to the Christian slaves inside and outside the citadel, providing food and clothing according to their need.

These are the principal offices at the court. There are other honourable officials, but of lower importance, such as the masters of the stables and wardrobe, the chaplain, the army judge, the tutor of the royal children, and the captain of the grooms and the various other attendants whom he commands through officials and governors. The king has 1,500 light cavalry, mostly converts from Christianity, and provides for them and their horses; he has a particular captain who hires and fires them at will. There are another 150 native Moorish cavalry, who ride with the king in war in battle formation, and he consults them on matters of war as commanders of the army. The king also keeps 100 crossbowmen, some of them Christian converts, who march near the king when he rides, whether in town or elsewhere. However, a private guard of cavalry rides closer to the king; they are Tunisian Christians, locals who live in the suburb mentioned earlier. Another guard of Turks, armed with bows and guns, marches in front of the king. The captain of the grooms rides ahead of the king's horse; beside him are men carrying his spear and shield, behind him a cavalryman bears the king's crossbow, and all around are attendants and mace-bearers who conduct the ceremonies. When the king wants to go to war, he recruits other, new soldiers and Arabs, and rides around his residence with great ceremony. He sends governors and viceroys to all the towns of his domain, to dispense justice and collect revenues and profits.

This is the general order, custom and way of life at the court of the king of Tunis. His way of life, however, is wholly unlike that of previous kings, for he is completely different in nature and habits, and governs differently. It would be a shame to speak of the specific vices of the rulers, and especially of the present king, since the author received some favour from him. Nonetheless, the king is good at finding and extracting money, which he spends on the Arabs and on fine edifices suited to indulging his desires and bodily pleasures with his women and slaves, to the music of every sort of instrument found in the region. Whether in his citadel or in his gardens and estates at Bardo, he bestows rich gifts on singers and musicians, both men and women. When he wants a man to sing for him, the king has him blindfolded like a falcon and brought into the room with the king and his women.

The kings of Tunis mint coins. A ducat weighs twenty-four carats, equivalent to one-and-a-third European ducats. They strike another, square, silver coin weighing six carats, about thirty to the ducat, sometimes closer to twenty-eight or thirty-two. They also make smaller coins, worth a half, a third or a sixth of the silver coins. The silver coins are called *nasri*, and the ducats are called *duppuli* in Italy.[39]

In brief, these are the details of Tunis and its distinctive features.

2.4.1.23. Napoli[40]

This is an ancient town built by the Romans on the Mediterranean near La Goletta, around two miles east of Tunis. The Moors call it Nabel. It was once cultured and well populated, but now nobody lives there except flax farmers, for nothing else grows there due to the land's sterility.

2.4.1.24. Gammarth

Gammarth is another town just as ancient, near Carthage eight miles north of Tunis. It is inhabited by gardeners who take their produce to Tunis. Much sugar cane grows in the countryside, which is sold in Tunis to suck on after dinner, although they do not know how to get the sugar out of it.

2.4.1.25. La Marsa

This is a small ancient town built by the Mediterranean on the site of Carthage's shore, that is, its port. It was ruined long ago, but a few inhabitants remain, all of whom are either fishermen, farmers or fullers. Nearby are many royal buildings and farms, where the current king stays for most of the summer.

2.4.1.26. Ariana

This is a small ancient town built by the Goths eight miles north of Tunis; nearby are many gardens of fruit, especially carob. Its walls are very ancient and the inhabitants all farmers. There are many other ancient little towns near Carthage, some inhabited and others not.

2.4.1.27. Al-Hammamet

This is a modern town with strong walls, built in the Muslim era fifty miles from Tunis. Its inhabitants are destitute; they are all starving and work in menial jobs as fishermen, boatmen, charcoal-makers or fullers. The ruler taxes them so heavily that they are like beggars compared to the others.

2.4.1.28. Hergla

This is an ancient little town built by the Romans on a hill by the sea, but it was destroyed by the Arabs.

2.4.1.29. Soussa

Soussa is a great ancient city built by the Romans on the Mediterranean 100 miles from Tunis. When the Muslims conquered the town and coast, they installed their viceroy here, and the ruler's palace is also here, although it has since become a monastery. The town has fine walls and a large, strong citadel, and is itself beautiful and well situated; it was once well populated and cultured, with elegant buildings, some of which still survive. There is also a splendid temple. Outside town are plenty of olive and fig groves, from which they extract a good deal of oil, as well as a great many barley fields, but they cannot farm them due to great oppression by the Arabs. The townsfolk are friendly and humane, warmly welcoming foreigners; most of them are sailors who travel in merchant ships to the Levant and Turkey, or operating as corsairs to the nearby towns of Sicily and other parts of Italy. The rest are either cloth-weavers, cowherds or potters who make earthenware pots, pitchers, tankards and all sorts of unglazed vessels, supplying the whole coast, including Tunis. But the wretched town is now almost entirely uninhabited due to the violence and oppression of the rulers; only a fifth of its settlements remain, and no more than five or six shops in the whole city, including food shops, apothecaries, greengrocers and other mean shops. The author arrived in this town due to a storm, and everyone felt great compassion and pity at seeing it treated this way.

2.4.1.30. Monastir

Monastir is an ancient town built by the Romans on the sea twelve miles from Soussa; it has strong, high walls, and the houses inside are built in an elegant style. The inhabitants are extremely poor, almost all beggars, wearing roguish clothes and slippers of spiny rushes. Most are cloth-weavers and fishermen, eating nothing but barley bread and *bazin* with oil, like in all the towns on the Tunis coastline, for nothing grows in the area but barley. The author once happened to find himself on board a galleon bound for Turkey with the town's ambassador, and they began to talk. He asked what provision the king gave the town, and the ambassador replied that the king gave them a few ducats and twenty-four bushels of barley a year. The author, being unfamiliar with the region, said, 'Ah, so perhaps you have lots of horses?' He replied that there were no horses at all.

'Then what do you do with all that barley?'

'Our people eat it.' He seemed ashamed to say so, and the author was even more ashamed to have asked so forwardly, but he had only done so because he assumed that only the poor ate barley.

Outside town are countless farms of apricots, figs, apples, pears, pomegranates and especially olives, but still the ruler oppresses the wretched inhabitants.

2.4.1.31. Teboulba

Teboulba is an ancient town built by the Romans on the Mediterranean, two miles east of Monastir. It was large, well populated and cultured, and still has many farms of good fields and olives, but they are now all abandoned due to the violence of the Arabs and the oppression of the ruler of Tunis. There are barely forty households in the town, and they live like religious folk, keeping a large house like a hospital to shelter all the foreigners who pass through. The Arabs often go to stay in the town; when this happens the townsfolk, being as few as they are, give them no trouble.

2.4.1.32. Mahdia

The city of Mahdia was founded in modern times by al-Mahdi, the first heretical caliph of Kairouan,[41] who built it on a branch of the mountains stretching into the Mediterranean. It has high, strong walls with sturdy towers that securely guard the port, and all its gates are well barred. Al-Mahdi came to these lands in the guise of a pilgrim, telling the local elders that he was a princely scion of Muhammad's family; they believed him and showed him great honour and welcome, rebelling against the viceroy of Kairouan and making al-Mahdi their prince. To increase his support, he had them call him Khalifa al-Mahdi, that is, 'The Guided Caliph'. With the help of one of their princes, he marched with an army against the viceroy and drove him out, entering Kairouan, where he was proclaimed secular and spiritual ruler. Then he went west through Numidia, forty days' journey from Kairouan, collecting tribute. He was captured and incarcerated by the prince of Sijilmasa. But the prince who had supported him before his caliphate, when he heard the news, at once gathered a large army, travelled to Sijilmasa and destroyed the prince's armies. He entered the city by force and rescued al-Mahdi from prison, bringing him back to his seat in Kairouan. But al-Mahdi, a wicked man, had his rescuer killed; the latter had put himself and his family in danger to help al-Mahdi, springing him from prison and making him caliph twice, and this is how he was rewarded. Al-Mahdi may be counted among those who have repaid good with evil.[42]

After killing the prince, the caliph al-Mahdi became such a cruel tyrant that he knew the people hated him, so he began to have the city built up like a fortress to keep himself safe in times of need. For having killed the prince, he learned that a preacher in Numidia was going to rebel against him in revenge for his treachery. This preacher, Abu Yazid, who was known as the Knight of the Ass because he always rode a donkey, assembled 40,000 warriors and marched on Kairouan.[43] Al-Mahdi, when he saw the size of the army, only just managed to escape, fleeing with his family to Mahdia and fortifying himself there. Abu Yazid followed with his army and laid siege to the city, but al-Mahdi had already requested help from the caliph of Córdoba, who sent thirty ships of well-armed and provisioned men and horses. The preacher was defeated and killed, along with his son and their army. Then the caliph al-Mahdi returned to Kairouan and maintained it in peace with all the western regions until he died. The rule remained in his family until one of the kings went to Egypt, as has already been said at the start of this work.[44]

One hundred and thirty years later, Mahdia was attacked by the Christians and finally captured, remaining in Christian hands for many months until the arrival of 'Abd al-Mu'min, king and caliph of Marrakesh, who reclaimed it by force. It was resettled and has been inhabited ever since. The king of Tunis kept a governor and castellan there, but did not impose any taxes on the townsfolk except the expenses for his two officials. The inhabitants used to trade by sea, and always kept many ships. They were very hostile to the Arabs, so they could not work on any of their farms, living instead on trade and crafts. In modern times Count Pedro Navarro came with nine ships, thinking he could capture the town, but it was defended with artillery at the entrance to the port, and only a few of his boats were not sunk. This happened in AD 1519.

2.4.1.33. Sfax

Sfax is an ancient city with high, strong walls, built by the Africans on the Mediterranean during the wars with the Romans. It is large and was once very cultured, but at present is almost abandoned; there are no more than three or four hundred homes and very few shops, because it is greatly oppressed by the Arabs and by the king of Tunis. Most of the inhabitants are cloth-weavers and sailors, and fishermen who work day and night catching an excellent fish that they call *spares*, a mongrel word neither Arabic, Berber nor Latin.[45] All of them are very poor and badly clothed, eating barley bread and *bazin*. There are a few merchants with ships that they use to trade in Egypt and Turkey.

2.4.1.34. Kairouan

The city of Kairouan was built by 'Uqba,[46] the army general sent from Arabia Deserta by 'Uthman, the third caliph. It is thirty-six miles from the Mediterranean and 100 from Tunis, for 'Uqba was wary of making his home in a town by the sea, fearing attacks from Italy or Spain as they were ruled by the Goths; he needed to keep himself safe, along with his army and goods, and the treasures he had robbed and pillaged from the towns of Barbary and Numidia. The city was soon surrounded with brick walls, and then he built a large, wondrous mosque on marble columns; two of these columns, next to the niche[47] where the imam stood, are especially remarkable, of an incredible size and colour, a perfect, lustrous red with white points like porphyry.

After 'Uthman's death, 'Uqba remained in Kairouan throughout the schism between Caliph 'Ali and Caliph Mu'awiya, giving tribute and obedience to neither of them, and waiting to see which would triumph. Mu'awiya, after his victory, sent a new viceroy[48] to Kairouan and confirmed 'Uqba as the general of his armies; the office remained in the family of Mu'awiya's viceroy for the entire period of the Umayyad Caliphate in Damascus.

But Caliph al-Walid ibn 'Abd al-Malik sent a great army with one of his servants, Musa ibn Nusayr, who stopped in Kairouan for many days until the army was well rested.[49] Then Musa marched west, robbing and pillaging many towns that he took by force, and continued on until he arrived at the ocean coast, riding into the water until his stirrups were wet, saying, 'Now I can tell my master al-Walid that I've conquered as many towns and lands as I could find.'

He returned to Kairouan, but sent one of his generals named Tariq (ibn Ziyad) to Mauretania; it was Tariq who made the treaty with Count Julian of Ceuta[50] that allowed him to cross to Baetica and conquer many towns and lands, as one reads in Ibn Hayyan[51] and other chroniclers of Baetica. When Musa heard of these victories he was envious, and he sent couriers to tell Tariq not to move without further orders or his own presence. So Tariq stopped on the coast of Andalusia, and two months later Musa arrived with a great army, crossing the sea to Baetica and joining the two forces together. They went inland to attack the armies of the Goths, who came to face them led by King Roderic, joining battle with the Saracen armies; but the unfortunate king was defeated and his entire army wiped out. Musa and Tariq pursued victory as far as Castile, taking the city of Toledo,[52] where they found huge treasures and precious goods, as well as many holy relics in the basilica, such as the table at which Christ dined with his apostles, and which was covered with gold and adorned with jewels, valued at half a million ducats.[53]

After the capture of Toledo, Musa left at once with a part of his army, bringing almost all the treasures from Spain, and crossing the sea to Kairouan. When he arrived, al-Walid sent for him, and he took all his treasures and precious goods and headed for Egypt; while he was in Alexandria, al-Walid fell seriously ill, and his brother Hisham,[54] who sought the caliphate for himself, sent to tell Musa not to come to Damascus, because al-Walid was about to die. For he feared that the riches that Musa brought, if they arrived before the death of al-Walid, would all be given away.

But Musa, caring little for Hisham, went to Damascus anyway, and the moment he arrived he visited al-Walid and handed over all the treasures. Al-Walid camped for five days and then died. His brother Hisham took power, depriving Musa of the viceroyalty of Africa[55] and tormenting him greatly; then he sent a new viceroy, named Yazid ibn al-Muhallab, who was a peaceful man. After Yazid's death his office and title passed to his family – his son, brother and nephew – lasting throughout the Umayyad Caliphate. The Abbasids then deposed that house by force of arms; when as-Saffah[56] came to power he sent another viceroy, named al-Aghlab ibn Salim, who governed on his own like a ruler, because the Muslim caliphs had moved their seat from Damascus to Baghdad, for the reasons narrated in the chronicles of the Muslims. After al-Aghlab's death he was succeeded by his son Ziyadat,[57] and the rule of Africa was passed down within the Aghlabid house for seventy years, until the last ruler was driven out by the heretical caliph al-Mahdi.[58]

In the Aghlabid era, the city of Kairouan grew so great in size, culture and power that it could not contain everyone. So the ruler had a separate city built nearby, calling it Raqqada, where he lived with his family, officials and chief generals.[59] During this period, Sicily was captured by his armies sent overseas under a captain called Halcamo, who built a town in the mountains for his protection, giving it his own name; even today the Sicilians call it Halcamo (Alcamo).[60] This town was besieged by the armies who came to Sicily's aid, so the ruler of Kairouan sent a larger army under a valiant captain named Asad[61] who refreshed the forces at Alcamo. Then they joined together and captured the remaining towns.

Because of such victories and the dominion of this island, Kairouan swelled in culture and size. It is situated in a sandy desert where no trees or grain grow; all the grain and fruit comes along the sea coast or from Soussa, Monastir or Mahdia. Two miles from the city is a mountain called Waslat where there are traces of Roman buildings, and many springs and gardens, especially of carob trees. The mountainfolk bring many goods to supply Kairouan, but Soussa, Monastir and Mahdia are forty miles away. There are neither springs nor freshwater wells in town, only the water from cisterns, but near the city are huge square reservoirs built by the ancients; these fill up in the rainy season, but in July one won't find a drop of water, for the townsfolk give it to their cattle to drink. Likewise, the Arabs go to stay around the city all summer, but they have a great abundance of meat and dates that they bring from Numidia, seventy miles away.

The town was a great centre for legal study, and even today most African scholars come from here; their names can still be seen in the epitaphs on their tombs. But, as was said above, when the Arabs invaded Africa the city was sacked and ruined, especially the town built outside. After many years it began to be miserably resettled, and the modern inhabitants are all poor craftsmen; most are tanners of lambskin and goatskin, and the rest are furriers. They export the pelts to the Arabs' fairs and the towns of Numidia, where there are no European fabrics, so the Arabs and Numidians wear the pelts without any fabric lining. The townsfolk make a living in this trade, but they are heavily taxed by the Arabs and by the ruler of Tunis, so they are reduced to great poverty, as the author saw in AH 922 (AD 1516–17) on his trip from Tunis to Numidia, where the king of Tunis was camped.

2.4.1.35. Gabes

Gabes is a huge city built by the Romans in a gulf on the Mediterranean. It has high, ancient walls of large, polished stones, especially around its citadel. A stream passes nearby, but its water is warm and a little brackish. The city was once inhabited and cultured, but after the Arabs invaded it was sacked, destroyed and abandoned. After many years it began to be resettled; then it was again abandoned, and its inhabitants moved to the farms outside town, where there were so many date palms it looked like a forest from a distance. No grain or trees grow in the fields except the palms, but the dates are not of the highest quality, for they do not last all year. However, there is also a great abundance of a fruit like the radish, but as small as a bean, that grows underground. These fruit are dried and eaten like almonds, which have a similar taste, throughout the kingdom of

Tunis. They are called *hab' al-'aziz*.[62] All the townsfolk are black; they are poor farmers and fishermen, greatly oppressed by the Arabs and by the king of Tunis.

2.4.1.36. Al-Hammah

Al-Hammah is a very ancient city built by the Romans five miles inland from Gabes. It is surrounded by beautiful walls of large, polished stones, and the inscribed marble tablets can still be seen over the city gates. However, the buildings and streets are hideous, and the inhabitants are destitute and wicked, all thieves and cut-throats. The soil is harsh and dry, and no grain or tree grows there except poor date palms around town. A mile and a half to the south is a great spring of boiling water that flows into the city by means of a wide underground canal; in it are buildings with separate chambers where one person can take a hot bath, for the floor is that of the canal. The water in the canal goes up to one's navel, but nobody dares to go in all at once, for it is scalding hot. The townsfolk drink the water, but it must be drawn in the morning to drink in the evening, and vice versa.

Outside town to the north, the water flows into a lake that they call 'the lake of the lepers', because it is used to cure leprosy and close up wounds. For this reason one finds many lepers in al-Hammah, though they stay not in the town itself, but in a suburb of huts on the shores of the lake. The water does wonders for invalids, but it tastes of sulphur, as the author can attest, so it will never quench a thirst.

2.4.1.37. Mahres

Mahres is a ksar built in modern times by the Africans fifty miles from Jerba, at the mouth of the Gulf of Gabes to guard it from enemy ships. It is inhabited by craftsmen who weave a certain kind of woollen cloth; all the others are boatmen and fishermen who do a great trade with Jerba, speaking the African language like them. The town has neither fields nor farms; all make their living from the sea.

2.4.1.38. The Island of Jerba

Jerba is an island just off the coast, all plains and sand, with countless groves of dates, grapes, olives and other fruit. It is eight miles in circumference, and all its settlements are separate villages; that is, each farm has a house where a family lives by itself, and there are a few villages with lots of homes together. The fields are very lean, growing a tiny amount of barley after frequent and laborious irrigation from deep wells, so there is a constant dearth of grain, which goes for six *duppuli* a bushel, sometimes more. Meat is also very expensive.

On the island by the sea is a citadel in which the ruler lives with his family. Near it is a large village in which Moorish, Turkish and Christian merchants stay; once a week it holds a market like a fair, for the whole island gathers there, and even the Arabs on the mainland nearby, bringing livestock and wool in bulk. The islanders mostly live on trading woollen fabrics and raisins, taking them to Tunis and Alexandria.

Fifty years ago the island was attacked by a Christian fleet who captured and sacked it, but the king of Tunis soon came to the rescue. It was then resettled and the citadel built, for before that there was nothing but villages. It was governed by two faction leaders from the two tribes who inhabited the island, but on behalf of the king of Tunis, who would send governors, judges and administrators. After 'Uthman's[63] death, his successors declined in power and the island became free, albeit under the control of the two faction leaders. Then one faction rose up and killed all the elders of the other faction, destroying the bridge to the mainland lest there be any suspicion of an army arriving by land. The island then remained under the control of a single leader, and his family has ruled ever since. But it was full of traitors: a son would kill his father for power, likewise a brother his brother, as happened recently, when ten rulers have been murdered for this reason in the space of five years. For the island brings in 80,000 ducats a year in tax and duty, due to the constant traffic of Alexandrians, Turks and Tunisians.

In recent years the island was attacked by a fleet sent by King Ferdinand of Spain under the duke of Alba's command.[64] They disembarked on the island and marched many miles inland, but they were repelled by the Moors and had to retreat, due to the heat and thirst, for no water was to be found between the ships and their point of arrival.[65] Still worse, the return journey was greater, for the soldiers had disembarked at high tide but the water ebbed while they were on land, uncovering four more miles. This only increased their suffering, and they were almost all either killed or taken captive, a few barely escaping to bring the ships back to Sicily.

Later, during the reign of his imperial majesty Charles, another fleet was sent with Don Novo, a knight and prior of the Order of St John in the city of Messina,[66] who, by his prudence and experience, made the Moors surrender without a fight; they were forced to pay a substantial tribute to his imperial majesty the Emperor, sending an ambassador to Germany to confirm the articles drawn up with Don Novo. The Emperor confirmed all the articles on condition that they pay 5,000 *duppuli* to the viceroy of Sicily, a truce that lasts to this day.

2.4.1.39. Zuwarah

Zuwarah is a little town with polished stone walls, built by the Africans on the Mediterranean fifty miles east of Jerba. Its inhabitants are poor because they have no livelihood but making lime and gesso; they have no fields to sow and are constantly wary of Christian corsairs, especially since Tripoli was captured by the Christians.

2.4.1.40. Lebda (Leptis Magna)

This is an ancient town built by the Romans and destroyed in the African rebellion. It formerly had high walls of large stones, but all its stones and columns were brought to build Old Tripoli. Nevertheless, it was resettled when the Muslim armies invaded, at least until the Arabs arrived, when it was destroyed a second time, as can be seen at present.

2.4.1.41. Old Tripoli

This ancient city was built by the Romans and later ruled by the Goths until the reign of 'Umar, the second caliph, when the first Muslim armies arrived. The grand duke had a great army himself, but, given the size of the Muslim forces, he dared not defend himself. They were besieged for three months, but, when he realised there would be neither help nor aid, he mounted his horse with his soldiers and headed for Carthage, abandoning the town. It was sacked and the inhabitants either killed or taken captive to Egypt and Arabia, as the African historian Ibn Raqiq has written.

2.4.1.42. Tripoli

Tripoli is a city in a sandy plain full of date palms, built by the Africans after Old Tripoli was ruined. Its walls are high and handsome but not too strong; the buildings are as fine as those of Tunis and the squares are well organised and supplied with every craft, especially cloth-weavers. The city has no springs or freshwater wells, but there are cisterns of rainwater. There is always a dearth of grain, for the countryside around town is all sandy, like that of Numidia. This is because the Mediterranean enters far to the south, so the places that should be temperate and fertile are flooded with water. The coastal dwellers believe that there used to be many fields stretching to the north, but due to the influx of the sea since better times,[67] the fields have been covered over with water. This is noted and acknowledged on the coasts of Monastir, Mahdia, Sfax, Gabes, Jerba and other towns to the east, where the sea is so shallow that one can wade a mile or two out without the water reaching one's belt; places like these are old fields that have been recently covered over. The inhabitants of Tripoli also hold that the town once extended further north, but the sea continually ate away at the walls and northern part, so they shifted gradually to the south. They say that buildings can still be seen underwater to this day.

In the city are large numbers of mosques, madrasas and hospitals for travellers and the poor. When it comes to food, the inhabitants live in great misery, eating barley *bazin* and *bsisa*, for supplies arrive only on a daily basis, and it is a lucky citizen who can amass a bushel or two of grain in his house – they store it in earthen pots, so one can imagine how little there is. However, the people trade a great deal, for Numidia and Tunis are nearby, and it is the last town on the way to Alexandria; it is also close to the islands of Sicily and Malta. The Venetian galleys once came to the port and did great business with the local merchants, and with those who travelled there every year to meet the galleys. The townsfolk are well dressed and cultured, like those of Tunis.

Tripoli has always been under the control of Tunis, except for a few days when Abu al-Hasan, the king of Fez,[68] attacked Tunis. The king of Tunis escaped with the Arabs to the desert, and later returned when Abu al-Hasan had been defeated and his army destroyed.[69] Tripoli rebelled against him and remained hostile for five years, at the end of which the king of Fez, now Abu 'Inan, attacked the kingdom of Tunis.[70] Abu-'l Abbas, the king of Tunis,[71] marched with his army against Abu 'Inan to defend it, but at the end of the battle he was defeated and escaped to Constantine. The king of Fez came and besieged him there, until the townsfolk opened the gates; Abu-'l Abbas was captured, brought to Fez and imprisoned in the citadel of Ceuta.[72] But just then Tripoli was attacked by a fleet of ten Genoese ships; it was captured, sacked, and its people taken captive. Hilal ibn Maimon – Abu 'Inan's viceroy in Tunis – wrote at once to his master with the news from Tripoli, and the king settled the matter with the Genoese with money, paying them 50,000 ducats to release the town and their captives, though they later discovered that half the ducats were false.

Tripoli began to be resettled. Later the king of Tunis was freed by Abu Salim,[73] the king of Fez; the two became family, and he returned to his kingdom. Tunis regained control of Tripoli, until the city rebelled against Prince Abu Bakr, son of 'Uthman, king of Tunis.[74] The prince was butchered along with one of his sons in the fortress of Tripoli, on the orders of his grandson Yahya, the new king.[75] Tripoli remained under Yahya's control until he was killed in battle by one of his cousins named 'Abd al-Mu'min,[76] who then succeeded to the throne.[77] 'Abd al-Mu'min was succeeded on his death by Zakariya, son of the slain king Yahya, and he ruled Tunis for many months until he died of the plague.[78] Then the people and princes of Tunis sought out Muhammad,[79] son of al-Hasan and a cousin of Zakariya, and installed him on the royal throne. He reigned for many months and began to exercise his power over the towns, especially Tripoli, which he taxed heavily.

Then the people drove out the king's governors and ministers and elected a burgher to govern Tripoli like a ruler, for treasures were given to him to dispense as seemed fit. The king of Tunis sent an army with his viceroy, who besieged Tripoli, but he was poisoned by the Arabs under an agreement with the ruler of Tripoli, and the camp was destroyed. After many months the elected ruler was murdered by his brother-in-law in revenge for his uncle whom the ruler had killed. Then the people elected as a ruler one who had formerly been the prince's courtier, but who had since become a hermit in the local manner; he was forced to rule for many months until Tripoli was captured by a Christian fleet dispatched by the Catholic king Don Fernando, led by Count Pedro Navarro.[80] The fleet arrived suddenly in the evening, and the next morning the town was captured and the people taken captive; none escaped. The ruler of Tripoli and his father-in-law, who had killed the previous ruler, were both taken to Messina and remained there as prisoners for many years; then they were brought to Palermo and freed by His Majesty the Emperor Charles (V). They went to live in Tripoli, hoping to resettle it, for it had been destroyed after it was captured by the Christians. The castle was fortified with strong walls and heavy artillery, as the author saw in AD 1515.

He also heard that the ruler of Tripoli has begun to resettle the town in the name of His Majesty Charles.

End of the tract on the kingdom of Tunis, there follows the mountains of this kingdom.

2.4.2.1. The mountains of Bejaia

The domain of Bejaia consists almost entirely of high, harsh mountains full of springs and forests. A rich, noble and generous people live there, keeping many goats, cattle and horses; they have almost always been free, especially since Bejaia was captured by the Christians. The inhabitants nearly all have a black cross on their cheeks, according to the ancient custom, as was described earlier.[81] They eat lots of barley bread, walnuts and figs, especially in the 'Zwawa mountains by the sea. In some of the mountains they mine iron, from which they make little pieces of half a pound which they spend like coins. The mountainfolk also strike silver coins weighing four grains each. A lot of flax and hemp grows there, from which they make a coarse cloth. The inhabitants are badly clothed, hot-blooded and brutish in their manners, but courageous. The mountains of Bejaia extend fifty miles along the Mediterranean and forty miles north to south; a separate tribe lives on each mountain, but there is no difference in their way of life, so they have not been discussed individually.

2.4.2.2. Aures mountains

This is a very high range, inhabited by a coarse, wicked people who are all brigands and thieves, for it is far from any city: eighty miles from Bejaia and sixty from Constantine, separated by other mountains and seventy miles across. To the south it borders the Numidian desert, to the north the territory of M'Sila, Setif, N'Gaous and Constantine. On its peaks are many springs, which spread out through the plains to form marshes, but when the weather heats up the marshes become salty. Neither the merchants nor the Arabs nor travellers can do business with the mountainfolk, who wish their lands to remain unknown, being enemies of the Arabs and the nearby rulers, such as the king of Tunis and others.

2.4.2.3. The mountains of the domain of Constantine

All the areas to the north and west near Constantine are extremely mountainous; they stretch from the borders of the Bejaia mountains thirty miles along the Mediterranean to the borders of Bona. The whole region is fertile, with many good fields in the plain between the mountains, producing enough olives, figs and other fruit to supply all the nearby towns, such as Constantine, Collo and Jijel, as well as the Arabs. The mountainfolk are a little more cultured than those of Bejaia, for they have many craftsmen, making a great quantity of cloth. They often war among themselves. Their women, when they dislike their husband, leave their children and flee to an enemy mountain to marry another. This is the cause of their disputes, which are sometimes settled by payment or bartering; for instance, the new husband may give one of his daughters or sisters to the man whom the wife left.

The mountainfolk are very rich because they are free; neither the king of Tunis nor the Arabs have anything to do with them. On the other hand, they cannot frequent the plain, for fear of being captured by the Arabs, still less the cities, for fear of the rulers. Each mountain holds a weekly market on different days; many merchants from Constantine and Collo are found there, but each needs the support of a friend from the mountain, or he will be robbed. If his friend wants to betray and rob him, nobody will speak up, and the merchant will have to put up with it.

The mountainfolk are divided into many tribes, each occupying their own mountain. They live like animals, without imams, judges or anyone who can read, so that to find a scribe they have to travel two, five or ten miles away. They have 40,000 warriors, 4,000 of whom are cavalry; if they got together they could conquer the whole of Africa, for they are very brave.

2.4.2.4. The mountains of Bona

To the north of Bona is the sea, and to the south and west are a few mountains, forming an alliance with the mountains of Constantine. But to the east are other mountains resembling hills with good fields full of cities and ksars built by the Romans; these are all currently ruined and their names unknown. The fields are uninhabited due to the violence of the Arabs, except a few strips farmed by a people who, like the Arabs, live in the countryside and protect them from the Arabs by force of arms. The hills have good fields that stretch eighty miles west to east, between Bona and Bejaia, and thirty miles north to south. There are also many sources of the rivers flowing through the plain between the hills and the Mediterranean.

2.4.2.5. The mountains near Tunis

Tunis lies in the plain, and there are no mountains nearby except certain branches along the sea to the west, like the one by Carthage. There is another very high, cold mountain called Zaghwan thirty miles south-east of Tunis; it is uninhabited except for the huts of a few peasants who keep bees and grow a little barley. But it was inhabited in antiquity, especially when the Romans ruled Africa, and they built many ksars and towns at the summit, on the slopes and in the foothills, the ruins of which can still be seen. There are lots of other traces, among them many Latin epitaphs that the author has seen; some of these were read and translated for him by a converted Sicilian. In antiquity, water was brought from this mountain to Carthage, as one can see from the aqueducts.

2.4.2.6. The mountains of
Beni Yafran and Nafusa

These mountains are separated by the desert thirty miles from Jerba and Sfax; they are inhabited by a brave people whom other Muslims consider heretics, belonging to the sect of the caliphs of Kairouan. All the lands in Africa have abandoned that sect except these people. The mountains are high and cold; only a little wheat grows there, and barley that scarcely lasts half the year. For this reason the locals often go to Tunis and other towns to earn a living at menial jobs, but they cannot reveal their belief in the heresy or they will be punished by the inquisitors.

2.4.2.7. Mount Gharyan

Gharyan is a high, cold mountain forty miles long and fifty wide, fifty miles from Tripoli and separated by sandy desert from other settlements. A large amount of barley grows there, and also excellent dates, but they have to be eaten fresh. There are plenty of olives, from which they press a lot of oil that they send to Alexandria and nearby towns. There are thirty or so poorly built villages and ksars. A huge quantity of saffron grows there, marvellous in quality and colour, and more perfect than that found anywhere else in the world, for while Italian or Greek saffron sells for ten *sherifi* a pound in Cairo and Tunis, Gharyan saffron goes for fifteen. The author has heard from a former deputy to the princes of Tripoli that the mountain brought in 60,000 *duppuli*, and that during his time there thirty *cantars* – five mule loads – were harvested in a single year. But it was always taxed by the kings of Tunis and by the Arabs, so the inhabitants are destitute and badly clothed.

2.4.2.8. Mount Beni Walid, Tunis

This is a mountain 100 miles from Tripoli, inhabited by a valiant and rich people who live at liberty and are allied with the other mountains bordering the Numidian desert.

End of the section on the mountains; there follows the provinces that have neither cities nor ksars, which are like villages, as will follow one by one.

2.4.3.1. Janzur

Janzur is a well-populated village near the Mediterranean, two miles from Tripoli. It is more cultured than the others, and there are many craftsmen and gardens of dates, pomegranates and quinces; but its inhabitants are poor, especially since Tripoli was captured by the Christians. They have made a treaty with the captain of Tripoli and so trade with the Christians, bringing some goods and fruits there to sell.

2.4.3.2. Zawiyat Ibn Yarbu'

This is another village not far from the sea, where some religious folk live with those who work their date farms, but there are very few fields for grain.

2.4.3.3. Amrus

This is a village six miles inland from Tripoli, surrounded by groves of dates and other fruit.

2.4.3.4. Tajura

Tajura is an area in the country three miles east of Tripoli, with many villages and gardens of dates and other fruit. The villages have become cultured, for after the ruin of Tripoli some of its townsfolk came to live here; the settlements are separate, but united by trade and government. It should be noted that all the villages under the dominion of Tripoli are inhabited by a lowly, ignorant and thieving people, whose buildings are made of clay with roofs of palm branches. All eat barley bread and *bazin* with oil, a wretched subsistence. All are subject to the king of Tunis, and to the Arabs, except Tajura.

2.4.3.5. Msallata

Msallata is a province on the Mediterranean thirty-five miles from Tripoli, with many villages and ksars; their inhabitants are rich because the land abounds with dates and olives. The people live at liberty; they have a leader who governs the province and deals with the Arabs in both peace and war. They number 5,000 warriors.

2.4.3.6. Misrata

This is a province on the Mediterranean 100 miles from Tripoli, with many villages and ksars both on the plains and in the mountains. The inhabitants are extremely rich because they are free and occupied in trade, taking goods that arrive from Europe on Venetian galleys and bartering them in Numidia for slaves, carpets, civet and musk from the Black Land; these they bring to Turkey, earning both on the outward journey and the return.

2.4.3.7. Al-Ghar

Al-Ghar is a village on the Mediterranean surrounded by date palms. It has a few miserable strips of land that must be irrigated; with difficulty a little barley can be grown there, with which the townsfolk are fed.

2.4.3.8. Ghar al-Ghar[82]

In this place there are many large and wondrous caverns that lead underground; it is here that the stones for building Old Tripoli were reputedly quarried, for the village is near Tripoli.

2.4.3.9. Sorman

This is a very large and well-populated town near Old Tripoli; it has many dates but no grain at all.

2.4.3.10. Ksar Ahmed

This is a ksar on the Mediterranean many miles from Tripoli, built by a general who went to Africa with the armies. It was later ruined by the Arabs.

2.4.3.11. Subeicha

Subeicha was a ksar built by the Arabs when the Muslims arrived in Africa. It was also ruined by the Arabs, but at present a few fishermen and other poor folk live there.

2.4.3.12. Ksar Hasan

This is another ksar on the Mediterranean built by a different Muslim general. It was also ruined by the Arabs.

End of the tract on the kingdom of Tunis; there follows the desert of Barca.

2.4.4.1. The desert of Barca[83]

Starting from the edges of the territory of Misrata, this desert extends eastward as far as Alexandria, around 1,300 miles in length. Barca is an empty wilderness without water or arable land; before the Arabs invaded Africa it was uninhabited, but since then the powerful have settled in the fertile lands, leaving the poor and powerless in the desert, barefoot, naked and starving, since they are far from any settlement. Out of dire necessity and misery, for nothing grows in this region, they pawn their sons for grain and other things they need to survive. Sicilian merchants bring the grain and goods from overseas and return with the hostages; but before they can leave the Arabs go and commit robberies in Numidia, and then redeem the slaves, rescuing their sons.[84]

The Arabs of Barca are the most treacherous thieves in the world, for they habitually ambush foreign travellers, and, far from stopping there, have them drink a great deal of warm milk and hurl them into the air, holding some by a foot, others by a hand, before suddenly releasing them. The poor wretches spew out their guts as soon as they are let go, and the Arabs search the mess for ducats, suspecting that the travellers had swallowed their gold when they found themselves in such a dangerous place. Often enough, they come across someone who does indeed have gold in his body. In this desert are many villages, as described above.

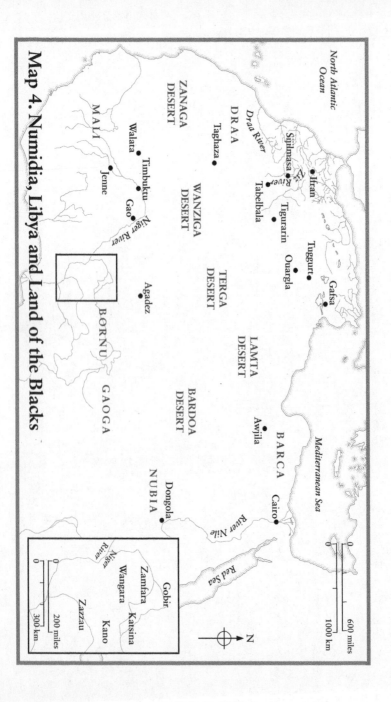

Map 4. Numidia, Libya and Land of the Blacks

BOOK 3.

NUMIDIA

As we already said in Part One of this book, Numidia is scorned by African cosmographers and historians for the reason we gave there.[1] Some of its towns are very near the Atlas mountains, and these are discussed in the second part of the book on Haha; similarly the provinces of Sous and Guzula, and al-Hammah and Gabes in the kingdom of Tunis. Others think that these towns are in Numidia, but the author puts them among the towns of Barbary because Ptolemy puts the entire coast of the kingdom of Tunis in Barbary. In this part, we will follow each place in turn.

3.1. Tesset

Tesset is a little town with rough stone walls on the edge of the Libyan deserts, built by the Numidians in ancient times; it has little culture, containing only 400 or so homes. There is nothing around it but sandy countryside, although there are a few wretched date palms, and stretches of land for sowing a little barley and millet, on which they support their wretched lives. From these farms, they pay heavy tributes to the neighbouring Arabs in the desert.

The inhabitants of the town often travel around the Lands of the Blacks and the province of Guzula as merchants, so you'll never find more than half of them at home. The men are quite brutish, dark-skinned and illiterate, and it is the women who study and work as schoolteachers for the girls and boys; however, when a boy reaches twelve his father will put him to work on the farm or land, or he will help hoe the soil or draw water from the wells to irrigate the fields. These people are very poor; they wear ragged clothes and have very few animals but goats and *adimmans* (Barbary sheep).[2] There are no oxen or sheep except the *adimmans*, and when they sow crops they use a horse or camel to plough, as is done all over Numidia. The women of the city are rather fat and paler than the men; they are all idle, except a few who study or spin a little wool.

3.2. Waddan

Waddan is a village in the Numidian desert bordering Libya, inhabited by a poor, brutish people; no grain or anything else good grows there, except a few dates and a handful of barley. The inhabitants are always fighting each other and the Arabs oppress them, so they are destitute and cannot trade, because of their hostile relations; they are more black than white and are wretchedly clothed, half-naked.[3] They use snares to hunt the wild animals of this land like *lamt* (oryxes)[4] and ostriches; no other meat is found in the area except game, although they do keep some goats for their milk.

3.3. Ifran

Ifran comprises around four ksars about three miles from one another, built by the Numidians on a river that flows in winter but is dry in summer; between them are many date farms. The inhabitants are quite rich, because they go trading all over the place; they trade with the Portuguese in the port of Gartgues-sen,[5] buying large reams of fabric and textiles and other merchandise, and bringing them to the Lands of the Blacks such as Walata and Timbuktu. In these ksars are many craftsmen, especially coppersmiths, for there are many veins of copper nearby in the foothills of the Atlas mountains, and they do a roaring trade in the Land of the Blacks. In one of the ksars they hold a market once a week, where all the inhabitants of the nearby villages and many Arabs gather. But the ksars, like those mentioned above, have very little grain and meat; nevertheless, the villagers have the authority and means to buy and bring back everything they need. They are well clothed and have a gorgeous mosque, where their imams are. There is a judge for debts and inheritances, but when it comes to crime their only punishment is to banish the wrongdoer.

3.4. Akka

Akka comprises three little ksars near one another in the Numidian desert on the borders of Libya; these ksars were once well populated but the wars between them emptied them out. By the author's time they had been largely abandoned, but a religious man went to live there, and by his effort and ingenuity began to make peace among the parties who had been at war for two years. He restrained them all with his smooth tongue and established families between them, so the ksars were resettled, and now they have him as their secular ruler. But the inhabitants are very poor and lazy, unable to do anything but work on the date farms and never leaving the village either for trade or anything else, since they were so used to war; as a result, you will never see a poorer or more brutish people than those of Akka.

3.5. Draa

The province of Draa extends 150 miles south from the Atlas mountains through the Libyan desert; it is quite narrow, for the settlements are on a river also called the Draa, which floods like a sea in the winter and ebbs in the summer so that one can cross it on foot. When it floods it irrigates the fields and the inhabitants immediately start sowing their crops; if it does not flood at the start of April, the crops are all lost, but if it does, the fields do very well. On the riverbanks are countless villages and ksars, all walled with rough stone or clay, and roofed with date palm beams; the planks are also of palm, but they cannot be made well because the wood is fibrous.

Also on the riverbanks, and stretching out five or six miles in every direction, are innumerable farms of huge, excellent dates, which can be stored for seven years without spoiling if the storehouse is on an upper level. The dates are of countless kinds and colours, and of various prices; some are worth a ducat per bushel, while others, worth a quarter of a ducat, are only good for feeding donkeys or horses, as is the custom in these lands. The date palms are of two kinds, male and female; the male produces only bunches of flowers, whereas the female produces the fruit. However, when the trees come into flower, one must take a bough of the male tree and graft it onto the female before the female flowers open; if this is not done, it will produce very poor fruit, meagre and coarse. The locals sustain themselves on the dates, especially during the day, to the extent of eating nothing else; they also eat barley soup and other wretched slop, rarely eating bread except at great feasts and weddings.

Most ksars in this land have little culture, except a few that contain larger settlements with many craftsmen and Jewish goldsmiths, especially in the foothills of the province near Mauretania, on the road between Fez and Timbuktu. There are also around three or four large towns where many foreign and local merchants live, and where they hold a market, with shops and well-furnished mosques. The largest of these is called Beni Sbih, which is divided into two parts by a wall and governed by various elders who often argue with each other, especially during the season when the fields are irrigated. For there is not enough water for both sides and so it has to go to each in turn, provoking grave disputes.

The inhabitants of the town are capable and generous; they will keep a visiting merchant in their house for a year or two at their own expense, and when it is time to leave he can repay his host at his own discretion. There are many faction leaders among the townsfolk and one faction is always in dispute with the others. They all enlist the help of the neighbouring Arabs, paying each horseman who fights for them an excellent salary: some half a ducat per day, others more, although they are only paid for the days they actually engage in battle. Twenty years ago the townsfolk learned to fire guns, and they are now excellent marksmen, able to hit the point of a needle, and many of them are killed by guns.

In these lands there also grows the indigo plant, a dye like woad that they barter with merchants from Fez and Tlemcen. Grain is very costly in this province, but they barter dates for it with the merchants from Fez and other nearby towns. They have little livestock. There are horses, to which they give dates instead of fodder, as well as hay like that found in the kingdom of Naples.[6] They also keep a few goats, which they feed with date stones that they break up first; they produce plenty of milk and grow quite fat. Meat, likewise, is quite expensive and the locals eat a lot of old ram and camel meat, a very pitiable thing. They also keep many tame ostriches, which they raise in their homes and kill and eat when they are mature; its meat tastes like chicken but is tough and foul-smelling, especially the sticky thigh flesh.

The women of this province are beautiful, voluptuous and friendly, and there are many prostitutes. The people keep plenty of black slaves, male and female, and marry with them, employing the fathers and sons to work on the farms; for this reason almost half the people are black or brown, and due to such mixing few are white.

3.6. The province of Sijilmasa

Sijilmasa is a province named after its principal city; it extends along the river Ziz from the gorge near the city of Gerseluin to the border of the Libyan desert, ten miles to the south. This province is inhabited by various Berber peoples; some are Zanata, others Sanhaja, others Hawwara. They were originally ruled by one of their own, but when Yusuf (ibn Tashfin), king of the Lamtuna, arrived with his people, he began at once to rule the province and had all those of the royal dynasty killed. When the Lamtuna lost the kingdom, the province was taken over by the Almohad dynasty and was always governed by the princes of their court; when the Almohads lost the kingdom, the province was ruled by the Marinids and was given to the king's family and sons to govern. It remained this way until the death of Achmad, king of Fez, when the province rebelled; the countryfolk outside the city killed the governor and destroyed the wall, and it has remained deserted ever since. Its inhabitants got together and built large ksars among the country farms of the province. After the city was ruined, some of the people were subjugated by the Arabs; others are free, but still governed by local chiefs, and they also pay some tribute to the Arabs.

3.7. Al-Kheneg

Al-Kheneg is a province or area on the river Ziz below the Atlas mountains, where there are many villages, ksars and date farms, although the dates are poor. The fields of this country are poor, meagre and narrow, all lying at the edges of the riverbanks up to the foothills of the mountains. Here and there is a patch of land a stone's throw in length, where a little barley can be sown. Some of those who live in the gorge are at liberty, others are vassals of the Arabs or of the city of Gerseluin; the vassals are destitute beggars, while the free men are wealthy and control the pass, charging the merchants who travel between Fez and Sijilmasa. In the gorge are three principal ksars. The first, Zehbel, practically touches the sky, being situated on a high cliff near the entrance to the pass, at the foot of which is a guard to which one must pay a quarter of a ducat per camel load. The second ksar, Gastrir, is around five miles from the first, but on the side of the mountain, almost on a plain; it is wealthier and more cultured than Zehbel. The third, Tamarrakesht, is around ten miles south of Gastrir on the main road. The rest are vassal villages and hamlets, as said above.

The inhabitants of the gorge have little grain but many goats, which they keep in large caverns in the winter, along with all their important goods. For the caverns, when needed, serve as their fortresses, with mouths high off the ground and deliberately narrow and precipitous paths; when even two people are in a cavern, no matter how many horses and men arrive from the provinces, they will never be able to approach because all the two have to do is hurl rocks down at them. This gorge extends around forty miles in length.

3.8. Matgara

This is another area that borders the previous one to the south, beyond the gorge, where there are many ksars on the river Ziz. The ruler of this country keeps his lodgings in Helel, the principal ksar; he is an Arab who maintains one household in the countryside with his people's tents, and another with his cavalry in the ksar, to hold the pass from the merchants. Merchants must apply for a safe-conduct when they travel near his domain, for if a caravan is encountered there without one, the merchants and wagoners are at once robbed and despoiled. There are also plenty of ksars and villages in the region, but without any culture or wealth; the people are lazy scoundrels.

3.9. Reteb

This area borders Matgara, extending fifty miles south along the river Ziz as far as the territory of Sijilmasa, where there are countless ksars and date farms. All the ksars are vassals of the Arabs, working entirely for their benefit; they can scarcely provide for themselves. To the east this area borders a desert mountain, and to the west a sandy plain where the Arabs lodge when they return from the desert. The inhabitants of this country are greedy and base; even a hundred of their cavalry would not dare stand up to only ten Arab horsemen. All of them work the fields and date farms, practically slaves of the Arabs.

3.10. The territory of Sijilmasa

The territory of Sijilmasa extends around twenty miles from north to south along the river Ziz, where there are many ksars and villages. There are three chief ksars. The first is Tanijiout, around a thousand homes and closest to the capital; this ksar is well populated and has some culture in the necessary arts. The second, Tabou'samt, around eight miles south of Tanijiout, is the largest and most cultured, and hosts many foreign merchants and many Jewish craftsmen and merchants; its inhabitants are richer than those elsewhere in the province. The third, al-Ma'mun, is very grand and large, with many wealthy inhabitants and lots of Jewish and Moorish merchants. Each ksar is governed by a faction leader, for they were once united, but a dispute has recently arisen and they are now constantly at war, each doing the worst they can against the others. They habitually destroy each other's aqueducts, which bring water from the river to irrigate the fields and cost much effort and expense to rebuild, and they cut down each other's date trees. The little ksars are often sacked by the country folk and the Arabs help them.

The people coin gold and silver money, making ducats like *bislacchi*[7] of impure gold and also coins of fine silver, each weighing forty grains, and eighty to the ducat. The Arabs take all the revenues that formerly went to the kings; the faction leaders have their own revenues, such as the tributes from the Jews, profits from the mint and the taxes on merchants, but the Arabs control the customs office. The people are ignorant, treacherous, greedy and base, and when they leave their lands they do lots of menial jobs. There are also rich and well-reputed gentlemen, and plenty of merchants who go to the Black Land carrying goods from Barbary and bartering them for slaves and gold. But the people are all badly clothed and they all have swollen eyes.

Throughout their ksars are swarms of scorpions, but no fleas. They all eat dates, but not much food made from grain; in the summer there is a burning heat and huge amounts of dust, and it is perhaps because of this that their eyes are all swollen. The water they drink from the wells is quite brackish, especially in the summer when the river is dry, but in other seasons they only drink river water. The territory is around eighty miles in circumference. The people were once united with the other ksars, and after the ruin of the city they walled the territory all around, albeit with cheap walls, so that cavalry could not pass;

in this way they achieved freedom. But when they split into factions, the people smashed up the walls and each faction brought
in a group of Arabs to aid them, so that they slowly became the
Arabs' vassals.

3.11. The city of Sijilmasa

This is a very ancient city built, according to some African historians, by a Roman general[8] who left Mauretania with a great
army against the Numidians, who were making trouble in his
regions; upon victory he headed west as far as Massa, which
was then the capital of that province. On his return he built a
city in the furthest part of the state of Massa and called it 'Sigillo Masse', since it was the last point of that kingdom, like a
seal. The phrase was then corrupted from Sigillo Masse to Sijilmasa.[9] Another opinion is that of the common people, and also
of the cosmographer al-Bakri, who did not have all that much
knowledge of history. They say that the city was built by Alexander the Great, who, after he returned from the west, built the
city in that place for the wounded and maimed men in his
camp. According to men who have studied the history of Alexander, however, there is no record that he arrived in these lands.
No other opinions have been found but these two, so let each
person choose the one he prefers.

In any case, the city was built on a plain on the river Ziz, and
surrounded with fine, high walls, as can be seen from the surviving fragments. When the Muslims invaded Africa, the city
and its domain were immediately conquered by Zanata rulers,
remaining under their rule until they fell to the Lamtuna under
the king Yusuf ibn Tashfin, as was said above. The city was very
cultured, with fine houses and wealthy inhabitants who conducted plenty of trade with the Land of the Blacks; it always
had just rulers and governors. The city was once adorned with
large, handsome mosques and madrasas, as can be seen in the
ruins today; there were many fountains that brought water
from the river, drawn up with large wheels that raised the water
onto the aqueduct leading to the city. The city is in a region of

good air, where few fall sick, except in the winter many come down with a cold because of the humidity; in the summer some are afflicted with eye problems, but they are soon healed.

At present the city is entirely empty, for its inhabitants have gone to live outside in villages and ksars, as was discussed above.[10] The author was there, and conversed with people in the city and its domain, which is well populated; he was also once in al-Ma'mun, one of the principal ksars, for seven months.

3.12. Essaoaihila[11]

This is a ksar, built by the Arabs in the desert around two miles south of Sijilmasa's territory, in which they keep their goods and food safe from their enemies. Around the ksar, however, there is only the curse of God, for there are no gardens or orchards or fields, nor anything good at all, but only black rocks and sand.

3.13. Oum al-Hadaj

This is another ksar, eight miles from Sijilmasa, also built by the Arabs in the desert where there are no fields to sow anything; therefore they constructed it like a fortress to store the goods that they couldn't take with them into the desert. However, around the ksar is a rough countryside where so much [. . .][12] grows that from a distance it looks like there are oranges scattered around the countryside.

3.14. Oum al-'Afen

This is a ksar around five miles from Sijilmasa, built by the Arabs in a harsh desert on the road between Sijilmasa and Draa, and walled with black stones that look like coal. In the ksar lives the guard of the Arabs who are its masters, exacting a quarter of a ducat per camel load, and the same from every Jew who passes through. When the author passed through, some of these guards went to ask his guide how many Jews were in their company; he replied that there were five, but they counted and found two more. When they told him this, the guide said, 'These two aren't Jews, they're Muslims.' The guards would not believe him, but wanted to take the tribute from them by force; then, a little while later, the ksar's chaplain came and tested them, making them recite a part of the Muslim prayers. The guard begged their pardon, and so at dawn they went on their way towards Draa.

3.15. Tabelbala

This is a settlement in the middle of the Numidian desert, 200 miles from the Atlas mountains and 100 miles south of Sijilmasa. It comprises three small but well-populated ksars as well as plenty of date farms and some patches of dry fields; they irrigate these with water from wells in the farms, so a tiny amount of barley can grow, but only with difficulty. They eke out their wretched existence with almost no meat, although they do hunt ostriches and deer; many of them go to the Black Land to trade, but they are quite poor, for they are vassals of the Arabs.

3.16. Todgha

Todgha is a little province on a river also called Todgha, where there are many groves of dates and other fruit, like peaches, grapes and figs. It comprises around four little ksars and ten villages inhabited by a poor people, all farmhands and curriers; they are around forty miles west of Sijilmasa.

3.17. Ferkla

Ferkla is another settlement on a brook, with many groves of dates and other fruit, but only wretched grain fields. The inhabitants are destitute, for they are also vassals of the Arabs; there are three ksars and around five other villages in the middle of the desert, around 100 miles south of the Atlas mountains and sixty miles from Sijilmasa.

3.18. Tazzarine

Tazzarine is a beautiful settlement with huge numbers of date farms along a brook, around thirty miles from Ferkla and sixty from the Atlas mountains; it comprises around five villages and six ksars, as well as two other ancient, ruined towns, built by unknown people. For this reason the settlement is called Tazzarine, which means 'the cities' in the African language, on account of the two ruined cities.

3.19. Beni Gumi

This is another settlement, on the river Ghir, with huge numbers of date groves. The inhabitants are poor and use their annual earnings to buy horses, bringing them back to the settlement for the merchants who go to the Land of the Blacks. There are eight little ksars and perhaps more than five villages, around fifty miles south-east of Sijilmasa.

3.20. Mazalig and Bouanane

These are two ksars in the Numidian desert, around fifty miles from Sijilmasa, where the wretched inhabitants live in the greatest misfortune and misery. They have some date trees, but not even a scrap of land for growing grain. The inhabitants are Arabs, but they were all at war with their kinsfolk and their camels were stolen; this disaster forced them to stay and live in the countryside, so they built the two little ksars on the banks of the river Ghir.

3.21. Al-Ksar

This is a little town in the Numidian desert twenty miles from the Atlas mountains. It contains a lead mine and another of antimony, and many mule-drivers arrive from Fez to take away the two metals; but nothing else of value grows in the vicinity, so the inhabitants all work in the two mines.

3.22. Beni Besseri

This is another settlement, of three ksars, in the foothills of the Atlas mountains, where there are many fruit farms, but no dates or grain fields. There is, however, a sizeable vein of iron that furnishes the entire province of Sijilmasa, and all the inhabitants work in the mine. They are all badly clothed, for nothing good grows on their lands and they are therefore vassals of the Arabs and of the ruler of Debdou.

3.23. Ouakda

This is another settlement, seventy miles south of Sijilmasa, comprising three large ksars and many villages, all along the river Ghir, where there are many date groves and a few grain fields. The inhabitants are neither poor nor rich, since they visit the Land of the Blacks to trade but must pay tribute to the nearby Arabs.

3.24. Figuig

These are three ksars in the middle of the desert, inhabited by a wealthy people who own plenty of date farms. Their women are very skilled at weaving blankets of wool that seem like silk, which they sell for a high price throughout the towns of Barbary, such as Fez and Tlemcen.[13] The men have great ingenuity, travelling to the Land of the Blacks to trade; they also go to study in Fez and Tlemcen, returning to Numidia with their degrees to become imams and preachers, and acquiring great wealth from this profession. These ksars are around fifty miles east of Sijilmasa.

3.25. Tesebit

Tesebit is a settlement in the Numidian desert fifty miles east of Sijilmasa, and 100 miles from the Atlas mountains. There are four ksars and many villages on the borders of Libya, along the route from Fez or Tlemcen to the kingdom of Agadez in the Black Land. The inhabitants of the ksars are very poor, for nothing worthwhile grows on their land except dates and a tiny amount of barley. The inhabitants are almost all black and the women are quite beautiful, but brown-skinned.

3.26. Tigurarin[14]

Tigurarin is another large settlement in the Numidian desert, fifty miles east of Tesebit, where there are fifty ksars and more than 100 other villages among the date groves. The people of this settlement are rich because they go to trade in the Land of the Blacks. Moreover, the Barbary merchants end their journey here with their goods, tying up their horses and waiting for the merchants from the Black Land; sometimes those of the Black Land await those of Barbary.

In these lands are many arable fields, but they need to be irrigated with water from the wells; they are very meagre, and it is a struggle to irrigate them and to enrich them with manure. The inhabitants let their houses to the merchants without rent, asking in return only for their horse manure – and their own. The worst insult a foreigner can give a householder is to empty his bowels outside the house; if the owner sees him he'll be furious, asking the foreigner, 'Is there really no latrine inside for you to empty your bowels?' The very poorest go around collecting the turds from the huts and wherever else they usually find them and taking them to the farms. Meat is very expensive here, since the land is too dry for them to keep any animals but some goats for their milk. They often eat camel meat, for many Arabs come here to buy the merchants' goods, which they barter for camels no longer up to bearing loads, as well as sheep. Due to the lack of meat, the merchants from Fez and Tlemcen bring countless loads of salted tallow, which they sell more than any other merchandise, and which the locals put in their wretched food.

In this country and in Tuat were many extremely rich men, but to their misfortune a preacher arrived from Tlemcen, who began to preach against the Jews; so the people rose up, robbed the Jews and killed most of them, bringing most of their riches to the preacher. This happened in the very year that they were driven out of Spain and Sicily.[15] The inhabitants of these lands are governed by faction leaders, but they are continually arguing among themselves and they kill each other like dogs. Nobody gives any hindrance to foreigners, who can converse with each faction without fear. The inhabitants also pay tribute to the nearby Arabs.

3.27. M'zab

M'zab is a settlement in the Numidian desert 300 miles east of Tigurarin and about the same distance from the Mediterranean; it comprises six or so ksars and many other villages. The inhabitants are very rich, for they are merchants who travel to the Land of the Blacks, and merchants from Algiers and Bejaia come to trade there with those of the Land of the Blacks. The inhabitants pay tribute to the nearby Arabs whose vassals they are.

3.28. Tuggurt

Tuggurt is an ancient city built by the Numidians on a mountain of tuff;[16] a stream flows past the lower part with a drawbridge over it. The lower town is surrounded by walls of clay and hard stones, but the side facing the mountain is not walled, for the slopes are enough of a defence. The city, which contains 2,500 homes, is 500 miles south of the Mediterranean, and 300 from Tigurarin. Its houses are all made of clay and unbaked brick, except the mosque, which is elegantly built of polished stone. The city is thronged with craftsmen and gentlemen who are rich in date farms, though they lack grain; nonetheless, the Arabs bring grain from the territory of Constantine and barter it for dates. The townsfolk are very warm to foreigners: they usually offer them rooms without charge, and give their daughters more willingly to them than to the locals, with their own farms as dowries, as is the custom in many lands and places in Europe. Likewise, they make gifts of important items to strangers whom they never expect to return and have no hope of seeing again; they are kind out of the goodness of their hearts.

The city was once ruled by the Lamtuna kings of Marrakesh; when they were deposed, it remained under the control of a governor who paid tribute to the kings of Marrakesh. When Marrakesh lost its kingdom, the city became a tributary of the kings of Tlemcen for a while. Then the kings of Tunis wanted it, so the ruler was obliged to pay 50,000 ducats to whichever king first arrived in the city with his camp. The king of Tlemcen lacked the strength to go, so the king of Tunis, who came in person, received the money. The current king of Tunis went there twice; the city's ruler paid him the ordinary amount and gave him additional sums as a gift.

Around the city are innumerable ksars and villages, which pay tributes to the city's ruler; there are also many settlements three or four days from the city, but under the governance of its ruler, who therefore receives revenues of 130,000 ducats. He keeps a guard of cavalry, crossbowmen and Turkish gunmen, who receive such a good salary that they all happily remain in his court. The present ruler, 'Abdullah, is young and generous; the author has stayed with him in his court and conversed with him, an agreeable and cheerful man who gladly receives foreigners.

3.29. Warjla (Ouargla)[17]

This is a very ancient city built by the Numidians in the desert, and walled with unbaked brick. The inhabitants are very cultured; there are many craftsmen and fine buildings, and around the city are innumerable date farms and ksars, and plenty of villages. The people of the city are very rich, for it lies on the borders of the kingdom of Agadez. Scores of foreign merchants are found there, especially from Constantine and Tunis, bringing goods from Barbary and bartering them with merchants from the Land of the Blacks. The city has little grain or meat, but the inhabitants eat camel and ostrich. Most of them are black, not from the air in the place but because they all keep black slaves and have children with them, with the result that only a fifth of them are white, and the rest black and brown. They are generous, friendly and welcoming to foreigners, for they would have nothing of value if it were not for them – no grain, salted meat, fabric, textiles, weapons or knives. The city is governed by a ruler whom the people hold to be a king; he keeps a thousand cavalry for his guard, as well as other light cavalry. The city is subordinate to the ruler and produces around 50,000 ducats a year, but he owes heavy tribute to the nearby Arabs.

3.30. The province of Zeb[18]

This province is in the middle of the Numidian desert, beginning to the west on the borders of M'Sila and bordering the foothills of the kingdom of Bejaia to the north; to the east it borders the Land of Dates near the kingdom of Tunis, and to the south the desert route from Tuggurt to Ouargla. The province is very hot and sandy, with little water and few fields for sowing grain, although there are countless date farms. It contains five cities and innumerable villages; below we will discuss the cities one by one.

3.31. Biskra

Biskra is an ancient city built in the era that the Romans ruled Barbary; it was ruined when the Romans left, and remained so until the Muslim armies invaded Africa, when it was rebuilt and resettled. However, it had to be re-walled with unbaked brick, for the ruin was so old that the new settlement was built far from it. Nowadays the city is quite cultured and populous, but its people are poor because nothing grows on their land except dates. Its tyrannical rulers greatly oppress the people, and the city has changed rulership more than any other town; even to count its royal buildings would be very tedious. In modern times it was controlled by the king of Tunis, but, after the death of 'Uthman,[19] the city's chief imam rebelled and, along with the people, drove out the king's officers; he took over the city's revenues and governed as a ruler belonging to the people. The kings of Tunis huffed and puffed to take it back but could never do it.

The city was always infamous for scorpions – whoever is bitten dies at once, and very few survive. In the summer, then, the townsfolk abandon the city and go live out on the farms until November, when they return.

3.32. Al-Borgi[20]

This is another town, fourteen or so miles west of Biskra, cultured and well populated, with many craftsmen and even more farmers. There is so little water that when the workers want to irrigate the fields, each person has the right to water his farm for an hour or two, depending (on the size of his field). The farmhands fill up water clocks, and when they are empty the time is up and they cannot take any more water; how many people die every year in disputes over the water!

3.33. Nefta

Nefta is a settlement comprising three large ksars, the biggest of which has an ancient citadel that looks like it was built by the Romans. The three ksars are well populated but have no culture; between them flows a stream warmer than others, which the locals drink from and use to irrigate their fields. The inhabitants once were rich, for they border Libya on the route from the Land of the Blacks. However, a century ago the people rebelled against the king of Tunis; more recently the king arrived with his army and besieged the settlement until he could take it by force, sacking it and ransoming the men for large sums of money. He then had countless people killed and smashed all the walls, so that all three ksars became a single village.

3.34. Tolga

Tolga is another city built by the Numidians and surrounded by poor walls; beside it flows a warm stream. The inhabitants are very poor, greedy and base; they are unwilling to meet foreigners, for they are heavily oppressed by the king of Tunis and by the Arabs. Around the city are countless date farms, and also a few fields where a little grain grows.

3.35. Doucen

Doucen is a very ancient town built by the Romans on the borders between the kingdom of Bejaia and the Numidian desert. It was ruined when the Muslim army invaded, for a Roman count lived there with many able-bodied men, and he would not give up the town to the Saracen generals, so it was besieged for around a year. Then the town was taken by force, the men were all killed and the women and children captured; the houses were destroyed but the walls could not be, because they were made of very large stones, requiring as much strength to destroy as to build. However, two sides have been destroyed either by design or by an earthquake. Near the town are other vestiges that seem like ancient tombs, and often, during the rainy season, hunters find large gold and silver coins with shapes and letters. But the author has never received any information about the meaning of these inscriptions.

3.36. The province of Bilad al-Jarid

This province extends from the borders of Biskra to those of the isle of Jerba; part of it is very far from the Mediterranean, such as Gafsa and Tozeur, which are 300 miles inland. The lands are very hot and dry, nothing but sand, where no grain grows but only countless excellent dates which are found all along the Tunis coast. In this country there are many cities, discussed one by one below.

3.37. Tozeur

Tozeur is an ancient city built by the Romans in the Numidian desert on a stream that descends from mountains to the south. The city was once surrounded by very strong walls and covered a large area, but when the Muslims came to rule they destroyed the walls and almost all the ancient buildings, although the walls were rebuilt with poor materials. The townsfolk are rich in farms and money, for every year they hold fairs at which a great throng of Numidian and Berber people gather. The locals are split into two factions, each living in one part of the city with a stream between them; one faction, the Fatnasa, are the true citizens, while the other, the Merdes, are the Arabs who remained there after it was captured by the Muslims. The two factions are always in dispute, and rarely obey the king of Tunis; but whenever he comes in person, especially the current one, he cuts their hearts out.

3.38. Gafsa

Gafsa is an ancient city built by the Romans, remaining under the control of certain dukes until the arrival of the caliph 'Uthman's general 'Uqba (ibn Nafi').[21] It was then captured by the Muslims and its walls destroyed, except for its very unusual citadel, which has fine walls fifteen cubits high, made of very large, dressed stones like those of the Colosseum in Rome. After some time had passed, the walls were rebuilt and the city began to regain its culture, until al-Mansur, king and caliph of Marrakesh, arrived, at which point the city walls were destroyed again, along with one side of the citadel wall. For a ruler from the family of the Lamtuna kings[22] still owned this land, conducting many attacks on the coast of Tunis with the Arabs' permission; so al-Mansur attacked the land with his army, and the ruler immediately fled with many Arabs to the desert. Al-Mansur claimed the province and returned to Marrakesh, whereupon the ruler came back from the desert and drove out al-Mansur's governor. After many years, al-Mansur returned to Gafsa with a large army, catching its ruler unawares in the citadel; he attacked relentlessly but the ruler held out, since the walls were strong enough to take on all the armies of Africa. However, the poor ruler ran out of food in the citadel, so one day he emerged, fully armed, with his sons and family, and they fought until they were cut to pieces.[23] Then al-Mansur destroyed the side of the citadel; he installed governors and officers in the province and headed back west, taking with him all the Arab princes who had caused the rebellion.

The city is now well populated, but has buildings of poor quality, except the grand mosque and other, smaller ones. The streets are wide and paved with black stones like those of Naples and Florence. The inhabitants are very cultured, but poor, since they are oppressed by the king of Tunis, effectively imprisoned in the citadel. In the middle of the city are well-built fountains in the form of wide, deep square pools with walls around them; there is an area between the walls and the edges where people can stand to wash their bodies, for the water is warm. They also drink from it, but have to leave the water to cool for at least an hour or two.

The air is very bad, and every summer half the population has a fever. They are a malicious people, wishing harm on foreigners and on each other; if a foreigner should live there even ten years, he will never make friends with a local, on which account they are much insulted by other Africans. Outside the city are many farms of dates, olives and oranges, a thing of wondrous beauty. The dates are the finest and largest anywhere in the province; likewise the olives are large and their oil has an excellent colour and flavour. There are, then, four excellent things in the city – dates, olives, cloth and pots. The inhabitants are well clothed; they wear shoes of tanned deer leather, but they make them quite wide so they can tighten them when they want to change the sole.

3.39. Nefzawa

Nefzawa comprises three ksars near each other, all teeming with people but surrounded by poor walls, and the houses are worse. The people are very poor and badly clothed, for they are heavily oppressed by the king of Tunis. Outside, around the ksars, are countless date farms and villages, but there is very little grain throughout the province. The ksars are around fifty miles from the Mediterranean, and from the cities of al-Hammah, Gabes and Jerba in the kingdom of Tunis.

In Numidia there are other settlements near the domain of Tripoli, as follows.

3.40. Tawergha

Tawergha is a settlement on the borders between the domain of Tripoli and the Barca desert, comprising three ksars and many villages, with a great quantity of dates, but there is no grain to speak of. The inhabitants are very poor in goods and money, for they are stuck in this desert, far from any place of culture.

3.41. Zliten

Zliten is a settlement of many villages and date farms on the Mediterranean. The inhabitants are of average wealth, for they are on the sea and can trade with the Egyptians and Sicilians.

3.42. Ghadames

Ghadames is a large settlement of many ksars and populous villages, 300 miles south of the Mediterranean. The inhabitants are rich in date farms and money, for they all travel to the Land of the Blacks to trade. Grain is very expensive there, as is meat. The people govern themselves and pay tribute to the Arabs, but they were formerly under the control of the king of Tunis, who answered to the viceroy of Tripoli.

3.43. Fezzan

Fezzan is a great settlement of large ksars and villages, all inhabited by a people rich in date farms and money, for it is at the edge of Agadez, on the borders between the Libyan desert and Egypt; it is around sixty days' journey from Cairo through the deserts, where there is no settlement except Awjila in the Libyan desert. Fezzan's ruler is a leading burgher; all the profits from the taxes and tributes from the farms pass to him and he spends them for the benefit of the land – that is, to content Arab allies and defend against enemies. Grain and meat are very expensive, but they eat plenty of camel meat, which is also very costly.

BOOK 4.

LIBYA: THE DESERT REGIONS

After Numidia, the second region of Africa, we will now discuss the deserts of Libya. These are divided into five parts, as noted at the beginning of this book. The five parts each take their proper name from the people who inhabit them: the first is where the Zanaga dwell; the second where the Wanziga live; the third, the Terga; and the fourth, the Lamta.[1]

4.1. The desert of the Zanaga

This dry and thirsty desert stretches from the ocean in the west to the salt mines of Taghaza in the east; the desert borders the Numidian provinces of Sous, Akka and Draa to the north, and extends south to the Land of the Blacks, that is, to the kingdoms of Walata and Timbuktu. In this harsh desert, especially along the way from Sijilmasa to Timbuktu, one can go 100 or 150 miles without finding water, and even then it is salty or bitter, and in very deep wells. There are wild beasts and snakes of many kinds, which will be addressed in the part on Africa's animals. One region, from the well of Azawad to that of Arawan, about fifty miles from Timbuktu, is cruel and unforgiving, without water or settlements; between these two wells many men and camels have been left for dead because of the unbearable heat and thirst, as described at the beginning of this book.[2]

4.2. The desert where the Wanziga live

This second desert, where the Wanziga live, begins to the west at the borders of Tegara and stretches eastward to the borders of Aïr, the desert where the Terga live; it goes north to the deserts of Sijilmasa, Tabelbala and Beni Gumi, and south to the edge of Ghir, a desert of the kingdom of Gobir, which offers no water or sustenance at all, being even harsher than that mentioned above. The merchants of Tlemcen cross the whole length of this dry, pitiless desert to reach Timbuktu, and many die along the way. Within this desert is a region named Gogdem,[3] where one can travel for nine days without finding any water except what the camels carry; occasionally one finds a lake after it rains, but only by chance.

4.3. The desert where the Terga live

This third desert begins at the borders of Aïr on the west, and goes east to the Igdi desert; on the north it borders the deserts of Tuat, Tigurarin and M'zab, and on the south the neighbouring deserts of the Agadez kingdom. This desert is not as cruel and harsh as those named above, since within two days one can find good water in deep wells, particularly in the region of Aïr, which is not an extreme desert; it has good air and grows plenty of grass. Closer to Agadez there is found a considerable quantity of manna,[4] a marvellous thing; the desert people go in the morning to fill their containers, bringing it fresh to the city of Agadez, where they sell one mug for a coin worth two *baiocchi*. The merchants drink it mixed with water and put it in their soup, which is excellent and refreshing, and because of it foreigners don't fall ill in Agadez as they do in Timbuktu, even though it has unhealthy air. From north to south, this desert spans about 300 miles.

4.4. The desert where the Lamta live

This fourth desert, where the Lamta live, extends from the borders of the Igdi desert to the edge of the desert where the Bardoa live; its northern border meets the deserts of Tuggurt, Ouargla and Ghadames, and it goes south to the desert of Kano, a kingdom in the Land of the Blacks. Merchant caravans travel through this extremely dry and hazardous desert from Constantine to the Black Land. It is also unsafe because its inhabitants are enemies of the prince of Ouargla; even though the current prince keeps to himself, his predecessors raided them, and even now there is such hostility that, when the locals encounter unlucky foreign merchants, they rob and ransack them without mercy – and kill those from Ouargla.

4.5. The desert where the Bardoa live

The fifth desert begins at the borders of the previous one, stretching east to the desert of Awjila. From the northern deserts of Fezzan and Barca it extends south to the desert of Bornu, another very dry country. The inhabitants are all bandits, and the only ones who travel the desert are the people of Ghadames, with whom the Bardoa are friendly because it is from Fezzan that they get provisions, cloth and other items necessary for the desert. The rest of the desert of Libya, from Awjila to the Nile, is inhabited by impoverished Arabs and by another African people known as the Lawata.

This ends the section on the deserts of Libya; the next addresses some of the settlements in these deserts.

4.6. The settlement of Nun[5]

In this settlement on the ocean shore, the villages are all inhabited by a very poor people; it is between Numidia and Libya, and closer to the latter. They grow only a little barley for grain, and dates of poor quality. The inhabitants are badly clothed and live in poverty, for the Arabs badly oppress them; some go to the kingdom of Walata to trade.

4.7. Taghaza[6]

In the settlement of Taghaza is a great vein of salt like marble, dug from vast caves. Outside the caves are huts inhabited by the salt miners. They do not keep their families there, since it is not their home. Instead, they try to arrange jobs with the merchant caravans, staying at the caves in order to work and keep a record until the next caravan comes along; these buy their salt to bring to Timbuktu, which has none, and load each camel with four slabs of it. The labourers only have whatever provisions arrive from Timbuktu or Draa, about twenty days' journey from Taghaza. They have often been found dead in their huts, for they use up their supplies and die of hunger when the caravans do not come. Sometimes south winds rise up in summer, bringing diseases that end up afflicting their knees or blinding them, so it is very dangerous to remain there. The author stopped in Taghaza for three days, until the merchants had finished loading up their salt; the labourers, meanwhile, constantly drank salt water from the wells around the caves.

4.8. Awjila

Awjila is a settlement consisting of three ksars and several other villages in the Libyan desert about 450 miles from the Nile. Around the ksars and villages are many date farms, but they grow no grain, which instead the Arabs bring from Egypt. The settlement is on the main road through the Libyan desert to Egypt at the point it leaves Mauretania.

4.9. Sirte

Sirte is an ancient city which some say was built by the Egyptians, others by the Romans and still others by the Africans. However, when the Islamic armies invaded Africa, this town was already inhabited by the Africans, even if, as some say, it had been destroyed by the Romans. Thus Ibn ar-Raqiq says that, when the Romans ruled Egypt, an Egyptian nobleman escaped and made war on them, until they closed in on him and destroyed the city; even today one can see the remaining foundations of the walls, which can be nothing else.

4.10. Bardoa[7]

This settlement comprises three ksars and five or six villages in the middle of the Libyan desert, about 500 miles from the Nile; many excellent dates grow there. These three ksars were once unknown, but eighteen years ago they were discovered by a guide named Hammar, who had lost the way because of an eye ailment he'd picked up en route, and there was no other guide to help. After every mile, he went ahead on his camel and was given sand to smell; thanks to this practice he could say, when the caravan was forty miles away, 'We are near a settlement.' No one believed him, since Egypt was 480 miles ahead and they had just left Awjila, so they doubted that the caravan could have turned back there. Yet on the third day the caravan found itself next to the settlement, and each was astonished at the other – the caravan at the villagers, and vice versa. The villagers withdrew into the ksar and shut the gates, as did those in the villages, leaving behind their fields of ripe dates. The caravan needed water, but the wells were inside the ksar and the inhabitants would not open them; they stayed there all day with their Arabs, until their thirst drove them to attack the ksar. Many of them died because the villagers' arrows were poisoned; nevertheless they came out victorious, taking the ksar by force, seizing the water and killing some of those brutish people. They did no further damage, since they imagined the villagers might have others in the countryside who would pursue the caravan.

4.11. Al-Wahat

Al-Wahat is a settlement in the Libyan desert about 100 miles[8] from Egypt, with three ksars, several villages and many date farms. The inhabitants are black, base and greedy, but rich because they live on the road from Egypt to Gaoga. The people have a chief like a king, though he pays tribute to some Arabs nearby.

The ancient cosmographers such as al-Bakri and al-Mas'udi have written nothing of the Black Land except al-Wahat and Ghana, for in their day nothing was known about the other countries of the Blacks. Then in AH 380 (AD 990–91) several of them were discovered, for the Lamtuna and all the people of Libya became Muslims on account of a preacher[9] who sent the Lamtuna to rule Barbary.[10]

End of the section on Libya's settlements. The next takes up the Lands of the Blacks.

BOOK 5.

THE LAND OF THE BLACKS

5.1. [Introduction]

Just now the author said the Black Land was unknown to the cosmographers of Africa in detail, but their knowledge generally picked up after the Libyans became Muslim. At that point, the cosmographers began to acquire some details of these lands, where all the people lived as animals: they had no king, rulers, republic or even any culture, and scarcely knew how to sow grain; they went about clothed in the skins of their flocks. A man had no particular wife, but instead the men, women and children of a farmstead would go together all day to work, pasturing their animals, and then return home at night together, around ten or twelve of them sleeping under some sheepskins in a hut. They did not go to war or leave their own lands.

Some of those peoples used to bow down each morning when they woke up and saw the sun; everyone bowed in reverence to it, as their whole religion and ritual. Some people such as the Walata worshipped fire, since this was the religion of those living in Barbary, who perhaps taught them. Some others were Christians, namely those in Gaoga, who worshipped like Copts.

The Libyans have always had contact with these black peoples and traded with them. The Lamtuna then invaded Numidia and Barbary and subdued the region; after Yusuf (ibn Tashfin), the king and founder of Marrakesh, had captured and subdued his kingdom, the rest of his people returned to Libya and began to dominate the black peoples. For their preacher[1] had taught them to rule, and all the Libyans schemed to dominate those peoples. Thus most of the blacks became Muslims and began to learn the law, culture and useful crafts.

The inhabitants of Barbary – that is, the burghers – took up travelling to the Land of the Blacks for trade and learned their language; as a result, they divided these lands among themselves into fifteen kingdoms, such that each corresponded to a third of one of the Libyan tribes.[2] It remains so even today, with the exception of the current king of Timbuktu, Abu Bakr Askia.[3] He came from the black people and was the general of Sunni 'Ali, king of Timbuktu and Gao. After Sunni 'Ali's death, Abu Bakr Askia rebelled against his master's two young sons and destroyed their camp, seizing both and putting them to death. He then became king and freed the region from the kings of Libya's tribes. Then he followed up his victory and within six years acquired several more kingdoms. After bringing peace to his empire, Abu Bakr Askia made a pilgrimage to Mecca with a magnificent treasure; all told, the journey cost 150,000 ducats.

All fifteen kingdoms known to us stretch across both banks of the Niger and all the rivers that lead into it. The fifteen kingdoms are set between two extremely long deserts: one begins from Numidia and goes to the Land of the Blacks, while the other extends from their southern border towards the ocean, where there are many cultivated regions. Most of them are unknown to us, on account of the long and difficult journey and the variety of their languages and religions. They have no dealings with our people, nor ours with them; even the many Muslim merchants neighbouring the people by the ocean deal with them very little, due to the difference in language and religion.

5.2. The kingdom of Walata

Compared to other kingdoms, this one is in a poor state, for its only settlement comprises three large villages and some date farms with a few huts, 300 miles south of Nun, 500 miles north of Timbuktu, and 100 miles from the ocean. When the Libyans came to rule, they made this settlement their royal seat where the merchants of Barbary would go; but in the time of Sunni 'Ali, a great ruler, the merchants abandoned Walata and went instead to Timbuktu or Gao, so he became poor and powerless.

These people, who all speak the Songhay language, are lowly and of the darkest black, but very friendly, especially to foreigners. Their ruler pays tribute to the king of Timbuktu, because once, when the king came with his army, the ruler fled to his kinsfolk in the desert. Seeing that he could not hold the kingdom fast, since its ruler and his kin would harass him from the desert, the king agreed to a certain tribute and returned to Timbuktu, while the ruler returned to Walata. In their customs and way of life, these people are much like their neighbours in the desert. Not much grain grows in this country, only millet and a certain other round, white grain not found anywhere in Europe,[4] and meat is scarce. The women and men go about with their faces covered, and their settlements have no culture, craftsmen or scholars; their lives are wretched and poor.

5.3. The kingdom of Jenne

The African merchants named this kingdom Gheneoa[5] and its inhabitants call it Gemni; the Portuguese and others from Europe know these lands as Ghenia.[6] It borders Walata, with about fifty miles of desert between them. Walata is to the north, Timbuktu to the east and Mali to the south. The kingdom extends 250 miles along the Niger river, down to the ocean where the Niger enters the sea. The land is lush with wheat, barley, livestock and cotton, and its inhabitants are very wealthy because they do a good trade in cotton fabrics. Barbary merchants sell many wares in this kingdom, especially European textiles, copper, brass and weapons such as swords and lances. They pay with gold that has not been struck into coin, though for small things they pay in iron pieces, in units of a pound, half a pound, quarter pound, etc., which they use to buy bread, milk and honey. Fruit trees are nowhere to be found in the country; the only fruit are dates from Walata or Numidia.

The kingdom has no city or ksar, only a large village where the ruler, merchants and other notables live, such as scholars and imams. Their houses are like huts, walled in clay with thatched roofs. The inhabitants are cultured, and dressed well in black and blue cotton cloth; they also wear a black cloth on their heads, while imams and scholars wear white. For three months of the year, July, August and September, this large village is like an island, for then the Niger floods naturally, like the Nile in Egypt. In that season the merchants from Timbuktu bring their wares to this kingdom in canoes carved out of large tree trunks. They travel all day, but at night they tie their canoe to the bank and sleep on land.

This kingdom was once ruled by a dynasty of a people of Libya, but in Sunni 'Ali's reign the local prince came to pay him tribute. Sunni 'Ali's successor, Askia, deprived this prince of his lands and kept him prisoner in Gao until his death, installing one of his own viceroys in the region.

5.4. The kingdom of Mali

The kingdom of Mali stretches about 300 miles along a branch of the Niger. On the north, it borders Jenne; on the south, it borders the desert and dry mountains. On the west it borders wild woods, which extend as far as the ocean, while on the east it borders the territory of Gao. In this region is a huge village of about 6,000 homes called Mali, which gives its name to the whole kingdom, and the king and his court live there. The land overflows with grain, meat and cotton; in the village there are many foreign merchants, to whom the king and his men show more courtesy and honour than to the locals. The region's inhabitants are very wealthy, on account of their trade and easy passage by boat to Jenne and Timbuktu. The town has a number of mosques, imams and scholars; they hold lectures in the mosques, since they have no schools. The people are cultured like those of Jenne; they are considered more cultured and ingenious than people anywhere else in the region of the Blacks, since they were the first of the Blacks to become Muslim. In those early days, they were ruled by the prince of Libya, the uncle of Yusuf, king of

Marrakesh.[7] This dynasty ruled until the time of Askia, who demanded so much tribute that the king of Mali could not maintain his own household.

5.5. The kingdom of Timbuktu

The name of this kingdom is modern, from the name of the city Timbuktu which was built in AH 610 (AD 1213–14) by King Mansa Suleyman about two miles from a branch of the Niger.[8] The city consists entirely of huts made of beams covered in clay, with thatched roofs. In the midst of the city stands a mosque of stone and lime, built by a Baetican master from the city of Almería.[9] There is also a great palace made entirely by this master, where the king dwells.

In this city there are many shops of craftsmen and merchants, especially dealers in cotton textiles. Slaves and free women sell all manner of food. The men are well dressed in black or blue cotton and fabrics that come from Europe by way of Barbary merchants. The women have their faces covered, unless they are slaves. The inhabitants are very wealthy, especially foreigners living there, to the point that the present king has married off his two daughters to brothers who are among the city's richest merchants for their money.

There are many freshwater wells, but when the Niger rises it reaches the town through canals. The city has grain and cattle in plenty, and its people consume much milk and butter. They have a tremendous amount of fruit, but sorely lack salt, because it comes from Taghaza, nearly 500 miles from Timbuktu.

The king of Timbuktu[10] possesses enormous wealth in precious stones and gold bars, some weighing fifty pounds, others 300. His court is smartly liveried and when the king rides with his courtiers from one town to the next they ride the camels known as *mehari*,[11] having the grooms lead the horses by hand. But when he goes to war they tie up the camels and ride the horses, as they do when he rides for pleasure in town.

If someone wants to speak to the king, he must fall to his knees and sprinkle some dirt on his head and shoulders – the same obeisance is made by one who never spoke to him before and by an ambassador from a great ruler. This king has about 3,000 light cavalry and countless infantry who carry bows made from the branches of wild fennel, which shoot poisoned arrows. The king often makes war on enemies at his borders, and with those unwilling to pay him tribute. In victory, he takes the men, women and children captive to sell them in Timbuktu, where some are bought by the townsfolk and others by Barbary merchants.

No horses are reared in Timbuktu but little hackneys[12] that the merchants use for travelling, or courtiers for going through the city; real horses come from Barbary and are highly valuable in that region of the Blacks. When a caravan arrives from Barbary, the king sends a secretary to note the number of horses in the caravan, and after ten or twelve days the horses are brought before him; he takes those he likes and pays handsomely.

The king of Timbuktu is a mortal enemy of the Jews, such that none are to be found in his kingdom or around it; if the king finds out that any merchant of Barbary has traded with Jews, or done business in partnership with Jews, or using Jewish money, then he uses his authority to confiscate all the merchant's goods for the royal treasury, leaving barely enough money for him to return home.

In Timbuktu there are many scholars, imams and judges, all subsidised by the ruler, who greatly honours men of letters. Many books are bought and sold, especially manuscripts from Barbary; merchants earn more from them than from all their other wares. Locals weigh out gold in natural pieces and, for small things, use tiny shells from Persia,[13] worth 400 per ducat; six and a third of their ducats are worth one Roman ounce.[14]

The city's inhabitants are pleasant and cheerful, and from about ten o'clock at night to one in the morning they like to go throughout every quarter of the city singing and dancing. The people keep many slaves, male and female, whom they put to work as domestic servants. Around the city there are no gardens, vineyards or fruit trees. It is dangerous to make a fire in the city, since the smallest spark can jump onto a roof and swiftly set the city ablaze, especially when the wind is blowing. When the author was there on his second journey, half the city burned down in the space of five hours; the wind blew strong and the other half of the city began to rescue their belongings, fearing the whole city would go up in flames.

5.6. Kabara

This great city is built like a village, without walls, around twelve miles from Timbuktu along the Niger river; this is where the merchants embark for Jenne and Mali. This city's houses exactly resemble those of Timbuktu, just as the people do in culture and dress. Blacks of every tribe are found in this city, for in its port there are always countless boats from all manner of places. In this city lives a representative of the king of Timbuktu, so that people can find an audience with him without troubling to take the twelve-mile journey. In the author's time, this representative was a kinsman of King Abu Bakr surnamed Pergama,[15] who was very black, but most valiant, wise and just. In this city many diseases befall the people, for they eat fish, milk and butter together with their meat. Nearly all the provisions found in Timbuktu have come from Kabara by land.

5.7. Gao and its kingdom

Gao is a magnificent city, unwalled like Kabara, about 400 miles south of Timbuktu, towards the south-eastern side. Its buildings are poorly made, as in Timbuktu, but there are several beautiful houses that stand out among the usual buildings. The king lives in this city with his court, and its people are great and rich, all traders who travel far and wide; countless foreign merchants are to be found in the city, as well as those from the Black Land who bring huge amounts of gold to buy the goods of Barbary and Europe. But they always have more money than there are things to buy; most of these merchants return to their lands with half or two-thirds of their money, unable to find enough goods to purchase.

The city is very happy and cultured in comparison with other towns, with an overflowing abundance of bread and meat, though no wine or fruit trees. Some garden produce is available, such as excellent melons and watermelons, cucumbers, gourds and vast amounts of barley. The people drink from the many wells of fresh water throughout the city.

There is a grand square always filled with thousands of slaves, male and female, for sale. A girl or boy of fifteen is worth about six ducats; smaller children are worth about half. The king lives apart in a palace where he keeps countless women – wives, concubines, slaves – as well as many eunuchs to guard them; he also keeps a strong guard of cavalry and archers. Between the public and private gates of the palace is a large square walled around with a portico, where the king gives audience or pronounces judgements, carrying out all his duties in person, with many officials, ministers, counsellors, generals and agents.

The king's revenues are greater than any in Europe, but his expenditure is also greater, since the horses, which are foreign, each cost at least forty or fifty ducats, while in Europe they would be worth ten. Likewise, the roughest European cloth costs four ducats a *canna*, and fine *monachino* and *minino* fifteen ducats; a *canna* of fine Venetian cloth in scarlet, purple, deep blue or yellow costs thirty ducats.[16] Even the worst sword, which costs a third of a ducat in Europe, here is worth four, or at least three; the same is true of spurs and bridles. Utensils and apothecaries' goods all cost more than anything else in this city; a tenth of salt costs a ducat of their money.

The remainder of the kingdom is villages where farmers and shepherds live, wearing the skins of their livestock, so that in spring and winter they wear only a small loincloth, going otherwise naked, their heads uncovered and either barefoot or shod in sandals of camel hide. They are ignorant and illiterate: in a hundred miles you won't find one who can read or write. The king treats them as they deserve, keeping them like slaves, their toil and labour only just enough to yield the tribute they pay him.

5.8. The kingdom of Gobir

This province is about 300 miles east of Gao. Between these two kingdoms lies a desert where there is little water, since it is forty miles from the Niger. Several high mountains surround the kingdom, which has countless villages where shepherds and cattle herders live, though the cattle are small. The inhabitants are more cultured than those just mentioned, having many craftsmen, weavers and cobblers. The shoes they make are in the style worn by the ancient Romans, and sold from Timbuktu to Gao. They grow plenty of barley, millet and other grains found in Spain but not Italy. When the Niger floods, the water covers the plain where the people live, and they sow their seeds on the water.

In this settlement is a very large village of about 6,000 houses, where the local and foreign merchants live and the king has established his home and court. Recently the king was seized and deposed by Abu Bakr Askia, king of Timbuktu; after he was killed, and his young sons castrated and made servants in the palace, Askia maintained his rule over the kingdom and installed one of his brothers as viceroy. The latter heavily oppressed the people and extracted massive revenues, since the land is very profitable; but once Askia took power, these revenues fell by half, because he took a large number of the people into captivity.

5.9. Agadez and its kingdom

The walled city of Agadez was built by recent kings on the borders of Libya. It is closer to the lands of the whites than to those of the Blacks, other than Walata. Its houses are well built in the Berber style, since the inhabitants are nearly all foreign merchants, with few locals, all of whom are craftsmen or soldiers to the king. There are very rich and cultured men with a great number of slaves, for it takes force of arms to travel across the region from Agadez to Kano or Bornu. This is because along the way are countless desert folk like the wretched gypsies, who are always ambushing merchants; to defend themselves, the merchants bring slaves with bows, spears and swords, and lately even crossbows. When the merchant comes to a city where he wants to stay, all his slaves set to work at their crafts and professions, earning their keep, while ten or twelve attend to the merchant's goods and person.

The kings of Agadez keep a large guard and a fine palace in the city, but because they are of Libyan origin, as mentioned earlier, most of their armies live in the desert. Sometimes the desert dwellers favour one or another of the royal family, driving the king out and setting the other in his place, usually without killing anyone; whoever keeps the desert folk happy can reign in Agadez.

The rest of this kingdom, towards the south, consists of shepherds and cattle herders, living in huts made of sticks or matting, which they put on oxen and move from place to place to pasture their sheep and cattle, as the Arabs do. The king levies a heavy tax on foreign goods and local produce, paying about 150,000 ducats per year to the king of Timbuktu.

5.10. Kano

Kano is a large province about 500 miles east of the Niger, with a large settlement where many people live in villages. They herd sheep and cattle, and work the land, growing wheat, barley and cotton. In this province are desert mountains with many springs and woods where wild oranges and lemons grow; they taste just the same as domestic ones, differing only in having a stalk. In the middle of the province is a city called Kano, from which the kingdom gets its name. The city is walled with beams and clay, as are all the buildings, and the inhabitants are all cultured craftsmen and rich merchants.

The king was very powerful; he maintained a magnificent court, with many cavalry, so widely admired that he often received tribute from the kings of Zazzau and Katsina. Askia, the king of Timbuktu, tricked these two kings by helping them against the king of Kano but, spotting an opportunity, he betrayed and killed them. For three years he ruled the two kingdoms in his own name, and then began to attack the king of Kano, besieging him for six months until they agreed a treaty in which the king of Kano took one of Askia's daughters for his bride and gave up a third of his kingdom's revenues. Then the king of Timbuktu returned to his own kingdom, leaving several of his administrators and treasurers to collect the revenues for him.

5.11. Katsina and its kingdom

The kingdom of Katsina borders Kano on the east; there are many mountains and the soil is hard, though good for barley and millet. The people are pitch black, with thick noses and lips. All the settlements in this country are small villages, none larger than 300 homes, and all wretched huts. The people are poor and base, and were once ruled by their own king; in Askia's time they were almost destroyed and the king killed. When Askia returned to Timbuktu, he left a kinsman as a viceroy in the kingdom.

5.12. Zazzau and its kingdom[17]

This region borders Kano to the south-east, and is about fifty miles from the border of Katsina. This land is well settled by a wealthy people who trade everywhere. Their land lies partly in a plain and partly in the mountains; the plain is very hot, while the mountains are cool, so in winter the inhabitants, not having beds, set braziers under the tall cots on which they sleep. The countryside is fruitful, full of water and grain; all its inhabitants live in villages like those noted above. The region did have a king from their own people, but Askia, king of Timbuktu, seized and killed him, so it remains under his rule.

5.13. Zamfara[18]

Zamfara, which borders Zazzau on the east, is inhabited by many base people. Their country is full of wheat, barley, millet and cotton. They are tall, but very black; they are brutish people with wide faces. Nearly all were destroyed by King Askia and the kingdom remains his, because he had the king of Zamfara poisoned.

5.14. Wangara and its kingdom

This region borders Zamfara to the south-east; a great people live there, ruled by their own king, who can summon 7,000 archers and 500 foreign cavalry, and commands a large revenue from trade and taxes. All the settlements in this kingdom are villages of huts, except one more beautiful than any other in the kingdom. The inhabitants of the region are quite rich, on account of their trade with distant lands. On the south, they border lands where one can find much gold, but recently they have no longer been able to do business beyond these borders, because the king has two enemies: King Askia of Timbuktu to the west, and the king of Bornu to the east.

When the author was in Bornu, King Ibrahim of Bornu[19] gathered a large army to lead against the king of Wangara, but, when he came near, news arrived that 'Umar, ruler of Gaoga, was on his way to attack Bornu. Immediately, he abandoned his plan and returned swiftly – how lucky for the king of Wangara.

When Wangara's merchants trade with their gold-rich neighbours, they have to cross mountains that their animals cannot climb, and instead have slaves carry their goods. These slaves put these goods into large, tall vessels made of gourds, which they set on their heads and carry for ten or twelve miles, each slave bearing a burden of more than a hundred pounds. The author has seen slaves who have returned from this journey; they no longer have hair on the top of their heads, on account of the great weight. As well as the goods, they carry provisions for themselves, their masters and the slaves who accompany the merchandise as an armed guard.

5.15. Bornu and its kingdom

Bornu is a kingdom or province which borders Wangara on the west and extends east for about 500 miles; it is situated about fifty miles from the source of the Niger. On the south, it borders the desert of Seu; on the north, the desert towards Barca. Its terrain is varied: some parts are mountainous and some are plains. In the plains are large villages where the cultured people live alongside white and black foreign merchants, and the fields are rich with grain; the king lives in one of these villages with his soldiers.

In the mountains live a people who keep animals such as goats and cattle, and who sow millet and various other, unknown grains. In summer the mountainfolk all go naked, with a leather loincloth covering their modesty; in winter they wear sheepskins, which they also use for their beds. Some of them are like animals with no religion, whether Christian, Jewish or Muslim. They also have women in common, working alongside the men, and they all live in villages of stick huts; the inhabitants of each live together like a single family. Disputes do arise among these mountain people, but their only weapons are wooden bows and arrows without iron but with poisoned tips. The author has heard something marvellous from a merchant who often deals with these mountainfolk and knows their language: they do not give people proper names, but name them by their appearance, or by some blemish or feature. For example, a tall man is named 'Tall', a short one 'Short', a cross-eyed one 'Cross-eyed', a fat one 'Fat', and so on.

The province of Bornu is governed by a mighty ruler from the Bardoa of Libya; he keeps about 3,000 cavalry and as many foot soldiers as he wants, since all the people are at his service, to do his bidding. Yet he burdens them with nothing except a tithe of their land's produce; his only revenue is from raiding the enemies at his borders, who belong to the countless black peoples that live beyond the desert of Seu. They used to cross that desert on foot, to do their worst to the province of Bornu. After they had eased off, however, the kings of Bornu bade the merchants come from Barbary, to bring horses in exchange for slaves, paying ten, fifteen, or twenty slaves, and also gold, for each horse. But the king would make them wait, buying the horses and immediately setting off on campaigns against his enemies. It would take two or three months for him to return, and when he did he sometimes brought enough to pay the merchants, and sometimes not. Then the merchants would have to wait another year, since the king could only campaign once a year without danger. For this reason the merchants stopped trading with him and his country, so that eventually, when the author was there, the king received the merchants' wares, but while a merchant awaited payment the king was obliged to cover his expenses.

The king is thought to have a huge treasure, for at his court all the horse equipment – stirrups, spurs and bridles – is golden, and in his palace the wooden bowls and dishes are covered over in gold plate, just as the dogs' chains are all of fine gold. But he is reluctant to use gold to pay off his debts to merchants; he would rather maintain them at his expense for a year, so he can pay in slaves instead. He rules several domains, but the whites know his lands all together as Bornu, for they have not done enough business with them to know their particulars; not least the author himself, who stayed in the province for only a month.

5.16. Gaoga and its kingdom[20]

This province borders Bornu on the west and stretches east to the borders of Nubia on the Nile. The south ends in a desert bounded by a turn of the Nile; to the north it borders the desert of Sirte in the foothills of Egypt. From east to west, the province extends about 500 miles, utterly devoid of culture, learning and governance. The inhabitants are less reasonable than others, especially those who live in the mountains, who go naked in all seasons with only a leather loincloth to cover their modesty. They keep many animals, both sheep and cattle, and they all live in stick huts, which often catch flame and burn down whole villages, especially when the wind blows.

This tribe was free, but a century ago they began to raise up kings. The first among them, it is said, was a black slave who had been brought back to the country by a wealthy merchant; when they approached his homeland, the slave attacked and killed his master by night, fleeing with the money and goods, including several loads of cloth and weapons. The slave came home and set about gaining favour by giving his friends the stolen goods, buying horses from white merchants, and launching campaigns against their enemies. He earned victory after victory, since he and his men had weapons and horses, while their enemies had only wooden bows. After a little while, the slave became a great ruler, having taken many of his enemies captive to barter for horses from Egyptian merchants. On his death, he was succeeded by a son who was as powerful and wise as his father, and he reigned for forty years; then his brother Musa reigned, also just, powerful and wise. When Musa died, his nephew 'Umar, the present king, came to rule.

'Umar is fearsome and powerful, and in a short time has devised many ways to make his kingdom better than it was under his predecessors. He has established goodwill with the sultan of Cairo, sending him such excellent gifts that the sultan gives him what he wants from Cairo: cloth, weapons and horses. As well as being generous and pleasant, he pays on time, and so has earned such a good reputation that all the merchants of Egypt go no farther than his court; likewise, many of the poor of Cairo and elsewhere come to his court bearing gifts that seem to those of that country to be of wondrous beauty. 'Umar offers astounding rewards of slaves, gold and camels, such that every foreigner leaves his court happy. He greatly honours learned men, particularly the descendants of Muhammad. Once the author was present when a nobleman from the city of Damietta presented 'Umar with a horse, a Turkish sword, a shirt of chain mail, a gun, some lovely mirrors, combs, crowns of coral and various knives – altogether these objects were worth about fifty ducats in Cairo. 'Umar gave him five slaves, five camels and 500 local ducats, along with more than a hundred large elephant tusks.

5.17. Nubia and its kingdom

From its western deserts, bordering Gaoga, the kingdom of Nubia stretches across the Nile. It borders the deserts of Gorhan to the south,[21] and Egypt to the north, although one cannot take a boat from this kingdom to Egypt, since the Nile flows across a plain in such shallow waters that animals and people can wade across. The kingdom's foremost city is Dongola, well populated with about 10,000 homes, though the buildings are all quite poorly made of beams and clay.[22] The inhabitants are cultured and wealthy, travelling to Cairo and all of Egypt's towns to buy cloth, weapons and other merchandise. The rest of the kingdom consists of villages along the Nile, inhabited by farmers. In the province of Nubia there is plenty of grain and sugar cane, which they blacken because they don't know how to cook it properly.

In Dongola one finds much civet, sandalwood and ivory, as many elephant hunters are there. One will also find the deadliest poisons, sold at the exorbitant price of 100 ducats per ounce; one grain will kill ten men in fifteen minutes, or one man in the time it takes to say the Paternoster. But they only allow foreigners to buy it, in order to keep people in their own country from harm. To buy it, one must pay the ruler a duty equal to the price, and the vendor cannot sell it privately, on pain of death.

The king of Nubia is always making war on the Gorhan people, who are like gypsies; they live idly in the desert and no one understands their language. He often makes war on another tribe living in the desert across the Nile to the east, towards the Red Sea. That tribe, near the borders of Suakin, speaks a mixed tongue which the author judges to be Chaldean, for it sounds similar to the language of Suakin and upper Ethiopia, the land of Prester John.[23] This tribe is known as al-Beja; they are unarmed, base and destitute, living on camel's milk and the meat of wild animals and camels. Occasionally they collect tribute from the rulers of Suakin or Dongola. They used to have a large town named 'Aydhab on the Red Sea, directly across from the port of Jeddah, which is forty miles from Mecca. But two centuries ago that tribe, defying the sultan, raided a caravan carrying goods and provisions to Mecca. As a result, the sultan sent a fleet on the Red Sea to raze the city and port of 'Aydhab,[24] and so that tribe, whose port had brought in about 200,000 ducats or *sherifi* a year, became beggars. Then they turned to scrounging around Dongola and Suakin, but lately they have often been attacked by the ruler of Suakin with the help of Turkish corsairs with guns and bows. Because the scoundrels go naked they lost around 4,000 people in one day, while a thousand were captured and brought to Suakin, where the women and children tied them up and killed them for their terrible deeds.

This is all the author could write about the Black Land and its various kingdoms. Even if he wished to say more, there would be no more to say, since in these kingdoms there are neither ordered cities nor regulated courts, and the lands are all the same; these fifteen kingdoms have the same terrain, and share their culture, customs and habits, especially because they have only four rulers. This is reason enough to see them as sharing one way of life and governance.

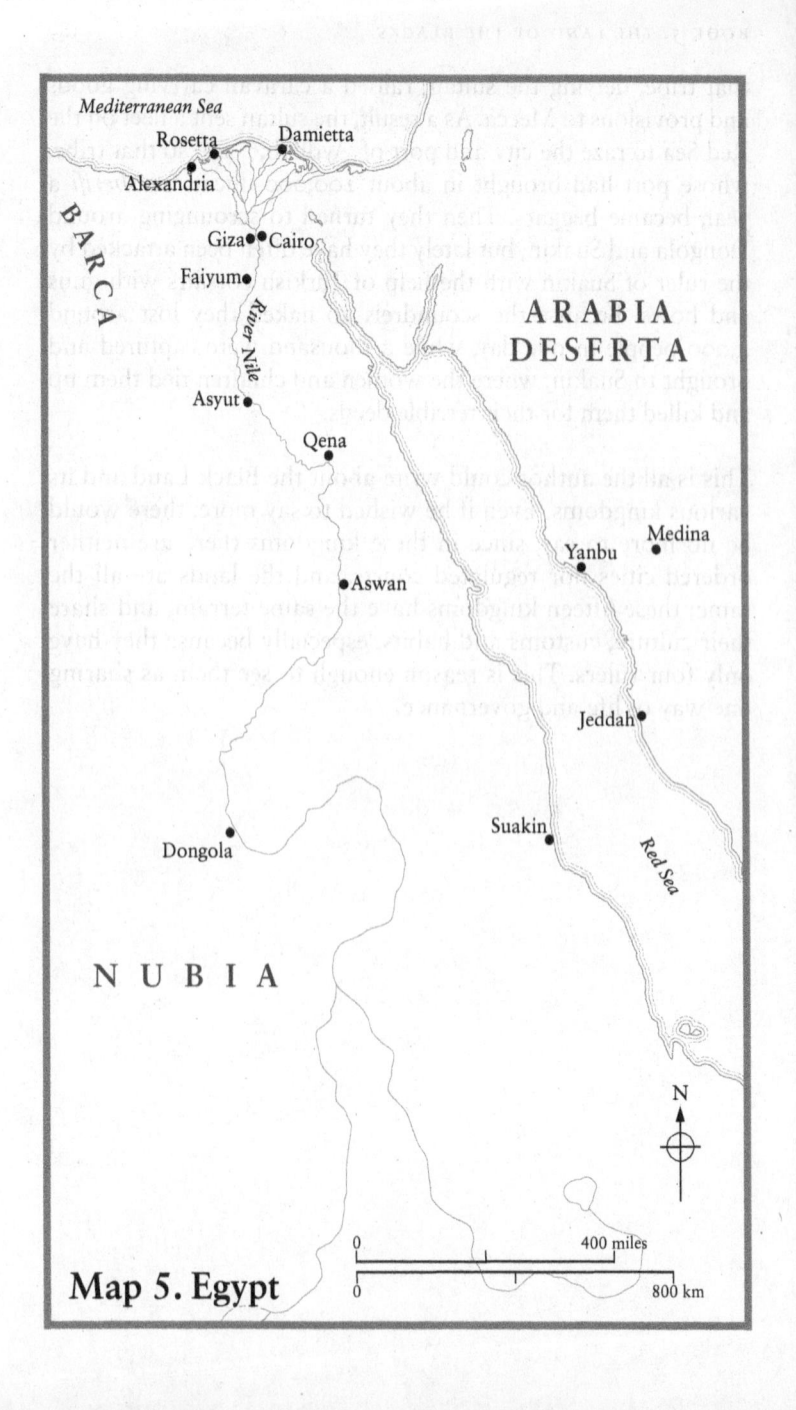

Map 5. Egypt

BOOK 6.
EGYPT

6.1. [Introduction]

Egypt is a very famous province, bordering the deserts of Barca, Numidia and Libya to the west, the deserts between Egypt and the Red Sea to the east, the Mediterranean to the north, and Beja on the Nile to the south.[1] From the Mediterranean to Beja the region extends around 450 miles, and is very narrow, there being no settlement or arable field except on the banks of the Nile, which flows between the dry mountains bordering the deserts just mentioned; the settlements and arable lands lie between the riverbanks and the mountains. It is true that the province widens a little towards the Mediterranean, for around eighty miles upstream of Cairo the Nile divides into two parts, with a branch that extends west and then returns to the main branch.[2] Then, around sixty miles past Cairo, it again divides into two parts: one branch goes to Rosetta and the other to Damietta. From the Damietta branch proceeds another that feeds into a lake,[3] and a strait connects the lake and the sea, upon which lies the ancient city of Tinnis. Egypt is enlarged by the divisions of the Nile into these parts.

The whole province is flat and fruitful, a place where much grain and gum grows, and where there are good pastures for animals and innumerable poultry, especially geese. The townsfolk are brown in colour, but the city folk are white. Almost all of them wear good, close-fitting clothes, fastened at the breast and open from there to the bottom; they have narrow sleeves, and on their head great turbans over round camlet caps. On their feet they wear sandals like people used to do;

some wear shoes, but they don't cover the whole foot, instead the instep is doubled back under the heel. In the summer they wear clothes of cloth and cotton worked in various colours; in the winter, short, full cotton robes, which they call *al-habara*, while the grand burghers and merchants wear robes of European cloth.

The people of this region are better, friendlier and more generous than others. They consume plenty of milk and fresh cheese, the milk rendered sharp and thick; likewise they put so much salt in their cheese that a foreigner won't dare try it, but to them it seems like nothing, because they are so used to it. They put the thick, sharp milk in almost all their soups.

6.2. The divisions of the region

In modern times, that is, since the Muslims began to rule, the region and kingdom of Egypt was divided into three parts: Cairo to Rosetta, called er-Rif, that is, the coast; Cairo to Beja, called al-Sa'id, that is, the ground;[4] and the part along the branch of the Nile to Damietta and Tinnis, called al-Behriyya, that is, the lake region. Each part is very fertile and fruitful, but al-Sa'id is the richest in wheat, beans, animals, poultry and flax, er-Rif in fruit and barley, and al-Behriyya in cotton, sugar cane and the *maus* (banana) fruit. The inhabitants of er-Rif and al-Behriyya are more cultured than those of al-Sa'id, for these two parts are near the sea and so have more commerce with travellers from Barbary, Europe and Assyria; whereas those of al-Sa'id are inland, south of Cairo, and so never see any foreigners except those from Ethiopia.

6.3. The origins of the Egyptians

According to the scriptures of Moses, the Egyptians are descendants of Mizraim, son of Cush, son of Ham, son of Noah, and the Hebrews call the ancestor and inhabitants by the same name, Mizraim. The Arabs likewise call the whole country Misr, but have another word for the inhabitants, namely al-Qibt;[5] they say that these were the first to rule and to build in the kingdom and so were called Qibt. The people also call themselves al-Qibt. The only true citizens are those who have remained Christian, but others became Muslims and mingled with the Arabs and Africans. The kingdom long remained under the government of the Egyptian Pharaohs, who were very grand, powerful kings, as their physical remains and written histories bear witness. Then the land fell under Roman control by the marriage of Queen [. . .][6] to a great Roman general, as is found in the histories; it stayed under Roman control for many years, and sometimes the Empire sent a viceroy to govern the kingdom.

After the birth of Christ, the Egyptians also became Christian and remained so under the Roman Empire; after the Empire began to decline, the emperors of Constantinople always took care to retain the kingdom, governed and pacified by their viceroys. But after the plague of Muhammad arrived, the kingdom was captured by a Muslim general named 'Amr ibn al-'As, who was sent with a great Arab army by 'Umar, the second caliph; when he captured the kingdom, the general allowed the people to practise their own religion, so long as they paid tribute. Amr built a small town on the Nile that the Arabs called al-Fustat, that is, the tent, for when he entered Egypt he had found that place deserted and uninhabited, sheltering there with his tents; after his victory he stopped there and began building houses where his tents had been. And so the town was called al-Fustat, but the people now call it Misr al-Atiqa, that is, the Old Town, for it is old compared to Cairo, which is modern.

Many excellent modern men – Muslims, Christians and Jews – are seriously mistaken, believing that Misr al-Atiqa is the city where the Pharaohs of Moses and Joseph lived, since the people speak of it using the word for 'old'. But the truth is that the town where the Pharaohs lived is across the Nile to the west, where the Pyramids are; scripture testifies to this, for the Book of the Generation says that the Hebrews were employed in building Apthum, the city Pharaoh built in the time of Moses.[7] This city is also along the Nile on the African side, around fifty miles south of Cairo on the branch that, as we said above, extends further west. There is further evidence that the city of the Pharaohs was there – still today, at the confluence of the two branches of the Nile, is a very old building called Joseph's Tomb, dug before the Hebrews left Egypt, although, when they left, Moses had his body carried to the tomb of his ancestors.[8] Therefore Cairo and its environs have nothing to do with the lands of the ancient Pharaohs.

It should be noted that in the time of the Egyptian kings the culture of the region centred on al-Sa'id, from Cairo upriver: Faiyum, Memphis, Akhmim and other famous cities. But when the kingdom was captured by the Romans, its culture shifted towards er-Rif, the sea coast, where Alexandria and Rosetta are. Even today many towns are found with Latin names, as will appear in the following; when the Empire was translated from Rome to Greece, the culture narrowed towards el-Behriyya, and the emperor's viceroy appropriated Alexandria for his own. When the Muslim armies arrived, they settled down in the middle of this kingdom, seeing two benefits in the decision: first, it brought peace to the kingdom on both sides, and, second, they did not want to be on the coast, fearing the assaults of the Christians.

6.4. The air in Egypt and its qualities

The air of Egypt is very hot and cruel; it rains only on rare occasions, and, when it does, many come down with a cold or fever; there are others who suffer swollen testicles, an extraordinary matter that the local doctors blame on salted cheese and buffalo meat. In the summer the country is scorched by the searing heat of the air. The Egyptians in every city, therefore, make use of high towers with one door at the top and another at the foot opening onto the rooms of the house; the wind enters the top of the tower, bringing in fresh air, without which they would die from the heat.[9] Sometimes the plague kills many people, especially in Cairo, where on one occasion 12,000 people died per day. As regards the French pox there is no country on earth so infected with it as Egypt, so that in Cairo there are many who have been crippled by the disease.[10]

All the grain is reaped in April, and part of it is threshed the same month, the other part in May; by 10 May there remains no grain at all in the countryside. In June the Nile begins to flood for forty days, then it recedes for another forty days, and over these eighty days all the cities and farms of Egypt resemble islands; one can go from place to place only by boat. But during this season they have the convenience of being able to load large cargo boats, each of which can carry six or seven thousand bushels of grain and hundreds of sheep. These huge boats, when loaded, can travel only during the flooding season, and with the current, whereas they are barely able to return empty against the current. In this season the Egyptians know the value of the grain for the entire year; they do not have to wait for the harvest season, as will be seen in the passage on the Nile and its islands next to the Old Town, where the Nile is measured.[11]

However, we will not give an account of all the particular towns of Egypt, since they are not all in Africa, and especially since many cosmographers say that Egypt is not in Africa, whereas others say that it is. Some claim that the part towards the Barbary desert, Numidia and Libya is indeed in Africa, while others argue that all the settlements on the principal branch (of the Nile) are in Africa and those on the other branch are not, such as Memphis, Faiyum, Samannud, Damanhur, al-Burullus, Tinnis and Damietta. For many relevant reasons, this last is the opinion of the author, as will be seen when he discusses the towns on the principal branch, such as Rosetta and others.

6.5. Abusir

Abusir was an ancient city built by the Egyptians on the Mediterranean, around ten miles west of Alexandria; it had very strong walls and beautiful buildings. Around it are plenty of date groves, but nobody owns them, for the city was abandoned when Alexandria was assaulted and sacked by the Christians, and the inhabitants of Abusir fled to the al-Buhaira lake.[12]

6.6. Alexandria

Alexandria is a great city built with the help of architects by Alexander the Great, son of Philip of Macedon, magnificent in appearance and on a fine site, on the edge of the Mediterranean forty miles west of the Nile. The city had a thriving culture and beautiful houses and other buildings; its great renown lasted for many years. But after it was captured by the Muslims the city's culture was diminished for many years, for at first it was frequented by no ship either from Greece, Italy or any part of Europe, and was almost entirely abandoned. But a shrewd caliph in those days came up with a good ruse in the form of a prophecy by Muhammad; he said that a great dispensation would come to those who lived in Alexandria, those who spent a few days looking after the city and those who gave alms for its preservation. Because of this the Egyptians and others began to inhabit the city again, and it was always full of foreigners who came for that dispensation, for whom many rooms were created in the towers on the city walls; many colleges were built for scholars and students, and many monasteries for the devout who went to stay in the city.

The city is square in plan, with four gates – one to the east by the Nile, another to the south at the lake called al-Buhaira, the third to the west by the desert of Barca and the fourth by the docks, where there is a port. At this last are stationed guards and customs officers, who search those who arrive by boat down to their underwear, for the customs office taxes even cash, like goods, at a fixed rate. Near the city walls are two gates separated by a corridor and a redoubtable citadel standing at the entrance to the port called Marsa al-Borji, that is, the Port of the Tower. To this port come the noblest ships and the most important merchandise, that is, the fleets from Venice, Genoa, Ragusa and elsewhere in Europe, for to Alexandria flock the ships of Flanders, England, Biscay, Portugal and all the coasts of Europe, but above all the Italians, and especially the Apulians and Sicilians. The Greek ships, that is, the Turks, are also drawn to this port for safety from pirates and storms. The other port is called

Marsa as-Silsila, that is, the Port of the Chain, at which arrive fleets from Barbary, such as Tunis, the isle of Jerba and other places. As they enter or leave, the Christians pay about ten per cent in customs, whereas the Muslims pay five, but it is free to take goods out of the city over land to Cairo. The city now has no great reputation or renown, except the port for its proximity to Cairo where countless goods are sold, since crowds of people convene at the port from all over the world.

At present the city itself is not very cultured or much inhabited, except for a long street running from the east gate to the west gate, and another area near the gate to the docks, where there are many shops and warehouses in which Christian foreigners stay. These two places are well populated, but the rest of the city has been empty and ruined since it was attacked by the Christians after Louis IV of France was freed by the sultan.[13] The king of Cyprus[14] arrived together with Venetian and French fleets and attacked Alexandria without warning, sacking it and killing untold numbers of people. But the sultan went at once to rescue the city, and the Christians, the moment they realised they would be unable to hold it, lit a fire and burned all the houses before boarding their ships. The sultan then began to provide for the city, that is, the fortifications of the walls, having the citadel built above the port and putting a substantial guard in the city; from that time on it began to be inhabited again.

Within the city is a very high mound – like the Testaccio in Rome, which contains many fragments of ancient pots below the ground – and nobody knows its history, although its position is certainly not natural. On it is a tower where an officer watches the sea for ships; whenever he sees one, he at once warns his superiors and receives six ducats for each boat he sees.[15] But if, for instance, he is asleep or off having fun and a ship arrives without his warning, he is fined twenty-four ducats, payable to the royal treasury, as well as losing his six ducats commission.

The city's houses are mostly built over large cisterns held up by great columns and arches, into which flows water from the Nile. When the river floods, the water travels by an artificial canal through the plain between the river and Alexandria, entering beneath the city walls and flowing into these cisterns under the houses.[16] However, over the years the cisterns have become so full of mud that they are practically bogs, with the result that in summer many people fall ill from the water. As regards its fertility, the city is in the middle of a sandy desert, in which are neither arable lands nor vineyards nor gardens; the grain has to be brought from forty miles away. And although there are little gardens and orchards beside the canal bringing water from the Nile, the fruit they produce is poisonous, for most of the townsfolk seem to develop a fever after eating them.

Beyond the city to the west, around six miles away, are certain ancient buildings among which is a very broad and tall column, called in the Arabic language 'Amoud al-Sawari, that is, Column of Trees.[17] For in accounts of the world's marvels, we read that in Alexander's time there was a philosopher named Ptolemy who made this column to protect the city from its enemies; at the top he built a huge mirror of steel, so that every boat passing the mirror was immediately scorched when it was uncovered. When the Muslims invaded Egypt the mirror was broken, and they told the story that it was broken by a Jew who rubbed it with garlic.[18]

In the middle of the city among the ruins is a little low house like a shrine in which there is a tomb much venerated and honoured by the Muslims, who burn candles there day and night. They say the tomb is that of Alexander the Great, who was a prophet and a king according to the madness of Muhammad in the Qur'an. All the foreigners who come to Alexandria visit this tomb, believing it a devout thing to do, and usually give alms to those who look after the place.

In the city live many Egyptian Christians, who are its oldest inhabitants; they are named Jacobites and have their own church, which once housed the body of St Mark the Evangelist, although it was later stolen by the Venetians and taken to Venice. All these Christians of Alexandria are craftsmen and merchants, but pay tribute to the king of Cairo. There are many other notable things in the city and beyond, but to discuss all of them would make this account too long-winded.

6.7. Abu Qir

This is an ancient town on the Mediterranean, around eight miles east of Alexandria; it remains in ruins from when Alexandria was assaulted, but there are many remnants of the walls and many date farms, among which are found the huts of the poor farmers. There is a tower on a dangerous shore where many merchant ships from Syria drown, for when they arrive at night nobody knows how to enter the port of Alexandria, and so they stop on that shore. Around the town is nothing but sandy countryside as far as the Nile.

6.8. Rashid, called Rosetta by the Italians

Rosetta is a city on the African side of the Nile, three miles from where it enters the Mediterranean. It was built by a caliph's slave, who was the viceroy of Egypt. The city has fine houses and buildings on the Nile, a huge square with various craftsmen and merchants, and a gorgeous, cheerful mosque with doors onto the square and others on the Nile, where one can descend beautiful stairs.[19] Under the mosque, a little further up, is a port where countless cargo boats gather, loaded with goods being brought to Cairo.

The city is not walled, but instead organised like a large village, around which are many buildings where rice is threshed with wooden implements; every month around 3,000 bushels are prepared. Outside the city is a little suburb where carriers keep mules and large donkeys for wagons, allocating them to people headed for Alexandria. One only has to ride, for the animals go carefully to the house where they are to be left, and with such speed that they cover forty miles from morning to evening along the sandy plains by the coast, with the waves lapping at their feet.

Around the city are plenty of date farms and excellent rice fields, and the inhabitants are homely and pleasant to strangers, happy to entertain them. The city has a good, handsome hammam, with hot and cold fountains inside, such a wonder of beauty and convenience that the like is not found in all of Egypt. The author himself stayed in this city when the Grand Turk Selim passed by on his return to Alexandria, entering the baths in person with his favourites and taking great pleasure in it.

6.9. Anthios[20]

Anthios is a fine town built by the Romans on the banks of the Nile, on the Asian side, where still today you can see many tablets with Latin writing. It is highly cultured and well populated, and endowed with all the arts; it has a splendid countryside for growing rice and wheat, as well as many date farms. The townsfolk are marvellous for their kind and pleasant natures, and they all earn their living by taking rice to Cairo.

6.10. Birinbal

Birinbal is an ancient town on the Asian side of the Nile, built when Egypt became Christian. The town is very handsome and fertile, especially for rice, and there are over 400 buildings where it is threshed. The rice threshers are all foreigners, mostly from Barbary, who earn more than they deserve and live a high life. For this reason all the prostitutes of Egypt converge on the town, trading on the lust of the threshers, tiring them out and ending up with all their earnings.

6.11. Thebes[21]

Thebes is a very ancient city on the Barbary side of the Nile. The cosmographers disagree as to who built it, some saying it was the Egyptians, others the Romans, others the Greeks; however, no ancient authority names it, so modern writers cannot judge the real truth of the matter, only making guesses from the many epitaphs in various languages, Egyptian, Greek and Latin, but one guess is as good as any other. The city now is in a poor state, with barely 300 homes, but it has fine storehouses with a great abundance of wheat, rice, sugar and delicious fruit called *maus* (banana). There are many craftsmen and merchants, but most of the inhabitants are farmers, so if you walk the streets during the day you'll only see women, who are pretty and friendly. Around the city are so many date farms that you can hardly see it until you are right next to it. Near the walls are plenty of orchards of grapes, figs and peaches, which they bring to Cairo. Outside are many traces of antiquity: columns, epitaphs and walls of huge dressed stones.

6.12. Fuwwah

Fuwwah is an ancient city built by the Egyptians on the Asian side of the Nile, around forty-five miles south of Rosetta; it is well populated, cultured and fertile, and has fine merchants' and craftsmen' shops, though the squares are narrow. The townsfolk are friendly and eager to please, and the women enjoy such a freedom that their husbands do not know where they are all day; you can imagine the rest. Outside the walls on one side is a district where the prostitutes live, and which amounts to a good portion of the city. Around the city are very many date farms and a good countryside for sugar cane and grain, but the cane does not produce a good sugar; instead of sugar, then, they make from it a sort of honey like grape syrup, which is used throughout Egypt, where there is little honey.

6.13. Jazirat adh Dhahab, the Island of Gold

This island is in the middle of the Nile opposite the aforementioned city; it has raised fields, with trees of every fruit except olives. On the island are many villages and fine buildings, but they cannot be seen through all the dates and other trees. The fields are very good for sugar cane and rice, and all the islanders work the fields and take the goods to Cairo.

6.14. Al-Mechella

Al-Mechella is a modern town built in the Muslim era on the Asian side of the Nile, surrounded with poor walls; it is well populated, but most of its inhabitants are textile workers and farmers, keeping countless geese, which they take to Cairo. Around the town are very good lands for grain and flax, but there is little culture or trade within.

6.15. Derot[22]

Derot is a noble city built by the Romans on the African side of the Nile; it has no walls, but it is highly cultured and well populated, with fine buildings, wide streets, good shops and a splendid mosque. The inhabitants are very wealthy, for they own many sugar cane fields; the city community pays the sultan around 100,000 *sherifi* a year for the freedom to grow the cane. They have a large building like a castle with presses and furnaces to boil the cane, many people working together on the same load in one place.

6.16. Mahallat Sa

Mahallat Sa is a modern town built in the Muslim era on the African side of the Nile, on a high hill; all its fields are raised too, so its farms serve as vineyards, for when the Nile floods it does not reach them. The town furnishes Cairo with fresh grapes for half the year, but it has little culture and the inhabitants are mostly boatmen, for they have little land to work or cultivate.

6.17. Cairo

Cairo's reputation as a huge, teeming, wondrous city has circled the globe; how it was built will shortly be told. Cairo is an Arabic name corrupted in Italian, or rather in all European languages; it ought to be spelled 'al-Qahira', which means 'compeller'. The city was built in modern times by a Slavic slave, Jawhar al-Katib, as was already mentioned in the first part of this book, in the chapter on the Arabs who live in tents in Africa.[23] The walled city currently contains around 80,000 homes of men of high estate; there are squares where riches from all over the world are sold, and important mosques, such as the renowned Jami' al-'Azhar, that is, the Shining Mosque, built by the Slavic slave with the surname Al-Azhar, 'Shining', one of his nicknames given by the caliph.

The city is built in a plain under the al-Muqattam mountain, around two miles from the Nile. It has high, strong walls and fine iron gates, the most famous of which are these three: Bab al-Nasr, the Gate of Victory, which faces east towards the Red Sea desert; Bab Zuweila, which faces the Nile and the Old Town; and Bab al-Futuh, the Gate of the Triumphs, which faces a lake and other fields and farms.

The city is well furnished with craftsmen and merchants of every sort, especially all along the road from the Nasr Gate to the Zuweila Gate, where most of the city's culture is.[24] Also here are madrasa buildings so stupendous and gorgeously ornate that no words suffice to express it, and huge, marvellous mosques like that of al-Hakim, the third schismatic caliph of Cairo. The city has other large and famous mosques but there would be no profit in mentioning them individually. Along this road are many hammams in the form of large buildings, and the Bain al-Qasrayn, district where there are sixty or so cooks' shops selling roast meat from tin containers. Other stalls, with valuable vessels of glass and worked tin, sell waters subtly flavoured with every kind of flower, enjoyed by all the nobles and gentlemen. Others fashion confectionery of honey or cane sugar in pretty shapes, different from those in Europe. Fruiterers sell fruit from Syria such as pears, quinces and pomegranates, since these do not grow in Egypt, and many other shops offer a variety of foods like bread fried in oil and fried eggs and cheese.

Past the food shops is another district of various craftsmen in noble arts, and beyond that the new madrasa built by Sultan (al-Ashraf Qansuh) al-Ghuri,[25] who died in the war with the Grand Turk Selim. Beyond the madrasa are the fabric bazaars, all of which contain countless shops. The first sells precious foreign textiles, such as that of Baalbec, a very thin cotton, and of Mosul[26] from Nineveh, both of which are wondrously thin and strong; all the nobles and city leaders use them for shirts and for the scarves on their turbans. Beyond this are the bazaars selling precious fabrics from Italy: satins, velvets, damasks, taffetas, brocades and so on. Then there are bazaars of woollen fabrics from Europe – Venice, Florence, Flanders, Mallorca and the Marches – and past those the shops of camlet and similar things. One shop after another, one arrives at the Zuweila Gate, where there are craftsmen without number.

Near the main street to the south is the Khan el-Khalili bazaar, where the Persian merchants live. It has the appearance of a great ruler's palace, tall and strong, with three floors; below it are rooms where the merchants give audience and barter copious amounts of merchandise. All the occupants have huge riches for sale – spices, gems and Indian textiles resembling crape. On another stretch of the road is an area where merchants sell aromatic substances like civet, musk, ambergris and benzoin; anyone who would buy an ounce of musk from a merchant will be shown a hundred pounds, an extraordinary thing. Further down is an area of merchants selling smooth white paper, and precious gems that dealers personally take door to door, and then an area where goldsmiths, most of them Jews, handle great riches. Elsewhere on the main road are ragmen who handle reams of precious fabrics owned by the townsfolk and city leaders, and we aren't talking about mere gabardines or cassocks or cloaks. Indeed, the author has seen in their quarter a tent, or rather, a canopy bed made entirely with needlework, covered on top with a fine net of pearls weighing forty-five pounds; even without the pearls, the bed went for 10,000 *sherifi*. He has seen other marvellous things in the shops at a similarly vast price.

In the city is a great hospital built by Baibars, the first Mamluk sultan.[27] It has an enormous income of around 200,000 *sherifi*; everyone can go there when they are sick, and be well looked after and healed by competent doctors, but, when a man dies there, if he has any possessions the hospital keeps them.

6.18. Bab Zuweila

This is a huge suburb of around 20,000 homes, extending west from the Zuweila Gate for around a mile and a half, and south as far as the sultan's citadel; it stretches a mile or so north, as far as the suburb of Bab al-Louq, where there is some culture as inside the city. Many keep shops in this suburb but live in the city, and vice versa. Here are also many mosques, monasteries and colleges, especially the famous madrasa built by Sultan (an-Nasir) Hasan, which is remarkable for the height of its vaults and walls; one sultan once rebelled against another, and the one outside the city dared to fortify himself in the madrasa and attack the royal citadel, for the two are about half a crossbow shot's length apart.[28]

6.19. Jami' Tulun

This large suburb borders with the previous one to the east and extends west as far as the ruins leading to the Old City. It was built in ancient times before Cairo itself, by Ibn Tulun, the slave of a caliph of Baghdad who became the viceroy of Egypt; a wise and prudent man, he left his home in the Old City and settled in the suburb, where he built a huge, gorgeous palace and a mosque likewise wondrous for its size and beauty. In this suburb are many craftsmen and merchants, especially from Barbary.

6.20. Bab al-Louq

This large suburb is around a mile from the walls of Cairo; in it are around 3,000 homes and all sorts of craftsmen and merchants. There is a large square with a huge palace and a marvellous madrasa built by the mamluk Azbak (al-Yusufi), an adviser to a former king;[29] in this square, the Azbakeya, all the people of Cairo assemble every Friday, after the sermon and prayers, for in the suburb are dishonourable things like taverns and prostitutes.

In the middle of the square gather many mountebanks and musicians, as well as those who make camels, donkeys and dogs dance – an extraordinary spectacle, especially the donkeys, for after one dances a little its master will say, 'Well, my dear donkey, this is new: the king wishes to build something, and plans to use all the donkeys in Cairo to carry mortar, stones and such like.' Hearing these words, the animal at once falls to the ground, sticks its legs up in the air, puffs out its belly and shuts its eyes as if dead.

The master then says to the crowd: 'O my lords! I've lost my donkey to please you; I pray you repair the loss!' The bystanders all know the custom, giving him a penny or two, until he has finished the collection. Then he says, 'My lords, don't worry! I think my donkey isn't dead, but he knows how poor his master is and is putting on this show until I have enough cash to buy his fodder. Now watch, my lords!' Suddenly he calls, 'My donkey!' It continues to play dead, and he beats it but still it doesn't move, until he says, 'My lords, have you heard the news?'

They reply, 'Tell us, maestro!' and he announces, 'My lords, his majesty the sultan has decreed that all the people of Cairo leave the city tomorrow morning to watch his procession, and that all the city's noblewomen and beauties ride fine donkeys and give them good barley and water from the Nile.' The donkey leaps to his feet and swaggers about, full of joy.

Then the master adds, 'But, unfortunately, the warden of the district where I live has asked to borrow my donkey for his aged wife.' When it hears these words, the donkey at once starts limping as if in pain.

The master exclaims, 'Look, my lords, my donkey doesn't want the old woman!' And then: 'My donkey, would you like to marry?' The animal replies by nodding its head, and its master says, 'Well then, look around for a woman who pleases you more, show her to me!' The donkey goes around the crowd, peering at the women who stand around watching it, and when it sees one who is younger and more honourable, it touches her with its head. All the bystanders cry out loudly and tease her, 'Hey look, it's the donkey's wife!' And in a trice the master mounts his animal and rides off to perform another trick elsewhere.

On Fridays you find people in the square who keep little birds in cages like cupboards; the birds bring fortunes to those who give them a penny, for their owner has put many written slips in their cages with good or bad predictions. When a man comes to learn his fortune, the owner tells him to place a penny in front of the little bird; it takes the coin in its beak at once and goes into the cage to deposit it, bringing out one of the slips for the customer to read. The predictions are sometimes good, sometimes the opposite.

Other entertainers in the square fence with sticks, fool around with their fists or recount the histories of the Arabs and Egyptians from when the Arabs conquered Egypt. How many absurdities and lies are uttered, how many wicked things done in that square! A wondrous and enjoyable spectacle – but it can't all be told in a little work like this.

6.21. Boulaq

Boulaq is a substantial suburb around two miles from the walls of Cairo, and the road is lined with houses and mills worked by animals. It was built in ancient times on the banks of the Nile, and contains 4,000 homes, with many craftsmen and merchants, especially of grain, oil and sugar cane. There are fine mosques and madrasas and plenty of fine buildings, especially on the banks of the Nile; it's a great pleasure to stand at their high windows and watch the ships arriving at the city port in this suburb, which sometimes contains thousands of boats, especially during the grain harvest. There are galleys full of merchandise on their way from Alexandria to Damietta, but they pay little customs, for they have already paid the office on the coast; goods from the smaller towns, however, incur the full tax.

6.22. Al-Qarafa

Al-Qarafa is a suburb like a city itself, only a stone's throw from the mountain, around two miles from the walls of Cairo, and a mile from the Nile. The suburb is well populated, with 2,000 homes; it has plenty of culture, but was once more inhabited than at present, since almost half of it has been lost. There are many tombs of men reputed holy by the foolish common folk; they are built like the high cupolas of strong buildings, and they are richly adorned inside with various techniques and colours, and furnished with carpets around the walls and on the ground. Every Friday morning the people come in droves from Cairo and other suburbs to visit the tombs and give alms.

6.23. The Old City, known as Misr al-Atiqa

This was the first city built in Egypt during the Muslim era by 'Amr (ibn al-'As), the general of 'Umar, the second caliph, for he built it on first arriving at the Nile. The city is not walled, but arranged like a large suburb along the Nile. It has 5,000 homes and many tall, fine buildings, especially those on the river. The town is filled with all kinds of craftsmen and merchants, as many as it can hold; there is also a mosque called Jami' Amr, marvellous for its grandeur, beauty and strength.

In addition the city contains the tomb of the famous Muslim holy woman Saint Nafisa, the daughter of Zayn al-Abidin, son of Husein, son of 'Ali (ibn Abi Talib), fraternal cousin of Muhammad.[30] When her family was deprived of the caliphate by hostile kinsfolk, Nafisa in desperation left Al-Qufa'ah, a city in Arabia Felix, and arrived in Cairo; because she was a descendant of Muhammad and led an honourable life, the common people of Egypt have esteemed her very holy. This has been especially true since the heretical caliphs began ruling Egypt, for they were her descendants; they built a fine tomb over her body and adorned it with many decorations, silver lamps and silk carpets, so that from that time until today her reputation has only grown. All the merchants who come to Cairo by sea or land bring the tomb a great offering, and the locals give many alms, so it receives about 100,000 *sherifi* a year, which are spent on repair and on sustaining the many poor among Muhammad's descendants; the money is also given to those who help preserve and look after the tomb, and who daily repeat lies about the miracles the holy body supposedly performs. On the entry of the Grand Turk Selim into Cairo, his janissaries looted the tomb, finding there around 500,000 *sherifi* in cash, not counting the lamps, chains and carpets, although Selim returned many of these. Those who have written the lives of the Muslim saints have made no mention of Nafisa, saying only that she was an honourable, chaste and noble woman of the house of 'Ali; but the simple people have invented many miracles, innumerable things dreamt up by the caretakers of that cursed tomb.

Above the suburb, along the Nile, is the customs office for goods coming from al-Sa'id, with many officers to collect the profits. Far to the east outside the walled city are the impressive and wondrous tombs of the sultans, many in number, fashioned like very high cupolas, well built and splendidly adorned within. One modern sultan made a passageway between two high walls stretching from the city gate to the place of the tombs; at either end is a soaring, well-built turret where a guard stands to take account of the Muslims and merchants arriving from the port of Mount Sinai.[31]

Around a mile-and-a-half from the tombs are the orchards of El Matareya, where the garden of the balsam tree is. This little tree is unique, and not found anywhere else in the world; it is not too large, with small leaves when it blossoms, and has been planted at the mouth of a fountain like a well. The garden is well walled and looked after, and nobody can get in without a favour or a bribe to the guards. If for any reason the fountain should stop, the tree will dry up at once, and it will only grow worse if watered with any other water – a marvel of nature.[32]

In the middle of the Nile opposite the Old City is an island called Al Miqyas,[33] that is, the Nilometer, by which it is known if there should be a dry or fertile season in Egypt; it is one test that never fails, having been invented by the ancient Egyptians.[34] This island is well populated and cultured; it has around 1,500 homes and at the top is a very large and beautiful palace built by a modern sultan. Next to the palace on the Nile is a splendid mosque, quite large and cheerful. In another area is a closed, stand-alone chamber, the middle of which is open, revealing a well-built square pit, around eighteen cubits deep. At the bottom on one side is an underground channel leading to the Nile shore, and set in the middle of the pit is a column with markings of every cubit and finger, reaching to the top of the pit, marked at eighteen cubits.[35] When the Nile begins to flood, the water flows through the channel into the pit, sometimes rising two fingers a day, sometimes three, sometimes half a cubit. Every day chosen officers go to see how much the Nile has risen, and the minute they've seen it they inform boys wearing a yellow cloth on their shoulders as a badge of office, who go around Cairo and its suburbs announcing how much the Nile has risen; they are tipped each day the Nile floods by the craftsmen, merchants and women. If the Nile reaches fifteen cubits on the column, it will be a most fertile year; if between fifteen to twelve, the year will be average, neither lean nor fertile; if it reaches only between twelve cubits and ten, the grain will fetch ten ducats per bushel, a great famine; if the water reaches fifteen to eighteen, the flooding will cause great damage; and if it passes eighteen all the settlements of Egypt will be in danger of drowning, with the water flowing from one mountain to another, between which the river and settlements of the country lie. The officer must announce such a sign, and that very day the boys go tell the people: 'Fear God from mountain to mountain!', meaning that the water will stretch from one mountain to another. The people will be very frightened and give many alms.

The Nile floods for forty days straight, beginning on 7 June, and recedes for another forty;[36] during these floods there is no lack of food, for in this period bakers and other food merchants are free to sell their goods for however much they want, although they use their discretion. After the eighty days are over, however, the consul of the squares determines the price of the foods, especially of bread; he does this only once a year, for these officers are appointed after the flooding of the Nile.[37]

Some lands are well irrigated, others have too much or too little, for they are in various positions, some high, others low, others in the middle, and they fix the price of grain accordingly. After the forty days of flood they hold a huge festival, turning Cairo upside down in revelry, cries and music, for on this day each family takes a boat, adorns it with many precious fabrics and fills it with delicious food – poultry, meat, confections – and they carry torches; all the people are found in boats that day, everyone according to his means. The sultan goes in person with his chief officers to a walled canal, called 'the greater canal'; he takes a hoe and starts smashing the wall, and his officers follow suit.[38] They each smash a bit until the wall is destroyed, and the Nile water at once rushes through and flows into other canals, passing through all the canals in all the suburbs and the city; on that day Cairo becomes a Venice, for one can go by boat through all the settlements of Egypt. The festival lasts seven days and seven nights, and in that one week a merchant or artist will spend his annual salary on food, pleasures, torches, perfumes and music. This was one of the customs surviving from ancient Egypt.

Outside Cairo to the south, bordering the suburb of Bab Zuweila, is the sultan's citadel built at the edge of the mountain al-Muqattam; it is surrounded by fine, high and strong walls, and within are marvellous buildings in a lavish style, which we'll ignore here for the sake of brevity.[39] But in short all the buildings and courtyards are paved with marble of various colours, made piece by piece, and the roofs are all painted with gold and fine colours; their beautiful windows are glazed in different colours, as in some parts of Europe. The doors are all of inlaid wood, adorned with gold and other fine colours. The buildings are bestowed on the sultan's family, some for the wives and others for concubines, eunuchs and guards. There are places where the sultan eats in public, where he gives audience to the ambassadors of great rulers and where he demonstrates his splendour in ceremonies.

6.24. The customs, clothes and practices of the people of Cairo and its suburbs

The Cairenes are likeable and jolly, talking endlessly but getting little done, as in all large cities. Some busy themselves in trade and arts, but rarely venture outside their districts; many spend their lives studying law, and a few study the arts, but the colleges are full of scholars, even if little profit is to be had there. The townsfolk are well dressed in winter with woollen fabrics and full cotton robes; in summer they wear thin linen shirts, and over that another garment of cloth mixed with stripes of coloured silk. Some wear camlet, and large turbans of Indian crape on their head. Women adorn themselves with many riches, especially garlands of gems on their necks and foreheads, and on their heads other precious items, long and narrow like a cannon a palm high. They wear little dresses with narrow sleeves of every kind of worked, embroidered cloth and fabric, a marvel of beauty, and cloaks of a very fine, smooth cloth made from Indian cotton. Over their faces are very thin, coarse black veils, made of what looks like human hair, so that they can see everyone else but nobody can see their faces.[40] On their feet they wear buskins and pretty shoes like the Turks.

The women are rather proud and have a high reputation, and, since none of them deign to spin or sew or even cook, their husbands buy everything already cooked; few except large families even have a kitchen in their house. These women have great freedom and authority over the men, so while the husband goes to his shop his wife gets dressed, fits herself out, puts on perfumes and rides a donkey into town to have fun visiting her family – or rather her friends. Both men and women ride donkeys, and some make a living by providing for transport large ones like hackney horses,[41] well furnished with nice trappings. The Cairenes ride often, paying a wagon for half the day; men ride alone, but women take a wagon boy with them. There are countless people in the city who barely go a quarter of a mile without riding their donkeys.

In the streets are innumerable people selling goods like fruit, cheese, raw and cooked meat; there are also water-carriers with heaps of large skins carried on camels and other animals, for the city is around two miles from the Nile.[42] Many poor men carry around their neck a single skin fitted with a brass tube at its mouth, and pretty damascened cups; they cry in the square 'Who wants a drink?' and earn a living by charging half a penny per cup. They don't get their water from the river but buy it from the water-carriers, keeping it in earthen pots in their shops, and whenever a skin is empty they go fill another up from the shop.

Throughout the city are huge numbers of poulterers who sell chickens that they hatch easily.[43] Some in this profession take

5,000 eggs or more and put them together in multi-layered ovens, with each level having its own opening; under the oven they lay a fire of moderate heat, and finally after seven days the chickens hatch quickly and leave the oven through the opening. Their owners collect them in large vessels and sell them on to retailers; they put a bottomless measure in the buyer's basket and fill it with chickens, then they remove the measure, leaving the chickens in the basket without disturbing or exciting them. The buyers grow them in their house until they are large enough to sell in the city. Those who hatch the chickens similarly earn a good living, but pay a substantial tribute to the ruler.

The stalls in the city shops stay open until midnight, at least the ones that sell food, but the other craftsmen and merchants close up before 11 p.m. and go making merry in one suburb after another. The Cairenes are disreputable in their conversation and have no shame with each other; a father will ask his son how many times he screwed his wife last night, a son will like-wise ask his mother how many times his father banged her, and a mother grumbles to her son that his father never lasts long enough to give her pleasure. Every day husbands go before a judge with their wives – the wife complaining that she gets it only once a night, the husband denying it and says he does more – so divorces happen daily, and everyone changes their partner, as will be explained later in the present work on the laws of Muhammad. Moreover, the author has seen dishonour-able things in the city that it would be very shameful to relate.

The city's craftsmen hold a procession for one of their own when he invents some elegant or ingenious thing or triumphs in something: they dress him in a brocade tunic and lead him accompanied by pipers and trumpets and drummers, receiving money from every shop with which to reward him. The author has seen one celebrated for forging a chain for a flea and putting it in chains on a piece of paper, and he went around showing it off and getting money for it.[44] Likewise, he saw some fool, one of those who carry water skins on their necks, challenged by another to carry a full calfskin fixed with an iron chain; it hung down and he bore the chain on his bare shoulders for seven days in a row, from morning to evening. On the last day the chain cut into his shoulder, but he kept up the pretence, so he won and triumphed in pride, accompanied by various musicians and by all the water-carriers of Cairo – perhaps more than 3,000.

By and large, the city dwellers are timid, keeping no weapons, barely even a cheese knife, in the house; when they fight they use their fists, but there are hundreds of men around to watch the dispute, and the quarrellers do not leave until they've made peace. The people eat plenty of buffalo meat and beans; small families dine at a round table, whereas larger ones use a long table, as at court and during celebratory meals.

One legal school of the Moors,[45] called al-Hanafi, permits the eating of horsemeat; when a horse is crippled the butchers of that school buy it, fatten it and then kill it, and the meat flies off the shelves. The Turks, Mamluks and most of Asia are of this school, but, although the Turks are allowed horsemeat, they do not touch it. In this city, or rather throughout the kingdom of Egypt, there are four schools, each different from the others in the ceremonies of sharia law – that is, the prescriptions of both civil and canon law – yet all are defined and bound by Muslim scripture.[46] For in ancient times there were four teachers with the ingenuity to define particular things in terms of universals, but each understood the scripture differently from the others; these four had great esteem and their rules were named after them. Muslims follow one of the four teachers, but nobody can change from one school to another, except learned men who understand the first principles of things.

In the city are four chief justices,[47] who give judgements on important matters, and under them are innumerable judges; in every district are found two or three judges for lesser matters. If a person from one school brings a suit against a person from another, the plaintiff goes to his own judge, but the defendant can appeal to the head of the four, who is of the Shafi'i school. If someone wants to do something forbidden in his school and permitted in another, it will be discovered, and his own judge will severely punish him. Likewise, there are also different imams; each school prays in its own way, but, although there are differences, they express no hatred or hostility on this account, and this is especially true of the common folk. Admittedly, the teachers often speak with one another, arguing on particular matters, and each seeks to defend his own teacher's rule, but none of them will speak ill of the opposing teachers, because doing so entails a very serious corporal punishment. All are equal in religion, for they keep to the rule of (Abu 'l-Hasan) al-Ash'ari, their leading theologian, whose rule is observed in Africa and Asia, except among the heretical Sufi, who stand outside the four schools and the rule of al-Ash'ari. To detail the causes of the differences between the four teachers would be too difficult and tedious, for those causes are contained in the author's little work on 'The Religion and Law of Muhammad According to the School of Maliki'. That school is followed all over Africa, and also in Egypt, Syria and Arabia; Maliki was a great teacher of the Moors in Medina, where Muhammad's body lies.

In Cairo they subject wrongdoers to cruel punishments, especially those sentenced in the sultan's court. They hang robbers, and, as for murderers, traitors and those who disobey the sultan's orders, they cut them in half crosswise: two servants of the ministry of justice hold the victim down by the feet and head while the executioner strikes him hard with a two-handed sword, and, when he is cut in two, they put the upper part on quicklime so that he survives for a quarter of an hour, talking – a fearful thing to see and hear. Brigands and rebels against the sultan they flay alive, filling their skin with bran and sewing it up to look like a living person; then they put it on a camel and lead it through the city, calling out his crime. This is the cruellest justice in the world, for the man is in agony while the executioner works, dying only when he reaches the navel; if the executioner wants him not to suffer, he can begin flaying at the navel, but not without his superiors' permission. As for those in prison for a debt they cannot pay, the prison captain will satisfy the creditor and then hold the debtor prisoner for ever, claiming four times what he paid for him. Every day he releases him from prison, bound to a companion by the neck on a short chain locked with iron links, and a servant goes with them; all day long they go begging for the love of God, and in the evening they bring back what they've earned, but the captain keeps one part for his expenses, and another for the lodging, and another to pay the servant who accompanies

them, leaving only a little to pay the poor men's debts. Sometimes the earnings don't cover the expenses and so the same
thing happens to them as to those who must pay a fine but don't
have the money: the captain buys them from the officers for a
lesser sum and holds them for ever his prisoners and debtors.
Wicked captains make a lot of money from this line of work.

In the city old women go crying through the streets, but it is
impossible to understand them, for they are like barbaric masters: their job is to cut the tips of the crests of nature from
women, as is the custom in Egypt, and as they are commanded
to do by Muhammad, but they only do it in Egypt and the land
of Syria.

6.25. The sultan, his principal ministers, and other officers, rank by rank

In AD 1517, he[48] was deprived of his title and authority by the
Grand Turk Selim, who changed all the sultan's hierarchies and
laws. But because the author lived in the time of the sultan,
making three journeys to Egypt, he witnessed and studied its
life and customs, as has already been narrated in the present
work, and likewise he informed himself of the court and the
sultan's hierarchy, as follows now.

6.26. The sultan

A highly esteemed mamluk, the sultan would be elected from
the principal ministers who are also mamluks. These mamluks
are Christians from the province of Circassia above the Black
Sea, which the Tartars would often raid, kidnapping men and
boys and taking them to the city of Caffa,[49] where they would
be sold on to merchants who brought them to Cairo. The sultan buys them and at once makes them renounce their faith,
teaching them to read and write in Arabic and to speak Turkish, and step by step they rise in rank and title. The custom that
the sultan should be a mamluk is modern – only about 250 years

old – and was brought about by the decline of the house of Saladin, a sultan from the Asian nation of al-Corduli,[50] who live in tents like the Arabs.

This occurred in the time of [. . .],[51] the last king of Jerusalem, who wanted to capture Cairo and had already received tribute from the caliph, an imprudent man.[52] The legal scholars and judges of Cairo, with the caliph's consent, summoned Asad ad-Din (Shirkuh) and his son Saladin from Asia,[53] appointing one of them captain general against the king of Jerusalem. Asad ad-Din, the prince of the Kurds, arrived in Cairo with 50,000 of his own cavalry,[54] but the caliph appointed Saladin captain general, giving him the authority to collect and spend the revenues from Egypt. Saladin began to organise his armies, and then attacked the Christians, pursuing them until the sack of Jerusalem and all of Assyria. On his return, he plotted to murder the captains of the caliph's two guards – the guard of Ethiopian slaves and that of Slavic slaves – who were the caliph's ministers and state governors. When he'd killed the two captains of the guard, the caliph, seeing that he now had no defence against Saladin, had the idea of poisoning him; but Saladin, out of caution, killed the caliph of Cairo and demanded obedience to the caliph of Baghdad.[55] Thus the schismatic caliphate of Cairo fell, having reigned for 230 years, and there remained only the true caliph of Baghdad.

But after this schism ended, another arose among the kings, for the grand sultan was in Baghdad, and Saladin, when he killed the caliph, saw his own power and made himself sultan. The sultan of Baghdad was from another Asian nation who ruled Mazandaran and Khwarazm, two provinces on the river Gance.[56] The two sultans wanted to go to war with each other, but, before they could, the sultan of Baghdad was put to the test, for during his reign the Tartars began to cross the river Gance and enter Khorasan, so he was forced to defend it.[57] At that time the sultan of Egypt could not leave his state, fearing the Christians would return to Syria for revenge.

Saladin realised that he had lost most of the men he'd brought from Asia: some were killed in the wars with Christians, others died of plague and the rest had become ministers of the kingdom.

He was therefore lacking soldiers, and began to buy slaves from Circassia, whom the rulers of Armenia would capture and sell in Cairo. Saladin acquired a great number of them, making them renounce their faith and learn the practice of arms and the Turkish language, which was his own; within a few years there were an infinite number of these slaves, all of them capable and competent, so he began to appoint them as generals and ministers. Upon his death the state remained under the control of his house for around fifty years, and his successors also bought these slaves and increased their race, so that one day, when Saladin's house fell, the slaves elected an esteemed mamluk named Baibars. From that time until the present, when one sultan died the mamluks elected another, rather than passing the kingdom from father to son; nor would they elect a mamluk who had once been Christian but then renounced, nor one unable to speak Circassian and Turkish. Many kings sent their young sons to Circassia to learn its language and rustic customs in the hope that they would become sultan, but their hopes were never realised, for the mamluks would never consent to it. This is the origin of Mamluk rule, and of their princes, called kings, from the beginning to the present.

6.27. Ad-dawadar

This is the second rank after sultan, appointed at the sultan's discretion, and given the authority to command, report back to him, assign and cancel duties, organise and send away provisions, as if he spoke in the sultan's person; he holds a court not too different from that of the sultan.

6.28. Al-amir al-kabir

The third minister of the kingdom, roughly the same as a captain general. He leads armies against the Arabs and rebels, and installs castellans and town governors; he has freedom in the treasury, spending money on whatever he deems necessary.

6.29. Na'ib al-saltana

The fourth minister, who serves as the sultan's deputy in Syria, governing that whole state as if in the sultan's person; he collects and spends its revenues as he sees fit, except for the citadels of Syrian cities which are guarded for the sultan by their castellans. This deputy sultan of Syria is obliged to give so many thousands of *sherifi* each year.

6.30. Ustadar

The fifth officer, who governs the sultan's house and takes care of furnishing the sultan and his family with food, clothing and household items. A sultan always appoints, from those he esteems, an old man who raised him since boyhood and taught him virtue.

6.31. Amir akhur

The sixth officer, entrusted to furnish the sultan's court with horses and camels to carry loads, as well as their provisions and food; he distributes horses among the sultan's family according to his judgement and their rank.

6.32. Amir alf

The seventh rank, held by certain great mamluks, equivalent to the colonel in Europe. Each of them is captain of 1,000 mamluks; there are many of them, and they direct battles and have the freedom of the sultan's armoury.

6.33. Amir mi'a

These are officers of the eighth rank, equivalent to constables; each of them is captain of 100 mamluks accompanying the sultan when he rides, and similarly when he engages in combat.

6.34. Khazindar

The ninth rank is the treasurer, who keeps the accounts of the kingdom's revenues and collects the state's ordinary revenues from the officers; he is obliged to give an account to the sultan of all the revenues that he handles. He deposits any money to be spent with the bankers, and the rest he keeps in the sultan's citadel.

6.35. Amir silah

This great officer of the tenth rank takes care of the sultan's weapons; everything under his authority is locked in a large room and he looks after it, cleaning, preparing and restoring items. There are many mamluks under him in the governance of the grand sultan's armoury.

6.36. Tasht khanah

This grand office is the wardrobe keeper, who keeps the sultan's clothes well sewn and in good repair; he receives a suitable amount from the ustadar, spending it according to the sultan's orders, for at court they give each person with an office or title a livery – a robe of brocade, velvet or satin. On the day he receives his robe, an officer will go through Cairo, accompanied by many mamluks, showing himself off as an officer and servant of the sultan.

There are countless other officers, as for instance one who is in charge of the sultan's drink, carrying clean water and water mixed with sugar and other flavourings. Other officers are called *farashin*, chamber-grooms, who are in charge of dressing rooms with arrases and carpets, furnishing and removing items, and tending the wax candles, which are mixed with ambergris to give off light and scents as they burn.

Other officers, the *shababatiyya*, are grooms who accompany the sultan on foot when he rides; the *tabarkhania* carry halberds, and also accompany him when he rides or gives audience. The *ad-dawiyya* carry lights in front of the sultan's carriage when he travels through the countryside; from among these officers they choose an executioner when one is needed, because every time he carries out public justice they go with him to learn the trade, especially that of flaying men alive, and torturing them for a confession. Others are called *su'a*, who carry letters from Cairo to Syria on foot, each of them going sixty miles a day, for there is no mountain or swamp between the two – the country is all sand. There are others who also carry letters, but ride camels and go on matters of the most importance.[58]

6.37. The sultan's soldiers

The sultan's soldiers are divided into four parts. The first are *khassakiya*, that is the cavalry, who are capable and competent at arms, and from these are drawn the city's castellans and captains of the guard. They march in the sultan's armies; some are paid by the treasury in ready cash, others receive income from vassal towns and ksars. The next group are the *sayfiya*, who only carry swords and go on foot; they are paid by the sultan's treasury in ready cash. Then there are the *qaranisa* or 'prospective ones', who are not among the paid soldiers; they receive only expenses, but when a paid mamluk dies one of them takes his place. The last are *al-jalab*, new mamluks who have studied neither the Turkish nor the Moorish languages, and have not achieved any excellence.

The officers appointed to govern the most general things

6.38. Nazir al-khass

This is an officer like a constable or rather a chamberlain, whose job it is to administer the customs and taxes from the sultan's entire state, collect the profits and then sign them over to the treasury. He also runs the Cairo customs office personally, earning hundreds and thousands of *sherifi* from it; but he pays a million *sherifi* upon taking up the position, which he earns back within six months.

6.39. Katib as-sirr

This is the sultan's secretary, who has the job of replying to letters, drawing up briefs on the sultan's behalf, keeping census records on the Egyptian fields, and collecting the profits from the administrators under his authority.

6.40. Al-muaqqi

This is another secretary of lower rank but more faithful to the sultan; his job is to look over the briefs to see if they match the sultan's commission. Then the sultan puts his signature in the space left below by the secretary. But the secretary employs many scribes who keep to a rule in writing the briefs, and the *muaqqi* rarely finds something to cancel, for they have already done their job.

6.41. Al-muhtasib

This is an important official, like a consul of the square, who has the authority to govern food prices and weights and measures; he keeps a court where he punishes and fines those who break the established rules. He also raises and lowers food prices depending partly on how much the ships supply from al-Sa'id and er-Rif, but more importantly on the flooding of the Nile. In Cairo the author has heard that this official raises 1,000 *sherifi* a day in his position, not only from Cairo itself, but from all the officials in all the towns of Egypt, who pay him tribute.

6.42. Amir al-hajj

This is a changing office, but one of great dignity and importance; he leads the caravan that goes to Mecca once a year. The sultan chooses the richest and most competent mamluk and appoints him to the job; the amir spends countless ducats on the journey, for he wants to travel in splendour and comfort, bringing other mamluks to look after the caravan, which goes out and returns after three months. You can hardly imagine the harm, the inconvenience, the stress and effort that afflict the leader on the journey, not even counting his enormous expenditure that affords no benefit to either the sultan or the merchants of the caravan.

There are other officers, but it is not important to discuss them here.

6.43. Giza

Giza is a town on the Nile opposite the Old Town of Cairo, and an island separates the two. It is cultured and well populated, with many fine buildings erected by the great Mamluks for their pleasure outside the bustle of Cairo. There are many craftsmen and merchants, especially of livestock, which the Arabs bring from Barca; but it upsets the animals to go by boat, so the merchants buy them and lead them to Cairo. The Cairo butchers also visit every day to trade.

On the Nile are the city mosque and other handsome, cheerful buildings, and around them many gardens and date farms. Many of the townsfolk go to Cairo to conduct their business, returning home in the evening. If anyone should wish to visit

the Pyramids the route goes through the town, but between them is only a sandy desert, although there is water that remains from the flooding of the Nile. However, whoever wants to travel without trouble will bring someone from Giza as a guide.

6.44. Al Mu'allaqa

Al Mu'allaqa is a little town around three miles from the Old Town, built on the river Nile by the Egyptians; it has some culture and fine buildings, especially the mosque on the Nile.[59] Around the town are many groves of dates and Egyptian figs. The inhabitants follow roughly the same customs as those of Cairo.

6.45. Khanka

Khanka is a large city built at the edge of the desert leading to Sinai, around six miles from Cairo; there are fine buildings and two handsome mosques and madrasas. Between this town and Cairo are many date gardens, but there are no settlements from the town to the port of Sinai, which is around forty miles. The inhabitants are rich, for they sell many goods, especially when the caravan departs for Syria; the groups assemble here, so there is always a greater need than in Cairo, which supplies this town with all its food and other things. Around it nothing grows but date trees.

In the town are two main roads, one going to Arabia and the other to Syria. There is no other water but what remains in the canals; when the Nile floods the canals are filled up, spreading out through plains and forming little lakes, from which the water reaches the town, entering the reservoirs by pipes.

6.46. Al-Massarah

Al-Massarah is a little town built after Cairo on the Nile, around thirty miles from Cairo on the east bank; a great quantity of sesame grows there, and there are many mills working to make oil from the seeds. All the inhabitants work on the farms, except for a few who keep shops.

6.47. Beni Suef

Beni Suef is a little town built on the African side of the Nile around 120 miles from Cairo; around it is a fine countryside for growing flax and hemp; the town's excellent flax, from which a wondrously durable linen is made, supplies all of Egypt and is sold as far off as Tunis in Barbary. However, the Nile continually shrinks the town's fields, especially the year the author was there, when the river carried away part of the date groves, and

almost a third of the land. The townsfolk all work the flax –
some sow it, some pull it up, some scutch it, some dry it and
some take it to Cairo. Upriver from the town are found crocodiles who eat humans and other animals, as will be seen at more
length in the section on animals below.

6.48. Al-Minya

Al-Minya is a splendid city built in the Muslim era by a viceroy
named al-Khasib, the close associate of a caliph of Baghdad;[60]
it is high up on the African side of the Nile, and around it are
many gardens and vineyards producing excellent fruit, much of
which goes to Cairo, although it does not arrive fresh, for the
town is eighty miles away. There are fine buildings in the town:
palaces, mosques and some ancient Egyptian ruins. The inhabitants are rich in land and money, for they go to trade in Gaoga
in the Black Land.

6.49. Faiyum

This ancient city was built by a Pharaoh who lived before the
Hebrews left Egypt; using the Hebrews to make bricks and
perform other labours, he had the town built on a branch of
the Nile, high up where there are countless fruits and olives,
although the olives are only good for eating, not for oil. Joseph,
son of Israel, was buried here, though his body was later taken
away by Moses when the Hebrews fled Egypt. The city is highly
cultured and well populated and there are many craftsmen,
especially cloth-weavers.

6.50. Manfalut

Manfalut is a huge ancient city built by the Egyptians and
destroyed by the Romans; in the Muslim era it began to be resettled, though hardly at all compared to its original state. Traces of

the Egyptians can still be seen today: tall, broad columns and other porticos with verse inscriptions in the Egyptian language, and beside the Nile a large, ruined building, apparently a temple. The townsfolk are always finding stamped coins of gold, silver and lead, with Egyptian letters on one side, and the heads of ancient kings on the other. The town's fields are very fertile, but it is extremely hot and the crocodiles do great damage, for which reasons the Romans abandoned it. The modern inhabitants are rich, for they go to trade in the Land of the Blacks.

6.51. Asyut

Asyut is a very ancient city built by the Egyptians on the Nile, around 150 miles from Cairo. It is a city wondrous for its size and its ancient ruined buildings, on which are found countless epitaphs in the ancient Egyptian script. In the Muslim era the city was inhabited by many nobles and knights, and there is great nobility and wealth even today. There are a hundred or so Coptic Christian households, and three or four churches; outside is a Christian monastery where more than a hundred monks live, who never eat meat or fish, but only bread, herbs and oil – a delicate diet with no grease at all. The monastery is very wealthy; the monks give food to every passing traveller, for they keep a great number of animals and dovecotes with which to feed others, who are also permitted to stay there for three days at the monks' expense.

6.52. Akhmim

Akhmim, around 300 miles from Cairo on the Asian side of the Nile, is the oldest city in Egypt, built by Akhmim, son of Mizraim, son of Cush, son of Ham.[61] It was already ruined when the Muslims first arrived in Egypt, for the reason mentioned above, so that only traces of the city remain, that is, the foundations of walls. However, its columns, porticos and large stones were all carried across the Nile when the city of El Mansha was built on the other side.

6.53. El Mansha

El Mansha is a modern city built on the African side of the Nile by a caliph's viceroy; he had the columns and large stones carried over and constructed the city with them. But it enjoys neither beauty nor a good location; all the streets are narrow and in the summer one can't go out because of the dust, but it has a great abundance of grain and animals. The city and its territory have an African ruler from the Hawwara Berber people; he succeeded to this rule from a line of Hawwara princes who helped Jawhar, the slave who built Cairo. As soon as the caliph al-Qa'im arrived at Cairo, he gave the territory of Akhmim as a reward to the Hawwara prince; building Akhmim did not give the prince any pleasure, because the Arabs made it hard for him, so he fled them and built El Mansha on the other side. The territory has remained in his house ever since, and they have always paid taxes to the sultan; but in the time of Suleiman, the new emperor of the Turks,[62] the house has been deprived of its rule and everything was confiscated for the Turkish treasury.

6.54. Girga

Girga was a very rich Christian monastery named after St George, around six miles from El Mansha; it was surrounded by a sizeable territory, with fields and pastures. More than 200 monks lived there, giving food to all the passing travellers, and sending the rest to the patriarch in Cairo, who distributed it to the poor Christians there. Around a century ago there was a terrible plague in Egypt, and all the monks died, leaving the monastery deserted for three years;[63] nobody would go to live there, so the ruler of El Mansha put up walls and many houses, which he gave to labourers, craftsmen and merchants as a large town. He went to live there in person, for there were beautiful gardens on high hills from the time of the monks. Then the Jacobite patriarch[64] complained to the sultan about this ruler, so, to appease both parties, the sultan ordered the ruler to build another monastery outside the new town, and to pay it a pension from the fields large enough to sustain thirty monks.

6.55. Al-Khiam

Al-Khiam is a little town on the Nile built in the Muslim era, but only Christian Jacobites live there; they all work in the fields, raising chickens and geese and keeping countless dovecotes, selling ten pigeons for around two *baiocchi*. Around the town are some Christian monasteries where foreigners can stay, and there is no Muslim except for the commissioner and his family.

6.56. Barbanda[65]

Barbanda is a city built by the ancient Egyptians on the Nile, around 400 miles from Cairo. It was destroyed in the Roman era, and at present only ruins can be seen, but its nobility moved to a city named Esna. In the desert around the town one finds many ancient gold and silver coins, as well as many excellent emeralds.

6.57. Qena

Qena is an ancient town built by the Egyptians on the Nile opposite Barbanda, walled with unbaked bricks; it has a great abundance of grain but little culture, and its wretched inhabitants do nothing but work the fields. In the town they weigh the merchandise that comes by river from Cairo to Mecca, for it is around ten miles from the Red Sea through the desert, where there is no water; on the coast is a port called El Qoseir, where there are many huts for unloading the merchandise. The houses and shops of the port are all built of matting and much good fish is caught there. Opposite the port, on the Asian side of the Red Sea, is another called Yanbu; here they weigh (goods) to go to Medina, where the body of Muhammad lies. The city of Qena gets its grain from Mecca and Medina, for it has little of its own.

6.58. Esna

Esna was formerly called Syene,[66] but when the Arabs took over they gave it the new name, for Arabic has a word like Syene that means 'ugly', whereas Esna means 'shining', and the city is now deservedly called the shining city. It was built on the African side of the Nile and it has since fallen into ruin; when the Romans lost Egypt it remained deserted, but was resettled in the Muslim era, though much less than in ancient times, as one can still judge from the huge circumference of the wall foundations. There are large buildings and marvellous tombs with epitaphs, some in Egyptian letters and others in Roman. The inhabitants are very rich in grain, animals and money, for they go to trade in the kingdom of Nubia, both on the Nile and through the desert.

6.59. Aswan

Aswan is a large and ancient city, surrounded by fertile grain fields, built by the Egyptians on the eastern bank of the Nile around eighty miles from Esna. The town is richly populated and commercial, for it is on the river and borders the kingdom of Nubia. But one cannot navigate past the city on the Nile, for it spreads out in the plains and its shallowness does not permit sailing. Aswan likewise borders the desert leading to the city of Suakin, where Ethiopia begins along the Red Sea; in the city it is very hot in summer. Its inhabitants are almost all brown-skinned, because they are mixed with the people of Nubia and Ethiopia. There are many ancient Egyptian buildings and high towers that the Egyptians call *barba*.[67] Beyond the city to the east there are no cities or any other cultured settlements, only villages inhabited by a brown-skinned race who speak their own language, mixed with Arabic, Egyptian[68] and Ethiopic; these families are subject to the Beja, who live and travel like Arabs in the countryside. The sultan's domain ends with this city.

These are the most famous cities on the main branch of the Nile that the author has seen. Some of them he has visited, others only passed by, but he has been fully informed by their inhabitants and by the boatmen who took him from Cairo to Aswan and back to Qena. From there he crossed the desert to the Red Sea and sailed over to the ports of Yanbu and Jeddah in Arabia Deserta, which may be omitted here as they are in Asia, not Africa. But the author, God willing, has a great desire to discuss in another work the parts of Asia he has seen, such as Arabia Deserta, Felix and Petraea; likewise the Asian part of Egypt, Babylon and parts of Persia, Armenia and Tartary, all of which the author visited in his youth. Similarly the many islands he saw on his last journey from Fez to Constantinople and then to Egypt by sea, and on his return from Egypt to the parts of Italy. When he has returned, by the grace of God, safe and sound from his voyage in Europe, he will at once, with careful consideration, arrange his little book in a good order; first will come the noblest and most worthy part, which is Europe, then with all his labour and diligence he will put Asia next, and finally the present work will appear as the third part.

BOOK 7.

RIVERS, ANIMALS, PLANTS

Here begins the discourse on Africa's famous rivers, starting with the west coast of Barbary.

7.1.1. The Tensift

The Tensift is a great river beginning in the Atlas mountains to the east, near the town of Animmei in the territory of Marrakesh, and extending north across the plains until it enters the ocean near Safi in the Doukkala region. Several rivers flow into it on its course to the sea. One is the Assif el-Mal, which begins on the Hintata mountain near Marrakesh and descends through the plains until it enters the Tensift; another is the Nfis, which starts in the Atlas near Marrakesh and flows rapidly through the city until it enters the Tensift. The Tensift itself is very deep, but in several places one can cross on horseback, even though the water reaches above one's stirrups. On foot, one needs to strip off one's clothing to cross. Near Marrakesh is a bridge built by al-Mansur, the king and caliph of that city; it has five arches, more beautifully constructed than anything else in all Africa. Three arches were destroyed by Abu Dabbus,[1] the last king and caliph of Marrakesh, in an effort to stop the advance of Yaqub, founder of the Marinid dynasty. His plan did not help him at all.

7.1.2. Tassawin

Tassawin comprises two rivers that begin in the Ghojdama mountain, about three miles from one another; they flow through a plain in the province of Haskoura to join the Oued el Abid. These two rivers share a name, which is Tassawt in the singular and Tassawin in the plural, meaning 'heads' in the African language.

7.1.3. The Wad al-Abid (Oued el Abid), or the River of Slaves

This river begins among high, cold mountains in the Atlas, passing through arduous valleys on the borders between Haskoura and Tadla, flowing north across the plains into the river Oum Er-Rbia. It is rather large, especially in May when the mountain snows melt.

7.1.4. The Oum Er-Rbia

The Oum Er-Rbia is a great river that comes from the high Atlas mountains along the border between Tadla and the region of Fez, flowing out across the plains known as Adekhsan. From there it flows through narrow valleys where there is a bridge built by Abu al-Hasan, fourth king of the Marinids. Beyond the bridge to the south, the river crosses the plains between Doukkala and Tamasna, finally meeting the ocean near the walls of Azemmour. In winter and spring, one cannot wade across the river, but those living in the villages along the banks often make large rafts of inflated bladders to move people and possessions across.[2] Various small streams likewise flow into this river. When the rainy season begins in Africa, late in May, one can catch great numbers of fish called *alaccia* (round sardinella) in Italy, disliked by the whole population of Azemmour. Many caravels transport these fish in salt to the kingdom of Portugal, as mentioned regarding the city of Azemmour.

7.1.5. The Bou Regreg

This river begins in one of the Atlas mountains, flowing through many valleys and forests until it emerges among the hills and extends across a plain to the ocean, where the two cities Salé and Rabat are situated, at the edge of the kingdom of Fez. The cities have no port but the river mouth itself, which is difficult to enter by boat. The boat must be navigated by an expert or it is sure to run aground on the sand. If this river weren't so hard to navigate, these two cities could not keep themselves safe from even the smallest fleet of any powerful Christian king.

7.1.6. The Baht

This river flows north from the Atlas among mountains and woods, emerging among hills, and then spreads out into a plain in the province of Azgar, feeding into marshes, valleys and lakes. These lakes contain innumerable fish, amazingly large and plump – sardinella, eel and nase.[3] Arab shepherds dwell among the marshes and lakes, living off their flocks and the fish; they eat so much fish, milk and butter that many of them fall sick with morphoea. There are known fords where one can wade across the river at any time except in the flood season or when the snow is melting. Several streams from the Atlas mountains feed into this river too.

7.1.7. The great Sebou

The Sebou has a similar name,[4] and begins in a mountain called Selelgo in the province Al Haouz, in the kingdom of Fez. It arises from a huge spring in a forbidding forest, flows past many valleys, mountains and hills, and extends across the plain six miles from Fez. After crossing the plain between the regions of al-Habat and Azgar, it continues to the ocean near al-Ma'mura, near the city of Salé. Several streams lead into the river; the Ouergha and Aodor come from the Ghomara mountain, and several others from mountains in the region of the city of Taza. The river has a strong current, but there are several places for wading across, though not in winter or spring, when one can only cross in rickety little boats. It is joined by the river that flows past Fez, in their language called 'The River of Pearls'.[5] The Sebou is full of fish, especially during the season for sardinella, which, as I described in the section on the culture of Fez,[6] they catch in such great numbers that they sell for very little. Since the river mouth is very deep and wide it can receive large ships, as the Portuguese and Spanish have often shown. The river is perfectly navigable, but because the locals don't realise it they have no barges or boats for cargo. If the people of Fez were to use this river, grain would cost a fraction of its usual price; the author himself has seen grain brought on wagons from Azgar to Fez, each load charged one load for transport and sold for a third of a ducat, whereas if it were taken by boat it would sell for barely a quarter of a ducat.

7.1.8. The Loukkos

The Loukkos is a river beginning in the Ghomara mountains, extending west across the plains of al-Habat, where it flows from Azgar next to the city of Ksar el-Kebir, and ending at last in the ocean by the city of Larache, on the borders between Azgar and al-Habat. At the river mouth the city has a port, but it is very difficult to navigate, especially for someone inexperienced.[7]

7.1.9. The Mouloula

The river Mouloula begins in the Atlas mountains, on the borders between Taza and Debdou, but nearer the latter; it flows through harsh, dry plains called Terrest and Tafrata, before joining the river Moulouya.

7.1.10. The Moulouya

The Moulouya is a great river springing up in the Atlas, in the region of Al Haouz, fifteen miles from the town of Gerseluin. It flows through harsh, dry plains before entering an even harsher plain in the middle of the deserts of Angad and Garet. From there it flows below the mountain of Beni Iznassen and enters the Mediterranean not far from the city of Cazaza. One can always wade across this river in the hot season, and near the sea it has excellent fish.

7.1.11. The Za

The Za is a river beginning in the Atlas mountains, flowing through the desert of Angad on the borders between the kingdoms of Fez and Tlemcen. The author has never seen this river full, but it is very deep and has plenty of fish, even though the ignorant people of the region cannot catch them, for two reasons: first, they do not have the gear, and, second, the water is very clear and therefore bad for fishing.

7.1.12. The Tefna

The river Tefna is rather small, beginning in mountains on the borders of Numidia. It flows north through the desert of Angad, and it ends in the Mediterranean about five miles from the city of Tlemcen. It has no fish, except for very small ones that aren't any good.

7.1.13. The Mina

The Mina is a rather large river which comes down from the mountains near the city of Tagdemt, flowing across the plains by the city of al-Batha, then north into the Mediterranean.

7.1.14. The Chelif

The Chelif is a great river beginning in the Ouarsenis mountains; it descends through the desert plains on the borders of Tlemcen and Tenes, reaching the Mediterranean, where it separates the towns of Mazagran and Mostaganem. Huge numbers of excellent fish of all kinds and sizes are caught at its mouth.

7.1.15. The Sefsaia[8]

The Sefsaia is a river of middling size that starts in the Atlas mountains and flows across the Mitija plain near the city of Algiers. It enters the Mediterranean near the ancient city of Tamentfoust.

7.1.16. The Greater River[9]

From the highest mountains bordering the province of Zeb, this river flows down into the Mediterranean about three miles from the city of Bejaia. It does not swell with the rainy season or with snow. Fishermen from Bejaia rarely fish in this river, preferring instead the sea next to it.

7.1.17. The Suf-Jimar[10]

This river begins in mountains near Mount Aures and flows through dry countryside before entering the territory of

Constantine and passing below its cliffs; there it is joined by another stream and flows north among hills and mountains to end in the Mediterranean, dividing the territory of Collo from the ksar of Jijel.

7.1.18. The Yadugh[11]

This river, which is not very large, comes from mountains in the Constantine region and flows down eastward until it enters the Mediterranean by the city of Bona.

7.1.19. The Wad al-Barbar

This river begins in mountains bordering the territory of Urbs, flowing among hills and mountains and snaking around so many times that those travelling between Tunis and Bona must cross it two dozen times, without bridge or boat. Eventually it enters the Mediterranean by the deserted port of Tabarka, five miles from Beja as the crow flies.

7.1.20. The Mejerda

The Mejerda is a rather large river, with its source in the mountains that border the province of Zeb near the city of Tebessa. It flows north to the Mediterranean near Ghar al-Melh, forty miles from Tunis. During the rainy season the river swells to such an astounding degree that merchants and travellers sometimes wait two or three days for the water to subside, since there is no boat, even though the ford is six miles from Tunis. From this one can conclude that the Africans are an incompetent bunch with little brains or ingenuity.

7.1.21. The Gabes

This river begins in a desert to the south, and flows down through a sandy plain before entering the Mediterranean next to the city of Gabes. Its water tastes of sulphur and is very hot, so it needs to be left to cool for an hour before it is drinkable.

These are the notable rivers of Barbary; there are many other large ones (which we shall omit) from the present work to avoid describing unknown things at tedious length.

Here ends the section on the rivers of Barbary; next the rivers of Numidia, beginning with the river Sous.

7.2.1. The Sous

The great river Sous begins in the Atlas mountains that divide the region of Haha from that of Sous. It flows south among the mountains, emerging in the countryside, and flowing west into the ocean by Gartguessen. In winter the river swells enough to carry away and destroy many fields; in summer it stays quite low, so that one can easily wade across in several places.

7.2.2. The Draa

This river begins in the Atlas mountains at the border of Haskoura, flowing south through the province of Draa, then across the desert, emerging in the countryside, where grass grows in spring and the nearby Arabs come to pasture their camels. For the sake of this grass the Arabs start many murderous wars. In summer the river runs dry and one can cross on foot, but in winter it swells so much that one cannot cross at all, even by boat. In hot seasons the river water tastes of salt.

7.2.3. The Ziz

This river begins in the Atlas mountains where the Zanaga live,[12] flowing south among many mountains, passing the city of Gerseluin and then the countryside around al-Kheneg, Matgara and Reteb. From there it flows through the territory of Sijilmasa and among its farms, emerging in the desert and passing the ksar of Essaoaihila. It then forms a lake in the middle of a sandy desert where no one lives, although Arab hunters go to its shore, where they find plenty of excellent game.

7.2.4. The Ghir[13]

The Ghir is a river that also begins in the Atlas mountains and flows south through various deserts, passing through a settlement called Beni Gumi before becoming a lake in the middle of the desert. As was already mentioned in the first part of this work, Ptolemy calls it the Niger in his treatise on the divisions of Africa.[14]

7.2.5. The great Nile

The Nile and its courses are truly astounding, as are its animals, such as the sea horses and sea cows, and the vast numbers of savage crocodiles, as described in the chapters on the river Niger and the strange beasts of Africa.[15] In the Egyptian and Roman eras the crocodiles caused little harm, but they became worse when the Muslims conquered Egypt. In his treatise on wonders discovered in modern times, al-Mas'udi says that at the time of Ahmad ibn Tulun, viceroy of Egypt on behalf of Ja'far (ibn Muhammad) al-Mutawakkil, caliph of Baghdad in AH 270 (AD 883–84),[16] there was a large lead statue of a crocodile on which it was written in Egyptian letters that it had been found in the foundations of a temple of the pagan Egyptians. The viceroy had the statue destroyed and later that year the crocodiles began to do great damage; because of this the people believed that the statue had been fashioned under a particular constellation of the stars that protected against the animal.[17] It is also a miracle that the crocodiles in the Nile between Cairo and the sea do not hurt anyone, while those upstream of Cairo cause great harm.

Every year, the Nile floods Egypt beginning from 17 June, rising continually for forty days, before receding for another forty days. For they say that in Upper Ethiopia there are astonishing downpours at the beginning of May, but the currents of the river coming into Egypt slow down through May and into June. There are many opinions on where the Nile begins: some say in the Mountains of the Moon, others from many large springs, each far from the others, in the desert plains at the foot of that mountain. Those of the first opinion say the water flows so fast down the mountain that it goes underground and shoots up in these springs. Both opinions are guesses, since no one has ever seen it, nor is there any place from which one could see it. However, Ethiopian merchants doing business in Dongola say that towards the south the river opens into a lake, making it difficult to know where it comes from. Further south it divides into many branches, east and west, preventing people from travelling the full length of the Nile. Many Ethiopians who cross the countryside like Arabs say they sometimes lose their camels during mating season and journey a thousand miles south to find them; they have only ever seen the river as similar streams and lakes among dry mountains and deserts.

Al-Masʿudi says that in those mountains are wild men who run about like goats, eating grass and living in the desert like beasts.[18] This may be a lie, spread as it is by those who give the chronicler a little trust and credit. He also says that many emeralds can be found in those mountains, and this may be true.[19] If all that the cosmographers have said about the Nile were retold, everyone would be stupefied and astonished, and might not even believe it. Therefore no more mention will be made of it, lest any time should be wasted on implausible things.

Here ends the section on Africa's famous rivers. The next takes up the exotic, terrifying animals only found in Africa.

7.3

To avoid being too long-winded, this section will not mention all the animals of Africa, but only those not found in Europe or differing somehow from European animals: first the tame and wild beasts, then the tame and wild birds, then those living in and around the water, and finally the snakes and reptiles, both venomous and not, beginning with the largest. Despite the expectation that these should be written about as Pliny has done in his well-known work,[20] since he was so great and worthy a scholar of the arts and sciences – nevertheless, he was deceived on a few details, especially concerning Africa. The author does not blame Pliny himself, but rather those who related to him things that turn out not to be true, and those who wrote before him. But as the common Arabic proverb says: 'How can a child's piss foul the high seas?'

7.3.1. The elephant

The elephant is a wild but tameable animal, found in large numbers in the forests of the Land of the Blacks. They usually go in small groups and when they see people they avoid them, but if someone provokes an elephant it will grab him, throw him to the ground, flatten him underfoot and leave him stone dead. In Ethiopia, elephant hunters use a trick to catch them. They go to the deep forest and weave branches between the trees to form a large pen, leaving an opening between two trees. In that opening they make a door lying on the ground like a grate, which lifts up and closes at the pull of a rope. One of the hunters climbs a tree and holds the rope. When it gets dark the elephants come to sleep, and the moment they pass through the two trees of the gate, the hunter pulls the rope, trapping them and securing the rope. He then goes to call the other hunters, who come with their bows and shoot the animals with large arrows. Once the elephants are killed, the hunters cut out their tusks and sell them. These hunters ply a dangerous trade, for the elephants often escape the pen and kill everyone they find nearby. This is the way they hunt elephants in African Ethiopia, but there is another method in India and Upper Ethiopia.[21]

7.3.2. The giraffe

This animal is so wild that one rarely sees it, because it normally remains hidden in the woods and lives in deserts unfrequented by other animals. Whenever it sees people it flees, although it cannot move very quickly. It has a head like a camel, ears like an ox and feet like a [. . .].[22] Hunters do not capture adults, but obtain the young where they rest.

7.3.3. The camel

This tame and friendly animal is often encountered in Africa, especially in the deserts of Numidia and Libya, and also in Barbary in great numbers. The Arabs keep these animals as wealth and property, so, when they want to describe the wealth of a prince or noble, they do not speak of money or houses, but say: 'This person has this many thousand camels and that person has so many.' The Arabs who possess camels are all lords or at least free men, for with them they can live in the deserts where it is too dry for kings or rulers. The animals are found throughout Asia and Africa, and even in some parts of Europe. In Asia they are kept by the Tartars, Kurds, Daylamites and Turkomans, and the Turkish rulers in Europe keep them to carry supplies. In Africa they are kept in large numbers by the Arab and African tribes living in the Libyan deserts, and by the Arabs in Barbary. The kings of Barbary all use these animals to carry supplies and food.

The camels of Africa are better than those of Asia, namely of Arabia and elsewhere, for the latter need fodder every night to keep carrying their loads, while those of Africa can carry loads for forty or fifty days straight without fodder; all they need is to be relieved of their load in the evening and left to graze in the field on grass, thistles or branches. At the start of the journey the camel has to be fat on its sides and belly and in its fatty hump. Experience shows that, when this animal journeys with a full load for fifty days, it loses fat from its hump first; after another five days it loses from its belly, and, after another five, from its sides. When it has lost all its fat, it cannot even carry a hundred pounds of cargo. Asian merchants who make extended journeys give their camels grain along the way, even though this is very expensive, since each camel with cargo requires another to carry its grain; but the merchants are forced to do this because the camels are loaded with cargo each way, and therefore must be kept fat enough to make the return trip. The African merchants who travel to Ethiopia don't worry about the return, because the camels are loaded up only on the outward trip and are practically empty on the way back, since what they bring back from Ethiopia is much less than their cargo from Africa. As a result, when the camels arrive in Ethiopia they are thin and their backs are sore, so they are sold cheaply to the African desert-dwellers, who fatten them up. When the merchants want to return to Barbary or Numidia, just a few camels are enough for riding and carrying food, gold and a few light possessions.

These camels are divided into three kinds. The *hujun* are as tall as people, good for bearing loads, though they cannot do so until they are four years old.[23] An average one can carry at least a thousand Italian pounds. When one wants to load it up the camel must lie down on its belly; once loaded, it gets up. To make it lie down, one taps its knees or neck with a rod and it naturally does so. In Africa and elsewhere, they have castrated all the camels they want to keep strong for bearing cargo, retaining only one male for ten females. Camels with two humps are called *al-bakhti*; they are good for cargo and riding, but only found in Asia.[24] The third kind, the *rawahil*, are shorter than people, with slender legs, and only good for riding.[25] They run very swiftly, and many can ride 100 miles a day, some even more. All the Arab and Numidian nobles, along with the Africans of Libya, ride these camels, making journeys of a week or ten days through the desert with hardly any provisions. When the king of Timbuktu wants to send the merchants of Numidia a message, he sends one of these all the way from Timbuktu to Draa or Sijilmasa, covering 900 miles in seven or eight days. Those who carry out such tasks must have experience in the desert, and they demand 500 ducats to make the journey there and back.

These animals are in heat at the beginning of spring. Their herders take good care when one male is near another, for it will kill the other if it can. Woe to the herder who has ever mistreated the animal in the past, for if it remembers that beating it will seek revenge as if it were human, seizing his hair or shoulder in its mouth, tossing him up and letting him fall; then it will try to flatten him with its feet, leaving the poor herder dead on the ground. The mating season lasts at least forty days, and then they become gentle again.

While a camel can put up with hunger, it tolerates thirst even better, since it can go fifteen days without drinking. If the herder gives it water every three days the camel is harmed; he needs to give it water every fifth day, or every ninth, or at most in extreme situations every fifteenth. Camels are sensitive by nature and have some understanding. On several occasions, the author has seen that drivers who lead the camels from Ethiopia to Barbary, when they need to cover more ground for some reason, don't force their camels by beating them. Instead, they sing in a way especially suited to the camels, which start to lengthen their strides, speeding up without being struck or berated. These drivers achieve more by singing than horse-riders do by spurring the flanks of their mounts, and the latter can hardly equal the camels in speed.

In Cairo the author has seen men make camels dance by playing drums, and earn their living by doing so, which is astounding. The author begged and bribed someone who kept dancing camels to explain how they are taught to dance. He said that they take a young camel and when they want to give it a dancing lesson they put it in a room made just for this purpose, heated like a hammam so the floor burns the little camel's feet while they beat the drum. The young camel jumps about, lifting one foot after the other; they keep at it for a half hour, and then set it outside and give it food to eat. They keep up this lesson for ten months or a year, so that the camel acquires the habit of lifting its feet when it hears the drums, since its memory brings back the heat it felt in the hot room. Thus they earn a wretched living from the rabble. There are plenty of marvels to relate about this animal, but this is not the place to say more about it.

7.3.4. The Barbary horse

These horses are known in Italy and throughout Europe as Barbs, as they are from Barbary. But the name is erroneous, since the common horses in Barbary are like those everywhere else, but in Africa the ones of this breed are known in Arabic as 'Arabian horses', just as they are called in Syria, Egypt, Arabia Deserta and Felix, and even Asia. The African historians believe that this breed of horse lived wild in the Arabian deserts and then in modern times, after the Ishmaelites arrived,[26] the Arabs tamed and rode them. Then they grew in great numbers and spread throughout Africa, especially after the Arabs invaded. The author holds this view, since nowadays some of these wild horses are seen in the deserts of Arabia and some deserts of Africa; on his second trip to the Numidian deserts, he saw, only a stone's throw away, a colt of one-and-a-half years that was white with a curly mane, looking like a wild horse. The greatest test of speed for one of these horses is to see if it can overtake the *lamt* (oryx) or the ostrich; when it has done one of these it is valued at 1,000 ducats. The desert Arabs, like the Libyans who raise these horses, do not ride them for travel or war, but only for hunting. There are few of them in Barbary. The desert Arabs give these horses nothing but camel's milk once a day and once a night; this keeps them strong and lean, if a little thin, and when there is grass they let them eat it, but then do not ride them. Those kept by the kings of Barbary are less swift but more sleek and handsome, for they feed them grain. When needed, these horses are good for escaping raging enemies.

7.3.5. The wild horse

The wild horse is considered a savage animal and is not often seen. The desert Arabs hunt it for food and say it has tasty flesh, especially when young. One can catch it rarely, and never with dogs or horses. The Arabs catch them in traps set near the water that the horses frequent and cover them over with sand; when the horses set foot in the snare, it tightens and holds them fast – and they are caught.

7.3.6. The *lamt* (oryx)

This animal has the shape of an ox but is somewhat smaller, with horns and a softer hide, nearly white in colour, with pitch-black hooves. It runs so swiftly that no animal can match it except some of the Barbary horses mentioned above. Like wild goats or deer, it is caught more easily in the summer, when its hooves break due to the heat of the sand and its swift running, stopping it in its tracks; the hunters then catch it without much effort. In Africa this animal's hide is used to make tough shields, which only well-made guns can pierce, and which are worth a great deal.

7.3.7. The wild ox

This animal is just like an ox but smaller, and almost all of them are grey. It runs very fast and is found only in and around the desert. Its meat is delicious.

7.3.8. The wild donkey

In and around the deserts are found many of these grey donkeys. They run with great speed, able to outrun any animal but the Barbary horse. If one spots a human, it begins to bray and kick its heels, and then stops, so the person supposes he can approach and touch it – and then it runs off. These animals usually run in groups, especially when they graze and drink. The desert Arabs catch them with traps and other tricks. The meat of these donkeys is good, but when hot it smells bad and tastes rather gamey; if left to cool for two or three days after cooking, it is very good and flavourful.

7.3.9. The mountain cattle of Africa

All the domestic cattle from the mountains of Africa are rather small, about the size of two-year-old calves of other cows. The people living in the mountains use them to plough the land, saying they are tough and can withstand hard labour.

7.3.10. The *adimman* (*Ovis longipes* or Guinea sheep)

This is a very tame animal, exactly the shape of a ram and the height of an average donkey, with rather long, dangling ears. The people of Libya keep flocks of these animals. They produce plenty of milk, good butter and excellent cheese, with exquisite wool of just the right length. Like the females, the males have no horns and are very gentle. In his wild youth, the author rode one of the rams for about a quarter mile, which just shows its strength. This animal is only found in the desert of Libya, at least in numbers, but in Numidia if they come across one they treat it as a marvellous monster.

7.3.11. The (fat-tailed) sheep

These sheep are much like others but with wide tails. As they get fatter, their tails get fatter too, some weighing twenty-five or thirty pounds, even when they fatten themselves naturally. In Egypt, however, there are people who fatten their lambs by raising them in pens on barley bran and grain; the tails grow so fat that the sheep cannot move on their own. Their keepers make little carts to which they cleverly tie the tail so they can walk about. In the Egyptian city of Asyut, on the Nile fifty miles south of Cairo, the author has seen one such tail that weighed eighty-five pounds; this aroused in him no little astonishment, but many locals said it was no wonder, since nearly every lamb kept on grain for six months would have a tail of that weight, and they had even seen some of 150 pounds. So the author had to shut up. These sheep do not have the fatty 'net' or entrails of other animals, since their fat goes to their tails. Sheep of this kind are only found in the kingdom of Tunis and in Egypt.

7.3.12. The lion

These animals are wild and dangerous to all other animals. They are more savage and powerful than other animals; they eat livestock and people whenever they find them, and attack herds of animals, seizing them and dragging them to the woods where they have their dens and their cubs. They take no notice of humans or dogs, but if one is threatened by someone, it will seize any chance it can get to attack and kill him. Sometimes people kill them, but ultimately, in certain notorious places, a single lion will be brave enough to attack 200 men on horses, killing four or five before escaping or being killed itself. Lions living in the snowy mountains are less daring and strong, and therefore less dangerous to people, but those in hotter areas rage more fiercely, such as those on the borders of Tamasna and the kingdom of Fez, in the desert of Angad near Tlemcen, and between Bona and Tunis. Lions in these places are more famous and savage than elsewhere, and in winter, during their mating season, they fight and claw, trying to strip the flesh from one another – woe to the person who comes across lions in heat, when they will devour him without mercy. There can be ten or twelve after a single lioness. The author has heard from many men and women that when a lion encounters a woman alone in a remote place, if she shows it her natural parts, the lion will roar, lower its eyes and leave without harming her at all. Anyone else the lion encounters it eats like other animals. Whenever it seizes a person or beast, even if it is a camel or a horse, the lion carries it around in its mouth like a cat with a mouse. Twice the author has escaped being eaten by lions, but he won't tell the story here, to avoid getting too long-winded and tedious for the readers of this work.

7.3.13. The leopard

These animals live in the woods of Barbary; they are very savage and powerful, but they only hurt humans if by misfortune they meet on a narrow path, where the person cannot escape it. Likewise, when a person sees it and cries out or gets in its way, it will leap and claw at his face, taking all the flesh it can, sometimes breaking the skull and killing him at once. This animal does not attack livestock too often, but dogs are its mortal enemies, which it kills and eats. Those living in the mountains of Constantine hunt them on horseback by driving them out of the bush, having surrounded the ways out with horses and men. The leopards run through the bush searching for a way out, escaping only to find a group of horsemen, and turn swiftly back, finding the same at the next way out; the hunters then round them up and kill them. Anyone watching the paths who lets one escape earns the penalty of providing a feast for the whole hunting party, even when it is a good 300 people.

7.3.14. The *dabuh* (hyena)

The *dabuh* is like a wolf in size and shape, with feet and legs similar to those of humans. The Arabs call it *dabuh* and the Africans call it *iesef*. It is harmless to livestock, sustaining itself by digging human bodies out of graves and eating them; the animal is rather vile and stupid, and many people hunt it in an amusing way. Having found out where it is, one of them takes a drum and enters the cave playing and singing while another holds a rope. When the drummer reaches the hyena he keeps playing as the animal listens, lulled by the sound, while the other slips around with the rope, step by step, setting a snare to catch it. They then go out pulling the rope, and the stupid animal suddenly notices and tries to escape, but it is already tied up, so the hunters kill it.

7.3.15. The rabbit

The rabbits of Africa are all wild, particularly those in the Ghomara mountains in Mauretania, where they are found in large numbers and hunted like hares. Many local geographers say that these animals were once tamed, but after the Romans and the Goths took over the African provinces they left many towns and ksars without inhabitants, and the rabbits there grew wild and entered the woods. It's impossible to say whether this is the truth or a lie, but it is plausible, if only because the meat of these wild rabbits is just like tame ones in colour and flavour. If these animals had been wild, their meat would be different from tame ones, so they are not naturally wild.

7.3.16. The ape

These animals are found in large numbers in the woods of Mauretania, and in the mountains of Bejaia and Constantine. Without a tail, they have feet and hands as well as hairy faces like humans, and, they are very clever and discerning. They eat grass and grain, and, when they want to steal the early shoots, twenty or thirty of them team up, leaving one outside the field to keep guard while the others harvest. The moment the guard sees a watchman or some other human, it shrieks and the others flee, climbing the high trees and leaping great spans from one tree to another. The females carry their young on their shoulders, carrying them as they leap.

7.3.17. The civet cat

These cats, found in the woods of Ethiopia, are naturally wild. Merchants catch them when small and raise them in cages, feeding them on milk, bran soup and meat. Two or three times a day, they extract the cat's civet, which is its pure sweat. To do this, the merchants use a stick to make them run around their cage until they sweat, then they take it out and wipe the civet from under its legs, thighs, neck and tail. All the merchants keep a great amount of this civet.

Here ends the author's work on the wild and tame beasts found in Africa. The next deals with animals that live in the water and some large fish, especially the whale.

7.4.1. The cachalot

The cachalot is a fish of fearsome shape and size, only seen when it is dead and the sea has cast it ashore. Its skin is extremely tough, as if it were stone. Some of these fish are twenty-five cubits long, others more or less. According to those living by the ocean, it is this fish that produces ambergris, though they disagree on whether the ambergris is its dung or sperm, as already mentioned in the section on the town of Massa.[27] This fish would be better called a whale, on account of its size.

7.4.2. The sea horse (hippopotamus)

In the river Niger and the Nile can be found an animal shaped like a horse, but the size of a donkey, with a smooth, very tough hide. It lives in the sea as well as on land, although it only goes on land at night. It is highly malicious and dangerous, especially to boats carrying goods on the Niger, for this nasty animal will come alongside the boat and give it a sudden shove with its back, turning it over. Too bad for those who cannot swim.[28]

7.4.3. The sea cow[29]

This is another animal that looks just like an ox, but rather small, about the size of a six-month-old calf. It is found in the Niger river as well as the Nile, and fishermen catch it and take it out of the water onto land, where it can live and move about for days. It has a very tough hide. The author himself saw one of these 'calves' in Cairo, led by a chain around its neck by its captors, who earned their living by parading it through the city before the gentlemen and merchants. The author asked the fishermen where they had caught it, and they answered the Nile, next to the city of Esna, 400 miles south of Cairo.

7.4.4. The desert tortoise

The African geographers say that this animal, which is more or less the size of a barrel, is found in the desert of Libya. The geographer al-Bakri, in his *Book of Roads and Kingdoms in Africa*, tells of a traveller in the desert who was exhausted by nightfall; seeing a rock sticking high out of the ground, he said to himself, 'I'll climb on this rock to sleep so I won't be bitten by the beasts of the sand.' And so he settled down to sleep on the rock. In the morning, to his astonishment, he found himself twenty-five miles from the place he had gone to sleep; when he got home he told his tale to someone experienced in desert life, who laughed and said, 'Don't you know what that rock was where you slept all night? It was a desert tortoise, which lies still during the day and at night gets up and moves to eat, but so slowly that someone on top of it won't notice, especially someone so exhausted.' The traveller didn't know whether to believe this or not, so the other went into his house and brought out a pair of large baskets, saying, 'These were once the shells of two tortoises, but they were quite young.' The traveller was stunned.[30]

The author has seen no tortoise that huge, but only ones the size of a large barrel. Those living in the desert say that if anyone has had leprosy for less than seven years, he can be cured in seven days by eating the meat of this tortoise. They also say the animal has many secret properties, which the author will not relate, or this work would become a medical tome.

7.4.5. The crocodile

This animal is found in the river Niger and also in the Nile. It is very hostile and dangerous, and rather large, some reaching twelve cubits or longer, with the tail making up half its length. Going on four feet, it is shaped like a green lizard, not too high, at most a foot-and-a-half, with a tail ridged all over and a hide so tough that a large crossbow will not pierce it. Some of these creatures eat only fish, but others eat people as well as animals, in the following way: the crocodile comes to the banks of a river where animals and people are playing, and, when it sees one coming near the edge of the water, it swiftly lashes out and surrounds it with its tail, drags it into the water and eats it. When it eats it moves only its upper jaw, because the lower jaw is conjoined with its chest bone. Not all crocodiles are of this nature, for if they were, nobody could live on the banks of the Niger or the Nile.

The author saw one with his own eyes on a boat trip from Cairo to Qena in Upper Egypt. One night, in the middle of the trip, about 400 miles from Cairo, there was a somewhat cloudy moon and a steady but gentle wind carried the boat along. All the crew and the passengers were asleep; only the author remained in his cabin, studying by candlelight. But then an old man of good living who had also been awake, silently reciting his prayers, called out to him, saying, 'My fellow, wake up some of your men, and come help me grab a large piece of wood which will be useful for cooking tomorrow.' Because it was the middle of the night, the author answered, 'I would sooner help you myself than wake anyone else at this time!' The other replied, 'Well then, I'll go see if I can grab it by myself.' As the boat approached the wood, he stretched his hand out to loop a rope around it, when suddenly it jumped from the water – five cubits of tail swept around him and tugged him down, so the poor old fellow fell in. The author at once cried out; everyone in the boat got up and he told them what had happened. The crew lowered the sails and secured the boat; some jumped into the water, swimming around to find him, and the boat remained still for a good hour, moored to the land, until there was no longer any hope. The old man remained with his wood. The author greatly thanked God that he had not troubled himself with this fine piece of wood.

On that trip he saw many crocodiles, ten or twelve together, on little islands in the middle of the Nile, with their mouths open in the sun, as white birds small as thrushes came and entered their mouths, staying for a while before flying out. Watching this marvel, everyone asked the crew what these birds were doing in the creatures' mouths, and they replied that the crocodiles ate plenty of fish and animals, the remains of which got stuck in their teeth and bred worms; the birds would see the worms in the creatures' teeth and fly in to eat them. The crocodile knows the benefit of the birds eating the worms, but when it feels that there aren't any more it closes its mouth to eat the bird. However, the bird has a very hard, sharp spur on top of its head, and when the crocodile closes its mouth the bird's spur cuts into its palate, so it opens its mouth and the bird escapes. As a result, the author has long sought for one of these birds to see its spur, but sadly he has never been able to get one; if he could only have held it in his hand, he would have been able to tell the story with greater certainty.

The animal lays its eggs on the ground and covers them with sand, and as soon as the crocodiles are born they climb down into the river. But there are some who do not go into the water and are not poisonous. The author has seen many Egyptians who eat the flesh of this animal; its fat is sold for a lot of money in Cairo, and they say it is very good for protecting against old and cankered wounds.

In Upper Egypt there are many crocodile-fishers who catch them in the following way. They get a rope 100 cubits long and tie one end around a thick tree or pillar planted by the river; to the other end they tie a hook a cubit long and as thick as a man's finger, with a sharp tip. To the hook they attach a lamb or goat,

which bleats loudly from the pain it causes; hearing this, the crocodile attacks it, seizes it, eats it in a trice, and so the hook enters its belly along with the rope, and fastens onto the creature's innards when it swallows the animal's flesh, or even earlier. The fishermen let out more rope as the crocodile sinks down into the water; once it is stretched out, the animal feels it pulling and wants to throw it off, but that only makes it worse, because with its movements the hook attaches itself still more strongly. When the fishermen see the rope jumping about, sometimes even moving the tree to which it is tied so tightly, they know that the crocodile is firmly stuck; it is then that they start pulling it back to land, and it comes obediently, because there is less pain from the hook when the rope does not pull. When they see that it has been pulled out of the water, it becomes frightened and turns around almost head to tail, heading back for the water; the sailors let it walk until the rope is stretched out again, doing this two or three times until it is almost dead with exhaustion. Then they pull it out of the water and kill it; they strike it with spears in the throat and under the arms and the thighs near the stomach, that is, in the places without any hide. Those who would kill it in any other way will need an arquebus or a falconet because of the hardness and thickness of its hide.[31]

The author has seen on the walls of Qena, fastened to the battlements, around 300 heads of these animals with their mouths open. Some of them could swallow an entire cow, and they have huge, sharp teeth. Whenever they catch one, the fishermen from these parts of Egypt cut off its head and put it up on the wall, just like the custom of hunters in Europe who hang the heads of wild beasts over the door when they return from their hunt.

7.4.6. The dragon[32]

In the Atlas mountains are certain caves where many of these huge animals are found. Most of them have heavy bodies and cannot move well, being fat in the middle and rather slender towards the tail and head. They are very poisonous and if anyone should accidentally touch the animal or be bitten, his body will immediately grow cold and soft as soap.

7.4.7. The hydra[33]

This is a short snake with a slender tail and head. Many are found in the Libyan desert, and it has an acute poison, as the author has seen himself from those African surgeons who, having seen someone bitten by this snake, immediately bind the limb above the bite and cut it off. They say there is no other remedy for this snake's poison.

7.4.8. The *dhub* (spiny-tailed lizard)

This is a desert animal like a gecko in shape but a little larger; it is the length of a man's arm and four fingers wide. It never drinks water, and if someone forces water into its mouth, it will die. It lays eggs like those of tortoises, and is not poisonous. The author has seen Arabs catch them in the desert; he himself found one to catch and cut its throat, but it bled only a little. After roasting it and peeling off the skin, they ate it, saying it tasted good, like a frog; even though it is quite the opposite of a frog by nature, they taste the same. The animal runs fast like a lizard; when it escapes into some hole leaving its tail outside, even the strongest man cannot pull it out, no matter how hard he tries, for it sheds the tail it leaves outside. Hunters bring shovels to enlarge their holes and dig them out. When they kill the animal, they leave it for a week or more, but even then, when they put its carcass on the fire, it begins to move as if it has just been killed.

7.4.9. The *waral* (varanus or monitor lizard)

The *waral* is like the *dhub*, but larger and poisonous in its head and tail. The author has seen the Arabs cut off the head and tail, and then cook and eat it. It has such an ugly colour and appearance that the author has not worked up the courage to taste its meat.

7.4.10. The chameleon

This is a hideous, hump-backed creature, with a very thin tail, as long as a rat's. It moves very slowly. It lives off the sun's rays, and when the morning sun rises the animal sets its mouth open towards the sun, and as the sun revolves the animal follows with its mouth. As the author has himself seen, it changes colour to match its place; if put on a piece of red cloth it goes red, or black on black, green on green. It is a great enemy of poisonous serpents and possesses a marvellous power: when it sees a snake sleeping under a tree, the animal climbs up and tries to judge from where it can strike the snake's head; it then emits a thread of spittle, as some frogs do. The thread goes straight down, with a droplet like a tiny pearl at its tip. If the thread does not drop precisely onto the snake's head, the chameleon shifts its footing until it does. Then it releases its thread onto the centre of the snake's head, piercing it and killing it instantly with the power nature has given it. The animal is small, the largest about the size of a green lizard. The Arabs have said enough about the properties and powers of this animal, which the author will not record here.

Here ends the author's treatise on the kinds of animals that live in the water, on the earth and in the desert. The next deals with the exotic birds, beginning with:

7.5.1. The ostrich

The ostrich is a wild bird with a large body, much like a goose in shape but with rather long legs and neck. It has a fat body and wings with large feathers, and, although it cannot fly, it moves its wings to help it run. The tail also has large feathers, and its wings are mottled black and white, like a stork.

This animal normally lives in dry deserts where it lays ten or twelve eggs together in the sand. The eggs are each as large as a cannonball, weighing twelve or fifteen pounds, although the younger ones lay smaller eggs. Once the animal has laid its eggs, it forgets where, but whenever a female comes across any eggs, whether its own or another's, it warms them. The moment they are born, they run all over the countryside in search of food. Their young run so fast, even before they have grown feathers, that a human cannot catch them. The desert dwellers say that the animal is extremely stupid and deaf, hearing nothing and eating everything, even pieces of iron, and that its meat is smelly and sticky, especially the thighs. The author himself tried this meat in Numidia, since the people there buy these birds young to raise and fatten, and then slaughter and eat them. The desert Arabs hunt and catch them in large numbers; for the birds go in flocks, and from afar they are mistaken for men on horseback. Seen from a distance, a herd often provokes alarmed chatter among the merchant caravans, who think they might be brigands – this happened many times when the author was present.

7.5.2. The eagle

These birds are of many kinds, distinguished by size, colour and other characteristics. The largest is called *nasr* in Arabic.

7.5.3. The *nasr* (vulture)

This is the largest bird in Africa, much bigger than the crane, but with shorter legs, neck and beak. The author has heard that Italians have the word *voltore* (vulture) for a bird he's never observed, which flies so high it cannot be seen, and when it sees a corpse it swiftly swoops down on it. These birds flock together and the older ones have cropped or bare heads that have lost their feathers. The Africans say that this bird reaches a great age, and many of the old ones, after losing all their feathers and plumage, remain bare in their nests as if they were chicks, brought food by their young. These birds live on the rocks at the top of the desert mountains, especially in the Atlas, but many experienced mountain dwellers reach their nests using their craft and wits and catch them.

7.5.4. The *bezi* (goshawk)

The *bezi* is called *astore* (goshawk) in Italian. It is found in Africa in great numbers, or at least the common one is; the more excellent and precious ones are white, which they catch in the mountains of the Numidian deserts. There are many kinds; some are used to catch storks, others to catch smaller birds, such as quail and partridge, others to catch hares. In Africa they train common eagles to catch wolves and foxes, and to fight one another. Trained eagles normally seize such prey by the shoulder in their talons and the head in their beak, so it cannot bite them. If the animal throws itself on its back, the eagle pays no heed, holding tight until it has killed or blinded it. Many Africans say that a male eagle can impregnate a she-wolf, which swells until finally a dragon bursts from its body, with a beak and wings like a bird, a tail like a serpent, feet like a wolf, and its body mottled over in various colours like a snake. They say this animal hasn't the strength to move much; it is only found in caves and is widely rumoured to have been sighted. Nonetheless, the author has never seen this creature, nor even met anyone who has, although he cannot deny it might exist.

7.5.5. The locust

Sometimes these animals travel through Africa in great swarms, and when they fly they block out the sun's light. They eat the grain, fruit and leaves from the trees and when they go they leave eggs, from which similar animals are born, though they are flightless and worse still than their parents, even eating the bark off the trees. Swathes of towns and settlements, especially in Mauretania, are constantly ruined by the famine these animals leave behind. But the people of the Arabian peninsula and Libya have better luck when they arrive, for they eat them boiled, or dry them in the sun, crushing them to make something like a flour, which they then eat.[34]

7.5.6. The bat

Common bats are found throughout the world, but these birds are found in certain caves on the slopes of the Atlas mountains; they are the size of doves, some larger, especially in their wings. The author has not seen them, but has heard about them from treasure hunters.

7.5.7. The parrot

This is another bird widely found in the woods of Ethiopia. They have many different colours, but the best are the green ones, because they have more wit for learning to speak like humans.

There are others, bigger than doves, but in various colours such as black, red, green and grey; these cannot be taught (to speak), but they have a sweet voice.

These are nearly all the animals and birds which are either not found in Europe or unlike those in Europe. The next section is about some substances found in Africa, as well as wild and domesticated fruit and trees.

7.6.1. Salt

In most of Africa all the salt comes, like rocks or marble, from mines dug out of caves; some is grey, some white and some red. One finds plenty in Barbary and enough in Numidia; in the Black Land there is none, especially in inner Ethiopia, where a pound costs half a ducat. This people do not put salt in their cooking pots; instead, each person of the household keeps a piece in their hand, and licks it whenever they take a mouthful, so as not to use up too much. In many parts of Barbary, such as near Fez, there are small lakes or marshes that become granular, white salt in summer.

7.6.2. Antimony

This comes from lead mines in several parts of Africa,[35] and masters of the craft use sulphur to separate the antimony from the lead. Great quantities are found at the southern base of the Atlas mountains, especially on the borders of Numidia and the kingdom of Fez. As said, in some places there is much sulphur.

7.6.3. Euphorbium

Euphorbium is prized by some as a wondrous solid substance, though it is less a solid than a gum deriving from trees that grow like heads of wild thistle.[36] Between the tree's branches grow fat green fruit like cucumbers, with seeds on them like cucumber seeds; the fruits are quite long, varying between a cubit and half a cubit. They do not grow on the branches, but are fixed in the ground like roots, and each head bears ten or fifteen or thirty fruits. When it ripens, the local peasants cut into it to draw out a sort of milk, which immediately thickens, and which they remove with their knives and bottle, once dried. These trees have plenty of sharp thorns.

7.6.4. Pitch

There are two kinds of pitch: one is a solid substance, collected on top of stones in the midst of certain springs where the water stinks and tastes of pitch; the other kind is artificial, extracted from the wood of juniper or pine trees by chipping them up, which the author saw done in the Atlas mountains.[37] First they build a deep, round furnace, with a hole in the bottom, constructed above a tub-shaped pit. They take green trees and cut them into small pieces, dumping them into the furnace and blocking up the mouth, and then bring the furnace to a medium heat. The material is distilled from the wood chips, coming out of the hole in the base and dropping into the pit below, from which they collect and bottle it.

[7.6.4b. The *maus* fruit (banana)[38]

This sweet, delicious fruit is the size of a small cucumber; it grows from a small plant with large, broad leaves a cubit long. Muslim scholars say that this was the fruit that God forbade Eve and Adam to eat. After eating it they sought to cover up their shame, and so picked the leaves of this fruit, which are more suitable than those of any other. Many grow in Salé, a city in the kingdom of Fez, but there is a greater supply in Egypt, especially in Damietta.]

7.6.5. Cassia

Cassia comes from large trees with leaves like mulberry bushes, and with huge flowers of purest white. The trees produce so much fruit that one must lighten them by picking much of it before it ripens, or else they snap under its weight. These trees only grow in parts of Egypt.

7.6.6. Terfezia

This is closer to a root than a fruit, and looks much like a truffle, but fatter and with a white skin. It grows in the sand in hot regions, and is recognised by seeing where the ground swells and cracks open a little. Some are the size of a nut, others are much larger, like oranges. Doctors say it is cooling and call it the *kam'a*. It grows plentifully in the deserts of Numidia, and the Arabs enjoy eating it like sugar cane, although it is also good roasted over coals, then washed and boiled in an oily broth or butter. The Arabs also eat it unwashed, just boiling it in water or milk. The terfezia is widely found in the sand around the city of Salé.

The fruit known as dates has already been described in the section on Sijilmasa, the city in Numidia.

7.6.7. The Egyptian fig, known as *jummeiz*

The *jummeiz* comes from a tree much like the fig, extremely tall and thick with similar leaves, except the fruit does not grow on buds among the leaves, but instead on the trunk where there are no leaves. It tastes much like a fig, with a thick, dark purple skin.

7.6.8. The thalh'ah tree[39]

This is a large, thorny tree with leaves like a juniper, producing a gum similar to mastic resin. African apothecaries use this gum to counterfeit mastic, since it has the same colour and even smells a little like it. These trees are found in the deserts of Numidia, Libya and also the Black Land. Those of Numidia, when split open, have white wood at the centre like other trees, while those of Libya have purple wood, and those of the Black Land are the darkest black. The black heartwood is called the *sangue* (blood) in Italian, and fine instruments are made from it. Likewise the author has recently seen doctors begin to use the purple wood in remedies for the French pox, so that it is commonly called 'French pox wood'.

7.6.9. Taserghint (*Corrigiola telephiifolia*)

This is a very pungent root found on the ocean shores to the west. Mauretanian merchants transport this root to the Black Land, where they use it as a perfume. They need not burn it, only keep it in their homes for its pleasant smell. In Mauretania one camel load is worth a ducat and a half; in the Black Land, it is fifty or sixty ducats, occasionally more or less.

7.6.10. Addad (*Atractylis gummifera*)

This plant is very bitter and its root is poisonous. One dram of liquid distilled from this root will kill a man within an hour, a fact commonly known in Africa even to women.

7.6.11. Surnag (possibly *Atriplex hymenelytra*)

This root grows on the western side of the Atlas mountains. People say it has tremendous power, for a concoction of it will stiffen a man's prick and keep him screwing all night. They also say that if a girl passes directly over the root, she will lose her virginity at once due to its power. Those living in the mountains claim that many girls have been deflowered in this way, going out to herd the goats and stepping over the root. As for the author, he believes they encountered not the root but young lads with stiff pricks, and no doubt lost their virginity to them; some cunning rogue having it off with one of the girls spread the story to spare them and their families from shame, not least because those people are so wild and jealous.

Because he can dredge up no more from his fleeting memory of various things strange to Europe, and even to Africa – trees, fruits, roots or minerals – the author now ends in silence.

Here ends the book or treatise of the author, Messer Giovanni Leone of Granada, on what is meant by Africa: its cities, deserts, mountains, settlements, villages, rivers, animals and their habits, likewise its unknown fruits and roots, in the manner of a cosmography. Rome, 10 March 1526

Notes

1   A Latinised form of *Ifriqis* or *Ifriqish*, a figure mentioned by several Arabic historians but dismissed as myth by Ibn Khaldun in the introduction to his *Muqaddimah*.

2   The name *Maghrib* (or *Maghreb*) means 'the West' (etymologically, 'setting', referring to the sun).

3   The straits of Gibraltar.

4   Perhaps Jebel Maïza or Mu'ayzah, present-day Tunisia, although it is 1,800 miles from Alexandria.

5   Now the Bab-el-Mandeb.

6   The fabled Christian king of an exotic land, variously India, Mongol Asia or Ethiopia; the legend dates from the twelfth century, when an invented Latin *Letter of Prester John* began circulating in Europe.

7   Leo's term *numidi* seems to lie somewhere between two closely related words, the Latin *Numidae* (Numidians) and the Italian *nomadi* (nomads).

8   Many scholars identify the Zanaga (Zenaga, Znaga) with the Sanhaja; others classify them as a subgroup. Across the *Cosmography*, Leo uses the forms 'Sanaga', 'Zanaga', 'Zenaga', 'Zanhaga', 'Zanhagia' and 'Sanhagia'; but he consistently uses 'Zanaga' in this context (cf. 1.20, 4.1), and 'Sanhagia' in his separate list (1.10) of the five great Berber groups (Sanhaja, Masmuda, Zanata, Hawwara, Ghomara). We have therefore retained the distinction in our translation, though it not always clear elsewhere which he means.

9   Épaulard identifies 'Bito' as Buré in present-day Guinea; 'Dauma' (tentatively) as Dahomey, present-day Benin; and 'Gorhan' as the region of the Gura'an people in Chad. Rauchenberger (*Johannes Leo*, pp. 190–91) plausibly identifies 'Jemiam' with the Yemyem or N'yemn'yem (i.e. Azande) people mentioned in 1841 by

William Desborough Cooley. 'Medra' may indicate the land of the Mandara.

10   Latin *barbarus* (*barbara* is feminine), from the Greek *barbaros*, means 'barbarous' or 'uncultivated', supposedly a representation of mumbling or incoherent speech (compare English *rhubarb*).

11   Morea: the Peloponnese.

12   In Genesis 10:6, Mizraim is Cush's brother, not his son. Genesis 10:14 notes that Philistim was the son of Mizraim's son Casluhim. Genesis 10:7 gives Sheba as the son of Raamah.

13   See the note on the name 'Zanaga' at 1.6 above (note 8).

14   The Oued el Abid: see 7.1.3 below.

15   Compare Leo's reasoning on rabbits in 7.3.15 below.

16   On this destruction, see further 2.2.1.2 below.

17   In fact, al-Mu'min belonged to the Kumya tribe of the Zanata.

18   Ibrahim ibn ar-Raqiq, an eleventh-century scholar whose history of the Maghrib is now lost, except in quotations in Ibn Khaldun and other later writers.

19   Hausa.

20   Kanuri.

21   That is, Arabic, Ethiopic and Coptic.

22   AD 670. For more details see 2.4.1.34 below.

23   The Fatimid Caliphate was founded by 'Abd Allah al-Mahdi in 910; see 2.4.1.32 below.

24   Bi-Amr Allah, aka Abu'l-Qasim Muhammad ibn 'Abdallah, 893–946, was the second Fatimid caliph. But Leo is in fact thinking of the third caliph after all, al-Mansur bi-Nasr Allah.

25   Al-Siqilli, aka Al-Qa'id Jawhar ibn 'Abdallah.

26   Perhaps Leo has in mind al-Hasan ibn Ubayd Allah ibn Tughj, r. 968–70, last of the Ikhshidid governors of Egypt on behalf of the Abbasid Caliphate.

27   Abu 'l-Qasim al-Fadl ibn al-Muqtadir, also known as al-Muti, r. 946–74.

28   See 6.17 below.

29   Compare Wellington's famous remark that Napoleon's presence on the battlefield 'made the difference of forty thousand men'.

30   Buluggin ibn Ziri, a Sanhaja Berber, was appointed regent of Ifriqiya in 972 by al-Mu'izz li-Din Allah, fourth Fatimid caliph, when he moved his capital from Mansouria (Tunisia) to Cairo.

31   The rebel was in fact not Buluggin but his great-grandson al-Mu'izz ibn Badis, who broke from the Fatimids in 1049 and allied with the Abbasids of Baghdad.

32 Al-Mustansir Billah, r. 1036–94.

33 Épaulard suggests that this is Abu Muhammad al-Yazuri, who served as vizier from 1050 to 1058.

34 The conventional date for the Bedouin migration into the Maghrib is around 1048.

35 AD 1057.

36 AD 1061. This sentence is the only use of 'Ifriqiya' after 1.1, and it is deliberate, for the word 'Affrica' has been crossed out.

37 The Zirids.

38 AD 1229.

39 Unidentified, and contrary to Ibn Khaldun's tripartite division of Sulaim, Hilal and Maqil. In general, Leo's classification of tribes in this chapter does not correspond neatly to that provided by Ibn Khaldun.

40 This insertion follows the classification in 1.17 below.

41 Épaulard identifies these as the Kinana, although the latter did not in fact migrate to Africa.

42 This sentence is in error: it should list the Oulad Dalim, Berabish, Udaya, Rahamna and 'Amr.

43 The famous corsair Oruç Reis, 1474–1518, known to Europeans as 'Barbarossa', came to power in the region in 1516. On the conquest of Algiers, see 2.3.25 below.

44 The Sabaeans were supposedly descended from Saba or Sheba (Genesis 10:7).

45 The source is Ibn Khaldun, *Histoire*, I.7, whose word *musta'jam* means literally 'becoming non-Arab'; de Slane's translation, 'Arabes barbarisants', derives directly from Leo's phrase *Arabi inbarbarati*.

46 Compare Alvise Cadamosto's description ('Voyage', 213–14) of Sanhaja customs.

47 Eid al-Adha.

48 This basket-like saddle is called a *basur*.

49 The two items are given in the manuscript as *fumo di galla* and *ferrocto*. Identification is uncertain; commentators have suggested nutmeg and galena (used in kohl) for the former, saffron (Ramusio's emendation) and fennel for the latter. However, the medieval geographer al-Mas'udi (*Prairies*, II.407) notes that oak gall mixed with iron sulphate produces a very black pigment.

50 See also 2.4.4.1 below for similar material.

51 Abu 'Abdallah Muhammad IV al-Mutawakkil, r. 1494–1526.

52   This is incorrect: St Augustine wrote against the Arian heresy in the early fifth century.
53   These 'schismatics', the Fatimid Caliphate, are discussed further in 1.13 above.
54   Épaulard identifies this as Sefrou.
55   Leo apparently changed his plan after writing this book: all the animals now appear in Book 7.
56   The kola nut. *Goro* is a Hausa word.
57   Aab-e Naysan. Nisan or Naysan is the Arabic equivalent of April.
58   Leo's name for Muslim Spain.
59   Six months have twenty-nine days, and the other six months have thirty days.
60   Ramusio supplies this lacuna with 'lakes'.
61   See, for instance, 2.1.3.15 below.
62   Épaulard suggests that Leo is misled by the accidental similarity between the Spanish *las bubas* (swellings, cognate with our 'bubonic' plague) and the Arabic *al-hoboub*.
63   Compare 6.4 below.
64   That is, they are cuckolds.

BOOK 2.1

1   Compare 2.2.2.12.9 below.
2   The *haik*, also referred to as the *safseri* or *sefsari* in Tunis, for which, see the end of 2.4.1.21 below. Duarte Pacheco Pereira (*Esmeraldo*, 60) calls these garments *alquyces*.
3   Leo means the *jizya* or tax on non-Muslims mentioned elsewhere in the book.
4   The asper was a Turkish coin, with 120 to a piastre; the fillér was a hundredth of a forint.
5   Present-day Souira Guedima.
6   AH 923 is in fact AD 1517.
7   Unidentified.
8   AH 922 is in fact AD 1516.
9   Unidentified.
10   Abu 'Abdallah Muhammad al-Qa'im, the emir of Sous and Haha, r. 1510–17.
11   Unidentified.
12   Unidentified.
13   This work, by the ninth-century scholar Imam Sahnun, compiles the writings of Malik ibn Anas, founder of the Maliki school a

century earlier; it was a standard legal textbook in Fez when Leo was educated there.

14 By 'endowments' (*beneficii*) Leo means the *waqf* (or *habs*), the charitable endowment in Islamic law.

15 One might wonder why Leo did not recognise the word, since the Berber word is borrowed from the Arabic *aj-jazzar*.

16 'Umar ibn Sulayman ash-Shayzami as-Sayyaf, d. 1485–6, a disciple of the Sufi mystic Muhammad al-Jazuli; in fact, as-Sayyaf slightly predated Leo's birth.

17 Ramusio adds that these Jews are reputed as heretics.

18 This passage, in Pory's translation, is quoted in Herman Melville's novel *Moby Dick*, chapter 104.

19 An Italian measure varying in length from about one to three metres.

20 Present-day Agadir.

21 Duarte Pacheco Pereira (*Esmeraldo*, 60) observed 'four villages: Taguaost, Haguost, Hahytemosy and Tyciguone, containing in all some fifteen hundred inhabitants, who are usually at war with one another.'

22 Épaulard renders this name Hankisa or Nguisa, and identifies it with the massif of Jebel el-Kest.

23 The name means 'Friday', suggesting a Friday market. Compare 2.1.5.5 below.

24 Perhaps a name related to that of the Algerian locale Medjadja.

25 On whom, see 2.1.1.13 above. Leo's date of 1494–5 cannot be correct, for as-Sayyaf died in 1485–6.

26 The Berber word for feather is *rriš* or *rric*.

27 Épaulard identifies this figure as Sidi Abu 'Abdallah Muhammad Kanoun.

28 Épaulard identifies the town as present-day Gmassa.

29 This is presumably the same encounter subsequently mentioned at 2.1.4.2.

30 That is, the Almohad Caliphate founded by 'Abd al-Mu'min. 'Almohad' is the Spanish form of the Arabic *al-Muwahhidūn*, which means 'the Monotheists'.

31 It is still today referred to as the Ben Youssef Mosque.

32 The Kutubiyya Mosque.

33 This mountain is probably Beni Mager, discussed in 2.1.4.13.

34 That is, from *kutubiyy*, bookseller, from *kitab*, book.

35 The date is impossible, as Yusuf did not come to power until AD 1061; Marrakesh was likely founded around 1070.

36   Abu 'Abd Allah Muhammad ibn Tumart, c. 1080–1130. Not to
be confused with the other figure Leo designates as al-Mahdi,
namely 'Abd Allah al-Mahdi, on whom see 2.4.1.32 below.

37   Amadori reads the date as AH 918, which is impossible; the
manuscript is worn here, and it seems likely either that the first
digit is in fact 5, or that it is a scribal error for 5. Ibrahim and his
nephew (not son) Ishaq were in fact killed in AD 1147.

38   The Marrakesh Kasbah.

39   The Kasbah Mosque.

40   Examples of these granaries or *ghorfas* still remain in some parts
of north Africa.

41   By 'the present king', Leo probably means the Berber emir al-
Nasr ibn Yusuf al-Hintati, although he was expelled by the
Sa'diyan (Arab) prince Ahmad al-Araj in 1524/5. Ahmad was
the son of Muhammad al-Qa'im, for whom Leo had worked a
decade before: see 2.1.1.8, 2.1.3.20 and 2.1.4.2.

42   The battle of Las Navas de Tolosa, 16 July 1212.

43   The Ourika.

44   Perhaps the *Alkaida* or *Creed* of Abu Hafs 'Umar an-Nasafi.

45   Present-day Sidi Rahhal.

46   *Asida*, on which see 2.1.1.3 above.

47   *Cazafrusti*, more properly spelled *cacciafusti*. Leo probably
means slings, as Ramusio has it.

48   On these figures, see 2.1.3.9 above.

49   Written indifferently as 'Hadimmei', 'Adimmei' and 'Adimmeni'.
Épaulard identifies the name with 'Animmei' (2.1.3.11 above).

50   Region of the Gaetuli.

51   Ilalen, on which see 2.1.2.8 above.

52   On this figure, see 2.1.1.8 above.

53   By June 1500. In September 1498, 'Abd ar-Rahman had driven
out his cousin Yahya az-Zayyat, according to a contemporary
report by the Portuguese envoy Diogo Borges to Queen
Leonora.

54   Sidi Yahya u-Ta'fuft.

55   The Portuguese chronicler Damião de Góis places the murder at
the end of 1506; Épaulard proposes April 1507 instead.

56   Sidi Yahya.

57   AD 1508.

58   For this latter figure, see 2.1.1.8 above.

59   At Tumeglast, for which see 2.1.3.7 above.

60   This is the key passage in the book for ascertaining the year of
Leo's birth. Unfortunately, it is riddled with textual problems. The

manuscript says that Leo visited Safi at the age of twelve, and that *four* years later he met Yahya, in the year 'AH 950', i.e. AD 1543–4, an impossible date. Ramusio, by contrast, says that Leo was twelve when Safi was captured by the Portuguese (i.e. in AD 1508), and that *fourteen* years later he met Yahya, in the year AH 920, i.e. AD 1514–15. Neither passage on its own is tenable, and every scholar has made different conjectures to square the evidence. It seems likelier to us that Leo was twenty-six (12 + 14) than sixteen (12 + 4) when he met Yahya on state business, so we have preserved Ramusio's 'fourteen'; moreover, AH 920 is a good date for the encounter with Yahya, and specifically AD 1514, since Yahya left for Lisbon that summer and remained there for two years. Therefore, if we ignore the capture of Safi and stay with the wording (but not the numbers) of the manuscript, Leo was twenty-six in 1514, and born in 1488. Rauchenberger, who always trusts the manuscript over Ramusio, prefers 'four years' (*Johannes Leo*, 33–4) and ultimately a birth date of Oct./Nov. 1494.

61 Miat Bir; compare 2.2.7.24 below for a place of the same name in the kingdom of Fez. Épaulard thinks the town of Sernou is meant.

62 'Ali ibn Washman, on whom see 2.1.4.2 above.

63 Mulay an-Nasir.

64 In fact AH 919 / August AD 1513. The expedition was led by the king's nephew Jaime, duke of Braganza.

65 Jebel Akhdar.

66 The fruit of the strawberry tree, *Arbutus unedo*.

67 The Italian is *lanze spezzate*, literally 'broken lances'.

68 Present-day Skoura.

69 Épaulard suggests an identification with present-day Demnate.

70 See the following chapter.

71 Unidentified.

72 For this aspect of the wedding ceremony, see 2.2.2.12.10 below.

73 AD 1515.

74 Unidentified.

75 The name means 'Friday', suggesting a Friday market. Compare 2.1.3.2 above.

76 This name does not appear elsewhere. It is identified by Épaulard with Ait Ouaouzguit, the mountain range west of Ouarzazate, where the local ruler mentioned in this chapter probably lived.

77 A dish of meat and noodles.

78 *Xylopia aethiopica*, used as both a spice and a medicine.

79   See 2.1.3.9 above.

80   Sandstone.

81   For the latter, see 2.1.1.4 above.

82   Unidentified.

83   According to Épaulard, actually Todgha.

84   For these baskets, compare 1.21 above, describing the practice of Arabs with camels. If this is what Leo has in mind here, the roof supports curve overhead like the frame of a modern camper's tent.

85   The great geographer Muhammad al-Idrisi, named here for his residency at the royal court in Sicily.

86   See 2.1.1.3 above.

87   Potassium nitrate, a key ingredient in gunpowder.

BOOK 2.2

1   Idris II: see 2.2.2.10 below.

2   In fact c. 925.

3   In fact, Ha-Mim, a prophet of the Majkasa tribe, died in 927/8. Leo has perhaps confused his followers with the older and larger confederation of the Barghawata (744–1058), an independent state in Tamasna.

4   The history is muddled; the Barghawata murdered 'Abdullah ibn Yasin, c. 1059, and Leo may be misremembering a campaign against them by Abu Bakr ibn 'Umar al-Lamtuni.

5   Present-day Casablanca.

6   AD 1468.

7   Unidentified, but Épaulard notes that the name in Berber means 'unused land'.

8   A silver coin worth ten baiocchi, named after Pope Julius II.

9   The Italian word is cornua; Ramusio has cornioli, cornel or cherry dogwood. However, this tree is not native to north Africa, and Épaulard offers sorbier, 'rowan', instead.

10   Wild jujube or Zizyphus lotus.

11   Duarte Pacheco Pereira (Esmeraldo, 42) remarks that Chellah 'was formerly the burial place of the Kings of Feez [i.e. Fez], their other burial place being in Hell' (tambem outra sepultura no inferno).

12   Brown, in his edition of Pory's translation of Leo, writes that three of these graves were intact in his day: that of Abu Yaqub Yusuf an-Nasr (d. AH 706 / AD 1307), and those of Abu al-Hasan

'Ali ibn 'Uthman (d. AH 752 / AD 1351) and his wife, in Brown's transcription Lella Chapa (d. AH 750 / AD 1349).

13   'Abd al-Haqq.

14   Also known as Abu Yaaza, Yalannur ibn Maynun, d. 1177. His grave is in Moulay Bouazza in Taghia.

15   Ibn al-Zayyat al-Tadili, d. 1230, author of a collection of hagiographies, *al-Tashawwuf ila Ridjal al-Tasawwuf*.

16   The fruit of the strawberry tree, *Arbutus unedo*.

17   Wild jujube.

18   Épaulard identifies this as the *Chamaerops humilis* or dwarf palm.

19   In fact 1260.

20   Alfonso X, r. 1252–84.

21   Ramusio: 'Marino'.

22   Ramusio identifies the king as 'Abulchesen', i.e. Abu al-Hasan 'Ali ibn 'Uthman, r. 1331–48.

23   'Uthman III, r. 1398–1420.

24   In fact the Nasrid king was Yusuf III, r. 1408–17.

25   The events described here are highly important to Leo, for he repeatedly mentions them as a reason for the destruction of the towns near Fez. The major source is Taqi al-Din al-Maqrizi's historical work *Durar al-'uqūd al-farīda fī tarājim al-a'yān al-mufīda* (*The Incomparable Pearl-Necklaces of the Useful Biographies of Famous Men*). According to this text (II.413–18), Yusuf's dispute with Abu Sa'id concerned Gibraltar; the latter's 'uncle' was in fact his cousin al-Sa'id Muhammad ibn 'Abd al-'Aziz (d. 1414), whom Yusuf released in November 1410. The siege lasted not for seven years but for two months, from March to May 1411.

26   Present-day Mehdya.

27   São João da Mamora. The king was Manuel I.

28   Mulay an-Nasir.

29   Ferdinand V, d. January 1516.

30   The Bou Fekrane.

31   His brother, Mulay an-Nasir.

32   Épaulard identifies this figure as Mulay Zayyan.

33   This is the literal meaning of Leo's word *agrra* (*agra*), but the sense seems doubtful.

34   That is, the Mosque of the Baths.

35   The mulberry tree was the preferred habitat of silkworms in Africa.

36   AD 1515.

37   In fact 789.
38   Idris was the great-grandson of Hasan, son of 'Ali and grandson of Muhammad.
39   Harun was the great-great-great-great-grandson of Abbas, Muhammad's uncle.
40   In fact, Leo is thinking of Harun's grandfather al-Mansur, r. 754–75.
41   That is, the first Abbasid caliph.
42   Again, al-Mansur.
43   Yahya ibn 'Abdallah, d. 803.
44   In fact, the concubine Kenza al-Awrabiya was not a Goth but a Berber.
45   Madinat Fas.
46   Al-'Aliya.
47   AD 1070.
48   See 2.2.2.14 below.
49   The distinction is between the *jami'* or congregational mosque, and the smaller *masjid*.
50   The *minbar*.
51   The Bou Inania Madrasa, built in 1350–55 by Abu 'Inan Faris, r. 1348–58.
52   The Wadi Lamtiyyin.
53   Leo is referring to the extraordinary wooden *muqarnas* or honeycomb vaults.
54   Ramusio: 'wooden nets like shutters', probably meaning a *mashrabiyya*.
55   Ramusio: 'ebony and ivory'.
56   Known in Arabic as *maristans*.
57   The Maristan of Sidi Frej.
58   This sequence of three rooms is modelled on the ancient Roman baths, with their *frigidarium* (cold room), *tepidarium* (warm room) and *caldarium* (hot room).
59   The present-day Palazzo della Cancelleria.
60   An al-Andalusi dialect word for sodomites.
61   *Giottoni*, a word in Italian slang with sexual, and especially homosexual, overtones.
62   Place Seffarine.
63   The *amin*.
64   The *muhtasib*; see 6.41 below.
65   A unit of dry volume, approximately thirteen litres.
66   Presumably a local name for a red spice.

67 The Sebou.
68 See 7.1.7 below.
69 See 2.2.5.30 below.
70 Duarte Pacheco Pereira (*Esmeraldo*, 57) notes that the Fez merchants prize Portuguese cloth and 'buy Dutch linens, fine handkerchiefs [*lenços*] and other coarser ones, which they call "bordateis".'
71 Souk El Attarine.
72 A cerate is a hard ointment made of wax and oil; an electuary is a medicinal paste.
73 *Azorro.* Ramusio: *aghi*, needlework.
74 Al-Andalusiyyin Mosque.
75 On the pits, see 2.2.2.13 below.
76 AD 1276.
77 The Bou Jeloud Mosque.
78 Leo's word is *cursori*, literally 'runners', meaning courthouse officials tasked with serving documents.
79 That is, the *muhtasib* or market inspector. Leo discusses this post in his description of Cairo: see 6.41.
80 Leo is describing the steamer or *couscoussier*.
81 The Finnish anthropologist Edvard Westermarck, in his eye-witness account *Marriage Ceremonies in Morocco* (London: Macmillan, 1914), relates many of the same rituals and objects as Leo describes below.
82 *Chiesia.* Presumably the mosque is meant.
83 *Mahr* or bride price.
84 The manuscript has *sacco*, the normal Italian word for a bag or sack. But every other instance of *sacco* in the book means the sack of a city, and Ramusio's word here is *iscacchiere* (chessboard), suggesting instead that the fabric is multicoloured in a checkerboard pattern – plausibly the better reading.
85 *Calzoni*, a word that usually means 'trousers' but could also mean 'underwear' in sixteenth-century Italian. Pory's word here is 'napkin', and this has been suggested as a source for the spotted 'napkin' or handkerchief on which the plot of Shakespeare's *Othello* turns. The public display of bloody garments or bedsheets was a common practice in both the Muslim and the Christian Mediterranean countries of the time. Westermarck records the name of the ceremony at Fez as *as-sarwal*, or, as he translates it, 'the drawers'.
86 A less terrible fate than the public stoning decreed in Deuteronomy 22:20–21.

87 The feast of John the Baptist is on 24 June; that of John the Apostle is on 27 December.

88 Ramusio has simply *dentilla*, from *dens*, 'tooth'.

89 Mawlid; in Sunni Islam celebrated on 12 Rabi' al-Awwal (the date accepted by Leo at 2.1.3.20 above), which can fall anywhere in the Christian calendar.

90 That is, before 1465.

91 The Chouara Tannery.

92 The word *fregare* means literally to rub, but also to copulate; the Arabic *sihaqa* (plural *suhaqiyat*), like the Greek *tribas*, means 'one who rubs'. Unsurprisingly, Ramusio and his translators pass over this material much more lightly.

93 An Islamic letter magic based in astrology. It is described in Ibn Khaldun's *Muqaddimah*, 6.28.

94 The great eighth-century grammarian al-Khalil distinguishes the peg (*watad*) from the cord (*sabab*); a peg is two syllables (short-long), while a cord is one short syllable, or one long syllable, or two short syllables. In the *at-Tawil* metrical form, a line (technically a distich) consists of the sequence, given twice, of peg-cord, peg-cord-cord, peg-cord, peg-cord-cord. Leo describes this and other metrical forms in his Latin work *De arte metrica liber*, for which see the Introduction, note 6.

95 Natalie Zemon Davis identifies this figure as Jamal ad-Din al-Marjani.

96 A century later, Abu Salim al-Ayyashi (*Voyage*, 77–8) notes that one needed an *ijazah* or licence to practise this and other occult arts; he mentions a marabout who had been sick for twenty-five years, supposedly for practising without a licence.

97 This seems to be a folk etymology from the Greek *sophos*, 'wise man'.

98 Leo's word here is *priore*, 'prior' or 'abbot'. The sheikh is in this sense the leader of a *tariqa* or Sufi order.

99 Better known simply as Hasan of Basra, 642–728.

100 Better known as al-Muhasibi, 781–857.

101 The name 'Caselsah' looks like that of Qizil [Shah] Arslan, r. 1186–91. But Qizil lived a century after Malik and was not his grandson. Nizam al-Mulk in fact served Malik's father, Alp Arslan, r. 1063–72, and then Malik himself, r. 1072–92.

102 Al-Ghazali joined Nizam's court in 1085.

103 Leo is probably referring to the *Ihyā 'Ulūm al-Dīn* or *The Revival of the Religious Knowledge*.

104 That is, the Mongols, under Hulagu Khan.

105 The work referred to is the *Maqamat* or *Assemblies* of al-Hariri of Basra (1054–1122). Davis suggests that the particular story is no. 10: see Thomas Chenery's translation (London, 1867), I. 158–63. As for the commentary, that of al-Sharishi (1181–1222) has been suggested as a likely candidate.

106 Shahab al-Din Yahya ibn Habash Suhrawardi, 1154–91.

107 The poem in question is the *Nazm al-Suluk* or *Poem of the Sufi Way*; the commentary was authored by Sa'id al-Din Mohammad Fargani, d. 1300.

108 Ahmad al-Buni, d. 1225.

109 Perhaps the renowned scholar and poet Elijah (or Elia) Levita, 1469–1549.

110 Muhammad ibn Ibrahim ibn al-Akfani, d. 1348.

111 These are Sunni and Shia Islam, respectively. Abu 'l-Hasan al-Ash'ari, 873/4–935/6, was one of the most important and influential theologians of Sunni Islam.

112 We follow Épaulard's rendering of this term (from the Arabic word for 'treasure'), though Gabriel Camps has suggested the alternative of *al-qanisin*, 'seekers'. The group is mentioned several times in the chapters following Fez.

113 Jabir ibn Hayyan, d. c. 806–16, a semi-mythical figure commonly known in the Western tradition as Geber.

114 This author is mentioned in Ibn Khaldun's *Muqaddimah*, chapters 6.29 and 6.32, but remains unidentified.

115 Leo's word is *ciarratani*, that is, *ciarlatani*, charlatans in the older sense of the word; as the quaint definition of the *OED* has it, 'A mountebank or Cheap Jack who descants volubly to a crowd in the street; esp. an itinerant vendor of medicines who thus puffs his "science" and drugs.'

116 Abu 'Abd Allah al-Sheikh Muhammad ibn Yahya died in 1504. The name of Muhammad's brother was Mulay an-Nasir.

117 Idris al-Wathiq or Abu Dabbus, r. 1266–9.

118 Yaghmurasen ibn Zyan, r. 1236–83.

119 Madinat al-Baida, built 1276.

120 This quarter is known as the Mellah.

121 In fact his son, 'Abd al-Haqq II, in 1438.

122 This tribute, paid by non-Muslim subjects, is called *jizya*.

123 Perhaps the Tommaso Murino or Marino mentioned at 2.2.2.2 above.

124 The Almohads.

125 That is, from Muslims. Non-Muslims are liable to secular taxes, such as the *jizya* mentioned in the previous chapter.

126 This tax is known as the *zakat*.

127 The tithe is known as *achour*.

128 The sovereign's enclosure is known as an *afrag* in Berber.

129 *Zawiya* is the Arabic word for a madrasa or religious hospice.

130 For this, see the main account at 2.3.10 below.

131 Épaulard identifies this town with the present-day Sidi Harazem, which still houses a bath complex.

132 The name is equivalent to the ancient Volubilis, but Leo has in mind the settlement now known as Moulay Idriss after the ruler buried there, two miles from Volubilis.

133 The extensive corpus reporting Muhammad's sayings and deeds is known as *hadith*.

134 The trope of the four world kings is common in early Muslim writing; see, for instance, al-Tha'labi, *Lives of the Prophets*, trans. William M. Brinner (Leiden: Brill, 2002), 125, 491. The two infidel kings are usually Nimrod and Nebuchadnezzar. Pharaoh may be a north African variant; it was recorded in Morocco in 1860 by the traveller James Richardson.

135 Dar al-Hamra.

136 The intended location is unknown, but Épaulard notes the nearby existence of an area named 'Bilad al-Mahaya', and suggests a play on the Arabic word *muhayaa*, 'to make someone blush'.

137 Épaulard suggests an identification with the river Mikkes.

138 See 1.15 above.

139 Muhammad ibn Idris, r. 828–36.

140 Moulay Bouchta.

141 For this cherry, see 2.2.1.13 above.

142 This seems to be a transcription of *jezirah*, 'island'.

143 Lixus.

144 The La Graciosa fortress.

145 The treaty of Xamez was signed on 27 August 1489.

146 'Ali ibn Abi Talib was the great-great-grandfather of Idris I.

147 In fact, Norman pirates.

148 In 844.

149 In fact 1471.

150 This seems to refer to the 1465 revolution; Ramusio says more accurately that Muhammad went to fight the rebels there.

151 The *sharif* Muhammad ibn 'Ali al-Amrani al-Joutey al-Idrissi, r. 1465–71.

152 Abu 'Abd Allah al-Sheikh Muhammad ibn Yahya, r. 1472–1504.

153 October 1508.

154 In Muslim mythology, Shaddad was the son of 'Ad, a great-grandson of Shem. The tale of his creation of a paradise on earth derives from the Qur'an, 89.6–8; for examples see Richard Burton's *Arabian Nights*, nights 277–9, and al-Bal'ami, *Chronique*, trans. Hermann Zotenberg, 4 vols (Paris, 1867–74), I.50–55.

155 AD 1437. The king was Edward, r. 1433–8.

156 Abu Zakariya Yahya al-Wattasi.

157 Actually in 1463.

158 AD 1458; the Portuguese king was Afonso V, r. 1438–81.

159 'Abd al-Haqq II.

160 'Civitas' means city in Latin; it is unrelated to the name Ceuta.

161 The offence was apparently Roderic impregnating Julian's daughter.

162 Belyounech.

163 John I, r. 1385–1433.

164 Abu Sa'id 'Uthman III, r. 1398–1420.

165 These details do not appear in the chief Arabic source on the conquest of Ceuta, namely al-Maqrizi's biography of 'Uthman in his *Durar al-'uqūd al-farīda* (see the note at 2.2.2.3 above), II.415–17. The conquest itself is noteworthy as the first event in the Iberian assault on north Africa, which lasted over a century; for the most important European source, see Gomes Eannes de Zurara, *Crónica da tomada de Ceuta por el-Rei D. João I*, ed. Francisco M. E. Pereira (Lisbon, 1915).

166 See 2.2.4.11 above. Leo here omits the key role of Abu Zakariya Yahya al-Wattasi, the governor of Salé who intervened in 1420 to act as vizier to the one-year-old 'Abd al-Haqq; Yahya would become the founder of the Wattasid dynasty that came to power in the coup described above.

167 In fact, Berber *tiṭṭawin* means 'eyes', plural, although the true sense here is 'springs'.

168 'Ali al-Mandri, in the service of Muhammad XII of Granada, r. 1482–3, known to Christians as Boabdil.

169 In 1471.

170 'Ali ibn Rashid al-Alami, also known as Barraxe.

171 Unidentified, but see Natalie Zemon Davis's discussion, *Trickster Travels*, 117–18.

172 Orlando (d. 778), traditionally called Roland in English, was a Frankish commander under Charlemagne who became the central figure in French chivalric romance. Ludovico Ariosto's comic addition to the story, *Orlando Furioso*, first published in 1516, was all the rage during Leo's stay in Rome.

173 Hisn al-'Uqab, the Arabic name for the Castillo del Ferral, not in
    Catalonia but on the border of La Mancha and Andalusia. The
    battle was the famous Las Navas de Tolosa, 16 July 1212 – the
    most decisive turning-point of the Spanish Reconquista – and
    the king was Muhammad an-Nasir.

174 This sentence indicates that Leo did not understand how to
    convert dates correctly: the Arabic date AH 609 is correct but the
    Christian equivalent is AD 1212.

175 See 2.2.2.2 above.

176 Abu Yaqub Yusuf al-Zuhayli al-Badisi.

177 Peñón de Vélez de la Gomera, constructed in 1508.

178 Site of present-day Torres de Alcala.

179 Al-Mazamma, the port of the ruined city Nekor (or Nakur), was
    eight miles south-east of modern Al Hoceima.

180 'Abd Allah al-Mahdi, r. 910–34, on whom see below, 2.4.1.32.

181 Presumably 'Abd ar-Rahman III, r. 929–61, though the history
    recounted here is doubtful.

182 Ramusio's text includes the claim that the women are all unfaithful
    to their husbands. Both texts feature two headings of 'Mount Beni
    Mansur' (2.2.5.9, 2.2.5.12); Épaulard suggests a simple mistake.

183 Épaulard identifies this with Jebel Sougna.

184 Zebibi (from Arabic zabib, 'raisin') is a raisin wine with a sweet-
    sour taste.

185 The kachabia.

186 Épaulard renders the name 'Aychtoum', but Pierre Morizot
    makes the suggestion that it represents the tribe of the Ngoucht,
    a branch of the Beni Ourtnaj.

187 Meli is Greek (mel in Latin), not Berber, for honey. The name in
    fact comes from Berber mlilt, 'white'.

188 See 2.2.1.2 above.

189 In fact in 1497.

190 AD 1497.

191 AD 1292.

192 AD 1504.

193 That is, the mountain of the Kebdana, a tribe of the Zanata.

194 See 2.2.6.5 above.

195 The mother of Abu Sa'id 'Uthman II (r. 1310–31) was Aishah,
    daughter of Abu Atiyah Mhalhal al-Khalti.

196 Present-day Metalsa.

197 In fact, 'Abd al-Haqq's four sons were, in order of rule, (1) Abu
    Sa'id 'Uthman, (2) Muhammad, (3) Abu Yahya Abu Bakr, (4)
    Abu Yusuf Yaqub.

198 The sense of this muddled passage seems to be that there are seven areas in Al Haouz; four were given to 'Abd al-Haqq's sons, and the remaining three were collectively redivided into six, four of which were given to Marinid tribes and two to related tribes. There were thus three domains (for the sons, for the Marinid tribes and for the related tribes) and ten parties (four sons, four Marinid tribes and two related tribes).

199 AD 1269.

200 In the manuscript, the two last paragraphs of this chapter appear by mistake at the end of 2.2.7.4. Ramusio, and all subsequent editors, have them in the correct place here.

201 Unidentified.

202 AD 1498–9.

203 Abu 'Abd Allah al-Sheikh Muhammad ibn Yahya, r. 1472–1504.

204 This was Jebel Matghara; see 2.2.7.7 below.

205 That is, in the kingdom of Fez.

206 See 2.2.7.5 above.

207 Ramusio's text is rather different here: 'they hold the rulers in such little esteem that, after their defeat of the king's army, they took one of his generals to the top of the mountain and cut him into a thousand pieces in view of the king. For this reason the king was never friendly with them again, but they did not care at all.'

208 Grape syrup.

209 *Calsamenti*; Ramusio's reading is *casamenti*, 'houses', for which see the next chapter.

210 The section in brackets does not appear in the manuscript, and has here been translated from Ramusio. Scholars disagree as to whether it was part of Leo's original text or added later.

211 Épaulard records the form 'Sliliou' from oral testimony in the region.

212 See note 35 above.

213 A natural ceramic material also once used in making cement.

214 Also known as Qala'at al-Mahdi.

215 Mahdi ibn Tuwala.

216 Perhaps cooled volcanic lava.

217 Jebel Miat Bir. However, there is also another Miat Bir, for which see 2.1.4.6 above.

218 For these people, see 2.2.2.12.21 above.

219 Épaulard identifies this with present-day Abekhnanes.

BOOK 2.3

1   The Hafsid monarchs Abu Faris Abd al-Aziz II (r. 1394–1434)
    and his grandson Abu 'Amr 'Uthman (r. 1435–88).

2   AH 893 (AD 1488).

3   See 2.3.23 below.

4   The famous corsair Oruç Reis, 1474–1518.

5   Abu Muhammad 'Abdallah II, r. 1527–41.

6   This passage poses a serious difficulty: the manuscript is dated
    10 March 1526, and the accession of Abu Muhammad was in
    AH 934 / AD 1528. These lines have not been added later to the
    copy, which implies that the manuscript itself is in fact later than
    the date given.

7   *Nadd* means 'equal' in Arabic.

8   Now Rachgoun Island.

9   Abu 'Amir Muhammad ibn 'Abdullah (938–1002), chamberlain
    to Caliph Hisham II.

10 AD 1318–37.

11 Abu Yaqub Yusuf an-Nasr, r. 1286–1307. The siege lasted from
    1299 to 1307.

12 A unit of dry volume, approximately thirteen litres.

13 Abu al-Hasan 'Ali ibn 'Uthman, r. 1331–48. The siege began in
    1335.

14 A regional gold coin, also called a Rhenish florin, worth between
    a third and two thirds of a ducat.

15 Abu 'Abdallah V, r. 1504–17.

16 Abu Hammu III, r. 1517–27.

17 See 2.3.1 above.

18 The Sufi master Abu Madyan, 1126–98. Ibn Battuta records
    visiting this shrine en route from Tlemcen to Fez (*Travels*,
    IV.924).

19 Francisco Ximenes, 1436–1517.

20 In fact, 17 May 1509.

21 Compare the similar remarks in 2.2.2.12.11 above about the
    forgotten origin of festivals in Fez.

22 The mulberry tree was the preferred habitat of silkworms in
    Africa.

23 The grandfather is Abu 'Abdallah Muhammad IV, r. 1468–1504,
    and his eldest son Abu 'Abdallah Muhammad V, r. 1504–17.

24 Ramusio identifies this figure as Abu Hammu III, r. 1517–27.

25 See 2.3.1.

26 According to Jean-Baptiste Gramaye (*Africa*, 36), who was imprisoned in Algiers a century later, there were over 14,000 gardens in the vicinity.

27 See 1.14 and 1.19 above.

28 'Tagdemt' is similar to the modern Berber word *taγdemt*, 'justice', of uncertain antiquity. Leo seems to be deriving the name instead from *[Tahert] al-Qadima*, Arabic for 'Tiaret the Ancient'.

29 I.e. ouds.

30 Zinc oxide.

31 See 2.3.23 above.

BOOK 2.4

1 This promise does not appear in the work itself; at 1.4 Bejaia is listed as part of the kingdom of Tunis.

2 Abu 'Inan, the Marinid king of Fez, r. 1348–58, ruled Tunis from 1357.

3 In fact, most likely in 1509.

4 See 2.3.25 above.

5 A century later, Jean-Baptiste Gramaye (*Africa*, 41) recorded the trade of leather and wax with the French at Jijel.

6 Now the Rhumel; see 7.1.17 below.

7 The last two clauses are difficult to translate: Leo says that the burghers of Constantine have a more *civile* way of life than others, but less *civiltà*.

8 The *qa'id* (commander) Abu 'l-Fahm Nabil, d. 1453.

9 This passage is corrupt in the manuscript, and we have emended from Ramusio.

10 The Greek word for apple is *mēlon*.

11 Present-day Annaba. As Ramusio adds, the town was once Hippo or Hippone, famous as the home and bishopric of St Augustine; this name is undoubtedly reflected in Leo's 'Orpona'.

12 According to Ibn Khaldun, a branch of the Riyah.

13 According to Épaulard, in AH 915 (AD 1508).

14 These are two verses, not four, each line here corresponding to a half-line in the original.

15 Lisan al-Din ibn al-Khatib, 1313–74. The work referred to is perhaps *Kitab Mi'yar al-ikhtiyar fi dhikr al-ma'ahid wa-al-diyar* (*The Choice Measure: An Account of Various Homes and Abodes*).

16 Present-day El Kef. The older name is rendered variously as al-Urbus, Alorbos and Laribus.

17   By coincidence, *Urbs* means 'city' in Latin.

18   This rudimentary philology is not far off the mark; the town was
     originally named Vacca or Vaga.

19   Unidentified.

20   Ramusio: twelve miles, which makes more sense of 'vast'
     (*larghissima*).

21   Unidentified.

22   Perhaps the same gilt-head bream as the *sparès* mentioned below,
     2.4.1.33.

23   This word is unattested elsewhere.

24   Morea: the Peloponnese.

25   On Ibn ar-Raqiq, see the note at 1.10 above.

26   That is, the twelfth-century geographer Muhammad al-Idrisi.

27   See 2.4.1.32 below.

28   The Aqua Claudia or Claudian Aqueduct, extended by Domitian
     to the Palatine Hill, which was known in the Renaissance as the
     Palazzo Maggiore.

29   That is, the Lake of Tunis. La Goletta, now more usually known by
     its French name, La Goulette, or in Arabic Halq al-Wadi, was and
     is the town's seaport, sitting between the lake and the Gulf of Tunis.

30   Contrast Leo's description of the allocation of endowments
     (*waqf*) at the al-Qarawiyyin mosque in Fez, 2.2.2.11 above.

31   This line is corrupt; lacking a good explanation, we have left it
     as it stands in the Italian.

32   See 1.13, and the note there.

33   Muhammad an-Nasir, r. 1199–1213.

34   That is, Leo's own lost *Epitome*.

35   Yusuf II, or Abu Ya'qub Yusuf, r. 1213–24, was actually an-
     Nasir's son.

36   Abu Muhammad 'Abd al-Wahid, son of Abu Yaqub Yusuf, who
     had been briefly a governor in Seville.

37   Abu Zakariya Yahya, r. 1229–49.

38   The Mosque of the Kasbah.

39   The silver *nasri* (or *nasari* in Leo's spelling) received their name
     from the Almohad king Muhammad an-Nasir, who occupied
     Tunis from 1203 to 1207. The word *duppuli* apparently denotes
     a Hafsid gold dinar.

40   The form Leo gives in Italian; like the Italian Napoli (Naples), this
     name was a corruption of the Greek Neapolis or 'new city', and was
     common to many Greek colonies. Today it is Nabeul. However,
     Épaulard observes that the location Leo gives matches that of
     Rades, whereas Nabeul is further south on the Gulf of Hammamet.

41   'Abd (or 'Ubayd) Allah al-Mahdi, r. 910–34, founder of the
      Isma'ili Fatimid Caliphate. Not to be confused with the other
      figure Leo designates as al-Mahdi, namely Ibn Tumart, on whom
      see 2.1.3.9 above.

42   Al-Mahdi's early supporter, Abu 'Abd Allah al-Shi'i, was no
      prince but an Isma'ili missionary from Yemen; the defeated
      prince of Sijilmasa was al-Yasa' ibn Midrar, r. 882–909. After the
      rescue, Abu 'Abd Allah and his brother were murdered by royal
      supporters in 911.

43   Abu Yazid Makhlad ibn Kaydad al-Nukkari, nicknamed Sahib
      al-Himar, 883–947. His conquest of Kairouan occurred in
      October 944; the caliph was by this time al-Mahdi's son, al-
      Qa'im bi-Amr Allah.

44   See 1.13 above. For the end of the Fatimid rule in Egypt, see
      Leo's discussion of Saladin at 6.26.

45   In fact the word is the Latin *sparus*, meaning the gilt-head bream.

46   AD 670.

47   Leo's word is *oratorio*, 'oratory' or 'chapel', but he is here refer-
      ring to the *mihrab* or Mecca-oriented niche in the mosque, which
      is indeed flanked by pillars of red marble breccia.

48   Leo is perhaps referring to Abu al-Muhajir Dinar, d. 683.

49   AD 706.

50   See 2.2.4.14 above.

51   Córdoban historian, 987–1075.

52   AD 711–12.

53   This fabled artifact is always referred to elsewhere as the Table
      of Solomon.

54   Hisham ibn 'Abd al-Malik, r. 724–43. However, Leo is thinking
      of his brother Sulayman, r. 715–17.

55   Here meaning the Islamic province of Ifriqiya.

56   Abu al-'Abbas 'Abdullah as-Saffah ('the Bloody'), r. 750–54, the
      first caliph of the Abbasids.

57   Ziyadat Allah I of Ifriqiya, r. 817–38, the grandson of al-Aghlab.

58   See 2.4.1.32 above.

59   Raqqada was built in 876 by Ibrahim II ibn Ahmad, r.
      875–902.

60   Leo's derivation of the name is almost certainly apocryphal.

61   Asad ibn al-Furat, d. 828.

62   The chufa or *Cyperus esculentus*.

63   Abu 'Amr 'Uthman, d. 1488.

64   The ship was commanded by García de Toledo, in fact the duke
      Fadrique's son.

65   AD 1510.
66   Unidentified.
67   Ramusio has 'per migliaia d'anni' ('over thousands of years')
      instead of 'infra li meliori anni'.
68   Abu al-Hasan 'Ali ibn 'Uthman, r. 1331–48.
69   AD 1348.
70   AD 1352.
71   Abu-'l Abbas Ahmad, r. 1346.
72   AD 1357.
73   Ibrahim Abu Salim, r. 1359–61.
74   Abu 'Amr 'Uthman, r. 1435–88.
75   Abu Zakariya Yahya II, r. 1488–9.
76   'Abd al-Mu'min ibn Ibrahim.
77   AD 1489.
78   AD 1494.
79   Abu 'Abdallah Muhammad IV al-Mutawakkil, r. 1494–1526.
80   AD 1510.
81   See 2.3.20 above.
82   *Ghar* is the Arabic word for cave.
83   Present-day Cyrenaica.
84   On this, see further 1.22 above.

BOOK 3

1   See 1.5 above.
2   On these, see 7.3.10 below.
3   If Waddan is to be identified with the 'Audem' mentioned
     by Duarte Pacheco Pereira (*Esmeraldo*, 75), there was appar-
     ently a large gold trade here; Pereira names the Arabs as the
     Udaya.
4   On these, see 1.21 above and 7.3.6 below.
5   For Gartguessen or Agadir, see 2.1.2.4 above. The name means
     'Cape Ksima'.
6   Ramusio identifies this fodder as 'farfa' or alfalfa.
7   A regional gold coin, also called a Rhenish florin, worth between
     a third and two thirds of a ducat.
8   Leo may be thinking of Gaius Suetonius Paulinus, who was sent
     to Mauretania in AD 41.
9   *Sigillum Mass[a]e* is the Latin for 'Seal of Massa'; *sigillo* is the Ital-
     ian equivalent of the first word. On this etymology see Daniel F.
     McCall, 'The Traditions of the Founding of Sijilmassa and Ghana',

> *Transactions of the Historical Society of Ghana* 5.1 (1961), 3–32,
> at 16–17.

10 In 1846 Adrien Berbrugger argued that Sijilmasa must have sur-
    vived in some form at least until 1710, possibly rebuilt after
    Leo's time.

11 Unidentified, but the name may represent as-Sawahila, 'people of
    the plain'.

12 Épaulard suggests that the missing fruit is the bitter apple (*Cit-
    rullus colocynthis*); the name of the ksar means 'mother of the
    bitter apple' in Arabic.

13 Compare 2.2.7.15.

14 Now Gourara, the locality of Timimoun, Algeria.

15 AD 1492–3.

16 A porous, volcanic rock.

17 Abu Salim al-Ayyashi, a Moroccan traveller who visited Ouar-
    gla in early 1663 (*Voyage*, 55), recorded heaps of clothes lying
    by the city gates, once belonging to those who had died of
    an illness.

18 Ziban.

19 Presumably Abu 'Amr 'Uthman, r. 1435–88.

20 Unidentified, but perhaps Bordj Ben Azzouz in the present-day
    Biskra Province.

21 Gafsa was captured in 667. On 'Uqba, see 1.12.

22 'Ali ibn Ghaniya.

23 The siege occurred in late 1187.

BOOK 4

1 Leo (or the scribe) here omits the fifth group, the Bardoa. For the
   classification see 1.6 above.

2 See 1.27 above.

3 Ibn Khaldun (*Histoire*, II.72, *Corpus*, 327) calls the desert of the
   Lamtuna 'Kakadam', which may be the same name as that of the
   town of 'Qoqadam' recorded by al-Idrisi (*Géographie*, I.206,
   Corpus, 128). Further tentative suggestions are made by Rauchenberger (*Johannes Leo*, 191).

4 R. A. Donkin, *Manna: An Historical Geography* (The Hague,
   1980), 68–70, identifies this as a plant sap.

5 Present-day Guelmim, in the Oued Noun region of southern
   Morocco and Western Sahara. The older Arabic name for the
   town was Nul.

6   In the north of present-day Mali. Ibn Battuta (*Travels*, IV.947) observed houses and a mosque built from blocks of salt with roofs of camel hide. Alvise Cadamosto ('Voyage', 214–17) has a more elaborate description of the salt trade here, and notes the local belief that, due to the intense heat near the equator, the blood would putrefy without the continual ingestion of salt.

7   For speculations about the intended location, see Gustav Nacht-igal, *Sahara and Sudan*, trans. Allan G. B. Fisher and Humphrey J. Fisher, 2 vols (London, 1980), II.459–61.

8   The manuscript says ten, but we emend on the basis of Leo's earlier statement in 1.3; Ramusio has '120'.

9   'Abdallah ibn Yasin, d. 1059.

10   Ramusio moves this paragraph to the start of Book 5. It seems to form a bridge between the two books, insofar as it locates al-Wahat in the Land of the Blacks, rather than in Libya; perhaps Leo meant to place it somewhere in the vast desert between the two. Épaulard, however, suggests that this appearance of 'Algue-chet' (al-Wahat) is in fact a mistake for 'Awdaghust'.

BOOK 5

1   See the note at 4.11 above.

2   The manuscript reads 'five kingdoms'; we have emended with Ramusio, on the grounds that Leo lists fifteen kingdoms in this book (Walata, Jenne, Mali, Timbuktu, Gao, Gobir, Agadez, Kano, Katsina, Zazzau, Zamfara, Wangara, Bornu, Gaoga, Nubia). For the five Libyan tribes, see the start of Book 4. Rauchenberger, who preserves 'five kingdoms' (*Johannes Leo*, 261), interprets the line to mean that these kingdoms formed a third of each tribe's land, along with their territories in Libya and Barbary.

3   Askia the Great, also known as Muhammad ibn Abi Bakr Ture, r. 1493–1528.

4   Perhaps sorghum.

5   This word may be identified with *gnawa*, the pejorative Berber term for West Africans.

6   This indicates a confusion with Guinea, a coastal region distinct from the town of Jenne.

7   The prince to whom Leo refers is Abu Bakr ibn 'Umar; however, the Almoravid dynasty did not actually hold power so far south as Mali.

8   The king, a brother of the fabled Mansa Musa, r. 1341–60.

9   Abu Ishaq Ibrahim al-Sahili, 1290–1346. On this figure see *The Negroland Revisited*, Masonen, 212–14.

10   Askia Muhammad I, r. 1493–1528.

11   The thoroughbred dromedary.

12   The *chinea* (a word that derives from the English *hackney*) is a mid-size horse adapted for journeys.

13   The use of cowrie shells as currency is also mentioned by Alvise Cadamosto ('Voyage', 219).

14   A unit of currency.

15   A mysterious word. Rauchenberger suggests that it represents the African title 'Farima'.

16   The *canna* is an Italian measure varying in length from about one to three metres. *Monachino* is a variety of coarse grey cloth; *minino* is unidentified, but the word may be related to *minio*, red.

17   Present-day Zaria, Nigeria.

18   Part of present-day Nigeria.

19   Leo means Idriss Katakarmabé, r. 1507–29.

20   The location of Gaoga has been a subject of considerable debate, but most scholars place it somewhere in present-day Sudan.

21   Now the Bayuda desert. For the Gorhan or Gura'an, compare 1.7 above.

22   Old Dongola is 80 km upstream of the present city.

23   By 'Chaldean', Leo means Ethiopic. For Prester John, see the note at 1.3 above.

24   This in fact occurred in 1426.

BOOK 6

1   That is, the territory of the Beja people, mentioned below at 6.59.

2   Leo seems to believe that this division occurs at Faiyum (see 6.3 below), though it is in fact at Dairut; it returns to the main branch at Al Misandah.

3   Lake Manzala.

4   The Arabic word really means 'highland', 'plateau', here indicating the altitude of Upper Egypt.

5   The Copts.

6   Cleopatra.

7   Leo is referring to the city of Pithom mentioned at Exodus 1:11.

8   See 6.49 below, where Leo identifies this place as Faiyum. In Faiyum is a canal called *Bahr Yussef*, 'Joseph's River'; some have identified Pithom as Faiyum.

9   These towers are called windcatchers, or in Arabic *malqaf*.
10   Syphilis.
11   See 6.23 below.
12   Lake Mariout. *Buhaira* is the Arabic for 'lake'.
13   Leo's history is confused here: the Alexandrian Crusade, which
      took place in October 1365, occurred over a century after Louis
      IX, not Louis IV, was captured by the Egyptian sultan.
14   Peter I, r. 1358–69.
15   Arnold Von Harff (*Pilgrimage*, 94) says that the official used
      flags to indicate the number of ships he saw. See also the obser-
      vation of Felix Fabri (*Evagatorium*, III.178).
16   The Mahmoudiyah Canal.
17   In fact, Column of Pillars; more commonly known as Pompey's
      Pillar and now located in the city. It was built around AD 300,
      although the sanctuary complex in which it was originally
      located was constructed in the third century BC under Ptolemy
      III Euergetes, around a century after Alexander the Great.
18   This section is substantially changed by Ramusio, who identifies
      Ptolemy, more accurately, as a king, and does not mention the
      garlic-wielding Jew at all.
19   This may be a form of simple Nilometer.
20   Perhaps Sindiyun ('Schandion' in Von Harff), but the location is
      not quite right.
21   The location of the ancient Thebes, far south of Cairo, was not
      known in the sixteenth century. Épaulard suggests Metoubes,
      but that town is on the eastern bank; it is more likely Leo had in
      mind a town, since lost, called Deyp by Von Harff, Dibi by Pierre
      Belon, and Débé by Edward Clarke in 1814.
22   Not the present-day Dairut far south of Cairo. It was apparently
      a common name (*Terōt* in Coptic); the famous Egyptologist Jean-
      François Champollion listed as many as five such places in Egypt.
23   See 1.13 above. The date of founding is 969.
24   This is Muizz Street.
25   Built in 1502.
26   Muslin.
27   Baibars was the fourth Mamluk king. The hospital Leo mentions
      is probably the Qalawun complex built in 1284 by al-Mansur
      Qalawun, the seventh Mamluk king.
28   The two buildings are about 500 metres apart, far further than any
      crossbow can shoot. Leo's description of the conflict is too vague to
      permit definite identification, but he is plausibly referring to the
      siege of the citadel during the insurgency of Kanṣawh Khamsumi'a

against King al-Nasir Muhammad in early 1497. Arnold Von Harff (*Pilgrimage*, 104–6) gives an eyewitness account.

29 Qa'it Bay.

30 Nafisa was actually descended from Husein's brother Hasan ibn 'Ali, and born in Medina.

31 Suez.

32 This tree and garden were frequently visited by Christian pilgrims, given the supposed connection to the Virgin Mary: see, for instance, Arnold Von Harff (*Pilgrimage*, 104–5 and 127–8), and especially Felix Fabri (*Evagatorium*, III.13–18), who identifies it as a scion of the balsam supposedly given to Solomon by the Queen of Sheba. Some time later the tree disappeared; Johann Michael Vansleb, who visited Cairo in 1672, noted its absence: see *The Present State of Egypt* (London, 1678), 141. A replacement exists today.

33 Now Roda Island.

34 A Nilometer at Memphis is mentioned in antiquity by Diodorus Siculus, *Historical Library*, I.xxxvi.11, and Pliny, *Natural History*, V.x.57–8. Shakespeare located the Nilometer in one of the Pyramids, for Antony explains (*Antony and Cleopatra*, II.vii.16–19): 'they take the flow o' the Nile / By certain scales i' the pyramid; they know, / By the height, the lowness, or the mean, if dearth / Or foison follow.'

35 The present structure, which Leo visited, was built on the southern tip of the island by the caliph al-Mutawakkil in 861.

36 Ramusio gives the date here as 17 June, in line with the date found before at 7.2.5. The flooding lasts far longer than eighty days, but perhaps the expression 'forty days' is used figuratively for a long period, as in the Bible.

37 For the consul or *muhtasib*, an important position, see 6.41 below.

38 This was the ceremony of *Fath* (or *Kasr*) *al-Khalij*, 'the opening of the canal'; it is attested as early as the tenth century, and lasted until 1899, when the canal (Khalij) was filled in.

39 Pierre Belon (*Travels*, 249 (II.36)) notes the marble-clad walls inlaid with mother-of-pearl, ebony, crystal, coral and coloured glass.

40 Pierre Belon, writing in 1547, thirty years after the Ottoman conquest of Egypt, remarks (*Travels*, 243 (II.35)) that the women wear different veils in different parts of the country; in the villages they wear an ugly cotton cloth over their whole face, but in the larger towns they follow the Turkish preference for a 'small veil woven from the hairs of a horse's tail'.

41 The *chinea* (a word that derives from the English *hackney*) is a mid-size horse adapted for journeys.

42 These water carriers are known in Arabic as *sakkas*.

43 The artificial incubation of chickens was widely commented on by travellers of the period: see Arnold Von Harff (*Pilgrimage*, 110), Felix Fabri (*Evagatorium*, III.57-9) and Pierre Belon (*Travels*, 237 (II.31)). The practice was evidently notorious in Renaissance England, for Ben Jonson (*The Alchemist*, II.iii.128) refers to it as a parallel to alchemy. Already Aristotle, *History of Animals*, VI.2, notes that the Egyptians artificially incubated eggs by burying them in dung.

44 Not an unknown parlour trick. Both the Italian polymath J. C. Scaliger, *Exoteric Exercitations* (Paris, 1557), fol. 444v, and John Stow, *Chronicles of England* (London, 1580), 1195-6, report having seen a living flea with a long chain around its neck; not to be outdone, the naturalist Ulisse Aldrovandi, *On Insects* (Bologna, 1602), 563, claims to have seen two.

45 Leo's word for 'legal school' is *religione*; it translates the Arabic term *madhhab*.

46 The four schools are Hanafi, Maliki, Shafi'i and Hanbali.

47 These are the *qadis*.

48 The Mamluk sultan, Tuman bay II, r. 1516-17.

49 Present-day Feodosia, Crimea.

50 The Kurds.

51 Amalric.

52 Al-Adid, r. 1160-71.

53 Saladin was in fact Asad ad-Din's nephew.

54 He arrived in 1164.

55 Al-Mustadi, who succeeded the Fatimids in 1171. Al-Adid died in 1171, but was not murdered. Leo may be thinking of the vizier Shawar, who was murdered, albeit by Saladin's uncle.

56 The identification of the river is unclear. Ramusio reads 'Ganges', which may be what Leo meant, although it is geographically inaccurate. It is more likely that he had in mind the Amu Darya, in medieval Arabic called 'Jayhun', the biblical Gihon.

57 This history is rather muddled. There was no such figure as 'the sultan of Baghdad'; Leo is perhaps conflating the Abbasid caliph an-Nasir li Din Allah (r. 1180-1225) and the Khwarazmian shah 'Ala ad-Din Muhammad II (r. 1200-1220), both of whom provoked Mongol ('Tartar') invasions.

58 These are the *barid*.

59   In fact, *al-Kanisa al-Mu'allaqa* (the Hanging Church) is a seventh-century Coptic church.

60   Al-Khasib ibn 'Abd al-Hamid was the Egyptian finance officer of Caliph Harun al-Rashid.

61   According to Genesis 10:6, Mizraim is Cush's brother, not his son; Akhmim is a later invention.

62   Suleiman the Magnificent, r. 1520–66.

63   Probably the plague of 1429–30.

64   Possibly the Coptic Pope, John XI of Alexandria.

65   Identified with present-day Denderah by Jean-Baptiste Bourguignon d'Anville in 1766.

66   In fact, Syene was Aswan, not Esna.

67   A word in Egyptian Arabic for any ancient monument, borrowed from the Coptic *perpē*, 'temple', ultimately from Egyptian *pr*, 'house'. Champollion, who was the first to suggest this identification in Leo's work, thought the reference was to the pylon gates of a vanished temple.

68   Coptic.

BOOK 7

1   Abu al-Ula al-Wathiq Idris.

2   Leo is describing the *kelek* raft.

3   The nase (*lasca*) is not native to Africa; Leo presumably means a fish resembling it.

4   Unclear; perhaps to a place or feature mentioned earlier in Leo's original notes.

5   The Oued al-Jawahir.

6   See 2.2.2.12.3 above.

7   See 2.2.3.3 above.

8   Épaulard identifies this as the Chiffa.

9   Probably the Kebir, which means 'great' in Arabic.

10   The present-day Rhumel. The first syllable is likely a form of the Berber word *asif*, river, and Henri Fournel suggests the meaning as 'the river of pebbles'.

11   The present-day Seybouse. Leo's name 'Iadog' is surely the same as that of the Yadugh or Edough mountains overlooking Annaba (Bona), recorded in the twelfth century by al-Idrisi (*Géographie*, I.268).

12   See 2.2.7.30 for more details.

13   Perhaps the Oued Guir.

14   *Geography*, IV.6.13–14, referring to the *Geir* and *Nigeir* rivers.

15   There is no chapter on the Niger; Leo must be thinking of the
     chapter on the crocodile below, 7.4.5.

16   In fact, Ahmad was sent to rule Egypt by al-Mutawakkil's son
     al-Mu'tazz in AD 868.

17   The tenth-century Arabic cosmographer al-Mas'udi has plenty to
     say about Egypt, the Nile and its crocodiles in his principal work,
     Murūj al-Dhahab wa Ma'ādin al-Jawhar (*Meadows of Gold and
     Mines of Gems*), but this anecdote does not appear. Leo may have
     dimly remembered an interview (*Prairies*, II.376–96) between
     Ahmad ibn Tulun and an unnamed Coptic sage, featuring much
     miscellaneous lore.

18   Perhaps *Prairies*, III.30–31, on the Zenj.

19   *Prairies*, III.43–50.

20   The *Natural History* was the life's work of the Roman polymath
     Pliny the Elder (AD 23–79), containing information on every
     branch of knowledge of the period. Book 5 is on Africa and the
     Middle East, Book 8 on land animals, including elephants and
     lions, and Book 12 on exotic plants.

21   Upper Ethiopia was not held to be part of Africa.

22   It is unclear what Leo had in mind; giraffes have rounded split
     hooves. However, he may not have seen one, for he does not
     mention the giraffe's most obvious physical feature, namely its
     long neck.

23   An inferior dromedary. Leo's word is the plural of *hajin* or
     hijan.

24   The Bactrian.

25   The plural of *rahila*, a female riding camel.

26   For this term, see 1.19 above.

27   See 2.1.2.1.

28   Ibn Battuta (*Travels*, IV.967) observes: 'They swim in the river
     [Niger] and lift their heads and blow. The boatmen were afraid
     of them and drew near to land to avoid being drowned by them.'

29   Uncertain: perhaps a pygmy hippopotamus or seal.

30   In al-Bakri's story a group of travellers mistake the tortoise for a
     rock, and rather than sleeping on it they leave their possessions
     on it overnight to avoid the termites in the sand; the next day
     they follow the animal's tracks and find their goods still on its
     shell. See the author's *Description de l'Afrique Septentrionale*,
     trans. William McGuckin de Slane (Paris, 1859), pp. 393–4.

31   Arquebus: an early musket. Falconet: a light cannon.

32   Perhaps a species of Varanus.

33 Perhaps a species of viper.

34 There is a nice description of this process in Chinua Achebe's novel *Things Fall Apart*, chapter 7.

35 See, for instance, 3.21.

36 The African spurge, *Euphorbia resinifera*. It is named for Euphorbus, physician to Juba II of Mauretania.

37 These two kinds are bitumen and wood tar respectively.

38 This chapter does not appear in the manuscript, but only in Ramusio; the omission is perhaps accidental, perhaps the result of censorship due to its theological content.

39 Difficult to identify confidently; perhaps *Acacia gummifera* or *Dracaena draco*.

Index of Places

This index lists the names found in the present book with their equivalents in Leo's original manuscript. Page ranges in bold indicate one or more chapters dedicated to that place or feature.